International Armed Conflict
Since 1945

A Bibliographic Handbook
of Wars and Military Interventions

Herbert K. Tillema

Westview Press

BOULDER • SAN FRANCISCO • OXFORD

D
843
T55
1991

Series on State Violence, State Terrorism, and Human Rights

This Westview softcover is printed on acid-free paper and bound in library-quality, coated covers that carry the highest rating of the National Association of State Textbook Administrators, in consultation with the Association of American Publishers and the Book Manufacturers' Institute.

Copyright © 1991 by Westview Press, Inc.

Published in 1991 in the United States of America by Westview Press, Inc., 5500 Central Avenue, Boulder, Colorado 80301, and in the United Kingdom by Westview Press, 36 Lonsdale Road, Summertown, Oxford OX2 7EW

Library of Congress Cataloging-in-Publication Data
Tillema, Herbert K.
  International armed conflict since 1945 : a bibliographic handbook
of wars and military interventions / Herbert K. Tillema.
    p. cm. — (Series on state violence, state terrorism, and
human rights)
  Includes bibliographical references and index.
  ISBN 0-8133-8311-0
  1. World politics—1945–   —Bibliography. 2. Military history,
Modern—20th century—Bibliography. I. Title. II. Series.
Z6204.T53 1991
[D843]
016.90982—dc20   91-14544
                                                                         CIP

Printed and bound in the United States of America

The paper used in this publication meets the requirements
of the American National Standard for Permanence of Paper
for Printed Library Materials Z39.48-1984.

10   9   8   7   6   5   4   3   2   1

Contents

PART FOUR
MIDDLE EAST

PART FIVE
ASIA AND OCEANIA

Preface

International Armed Conflict Since 1945 is a concise handbook that briefly describes each of 269 international wars and other war-threatening conflicts occurring between 1945 and 1988. It also includes select bibliographies that identify more than 1,000 books, articles and essays plus numerous news accounts especially useful to further study of each of these events.

This is part of the *Overt Military Intervention* project that hopes to trace paths to, through and away from contemporary war. The larger project aims also to compile machine-readable data describing more than 600 foreign overt military interventions conducted by more than 100 states since World War II. This volume, based on work in progress, is intended primarily for reference use by students and professional scholars of international relations, peace studies, comparative politics, national security studies and contemporary history. Among other things, it aims to draw attention to often forgotten conflicts that nearly brought war and to often overlooked aspects of familiar conflicts that apparently encouraged or constrained war. It is hoped that it will encourage further research in order to fill gaps in present knowledge.

I am grateful for support from many quarters. My daughters and spouse, Marie, Anne, and Susan, have shown great patience. Prior collaboration with John Van Wingen helped to shape essential ideas. Eric Anderson, Maqsood Choudary, and Yogesh Grover helped to gather data. Present and former colleagues at the University of Missouri-Columbia have given good advice, including Soon Sung Cho, Robin Remington, Paul Wallace and Birol Yesilada. Many others have encouraged the project from afar, including but not limited to Karen Feste, Charles W. Kegley, Jr., Frederic Pearson, J. David Singer, and Harvey Starr. Financial support from the University of Missouri has helped at crucial moments. Guidance and arduous effort by the staff of the University of Missouri Libraries made it possible to complete this book. Those who have given aid and comfort should be held blameless for any errors or omissions.

Herbert K. Tillema

PART ONE

Introduction

1

Introduction

Armed conflict pervades contemporary international relations. Frequent local and regional wars and military interventions that end just short of war repeatedly challenge the recent semblance of world peace. Nearly every world region has been afflicted since 1945. Most except the smallest states have forcibly intervened within foreign lands upon some occasion. A majority of independent states and non-self-governing territories have been recent targets of foreign military force at one time or another, including nearly all of the Third World.

Recent wars are noteworthy despite their ostensible limitations. The Korean War is believed to have killed more soldiers than any prior international encounter except World War I and World War II and contributed by memorable example to ensuing global belligerence between the "communist bloc" and the "free world". Millions died also during the Second Indochina War which dominated the world diplomatic agenda for more than a decade. Other major wars, including repeated conflicts between Israel and her neighbors and between India and Pakistan, have forcibly redefined the political geography of world regions.

Little wars and armed conflicts short of war are often important in themselves and are always significant for what they might become. Modern wars evolve. They do not, as did Pallas Athena, emerge fully grown and armor-clad from the brow of Zeus. Local wars typically begin with small engagements. Regional wars grow from local wars. World wars expand from regional wars. States aim toward war, whether or not they mean to do so, whenever they employ force within foreign lands. They do so frequently and the consequence is not always easily controlled. Serious local resistance, counterattack, or counter-intervention by third parties can quickly enlarge an initially isolated affair. Global conflagration has been avoided since World War II but force and war are still widespread. Why states resort to force and how war is contained represent crucial questions in the nuclear era. It would

3

help to know how major wars compare to little wars and to wars that might have been.

In one sense wars may be said to evolve through crises.[1] Costs and risks associated with war are too obvious and too great for most statesmen to embrace them casually. Conflicts among basic values and threats, real or imagined, often presage use of force. Crisis is ubiquitous within international relations, however. A short list of famous crises includes only a few of the many occasions when war was near. States threaten war and risk war whenever they forcibly intervene within foreign domains.

War and intervention are sometimes misrepresented as entirely separate phenomena. Such sharp distinction is due in part to anachronistic legalisms inherited from the nineteenth century. Legal publicists used to condemn unsanctioned interference among states that enjoyed normal diplomatic relations while at the same time tolerating the same or worse within a declared or otherwise rightful "state of war".[2] Artificial notions of a "state of war" are no longer commonly accepted: war is war without regard to legal niceties; and the same is true of intervention. War in the practical sense is simply destructive combat involving regular military forces.[3] International war, as opposed to civil warfare, includes at least one combatant clearly representing a foreign power. Intervention represents intrusive behavior both within and without war.[4] One form of it, overt military intervention, is essential to contemporary international war.

Overt Military Intervention

The hallmark of all contemporary international wars and of all conflicts immediately threatening international war is overt military intervention. Overt military intervention represents direct military operations openly undertaken by a state's regular military forces within foreign lands in such a manner as to risk immediate combat, hence war, merely if they encounter armed resistance. One may assume today that overt military intervention represents a deliberately authorized act of state. It is also a necessary condition for contemporary international war. Moreover, given that regular military forces are almost universally controlled by individual states today, overt military intervention is now a necessary condition for international war.

Military intervention is seldom ambiguous today as it may occasionally have been in the past. States can and do immediately control distant military forces, in part through electronic communications. The geographical boundaries of individual states are generally well-defined and nearly every spot of land is recognized as part of some state or state dependency. Such private or irregular armies as still exist are generally recognized as such and are seldom capable of waging war far from their home bases. These conditions did not necessarily prevail until the twentieth century, which may help to explain the eighteenth century European practice of declaring war (previously practiced also within ancient Greece) in order to help tell friend from foe. It is no longer necessary to declare war in order to demonstrate responsibility for regular military operations and few states continue to do so.

Contemporary states have more ready means to intervene than in the distant past. Modern technology permits far-flung operations by commandos, aircraft, and ground-based or sea-based artillery and rocketry as well as facilitates distant deployment of ground armies. Nevertheless, overt military intervention is readily recognizable within contemporary international society. It represents all combat-ready foreign military operations undertaken by regular military forces and only such operations. It includes all ground deployments of regular combat units abroad that involve direct operations such as alert patrol, offensive maneuver, riot quelling, armed seizure of territory, and battle. It includes also commando raids and other combatant small-unit actions, aerial attacks, ground-based artillery and rocketry, and naval bombardment if undertaken by regular foreign military forces. All such operations within any foreign state or non-self-governing territory constitute overt military intervention, including within non-self-governing territories administered by the intervenor as distinctive political entities. All such operations place foreign military forces at immediate risk of combat even if they do not actually lead to war.

States threaten and intervene in other ways but in doing so are one or more steps further removed from international war. A verbal or written threat, by itself, represents words not concrete action. Homebound military mobilization does no more than signal preparation for military operations. A show of force conducted outside its target, including upon the high seas or in the air, is momentarily safe unless others attack preemptively. Small-arms fire across an international border does not constitute modern warfare by itself although it may precede more serious actions. Forces deployed peaceably to foreign garrisons await orders to take up arms. Police, auxiliaries and other civilian agents are seldom equipped to make war abroad in the full sense of the term, nor are military technicians and advisors who provide merely noncombat services to someone else's armed forces. A state may plausibly deny authority for acts of unofficial parties, including of private bands that it may support covertly.

Overt military intervention is widespread today. Between September 1945 at end of World War II and the end of 1988, 105 states intervened one or more times within 131 other states and non-self-governing territories.[5] These actions represented at least 639 interventions.[6] Many amounted to little. A few led to major war resulting in military fatalities numbering thousands or even hundreds of thousands.

Seemingly inconsequential interventions do not necessarily differ from war-making ones initially. Israeli aircraft and commandos attacked territories of neighboring states many times. Most attacks ended quickly and represented isolated incidents but a few subsequently mushroomed into major offensives and serious warfare. Nor is there necessarily a fundamental tactical difference between interventions that prove costly and those that do not. The United States deployed thousands of troops to Lebanon both in 1958 and 1982–1984 under similar military plans that included occupation of Beirut airport by U.S. Marines. Two soldiers died by accident during the first intervention. Nearly 300 were killed during the second due primarily to greater local resistance.

States intervene cooperatively as well as aggressively. Cooperative intervention arises under various auspices, including at the specific request of a foreign state, at the behest of colonial administrators, or at invitation of the United Nations or other intergovernmental body. Aggressive attacks such as North Korea's invasion of South Korea are often blamed for war. Cooperative intervention is sometimes excused as mere peacekeeping. The United States was no less a warrior, however, when she battled within South Korea at the behest of that government under the U.N. flag, nor was France when she fought to retain colonial control of Indochina.

International Armed Conflict

Any overt military intervention creates international armed conflict and heightens risk of war. Each international armed conflict represents incipient warfare even if war does not immediately result. Many especially damaging wars grow incrementally by multiplying interventions. Most conflicts start simply when one state intervenes within a foreign territory. Subsequently, a state that is under attack may counterattack the territory of its assailant. Other states may join to support or oppose initial intervenors. Conflict may spread beyond original boundaries in the process. Regional wars, such as the Second Indochina War of the 1960s and early 1970s and the Third Indochina War of the late 1970s and 1980s, typically develop in these ways.

Big and complex wars often appear to have multiple causes due in part to their incremental evolution. A state may intervene initially for one ostensible purpose but find other reasons to continue when war expands. One intervenor's motivations are seldom identical to others'. Nor is it necessarily the case that states that oppose one another do so for exactly opposite reasons.

Some international armed conflicts appear to originate within territorial or policy disputes. Protracted border disputes are notorious for tempting arms and are associated, in one way or another, with a majority of major nineteenth and twentieth century wars.[7] Other international armed conflicts originate within civil strife. Civil violence invites international conflict in several ways. Foreign states may intervene in order to support established governments, to help insurgents, or in the name of neutral peacekeeping. Beleaguered governments may carry the fight to insurgents' foreign sanctuaries. Civil conflict may thus be overlaid by and eventually overshadowed by international war, as within South Vietnam during the 1960s. Most large and lasting civil upheavals involve foreign military intervention, at least episodically.

When a particular war begins or ends is sometimes arguable. Great battles and other memorable military engagements often represent merely a part of longer and larger international armed conflicts. Overt military intervention by both Taiwan and mainland China associated with the Chinese Islands Conflict persisted from 1949 to 1969. Dramatic crisis within the Taiwan Straits during 1954–1955 momentarily intensified this conflict but did not represent its bloodiest period. The Korean War involved a year and a half of border skirmishes costing hundreds of lives preceding North Korea's full-scale invasion of South Korea in June 1950. Four years of repeated low-intensity military operations preceded climactic battles of the Six Day War between Israel and her neighbors in June 1967. Somalia and Ethiopia continued sporadic military interventions for nearly seven years after the supposed end of the Ogaden War in 1978. Major battles are often surrounded by a halo of additional military interventions that involve other intervenors and other territories. The Third Indochina War involved armed conflict between China and Laos and Laos and Thailand as well as major battles involving Cambodia, China and Vietnam.

At least 269 international armed conflicts started between 1945 and 1988.[8] Some lasted longer than did others. Some involved one and others many directly related overt military interventions. Among them are all generally recognized international wars. Many others ended short of war.

Many seemingly inconsequential international armed conflicts offer insights into the process that makes war. Some represent small battles that almost got out of hand, including between Egypt and Libya in 1977 and between Mali and Upper Volta in 1985. Others appear to anticipate serious wars that follow at a later date. France intervened briefly within Morocco several times before becoming involved in protracted struggle during the North African War beginning in 1952. Libya participated in the Chadian Civil War during 1978–1980 prior to the much more costly Libyan-Chadian War of 1983–1987. Iran and Iraq fought over the Shatt El-Arab between 1972 and 1975 before the onset of the disastrous Persian Gulf War in 1979.

Nearly every world region has been afflicted by international armed conflict, small and large, since World War II. The Western Hemisphere and Europe have been comparatively fortunate but not exempt. Only North America has been entirely spared. The Caribbean has witnessed several minor engagements. Central America has suffered numerous civil conflicts that spilled over international borders, especially during the late 1970s and 1980s, as well as the serious Football War of 1969 between El Salvador and Honduras. Territorial disputes have brought trouble to South America, including during the Malvinas (Falklands) War in 1982. Europe, too, has experienced international armed conflict, most notably associated with the Greek Civil War during the late 1940s, the Budapest Uprising within Hungary in 1956, and recurrent strife involving Cyprus from the 1950s to the 1970s.

Africa has been a war-torn continent both before and after most states gained independence during the early 1960s. Within West Africa, Portugal fought into the 1970s in an effort to retain control of what became Guinea-Bissau. Internal strife within newly independent Central African states has provoked frequent international conflict, including the Congolese Civil War that brought U.N. involvement and recurrent conflict within Chad. Peace within the Horn of Africa has been challenged by competing claims of nationality, most notably between Somalia and Ethiopia but also growing out of the persistent Eritrean War. East Africa has suffered similarly from Madagascar to Mauritius to Rwanda and Burundi. Policy and territorial disputes also contributed to major war between Uganda and Tanzania. Southern Africa has been beset by long struggle against white rule, including during the Southwest African War, 1960–1988, embracing both Angola and Namibia, within Mozambique and also Rhodesia. The North African War spread throughout the Maghreb and beyond during the 1950s and early 1960s. It was followed by protracted warfare within the Western Sahara beginning in 1974.

The Middle East has suffered also. The Persian Gulf region has been the scene of repeated conflict, including growing out of Kurdish separatism and Iranian-Iraqi confrontations that culminated in the Persian Gulf War that killed hundreds of thousands of soldiers. Levantine states of the Eastern Mediterranean, including Egypt, Israel, Jordan, Lebanon and Syria, have conflicted perpetually since the Palestine War associated with the birth of Israel. Southern Arabia was highly unstable until very recently, resulting in the Aden-Yemeni War of 1961–1967 among other violent events.

Asia has been host to many especially destructive international armed conflicts. Southwest Asia experienced primarily minor disturbances until the Russo-Afghan War began in 1979. East Asia, on the other hand, witnessed the Korean War and protracted violence associated with the Chinese Islands Conflict and Tibetan Occupation until the 1960s as well as dangerous small battles between the Soviet Union and China in 1969. South Asia has been riven by repeated wars involving India and her neighbors, especially between India and Pakistan. Southeast Asia, particularly Indochina, has known little peace since World War II. International conflict has occasionally come even to Pacific Oceania since the late 1970s.

Cases of International Armed Conflict Since 1945

The following chapters include brief synopses of each of 269 international armed conflicts initiated between September 2, 1945, and December 31, 1988.[9] These include major wars, small wars and armed engagements short of war. Each is defined by incidence of foreign overt military intervention. Events involving non-self-governing territories are included but conflicts confined within fully integrated states are omitted except when foreign states overtly intervene. A few notable civil conflicts thus gain no mention here, including the Biafran War within Nigeria and continuing strife within Northern Ireland. International crises that may have threatened war but did not proceed so far as overt military intervention, such as the Cuban missile crisis of 1962, are also omitted.

Each chapter represents a geographic region. Individual conflicts within a region are arrayed chronologically. Each synopsis highlights who intervened where, when, how, under what circumstances and with what effect. Cross–references indicate previous related international armed conflicts. Estimates of military losses sustained upon foreign soil are included. Estimates of civilian losses and military losses upon home territory are also included if available. Synopses vary in length depending upon the complexity of conflict but in no case represent a complete account. They are intended primarily to facilitate further research. It should be apparent that many potentially significant minor conflicts are too often forgotten as are some aspects of otherwise well-known wars.

Selected references that may be especially useful to further research are listed for each conflict. References include primarily English-language materials that are readily available through North American libraries. Unpublished documents are generally omitted. Preference is given to recent items and to those that include further bibliographical references. In cases where secondary accounts are sparse, newspaper and other current events reports are also cited. Shortened references to particular items identify authors by last name and first initial, year of publication, title and page numbers as appropriate. These data will suffice to obtain materials in many cases. Full citations are provided within a comprehensive Bibliography at the end of the volume.

A summary list of International Armed Conflicts follows. It identifies individual conflicts in the same geographical and chronological order as they appear within particular chapters. Each intervening state and each target state or territory is also named.

A short list of General References is also provided. These include selected articles, serials or monographs that are especially useful to study of worldwide conflict or of conflict within particular regions. Many of these items are also mentioned elsewhere in connection with individual conflicts.

A comprehensive Bibliography includes full bibliographic information for all cited materials. Entries include unique identifiers such as International Standard Book Numbers (ISBN), International Standard Serials Numbers (ISSN), or Library of Congress (LC) card numbers. More than 1,000 periodicals, articles, edited books and monographs are listed in all.

Notes

1. Brecher, M., J. Wilkenfeld, and S. Moser. 1988. *Crises in the Twentieth Century*; Bueno de Mesquita, B. 1981. *The War Trap*; Maoz, Z. 1982. *Paths to Conflict*; Siverson, R., and M. Tennefoss. 1982. "Interstate Conflicts: 1815–1965." *International Interactions* 9 (#2): 147–178.

2. Brownlie, I. 1963. *International Law and the Use of Force by States*, 26–40; Hall, W. 1895. *A Treatise on International Law*, 297–309; Oppenheim, L. 1906. *International Law*, 2:181–191.

3. Most, B., and H. Starr. 1983. "Conceptualizing 'War'". *Journal of Conflict Resolution* 27 (March): 137–159.

4. Jaquet, L., ed. 1971. *Intervention in International Politics*; Moore, J., ed. 1974. *Law and Civil War in the Modern World*; Rosenau, J. 1969. "Intervention as a Scientific Concept". *Journal of Conflict Resolution* 13 (June): 149–171.

5. Territorial political units are generally defined according to Russett, B., J. Singer and M. Small. 1968. "National Political Units in the Twentieth Century," *American Political Science Review* 62 (September): 932–951. Exceptions include: (1) the Falkland Islands (1945–1985), Tibet (1945–1965), Hyderabad (1947–1948), Nyasaland (1953–1964) and Kashmir (1947–1948) are recognized as distinct political entities; (2) the brief unions represented by the Mali Federation (1960) and the United Arab Republic (1958–1961) are treated as extensions of their constituent territories, including Mali and Senegal in the first case and Egypt and Syria in the second; and (3) the Straits Settlements (1945–1946) and the Federated Malay States (1945–1946) are treated as parts of the Malayan Union formed in 1946. Generally recognized international borders are accepted except that authority within lands subject to active diplomatic dispute is defined according to de facto control. Names of non-self-governing territories are those current at the times of intervention. Names of independent states are generally those current as of December 31, 1988, the end of the period of study.

6. Foreign overt military intervention is operationally defined as direct combatant or combat-preparatory military operations conducted upon foreign territory by units of a state's regular military forces. It includes conventional deployments of ground combat units that involve such actions as alert patrol, offensive maneuver, riot quelling, armed occupation of territory, and battle. It also includes other, usually less intense combatant military actions, among them: commando or other small-unit raids; aerial bombing, strafing and rocketry; ground-based artillery or rocketry; and naval gunnery and rocketry. Overt military intervention includes all such operations within territories subject to other states' jurisdiction, and also within distinct non-self-governing territories such as colonies, protectorates, mandated or occupied lands not fully integrated within the generally recognized boundaries of a state. It excludes operations conducted by a state within its own integral territory. Overt military intervention excludes less blatant forms of international interference such as covert operations, military alerts, shows of force, garrison deployments or deployments of other forces not immediately prepared for combat, incursions across international borders that do not involve occupation of territory or other overt military actions, military assistance, and activities of police units, irregular forces, multinational peace forces and international observer groups that do not directly involve the overt military intervention as defined above. Overt military intervention also excludes incidents involving merely small-arms fire across international borders, engagements among vessels at sea, or encounters among aircraft in flight. An overt military intervention begins on the day of a state's first overt military action within a

foreign territory and ends on the day that activity ceases due either to withdrawal of military forces or subsequent inactivity among remaining forces. As a rule, all overt military operations conducted within six months of one another by one state within one foreign political territory are represented as one intervention. A few instances of quickly renewed intervention are treated separately due to historical familiarity. These include resumption of artillery exchanges among Israel, Jordan and Egypt within less than six months after the Six Day War of 1967.

7. Diehl, P., and G. Goertz. 1988. "Territorial Changes and Militarized Conflict". *Journal of Conflict Resolution* 32 (March): 103–122.

8. An international armed conflict is operationally defined to include all directly related foreign overt military interventions undertaken by one or more states within one or more foreign political territories. Foreign overt military interventions are deemed to be directly related to one another if: (1) they occur within six months of one another; and (2) they intersect tactically or strategically in the sense that they either combat one another, are operationally coordinated with one another, openly support one another, or openly oppose one another's visible military objectives. Onset of the first directly related foreign overt military intervention and cessation of the last intervention are taken as the beginning and the end of an international armed conflict.

9. These data expand upon a list of international armed conflicts, 1945–1985, previously published in Tillema, H. 1989. "Foreign Overt Military Intervention in the Nuclear Age." *Journal of Peace Research* 26 (May): 179–196.

PART TWO

Western Hemisphere and Europe

2

Caribbean

Recent Caribbean international armed conflict arose primarily from civil conflict. Unrest under colonial rule provoked brief interventions by the United Kingdom within Grenada (2.1), the Bahamas (2.2), Jamaica (2.3) and Anguilla (2.6), as well as by the Netherlands within Curaçao (2.7) during the 1950s and 1960s. Both Cuba and the United Kingdom intervened against Cuban exiles within the Bahamas in 1962 (2.4). The Dominican revolt of 1965 (2.5) attracted intervention by the United States and other parties as did the Grenadan coup of 1983 (2.8).

2.1 Grenadan Riots, 1951

The United Kingdom governed Grenada, one of the Windward Islands, from the eighteenth century. In February 1951 a strike by members of the Manual and Mental Workers' Union led by Eric Matthew Gairy turned violent. Several persons died during rioting. British Marines and sailors aboard ship in the vicinity intervened in support of local police. These guarded key installations for several days after coming ashore February 23 until police reinforcements arrived from Trinidad. No casualties are reported among British forces.

New York Times 2/24/51, 2:8; 2/26/51, 8:3; 2/27/51, 3:6.
Wallace, E. 1977. *The British Caribbean from the Decline of Colonialism to the End of Federation*, 69.

2.2 Nassau Strike, 1958

The Bahamas became a British crown colony in 1717. Immigration of freed slaves in the nineteenth century helped to produce an overwhelmingly black population. The Bahamas generally avoided major civil violence during the first half of the twentieth century except for riots within Nassau in 1942 contained by local police without

15

military assistance. In November 1957 Nassau taxidrivers staged a strike protesting policies instituted at a newly-opened airport. On January 13, 1958, the Bahamas Federation of Labour called a general strike to support the drivers. The United Kingdom flew troops in from Jamaica the next day to patrol the streets of Nassau. The strike proceeded peacefully except for occasional isolated violence. British troops withdrew at the beginning of February 1958 without fatality.

Blaxland, G. 1971. *The Regiments Depart*, 367–368.
Craton, M. 1962. *A History of the Bahamas*, 287–288.
Hughes, C. 1981. *Race and Politics in the Bahamas*, 62–66.

2.3 Rastafarian Violence, 1960

The United Kingdom acquired colonial control of Jamaica in 1655. She helped to develop extensive sugar cane plantations by importing African slaves. Slaves' descendents eventually constituted more than three-quarters of the population. Racial and labor tensions provoked violence and British military intervention during the late 1930s. The colony attained limited self-rule in 1944 and in 1956 joined the British West Indies Federation administered from Trinidad. The Rastafarian movement attracted a local following during the 1950s by emphasizing class and racial consciousness. Reverend Claudius Henry, a radical Rastafarian leader, attempted to organize a guerrilla campaign to overthrow the Jamaican government beginning in 1959. Jamaican police arrested Henry and some of his followers in April 1960. Other Henry followers orchestrated demonstrations and arson attacks during April and May. Jamaican police and small British Army units swept the Red Hills area June 21–27, 1960, and captured most hard-core insurgents. Two British soldiers died during the operation.

Barrett, L. 1977. *The Rastafarians*, 98–99.
Blaxland, G. 1971. *The Regiments Depart*, 368.
Lacey, T. 1977. *Violence and Politics in Jamaica*, 82–84, 106–107.
Norris, K. 1962. *Jamaica: The Search for an Identity*, 50–51.

2.4 Cuban Exiles Conflict, 1963

The Cuban government of Fulgencio Batista collapsed in January 1959 following several years of guerrilla warfare. Fidel Castro assumed power, promptly initiated a social revolution, and obtained economic and military aid from the Soviet Union. Cubans opposed to the Castro regime fled to the United States and some also to the British colony of the Bahamas. They harassed Cuba from bases in southern Florida and among lightly inhabited Bahamian cays. Cuba publicly objected to raids by exiles, especially after the United States pledged noninterference at end of the Cuban missile crisis in October 1962. Bahamian fishermen also objected to poaching by Cuban exiles. The United Kingdom deployed a frigate to the Bahamas in late 1962 and Royal Marines interned Cuban exiles discovered upon Bahamian cays from February to mid-August 1963. Cuban ships also operated in the area and seized Cuban exiles fishing within Bahamian waters near Elbow Cay in February. Cuban Marines also attacked Cuban exiles on Anguila Cay in August 1963. Cuban and British vessels did not engage one another directly and no fatalities are reported among Cuban or British military forces.

Butterworth, R. 1976. *Managing Interstate Conflict*, 318–319.
Cable, J. 1981. *Gunboat Diplomacy*, 240.
Hughes, C. 1981. *Race and Politics in the Bahamas*, 98.
Slater, J. 1967. *The OAS and United States Foreign Policy*, 149–161.

2.5 Dominican Revolt, 1965–1966

The Dominican Republic gained independence from Spain in 1821 and separated from its island neighbor, Haiti, in 1844. From 1916 to 1924 the U.S. Marine Corps occupied the Dominican Republic. General Rafael Trujillo Molina governed the state, directly or indirectly, from 1930 until assassinated in May 1961. A provisional Council of State succeeded Trujillo and paved the way for democratic elections. Juan Bosch, leader of the Revolucionario Dominicano party (PRD) was elected president in December 1962 and served until overthrown by a military coup in September 1963. A civilian triumvirate succeeded and by 1964 devolved into a two-man regime dominated by Donald J. Reid Cabral. On April 24, 1965, supporters of Bosch and the PRD, who called themselves "Constitutionalists," toppled Reid Cabral's government. Serious fighting followed within the capital, Santo Domingo.

U.S. military advisors encouraged field-rank Dominican military officers, including Colonel Pedro Bartolene Benoit, to declare a new government. Benoit requested American military support. U.S. Marines landed April 28, 1965, followed shortly by U.S. Army units. U.S. forces cleared most parts of Santo Domingo previously seized by

Constitutionalists. The Organization of American States sanctioned an Inter-American Peace Force to help maintain order. Small numbers of troops arrived from Brazil, Honduras and Nicaragua on May 23, 1965. A unit of Paraguayan soldiers joined them June 27. Brazil's General Hugo Panasco Alvim was named to command the IAPF and exercised titular authority over all foreign troops. A provisional government acceptable to both Constitutionalists and their opponents was established under Hector Garcia-Godoy September 3. The IAPF helped to contain occasional disturbances that erupted during following months. Juaquin Balaguer defeated Juan Bosch in June 1966 presidential elections. Paraguayan troops withdrew July 30 as did those from Honduras and Nicaragua on August 22. Remaining Brazilian forces withdrew September 20, 1966, as did U.S. troops the following day.

Approximately thirty American soldiers died during initial efforts to gain control of Santo Domingo. Neither Brazil, Honduras, Nicaragua nor Paraguay suffered fatalities.

Brecher, M., J. Wilkenfeld, and S. Moser. 1988. *Crises in the Twentieth Century*, 1: 274–275.
Butterworth, R. 1976. *Managing Interstate Conflict*, 400–402.
Draper, T. 1968. *The Dominican Revolt*.
Gleijeses, P. 1978. *The Dominican Crisis*.
Georgetown University Center for Strategic Studies. 1965. *Dominican Action, 1965*.
Lowenthal, A. 1972. *The Dominican Intervention*.
Moreno, J. 1970. *Barrios in Arms: Revolution in Santo Domingo*.
Rikhye, I. 1984. *The Theory and Practice of Peacekeeping*, 139–150.
Slater, J. 1970. *Intervention and Negotiation*.
Slater, J. 1978. "The Dominican Republic, 1961–66." In *Force Without War*, by B. Blechman and S. Kaplan, 289–342.
Small, M., and J. Singer. 1982. *Resort to Arms*, 231.
Szulc, T. 1965. *Dominican Diary*.
Tillema, H. 1973. *Appeal to Force*.
Wainhouse, D. 1973. *International Peacekeeping at the Crossroads*, 459–516.
Yates, L. 1988. *Power Pack*.

2.6 Anguillan Secession, 1969

The United Kingdom occupied the small Caribbean island of Anguilla from the mid-seventeenth century. She administered it as an appendage of the larger islands of St. Kitts (St. Christopher) and Nevis among her Leeward Islands possessions from the nineteenth

Century. St. Kitts-Nevis-Anguilla became a separate colony in 1956 and gained internal self-government in late February 1967. Previously, on February 4, 1967, demonstrations on Anguilla opposed association with St. Kitts and demanded separate colonial status. Local police assisted by police reinforcements from St. Kitts attempted unsuccessfully to find and arrest demonstration leaders. Sporadic violence occurred until St. Kitts police withdrew May 29, 1967. An Anguillan Peacekeeping Committee led by Ronald Webster and Walter Hodge established de facto control of the island. Hodge proclaimed Anguillan independence July 11, 1967, following a local referendum held that day. Protracted negotiations ensued involving Anguillan representatives, St. Kitts administrators and the United Kingdom. Eventually, on March 19, 1969, more than 300 British paratroops and marines landed and took control of Anguilla without bloodshed. Britain established a new administration separate from St. Kitts directly under authority of the crown. British soldiers remained to help assure security but encountered no violent resistance before withdrawing in September 1969.

Blaxland, G. 1971. *The Regiments Depart*, 373–374.
Brisk, W. 1969. *The Dilemma of a Ministate: Anguilla.*
Westlake, D. 1972. *Under an English Heaven.*

2.7 May Movement, 1969

The Netherlands conquered Curaçao in 1634 and later appended other small islands to this domain. She granted local self-government to the Netherlands Antilles with capital at Willemstad, Curaçao, in 1954. The Democratic party persistently dominated local government from 1954 to 1969. On May 6, 1969 indigenous workers at an oil facility associated with Royal Dutch Shell staged a strike demanding equal pay with foreign employees. Other labor unions lent support later that month. Several thousand workers and others marched upon the capital May 30 to protest alleged government complicity with oil companies. The march provoked rioting in Willemstad after Papa Godett, leader of the radical dockworkers union, was shot and Curaçao police arrested other labor leaders. Rioting continued the next day. 300 Dutch marines arrived from the Netherlands to assist police June 1, 1969. Labor leaders formed the May 30 Labor and Liberation Front (May movement) to promote political and economic reforms. The government resigned and new legislative elections were held September 5, 1969. The May movement won enough seats to take posts within a coalition cabinet. Dutch Marines stood down September 6, the day after the election. No Dutch military fatalities are reported.

Anderson, W. 1975. *Social Movements, Violence, and Change: The May Movement in Curaçao.*

Hoetink, H. 1972. "The Dutch Caribbean and its Metropolis." In *Patterns of Foreign Influence in the Caribbean*, ed. E. de Kadt, 103–120.

2.8 Grenadan Occupation, 1983

The small island of Grenada gained independence from the United Kingdom in 1974. Eric M. Gairy, who had encouraged labor demonstrations preceding British military intervention in 1953 (3.1), became prime minister. Maurice Bishop and the New Jewel movement overthrew Gairy in 1979 and proclaimed a People's Revolutionary Government. Bishop's regime accepted military and economic assistance from Cuba and the Soviet Union. Open rivalry erupted within the government in October 1983. The deputy prime minister, Bernard Coard, was forced to resign October 14 after allegedly plotting to assassinate Bishop. On October 17 army commander General Hudson Austin arrested Bishop and other government leaders. Soldiers loyal to Austin fired upon a crowd protesting Bishop's detention October 19, killing and wounding as many as 200 persons. The army also executed Bishop at about the same time. Austin and other officers formed a Revolutionary Military Council to govern the island on October 20.

On October 25, 1983, nearly 2,000 U.S. army paratroops and marines assaulted Grenada. The United States claimed to act upon request of the Organization of East Caribbean States (OECS) of which Grenada was a member. The Grenadan army resisted the American invasion. Several hundred Some Cuban construction workers present, a few of whom were professional soldiers, also took up arms in irregular fashion against U.S. forces. The United States secured the island by October 31 after capturing General Austin and Bernard Coard. Dominica, Antigua, St. Lucia and St. Vincent and the Grenadines, Jamaica and Barbados each provided small numbers of soldiers and police to constitute a several hundred-man Caribbean Peacekeeping Force. The Caribbean force organized as a police unit and undertook no overt military operations. Sir Paul Scoon, Britain's governor-general for Grenada, and an Advisory Council named by him formally constituted a new government November 15. U.S. combat troops withdrew by December 15,

1983.

More than 100 soldiers and civilians died during the American invasion. Official reports acknowledge nineteen U.S. military fatalities during operations. Unofficial estimates suggest that as many as forty-two American civilian and military personnel may have been killed.

Adkin, M. 1989. *Urgent Fury: The Battle for Grenada.*
Burrowes, R. 1988. *Revolution and Rescue in Grenada.*
Davidson, S. 1986. *Grenada: A Study in Politics and the Limits of International Law.*
Dominguez, J. 1989. *To Make a World Safe for Revolution,* 162–171.
Germain, L. 1985. "A Chronology of Events Concerning Grenada." In *American Intervention in Grenada,* ed. P. Dunn and B. Watson, 149–182.
Laffin, J. 1986. *War Annual 1,* 48–54.
Lewis, G. 1987. *Grenada: The Jewel Despoiled,* 1–112.
Manigat, L. 1988. "Grenada." In *The Caribbean and World Politics,* ed. J. Heine and L. Manigat, 178–221.
O'Shaughnessy, H. 1984. *Grenada: An Eyewitness Account.*
Payne, A., P. Sutton, and T. Thorndike. 1984. *Grenada: Revolution and Invasion.*
Sandford, G. 1985. *The New Jewel Movement.*
Schoenhals, K., and R. Melanson. 1985. *Revolution and Intervention in Grenada.*
Thorndike, T. 1985. *Grenada: Politics, Economics, and Society.*
U.S. Department of State and U.S. Department of Defense 1984. *Grenada Documents.*
Valenta, J., and V. Valenta. 1986. "Leninism in Grenada." In *Grenada and Soviet/Cuban Policy,* ed. J. Valenta and H. Ellison, 3–37.

3

Central America

Central America has been the Western Hemisphere's most unstable region since World War II. International armed conflict grew out of Costa Rica's civil war in 1948 (3.1, 3.2). The Honduran-Nicaraguan border dispute (3.3, 3.6) and Guatemalan claims to British Honduras (3.5) led to international incidents during the 1950s and 1960s. Panamanian opposition to American control of the Canal Zone fostered conflict in 1959 (3.4) and 1964 (3.7). El Salvador and Honduras fought the disastrous Football War in 1969 (3.8) and suffered further border conflict in 1976 (3.9). Civil strife within Nicaragua spilled over international borders during the late 1970s and 1980s (3.10, 3.11, 3.12), as did insurrection within El Salvador (3.13) and Guatemala (3.14, 3.15).

3.1 Quesada Incident, 1948

Costa Rica instituted democratic national elections in 1896, first in Central America. Costa Rican politics remained more personal than partisan, however. Rafael Calderon Guardia was elected president of the republic in 1940. In 1942 Jose ("Don Pepe") Figueres, who held no public office at the time, publicly protested alleged graft and corruption within Calderon's government and called upon the regime to resign. Figueres was arrested and then forced to flee to Mexico. Calderon continued to play a dominant role behind the scenes after Teodoro Picado Michalski was elected president in 1944 under the banner of Calderon's political coalition. In 1947 Figueres signed the Caribbean Pact with other Central American and Caribbean exiles and supported by President Juan Jose Arevalo of Guatemala, proclaiming the intent to overthrow all dictatorial regimes.

Calderon ran again for president in 1948 against Otilio Ulate. Ulate won a majority in February 8 popular voting but Calderon contested the count and President Picado delayed certifying the results. Figueres's previously organized National Liberation Army attacked Costa Rican government installations beginning March 11, 1948. Full-scale civil war lasted one month. Nicaraguan president Anastasio Somoza, also targeted by the Caribbean Pact, clandestinely supported Picado's losing effort, including by providing "volunteer" fighters. By April 13 Figueres's forces controlled most strategic points outside the capital, San Jose. Surrender negotiations began. The Papal Nuncio and ambassadors of the United States, Panama and Chile acting as intermediaries. Picado resisted Figueres's initial demand for unconditional capitulation. On April 17, 1948, Nicaraguan National Guard units entered Costa Rican border areas and also occupied Villa Quesada with approval of Picado's government. On April 19 Picado belatedly agreed to formal armistice. Nicaraguan forces withdrew April 21. Figueres entered San Jose April 24 to assume leadership of a new government.

A thousand or more persons are thought to have died during the Costa Rican civil war of 1948. No Nicaraguan regular soldiers are acknowledged killed although irregular Nicaraguan "volunteers" are known to have suffered casualties.

Ameringer, C. 1978. *Don Pepe*, 43–66.
Bell, J. P. 1971. *Crisis in Costa Rica*, 146–154.
Bird, L. 1984. *Costa Rica, the Unarmed Democracy*, 71–75.
Dunkerley, J. 1988. *Power in the Isthmus*, 130–131.
Millett, R. 1977. *Guardians of the Dynasty*, 212.

3.2 Costa Rican Crisis, 1948

Jose ("Don Pepe") Figueres was declared head of the Founding Junta of the Second Republic on May 8, 1948, at end of Costa Rica's civil war. Nicaragua's president Anastasio Somoza Garcia had clandestinely assisted the Costa Rican government's vain effort to resist Figueres's forces and also committed regular troops during the last days of the struggle (3.1). Costa Ricans committed to overthrow the new Figueres regime took sanctuary within Nicaragua and contributed to minor border incidents during the summer and fall of 1948. Nicaragua and Costa Rica each protested unsanctioned overflights by one another's military aircraft during October 1948. On December 10, 1948, armed exiles invaded Costa Rica from Nicaragua. Costa Rica alleged that Nicaragua supported the invasion and appealed for help from the Organization of American States (OAS). The Council of the OAS appointed an investigating committee December 14. On December 20, 1948, Costa Rican aircraft attacked Nicaraguan border territory used as base by exile rebels. OAS representatives mediated a cessation of hostilities and a Pact of Amity between Nicaragua and Costa Rica was signed February 21, 1949. No Costa Rican military fatalities are reported during raids upon Nicaragua.

Ameringer, C. 1978. *Don Pepe*, 76–84.
Bird, L. 1984. *Costa Rica, the Unarmed Democracy*, 104–117.
Brecher, M., J. Wilkenfeld, and S. Moser. 1988. *Crises in the Twentieth Century*, 1: 215–216.
Butterworth, R. 1976. *Managing Interstate Conflict*, 104–105.
Crawley, E. 1984. *Nicaragua in Perspective*, 109–110.
Hispanic American Report 1 (October 1948): 8–9; (December 15, 1948): 8.
Slater, J. 1967. *The OAS and United States Foreign Policy*, 67–72.

3.3 Mocoran Seizure, 1957

Honduras and Nicaragua disputed ownership of a small section of border territory north of the Segovia River since the nineteenth century. In 1906 Nicaragua rejected an arbitration decision offered by the king of Spain that favored Honduras. She maintained de facto control and a small military presence within the southern part of the disputed territory between the Segovia and Cruta rivers. Honduras effectively administered the northern sector. Honduras formally reasserted claim to the entire disputed territory in February 1947 when she proclaimed a new department of Cracias a Dios to encompass it. Nicaraguan National Guardsmen deployed along the Cruta River south of the Salvadoran populated town of Mocoran on April 18, 1957. Minor incidents followed. Nicaragua occupied the town of Mocoran on April 25. Honduras' army counterattacked Nicaraguan forces north of the Cruta River and her air force also attacked south of the river. Fighting continued until May 5 when a cease-fire and agreement for military withdrawal was signed following mediation by a commission appointed by the Organization of the American States. A month later Honduras and Nicaragua agreed to submit their dispute to the International Court of Justice. Thirty–five Nicaraguan soldiers were killed on Honduran territory. Honduras maintains that her regular forces suffered no fatalities.

Brecher, M., J. Wilkenfeld, and S. Moser. 1988. *Crises in the Twentieth Century*, 1: 234.
Butterworth, R. 1976. *Managing Interstate Conflict*, 225.
Crawley, E. 1984. *Nicaragua in Perspective*, 120.
Hispanic American Report 10 (April 1957): 179–181; (May 1957): 236–239.

3.4 Panama Incidents, 1959

The United States acquired control of the Panama Canal Zone in 1903 by agreement with a newly established government of Panama which the United States helped to secede from Colombia. The United States administered the zone as an overseas territory, including separate schools, police forces and large military installations. Growth of Panamanian nationalist sentiment after World War II challenged existing arrangements. One sensitive issue involved demands to fly the Panamanian flag within the zone. Panamanian university students implanted several flags in May 1958 which were peacefully removed. On November 3, 1959, flag-carrying demonstrators again attempted to enter the zone. They were turned back at the border by zonal police, sparking riots within neighboring Panama City. The United States Army took over border security later that day as incidents continued. The Panamanian National Guard interceded to disperse demonstrators on the Panamanian side of the border. American soldiers temporarily withdrew November 5 but returned later in the month as violence flared again. Incidents subsided November 30 and U.S. troops returned to barracks. More than one hundred persons were injured during November's disturbances, but no fatalities are reported.

Farnsworth, D., and J. McKenney. 1983. *U.S.-Panama Relations*, 36.
Kitchel, D. 1978. *The Truth About the Panama Canal*, 85–86.
LaFeber, W. 1989. *The Panama Canal*, 98-101.
Liss, S. 1967. *The Canal: Aspects of United States-Panamanian Relations*, 61–62.

3.5 Belize Incident, 1962

British Honduras (Belize) was settled from Jamaica beginning in the seventeenth century. The United Kingdom declared it a colony associated with Jamaica in 1862 and administered it separately from 1884. Neighboring Guatemala asserted claim to the territory after World War II. Britain deployed troops as a precaution in 1948 and maintained a company of regulars in residence thereafter. The garrison was reinforced in November 1961 in order to support rescue and reconstruction efforts following a major hurricane that hit the capital, Belize. In January 1962 twenty armed irregulars representing the Belize Liberation Army supported by Guatemala entered British Honduras. A platoon of British infantry moved to the border area and quickly captured nearly all of the invaders without fatality.

Blaxland, G. 1971. *The Regiments Depart*, 346–353.
Day, A., ed. 1987. *Border and Territorial Disputes*, 397–406.
Dewar, M. 1984. *Brush Fire Wars*, 45–49.
Grant, C. 1976. *The Making of Modern Belize*, 240.

3.6 Cifuentes Incident, 1962

Dispute between Nicaragua and Honduras over ownership of border territory north of the Segovia River provoked fighting around the town of Mocoran in 1957 (3.3). Following this engagement, the two states agreed to submit the issue to the International Court of Justice. The Court ruled in favor of Honduras in 1960. Disagreement followed concerning the status of Nicaraguan citizens and property previously settled within the area. Some residents were relocated and new boundary lines marked in March 1961. Nicaraguan National Guard units continued border patrols. In August 1962 Nicaraguan Guardsmen clashed with Honduran Civil Guards near the town of Cifuentes within Honduran territory. Four Nicaraguan soldiers were killed.

Hispanic American Report 15 (August 1962): 702.
New York Times 8/15/62, 3:4.
Times (London) 8/15/62, 9g.

3.7 Panama Flag Riots, 1964

Dispute concerning sovereignty within the U.S.-administered Panama Canal Zone provoked conflict in 1959 (3.4) and even more serious violence in January 1964. Panama and the United States agreed in 1963 to fly both Panamanian and American flags above some public buildings within the zone. American authorities began to implement the agreement in December 1963 despite resistance among some zonal residents. On January 7 American students at Balboa High School unilaterally raised the U.S. flag in front of their building. On January 9 two hundred Panamanians entered the zone and attempted to raise the Panamanian flag at the school. Riots ensued in Balboa, followed by riots elsewhere in the zone as well as in Colon and Panama City within Panama. The U.S. Army assumed responsibility for maintaining order within the zone the night of January 9. Cross-border sniping and incursions by Panamanian citizens continued for several days. The Army returned control to civil zonal authorities on January 16 after the Panamanian National Guard belatedly reasserted control within Panama and incidents ceased along the border. More than twenty Panamanians were killed, as well as four U.S. servicemen.

Dubois, J. 1964. *Danger in Panama.*
Ealy, L. 1971. *Yanqui Politics and the Isthmian Canal,* 122–125.
Farnsworth, D., and J. McKenney. 1983. *U.S.-Panama Relations,* 35–58.
International Commission of Jurists. 1964. *Report on the Events in Panama.*
Jorden, W. 1984. *Panama Odyssey,* 21–90.
Kitchel, D. 1978. *The Truth About the Panama Canal,* 86–87.
Knapp, H., and M. Knapp. 1984. *Red, White, and Blue Paradise,* 53–64.
LaFeber, W. 1989. *The Panama Canal,* ix, 105–113.
Liss, S. 1967. *The Canal: Aspects of United States-Panamanian Relations.*

3.8 Football War, 1969

El Salvador and Honduras disputed the location of border from the time of independence in the early nineteenth century. Negotiations eventually produced the Bonilla-Velasco agreement signed in 1895. The treaty was never ratified by either El Salvador or Honduras, however, and later negotiations failed to produce a permanent understanding. Beginning in the 1920s, thousands of land-poor Salvadorans immigrated to work or squat within Honduran territory. In January 1969 the Honduran government announced social reforms that, if fully implemented, would result in deportation of as many as 300,000 Salvadorans who had failed to establish legal residence.

In June 1970, Honduran and Salvadoran soccer teams met during elimination rounds of the World Cup competition. Matches in Tegucigalpa, capital of Honduras, June 8, 1969, and in San Salvador, capital of El Salvador, June 15 led to disputes, stadium violence, and rioting. El Salvador declared a state of alert. Formal diplomatic relations between the two countries were severed June 27. El Salvador moved troops to the border. These conducted small raids upon Honduran border positions beginning July 8. On July 14, 1969, El Salvador mounted a full-scale invasion that involved a combination of regular soldiers, designated militia and hastily recruited civilians. The Honduran Air Force undertook retaliatory attacks upon Salvadoran cities July 15 as well as attacked Salvadoran forces within Honduras. Fighting continued within Honduras until cease-fire was arranged July 18 with help of representatives of the Organization of American States. El Salvador withdrew from most of the territory she had conquered after a further agreement was reached July 30, 1969. Several thousand persons are believed to have died during the war. Nearly all were civilians. Fatalities among regular Salvadoran military personnel apparently amounted to no more than 200–300. Honduran casualties were generally lighter and included no reported losses within El Salvador.

Anderson, T. 1981. *The War of the Dispossessed.*

Brecher, M., J. Wilkenfeld, and S. Moser. 1988. *Crises in the Twentieth Century,* 1: 289–290.

Butterworth, R. 1976. *Managing Interstate Conflict,* 438–441.

Cable, V. 1969. "The Football War and the Central American Common Market." *International Affairs* 45 (October): 658–671.

Day, A., ed. 1987. *Border and Territorial Disputes,* 420–425.

Dunkerley, J. 1988. *Power in the Isthmus,* 358–359.

Durham, W. 1979. *Scarcity and Survival in Central America,* 161–165.

English, A. 1984. *Armed Forces of Latin America,* 290, 408–409.

Holly, D. 1979. "Le Conflit du Honduras et du Salvador de 1969." *Etudes Internationales* 10 (March): 19–51.

Keegan, J., ed. 1983. *World Armies,* 249–253, 495–500.

McClintock, M. 1985. *State Terror and Popular Resistance in El Salvador,* 154–157.

Small, M., and J. Singer. 1982. *Resort to Arms,* 94.

Webre, S. 1979. *Jose Napoleon Duarte and the Christian Democratic Party in San Salvadoran Politics,* 106–120.

3.9 Sazalpa Raids, 1976

Border dispute between Honduras and El Salvador and disagreement about the status of Salvadoran immigrants within Honduras contributed to the Football War of 1969 (3.8). El Salvador was induced to withdraw its forces from most captured territory at the end of July 1969. Negotiations ensued concerning a permanent border settlement. These eventually led to agreement in 1980. In the meantime, however, frequent minor border incidents occurred. During July 1976 Salvadoran troops also raided Honduran positions several times in the Sazalapa region and near Hacienda Dolores. On August 9, 1976, El Salvador and Honduras agreed to the emplacement of Organization of American States observers at tense border points and incidents abated thereafter. Two Salvadoran soldiers are reported killed during attacks upon Honduras.

Anderson, T. 1981. *The War of the Dispossessed,* 137.
Day, A., ed. 1987. *Border and Territorial Disputes,* 425–428.
New York Times 7/24/76, 2:7; 7/28/76, 6:5; 7/29/76, 10:7; 8/1/76, 7:1.

3.10 San Carlos Incident, 1977

General Anastasio Somoza Garcia, commander of the National Guard, assumed the presidency of Nicaragua in 1937 under auspices of the Liberal party. He dominated Nicaraguan politics until his assassination in 1956. The Somoza family continued to control

Nicaragua until 1979 when General Anastasio Somoza Debayle, Somoza Garcia's youngest son, surrendered to the Sandinista National Liberation Front. Nicaraguan-Costa Rican relations were repeatedly troubled from the late 1940s, including during and immediately after the 1948 civil war that brought Jose ("Don Pepe") to power within Costa Rica (3.1, 3.2). In 1955, Somoza's government clandestinely supported an unsuccessful attempt by Costa Rican exiles to topple the Figueres regime. Costa Rica and Nicaragua each backed other attempts to overthrow one another's governments as late as 1959.

Open hostilities recurred during the late 1970s. Several issues were at stake, including disputes about water rights and fishing zones. Incidents occurred in 1976–1977 involving allegedly illegal activities by fishing vessels of both countries. Costa Rica also permitted anti-Somoza dissidents to operate from Costa Rican territory. In October 1977 Nicaraguan rebels attempted to seize the Nicaraguan National Guard barracks at San Carlos near the Costa Rican border. The attackers were driven back across the Costa Rican border. Pursuing Nicaraguan aircraft strafed Costa Rican territory October 14, including an attack upon a river vessel carrying Costa Rica's security minister. No Nicaraguan military fatalities are reported within Costa Rica during this incident.

Dupuy, R., and T. Dupuy. 1986. *The Encyclopedia of Military History*, 1395.
Earley, S. 1982. *Arms and Politics in Costa Rica and Nicaragua*, 9–19.
Millett, R. 1977. *Guardians of the Dynasty*, 251–263.
Seligson, M., and W. Carroll. 1982. "The Costa Rican Role in the Sandinist Victory." In *Nicaragua in Revolution*, ed. T. Walker, 331–343.

3.11 Nicaraguan Civil War, 1978

The Somoza family dominated Nicaragua from General Anastasio Somoza Garcia's assumption of the presidency in 1937. Anastasio Somoza Debayle, youngest son of Somoza Garcia, became president in 1967 and was reelected in 1974. In 1961 radical opponents of Somoza rule organized the Frente Sandinista de Liberation Nacional (FSLN) modelled after the Cuban revolutionary movement. The FSLN adopted the name of the martyr Augusto Sandino who had forcibly resisted U.S. military administration of Nicaragua during the 1920s and its adherents came to be known colloquially as "Sandinista". The FSLN originally subsisted primarily among Nicaraguan exiles within Honduras and Costa Rica but gradually built support within Nicaragua. During the 1960s and early 1970s it conducted sporadic terrorist attacks upon government facilities and Somoza family holdings but its effectiveness was limited by division among rival ideological factions. A 1977 raid upon San Carlos near the Costa Rican border led to Nicaraguan air attacks upon Costa Rica (3.10).

Civil war began in earnest in 1978. Costa Rica served as sanctuary and supply conduit for many FSLN operations. On August 22, 1978, FSLN adherents under Eden Pastora attacked the National Palace in Managua and held it for two days until forced to withdraw. On September 7 the FSLN launched attacks within nearly every major Nicaraguan city. On September 12 the Nicaraguan air forces began counterraids upon Costa Rica by strafing the town of La Cruz. In mid-October Nicaragua initiated small-unit ground raids against FSLN supply points across the border. Nicaraguan air and ground attacks upon Costa Rican territory continued upon until November 21, 1978. Costa Rica severed diplomatic relations after an especially egregious incident that day, requested and obtained an investigating team from the Organization of American States. Costa Rica subsequently took steps to impede the flow of FSLN personnel and arms into Nicaragua. Minor border incidents continued as the war intensified in 1979 but Nicaragua refrained from further cross-border operations. The FSLN united factions in March 1979. Major fighting reached Managua in May. On July 16, 1979, Somoza Debayle fled Nicaragua, allowing the FSLN to establish a new government.

The Nicaraguan civil war is estimated to have cost more than 30,000 lives, primarily among civilians. No Nicaraguan military fatalities are reported during operations within Costa Rica.

Black, G. 1981. *Triumph of the People*, 100–181.
Booth, J. 1985. *The End and the Beginning*, 157–182.
Brecher, M., J. Wilkenfeld, and S. Moser. 1988. *Crises in the Twentieth Century*, 1: 334–335.
Christian, S. 1985. *Nicaragua, Revolution in the Family*, 34–118.
Crawley, E. 1984. *Nicaragua in Perspective*, 162–168.
Diederich, B. 1981. *Somoza, and the Legacy of U.S. Involvement in Central America*.
Dunkerley, J. 1988. *Power in the Isthmus*, 247–260, 621–628.
Earley, S. 1982. *Arms and Politics in Costa Rica and Nicaragua*, 9–19.
Ignatev, O., and G. Borovik. 1980. *The Agony of a Dictatorship*.
Lake, A. 1989. *Somoza Falling*, 137–138.
Loveman, B., and T. Davies. 1985. *Che Guevara, Guerrilla Warfare*, 350–389.
Millett, R. 1977. *Guardians of the Dynasty*, 251–263.
Pastor, R. 1987. *Condemned to Repetition*, 49–187.
Seligson, M., and W. Carroll. 1982. "The Costa Rican Role in the Sandinist Victory." In *Nicaragua in Revolution*, ed. T. Walker, 331–343.
Small, M., and J. Singer. 1982. *Resort to Arms*, 232.
Somoza Debayle, A. 1980. *Nicaragua Betrayed*.

3.12 Contra-Sandinista War, 1980–1988

The Frente Sandinista de Liberation Nacional (FSLN) established a provisional Junta of National Reconstruction within Nicaragua on July 19, 1979. FSLN forces, known colloquially as "Sandinistas," had forced President Anastasio Somoza Debayle to flee the country at end of a bloody civil war. Jose Daniel Ortega became de facto leader of the original junta and was designated president of the republic in 1985. The new government committed itself to both economic recovery and social reform and received economic and military assistance from Cuba.

Violent resistance to the FSLN regime persisted in several quarters throughout most of the 1980s, including among former National Guard members who took refuge within Honduras following the civil war. Exile antigovernment forces, popularly referred to as "Contra-Sandinista" or "Contras," became more active after 1981 when the United States began significant covert military and economic support with Honduran cooperation. Diverse Contra factions based within Honduras formed the Union Nicaraguense de Opposition (UNO) in 1985 and formally combined with the smaller Bloque Opposition del Sur (BOS, or "Southern Bloc") based in Costa Rica and composed primarily of FSLN defectors in 1987. Miskito and other Indian minorities who resided primarily along the Atlantic coast also challenged the Sandinista government separately during the early 1980s.

Contra-Sandinista's activities provoked renewed border conflict from 1980 due in part to reliance upon their use of sanctuaries within Honduras and . International armed conflict flared previously on the Nicaraguan-Honduran border in 1957 and 1962 (3.3, 3.6), and also on the Nicaraguan-Costa Rican border in 1948, 1977 and 1978 (3.1, 3.2, 3.10, 3.11). Nicaraguan government aircraft repeatedly strafed and bombed Honduran territory beginning in November 1980, and engaged in small-unit ground raids into Honduras from December 1981. In late March 1986 Nicaraguan troops occupied part of the Las Vegas salient within Honduras and remained until driven out the following December. Honduran air and artillery intervened episodically within Nicaragua between May 1981 and March 1988. Nicaragua also attacked Costa Rican border areas by air beginning in September 1983 and by a commando raid at the end of May 1985. Serious incidents ceased on the southern front after 1985 when the Costa Rican government restricted rebel activities.

On August 7, 1987, President Oscar Arias Sanchez of Costa Rica and the Contadora Group of Latin American states proposed a comprehensive peace plan for the region. Negotiations began between

Contra leaders and the Nicaraguan government in late January 1988. Nicaragua halted raids upon Honduras after March 20, 1988, when a general cease-fire was agreed to take effect April 1.

The Contra-Sandinista War is believed to have involved as many as 20,000 fatalities, primarily among civilians. Nicaragua lost a score of soldiers on foreign soil between 1981 and 1988, half of these during 1986 operations within Honduras. Honduras apparently suffered no losses within Nicaragua.

Azicri, M. 1985. "Relations with Latin America." In *Nicaragua: The First Five Years*, ed. T. Walker, 499–522.

Cruz Sequeira, A. 1989. *Memoirs of a Counterrevolutionary*, 125–259.

Dunkerley, J. 1988. *Power in the Isthmus*, 312–327, 568–583, 640–648.

Gold, E. 1987. "Military Encirclement." In *Reagan Versus the Sandinistas*, ed. T. Walker, 39–56.

Gutman, R. 1988. *Banana Diplomacy*.

Kornbluh, P. 1987. *Nicaragua, the Price of Intervention*.

Laffin, J. 1986. *War Annual 1*, 118.

Laffin, J. 1987. *War Annual 2*, 157–168.

Laffin, J. 1989. *The World in Conflict 1989: War Annual 3*, 67–75.

Pastor, R. 1987. *Condemned to Repetition*, 230–261.

Robinson, W., and K. Norsworthy. 1987. *David and Goliath*.

Turner, R. 1987. *Nicaragua v. United States*, 98–108.

Vanderlaan, M. 1986. *Revolution and Foreign Policy in Nicaragua*, 265–371.

Vilas, C. 1989. *State, Class, and Ethnicity in Nicaragua*, 142–187.

3.13 Salvadoran Civil War, 1981–1982

A small oligarchy within El Salvador: controlled most land and most wealth from the nineteenth century. Large numbers of landless peasants emigrated to Honduras from the 1920s, contributing to the Football War of 1969 and later incidents between the two states (3.8, 3.9). Military figures generally dominated the El Salvadoran government from the 1930s, including by election under banner of the Partido de Conciliacion National (PCN) beginning in 1962.

Numerous small guerrilla groups representing different leftist tendencies organized against the Salvadoran government during the 1970s and mounted separate armed challenges from 1972. Right-wing terrorist groups developed as counterpoise, including groups such as the Falange which cooperated unofficially with elements of the Salvadoran military establishment. El Salvador was wracked by intense, sustained violence after 1976. Fighting within eastern and western provinces encouraged the flight of large numbers of refugees to Honduras. The Honduran army attempted to impede the exodus, including by stationing forces at the border and erecting barricades along the Sumpul River boundary. On May 14, 1980, Honduran soldiers forced 600 refugees back across the river where they were massacred by the Salvadoran army.

Several, but not all left-wing paramilitary groups combined operations under the Frente Farabundo Marti para la Liberacion Nacional (FMLN) in October 1980. In January 1981 the FMLN launched what it described as a "final offensive" which called for a general strike and made serious inroads within northern and eastern countryside. Salvadoran army counteroffensives included air attacks upon Honduran territory beginning in March 1981 and raids by small ground units from July 1981. The Honduran government did not officially sanction Salvadoran cross-border operations and lodged formal protests upon several occasions. Nevertheless, the two governments cooperated during July 1982 when more than 2,000 Honduran troops participated in a ten-day joint operation against guerrilla bases in border areas, including upon Salvadoran territory. The focus of fighting shifted away from the Honduran border by the beginning of 1983 and Salvadoran cross-border operations ceased after December 1982. The civil war continued into the 1990s.

The Salvadoran bloodbath is estimated to have cost more than 50,000 lives, primarily civilian, from the late 1970s through the late 1980s. No Salvadoran military fatalities are reported within Honduras. Nine Honduran soldiers died during July 1982 operations within El Salvador.

Baloyra, E. 1982. *El Salvador in Transition*, 125–143.
Day, A., ed. 1987. *Border and Territorial Disputes*, 425–428.
Diskin, M., and K. Sharpe. 1986. *The Impact of U.S. Policy in El Salvador*.
Dunkerley, J. 1982. *The Long War*, 162–205.
Dunkerley, J. 1988. *Power in the Isthmus*, 381–413.
Earley, S. 1982. *Arms and Politics in Costa Rica and Nicaragua*, 22–36.
Hadar, A. 1981. *The United States and El Salvador*, 42–68.
Loveman, B., and T. Davies. 1985. *Che Guevara, Guerrilla Warfare*, 390–417.
McClintock, M. 1985. *State Terror and Popular Resistance in El Salvador*, 286–325.
Montgomery, T. 1982. *Revolution in El Salvador*, 159–193.

3.14 Chiapas Raids I, 1982–1983

The United States covertly helped to overthrow of the elected government of Jacobo Arbenz Guzman within Guatemala in 1954. One repressive military regime succeeded another during ensuing years. Several left-wing groups mounted persistent guerrilla resistance from the early 1960s, including the Revolutionary Organization of the People in Arms, the Revolutionary Armed Forces, and the Guerrilla Army of the Poor. Persistent rebellion reflected in part deep social cleavages. Most guerrillas championed the plight of impoverished Indian peoples who represented a majority of the population. A Spanish-descended minority controlled most of the country's wealth and political power. General Efrain Rios Montt became president of Guatemala in June 1982 after another military coup. The new government resorted to draconian measures against opponents during the next two years and is thought to have killed as many as 10,000 unarmed civilians. As many as 100,000 Guatemalans fled to neighboring Mexico where they concentrated in refugee camps just across the border. From September 1982 to late January 1983, small units of Guatemalan soldiers repeatedly raided refugee camps within Mexico's Chiapas state. The Mexican government protested these actions but did not retaliate militarily. No Guatemalan military fatalities are reported within Mexico.

Dunkerley, J. 1988. *Power in the Isthmus*, 484–504.
New York Times 9/28/82, 4:3; 10/9/82, 2:3; 10/17/82, 9:1; 1/31/83, 5:2.
Walker, P. 1984. "National Security." In *Mexico, a Country Study*, ed. J. Rudolph, 315–373.

3.15 Chiapas Raids II, 1984

The Guatemalan government of General Efrain Rios Montt conducted raids upon refugee camps within Mexico that allegedly harbored dissidents in 1982–1983 (3.14), during Guatemala's protracted civil war. Refugee concentrations declined abroad in 1983 after Montt was ousted and the army adopted less stringent counterinsurgency policies. Mexico also announced plans to resettle refugees away from the border in 1983. The program was slow in starting and tens of thousands remained near the Mexican-Guatemalan boundary in 1984. At the end of April 1984 a small number of Guatemalan troops again raided a refugee camp within Mexico's Chiapas state. No Guatemalan military fatalities are reported.

Latin America Weekly Report (May 18, 1984): 11.
New York Times 5/3/84, I, 10:1.
Walker, P. 1984. "National Security." In *Mexico, a Country Study*, ed. J. Rudolph, 315–373.

4

South America

International armed conflict within South America was generally sporadic and isolated after World War II. The United Kingdom intervened briefly upon four occasions within British Guiana (Guyana) between 1953 and 1964 (4.3, 4.5, 4.7, 4.8) prior to independence. Civil strife within Paraguay contributed to an incident with Argentina in 1962 (4.6). In addition, territorial disputes provoked conflict upon several occasions. Argentine claims to the British-ruled Falkland Islands and Dependencies led to an armed incident in 1953 (4.2) and to the Malvinas War of 1982 (4.13). The disputed border between Ecuador and Peru contributed to an armed exchange in 1951 (4.1) and to repeated incidents from 1978 to 1984 (4.1, 4,11, 4.12, 4.14). Border disputes between Argentina and Chile (4.4), between Guyana and Surinam (4.9), and between Venezuela and Guyana (4.10) also led to occasional armed conflict.

4.1 Gualingo Raids, 1951

From the time of independence in the early nineteenth century, Ecuador disputed Peruvian control of border territories that provided access to both the Amazon Basin and the Pacific. The two waged a minor war in the Amazon in 1941 that ended largely to Peru's advantage. Formal demarcation of the border proceeded under an agreement signed in 1942. The task was partially completed in 1951 when, following the discovery of a previously unknown river in the Amazon Basin, Ecuador pressed new territorial claims. Peruvian troops launched a series of as many as eight attacks over a period of a week in August 1951 upon Ecuadorian positions established in the disputed Gualingo area. No fatalities apparently resulted from these incidents, and Peru excused the actions as unauthorized conduct of drunken soldiers.

Butterworth, R. 1976. *Managing Interstate Conflict*, 29.
Day, A., ed. 1987. *Border and Territorial Disputes*, 420–425.
Krieg, W. 1987. *Ecuadorean-Peruvian Rivalry in the Upper Amazon*, 144–145.
Hispanic American Report 4 (August 1951): 25.

4.2 Deception Incident, 1953

The United Kingdom asserted formal dominion within the Falkland Islands in 1833. She appended other South Atlantic territories later in the nineteenth century, including the uninhabited South Sandwich Islands near Antarctica. Argentina refused to abandon her own claims to the area due to proximity and prior rule. Unoccupied Deception Island near Antarctica became one focus of rivalry after World War II. Argentina attempted to establish a civilian presence there in 1946 but was induced to withdraw. In 1948 Argentina publicized her claim to the South Sandwich group. She began again to build residence huts upon Deception in 1952. In February 1953 a detachment of British Royal Marines landed, arrested the Argentine inhabitants and destroyed facilities without casualty to either side.

Child, J. 1988. *Antarctica and South American Geopolitics*, 73.
Fox, R. 1985. *Antarctica and the South Atlantic*, 185.
Hispanic American Report 6 (February 1953): 31–32.

4.3 Jagan's Removal, 1953

The United Kingdom captured the colony of British Guiana (Guyana) from the Dutch in 1796. Population was augmented by imported African slaves and later by East Indian laborers. Successive waves of immigrants helped to form a culturally and racially divided society. Such divisions exacerbated tensions growing out of rising nationalism after World War II. Cheddi Jagan's radical People's Progressive Party (PPP) won the first national elections held under universal suffrage in April 1953 primarily due to support within the East Indian community. Jagan formed a government under grant of limited autonomy. He subsequently pursued policies that were offensive within both the black and British communities. A general strike and demonstrations in the capital, Georgetown, in October 1953, primarily involving East Indians, precipitated intervention by British troops. The United Kingdom suppressed the demonstrations and deposed the Jagan government. The British forces suspended operations by late October but remained in garrison thereafter. No British military fatalities are reported.

Blaxland, G. 1971. *The Regiments Depart*, 366–367.
Burrowes, R. 1984. *The Wild Coast*, 33–66.
Butterworth, R. 1976. *Managing Interstate Conflict*, 170–171.
Dewar, M. 1984. *Brush Fire Wars*, 63–67.
Henfrey, Colin V. F. 1972. "Foreign Influence in Guyana." In *Patterns of Foreign Influence in the Caribbean*, ed. E. de Kadt, 49–81.
Jagan, C. 1971. *The West on Trial*, 124–146.
Mitchell, H. 1963. *Europe in the Caribbean*, 146–147.
Reno, P. 1964. *The Ordeal of British Guiana*, 13–19.
Smith, Raymond. 1962. *British Guiana*, 168–180.
Spinner, T. 1984. *A Political and Social History of Guyana*, 33–47.

4.4 Snipe Island Incidents, 1958

Argentina and Chile disputed their southern boundary as well as other parts of their border from time of independence in the nineteenth century. Conflicting claims of rights among islands in the vicinity of Tierra del Fuego and Cape Horn, especially within the Beagle Channel, provoked repeated controversy. In 1958 Chile constructed a lighthouse on disputed Snipe Island in the Channel. A small party of Argentine Navy and Marines landed and destroyed the installation in May 1958. Chile rebuilt the lighthouse. Argentina dispatched military forces again in August 1958 and once more destroyed the facility. No fatalities are reported in these incidents.

Butterworth, R. 1976. *Managing Interstate Conflict*, 235–237.
Hispanic American Report 11 (May 1958): 275–276; (August 1958): 456.
Talbott, R. 1974. *A History of the Chilean Boundaries*, 113.

4.5 Georgetown Riots, 1962

The United Kingdom dispatched troops to the colony of British Guiana (Guyana) in 1953 (4.3) and unseated the local government recently formed by Cheddi Jagan and the radical People's Progressive Party (PPP). A small garrison of British troops remained thereafter. The PPP was resoundingly successful in the 1957 elections, gaining support from both black and East Indian communities. PPP support declined by the time of the 1961 elections and the party obtained merely a plurality of the vote, garnered primarily among East Indians. Jagan formed a new government on this basis. A general strike and sporadic rioting occurred in the capital, Georgetown, during February 1962. Demonstrations involved primarily black protest against Jagan's policies deemed to favor the East Indian community. British troops intervened again in support of local police. British military units were called into action upon several occasions as late as August 1962. No British fatalities resulted from these operations.

Blaxland, G. 1971. *The Regiments Depart*, 370–371.
Burrowes, R. 1984. *The Wild Coast*, 143–166.
Butterworth, R. 1976. *Managing Interstate Conflict*, 170–171.
Despres, L. 1967. *Cultural Pluralism and Nationalist Politics in British Guiana*, 262–267.
Dewar, M. 1984. *Brush Fire Wars*, 63–67.
Glasgow, R. 1970. *Guyana: Race and Politics Among Africans and East Indians*, 114–133.
Henfrey, Colin V. F. 1972. "Foreign Influence in Guyana." In *Patterns of Foreign Influence in the Caribbean*, ed. E. de Kadt, 49–81.
Jagan, C. 1971. *The West on Trial*, 205–221, 258–261.
Mitchell, H. 1963. *Europe in the Caribbean*, 149–150.
Newman, P. 1964. *British Guiana*, 91–95.
Reno, P. 1964. *The Ordeal of British Guiana*, 35–44.
Spinner, T. 1984. *A Political and Social History of Guyana*, 89–100.

4.6 Pilcomayo Incident, 1962

General Alfredo Stroessner, chief of the army, assumed the presidency of Paraguay in 1954. Exiles opposed to Stroessner's regime fled to Argentina. Relations between Paraguay and Argentina alternated between confrontation and accommodation during the late 1950s and early 1960s and Argentine support of dissident exiles waxed and waned. In December 1959 Paraguayan exiles attempted an invasion from Argentina but were repulsed. In May 1962 a small detachment of Argentine troops briefly occupied Remansito Paraguayo on the Pilcomayo River within Paraguay. The unit withdrew after a few days. The Paraguayan government minimized the significance of the incident by attributing it to an error by the local Argentine commander. No casualties are reported.

Hispanic American Report 15 (May 1962): 459.
New York Times 5/16/62, 12:5.

4.7 Guyanese Strike, 1963

Cultural and political tensions within the United Kingdom's colony of British Guiana (Guyana) called forth British military intervention in 1953 (4.3) and 1962 (4.5) and did so again in 1963. Cheddi Jagan and his radical People's Progressive Party (PPP) controlled local government from the 1950s based primarily upon consistent electoral support within the East Indian community. The PPP enjoyed much less support within the black community and among Europeans. During the 1960s the Jagan government increasingly pursued policies favoring East Indian interests. A general strike was called by Jagan opponents in April 1963. Riots erupted within the capital, Georgetown, in early May and spread to some outlying villages. Locally garrisoned British troops turned out immediately to help police contain violence. Additional troops were brought in at the beginning of July. Serious disturbances and military patrols ceased a few days later. No fatalities occurred among British forces.

Blaxland, G. 1971. *The Regiments Depart*, 371–372.
Burrowes, R. 1984. *The Wild Coast*, 167–187.
Butterworth, R. 1976. *Managing Interstate Conflict*, 170–171.
Despres, L. 1967. *Cultural Pluralism and Nationalist Politics in British Guiana*, 262–267.
Dewar, M. 1984. *Brush Fire Wars*, 63–67.
Glasgow, R. 1970. *Guyana: Race and Politics Among Africans and East Indians*, 114–133.
Henfrey, Colin V. F. 1972. "Foreign Influence in Guyana." In *Patterns of Foreign Influence in the Caribbean*, ed. E. de Kadt, 49–81.
Jagan, C. 1971. *The West on Trial*, 222–247, 262–266.
Newman, P. 1964. *British Guiana*, 96–100.
Reno, P. 1964. *The Ordeal of British Guiana*, 45–57.
Spinner, T. 1984. *A Political and Social History of Guyana*, 100–103.

4.8 Guyanese Emergency, 1964

The United Kingdom intervened within its colony of British Guiana (Guyana) in 1953, 1962 and 1963 (4.3, 4.5, 4.7) during recurrent political strife that reflected in part deep cultural and racial divisions within the society. Cheddi Jagan's People's Progressive Party (PPP) repeatedly won at least a plurality within local government elections from 1953. In power, Jagan tended to pursue policies favoring the East Indian population as opposed to other ethnic groups. Serious racial violence erupted again in May 1964. A state of emergency was declared and locally garrisoned British troops intervened once more in support of police. Soldiers remained on duty through the elections of December 1964 without suffering any fatalities.

Blaxland, G. 1971. *The Regiments Depart*, 372–373.
Burrowes, R. 1984. *The Wild Coast*, 187–199.
Butterworth, R. 1976. *Managing Interstate Conflict*, 170–171.
Despres, L. 1967. *Cultural Pluralism and Nationalist Politics in British Guiana*, 262–267.

Glasgow, R. 1970. *Guyana: Race and Politics Among Africans and East Indians*, 114–133.
Henfrey, Colin V. F. 1972. "Foreign Influence in Guyana." In *Patterns of Foreign Influence in the Caribbean*, ed. E. de Kadt, 49–81.
Jagan, C. 1971. *The West on Trial*, 305–319.
Reno, P. 1964. *The Ordeal of British Guiana*, 58–67.
Spinner, T. 1984. *A Political and Social History of Guyana*, 104–110.

4.9 New River Conflict, 1969

The Netherlands first settled Dutch Guiana (Surinam) in the early seventeenth century and ruled it continuously from 1816. The United Kingdom seized British Guiana (Guyana) from the Dutch in 1796. The boundary between the Guiana territories was determined by international agreement in 1814. Dutch authorities protested British Guiana's control of a triangular section of their southern frontier near Brazil after discovery of the New River tributary of the Corentyne River in the late nineteenth century. Dutch and British governments negotiated sporadically about the issue during the early twentieth century. The Netherlands granted local self-rule to Surinam in 1954 but retained colonial control until 1975. In 1962 the Netherlands formally reasserted Surinam's claim to the New River triangle. Unsuccessful negotiations took place in London in June 1966, three months after Guyana gained independence from Britain. Surinam commenced survey explorations of the New River area in conjunction with a hydroelectric power project planned within Surinam. Guyana expelled one survey party in December 1967. Further minor incidents followed. In August 1969 a small unit of Guyanese troops landed at and briefly occupied an airstrip at Tigri within Surinam. Guyana and Surinam agreed thereafter to reopen negotiations. No fatalities are reported during the 1969 incident.

Butterworth, R. 1976. *Managing Interstate Conflict*, 329–331.
Child, J. 1985. *Geopolitics and Conflict in South America*, 163–165.
Day, A., ed. 1987. *Border and Territorial Disputes*, 431–434.
Jeffrey, H., and C. Baber. 1986. *Guyana: Politics, Economics, and Society*, 168.
Manley, R. 1979. *Guyana Emergent*, 42–44.

4.10 Essequibo Incident, 1970

Venezuela and British Guiana (Guyana) disputed control of a substantial section border territory in the vicinity of the Essequibo River. An arbitral panel awarded most of the disputed territory to British Guiana in 1899. Venezuela formally accepted the arbitration decision in 1905 but revived its claim to territory west of the Essequibo in 1962. In February 1966 Venezuela agreed with the United Kingdom to recognize Guyana when it became independent later that year and to participate in a mixed commission to resolve boundary disputes. Numerous incidents followed Guyanese independence in May 1966. Venezuelan survey parties frequently crossed the Guyanese border, especially in and around the island of Amkoko which was thought to possess mineral potential. In July 1968 the Venezuelan government advanced additional claims involving territorial waters and also withdrew from the mixed commission subcommittee dealing with border claims. In January 1969 a two-week rebellion broke out within Guyana's Rapanuni district in the Essequibo region. Several hundred men led by Elmo and Jimmy Hart attacked Guyanese government facilities and attempted to foment secession. Guyana charged that Venezuela supported the secessionist movement, although Venezuela denied doing so. Further minor incidents in February 1970 led to mortar attacks by Venezuelan troops upon Guyanese border guards on March 22, 1970. Further incidents were avoided and on June 18, 1970, Venezuela, Guyana and the United Kingdom signed the Port-au-Prince protocol committing to a twelve-year cooling off period regarding border questions. No fatalities are reported in association with the March 1970 attack.

Braveboy-Wagner, J. 1984. *The Venezuela-Guyana Border Dispute*, 167.
Butterworth, R. 1976. *Managing Interstate Conflict*, 329–331.
Child, J. 1985. *Geopolitics and Conflict in South America*, 157–163.
Day, A., ed. 1987. *Border and Territorial Disputes*, 435–438.
Jeffrey, H., and C. Baber. 1986. *Guyana: Politics, Economics, and Society*, 167–168.
Liss, S. 1978. *Diplomacy and Dependency*, 208–216.
Manley, R. 1979. *Guyana Emergent*, 41–42.

4.11 Qualquiza Incident, 1978

Protracted border dispute between Ecuador and Peru dating from the early nineteenth century provoked war within the Amazon Basin in 1941 and further armed conflict in 1951 (4.1). Efforts to demarcate the border, begun after the 1941 war, effectively ceased after 1951, leaving part of the border through the El Condor Mountains unmarked. Minor border incidents occurred again in 1977 as Ecuador and Peru pressed forward to occupy new positions along the Maranon River. In mid-January 1978 a small unit of Ecuadorian soldiers attacked a Peruvian border post near Qualquiza. Peru refrained from direct retaliation at this time but minor incidents continued during 1978 and ensuing years.

One Peruvian died during the Qualquiza incident but no Ecuadorian fatalities are reported.

Child, J. 1985. *Geopolitics and Conflict in South America*, 92–98.
Day, A., ed. 1987. *Border and Territorial Disputes*, 420–425.
Krieg, W. 1987. *Ecuadorean-Peruvian Rivalry in the Upper Amazon*, 224–228.

4.12 Paquisha Incident, 1981

Border dispute between Peru and Ecuador relating to the Amazon Basin provoked armed conflict in 1951 (4.1) and 1978 (4.11). In 1980 Ecuador established forward posts and military encampments within disputed territory on the eastern side of the Cordillera del Condor at Machinaza, Paquisha and Mayaycu. A minor shooting incident occurred January 22, 1981, involving a Peruvian helicopter operating near Paquisha. On January 28 Peru launched major air attacks upon the three forward Ecuadorian encampments. Ecuador withdrew troops from her most advanced positions. Peruvian ground forces occupied the three posts two days later. Paquisha was taken without resistance but gun battles continued for a few days in the vicinity of Machinaza and Mayaycu.The Organization of American States encouraged a cease-fire effective February 1 and fighting ceased by the next day. At least one Peruvian soldier died during the fighting as did at least two Ecuadorians.

Child, J. 1985. *Geopolitics and Conflict in South America*, 92–98.
Day, A., ed. 1987. *Border and Territorial Disputes*, 420–425.
Keegan, J., ed. 1983. *World Armies*, 469–474.
Krieg, W. 1987. *Ecuadorean-Peruvian Rivalry in the Upper Amazon*, 271–319.

4.13 Malvinas War, 1982

Spain colonized the Falkland Islands in 1766 and remained until 1811. A British settlement also existed until abandoned in 1774. In 1820 Argentina proclaimed authority over the Islands (which she called Las Malvinas) shortly after gaining independence from Spain and remained until driven out in 1831–1832. The United Kingdom took formal possession of the lightly-inhabited Falklands in 1833 and later appended South Georgia and the uninhabited South Sandwich Islands. Argentina persistently refused to acknowledge British rule within the Falklands. In 1927 she also asserted claim to South Georgia and in 1948 to the South Sandwich Islands. Minor incidents occurred upon several occasions, especially after Argentina attempted to establish facilities upon the uninhabited Deception Island in 1946. In 1953 British Marines forcibly expelled Argentines from Deception (4.2). In 1973 the Argentine government pressed claim to the territories before the United Nations. Inconclusive negotiations followed as did repeated minor incidents. On March 19, 1982, a party of Argentine civilians landed upon South Georgia and raised the Argentine flag, ostensibly for purpose of collecting scrap from an abandoned whaling station. The United Kingdom demanded that the Argentine government of Leopoldo Galtieri arrange to withdraw its nationals. Argentina refused to do so.

On April 2, 1982, Argentina executed Operation Azul, a series of quickly successful amphibious assaults that resulted in military occupation of the Falklands, South Georgia and the South Sandwich Islands. Argentina refused to withdraw despite British protest, U.N. urging and mediation by the United States. The United Kingdom dispatched a large task force from Britain prepared to retake the islands by force. Upon arrival in the South Atlantic, British forces quickly recaptured South Georgia April 25. On May 2 a British submarine sunk the Argentine battle cruiser *General Belgrano* operating in international waters some distance from the Falklands. Argentina destroyed the British destroyer *Sheffield* two days later. British troops landed on East Falkland May 21 and in June attacked the main Argentine garrison at Port Stanley. Argentine forces on the Falklands surrendered by June 15. On June 20, 1982, Britain forced surrender on Southern Thule in the South Sandwich Islands, the last remaining Argentine position.

The casualty toll of the Malvinas War included nearly 1,000 killed. Approximately 250 British service personnel died, including aboard the *Sheffield*. Argentina lost nearly 700 soldiers, sailors and airmen including those who perished with the *General Belgrano*.

Calvert, P. 1982. *The Falklands Crisis.*
Charlton, M. 1989. *The Little Platoon.*
Child, J. 1985. *Geopolitics and Conflict in South America*, 112–130.
Cordesman, A., and A. Wagner. 1990. The Lessons of Modern War. 3:238–361.
Dabat, A. 1984. *Argentina, the Malvinas, and the End of Military Rule*, 63–124.
Day, A., ed. 1987. *Border and Territorial Disputes*, 387–397.
Dillon, G. 1989. *The Falklands, Politics, and War.*
Eddy, P., and M. Linklater, eds. 1982. *The Falklands War.*
Gamba, V. 1987. *The Falklands/Malvinas War.*
Gustafson, L. 1988. *The Sovereignty Dispute Over the Falkland (Malvinas) Islands.*
Hastings, Max, and S. Jenkins. 1983. *The Battle for the Falklands.*
Headland, R. 1984. *The Island of South Georgia*, 237–256.
Hoffmann, F., and O. Hoffmann. 1984. *Sovereignty in Dispute*, 152–171.
Keegan, J., ed. 1983. *World Armies*, 606–613.

Kinney, D. 1985. "Anglo-Argentine Diplomacy and the Falklands Crisis." In *The Falklands War*, ed. A. Coll and A. Arend, 81–105.
Middlebrook, M. 1985. *Operation Corporate*.
Moro, R. 1989. *The History of the South Atlantic Conflict*.
Rock, D. 1987. *Argentina, 1516–1987*, 374–383.
Watson, B., and P. Dunn, eds. 1984. *Military Lessons of the Falkland Islands War*.

4.14 Corrientes Clash, 1984

Protracted Peruvian-Ecuadorian border dispute contributed to conflict in 1951 (4.1), 1978 (4.11) and most seriously in 1981 (4.12). The primary area in dispute included a 50-mile-long zone that partially controlled river access to the Amazon Basin. Peru forcibly expelled Ecuador from most of the disputed region in 1981 but minor incidents continued intermittently. On January 15, 1984, a small unit of Ecuadorian troops assaulted Peruvian border guards near a Peruvian frontier post on the Corrientes River. One Ecuadorian soldier was killed and another wounded. No Peruvian fatalities are reported.

Child, J. 1985. *Geopolitics and Conflict in South America*, 92–98.
Day, A., ed. 1987. *Border and Territorial Disputes*, 420–425.
Krieg, W. 1987. *Ecuadorean-Peruvian Rivalry in the Upper Amazon*, 328.

5

Europe

The Greek civil war (5.1) represented continental Europe's most costly conflict after World War II and included low-intensity international armed strife. Efforts of the Soviet Union to maintain order within Eastern Europe included military operations within East Germany in 1953 (5.2), Hungary in 1956 (5.5), and Czechoslovakia in 1968 (5.9). Allied occupation of Trieste also called forth military action in 1953 (5.3). Cyprus suffered repeated civil strife and foreign intervention, including during the 1950s (5.4), the 1960s (5.7, 5.8), and Turkish invasion in 1974 (5.10). The United Kingdom also mobilized troops during demonstrations on Malta in 1958 (5.6). In addition, Egypt raided Cyprus (5.11) and Malta (5.12) during air hijack incidents in 1978 and 1985.

5.1 Greek Civil War, 1947–1949

Italy annexed Albania in 1939 and attempted to conquer Greece in October 1940. Greek and British forces drove the invaders back and captured a strip of southern Albania. Germany intervened in aid of Italy and captured Athens in April 1941. The government of King Georgios II fled to exile and eventually arrived in London. Both the Soviet Union and Britain encouraged resistance groups but left-wing groups organized first. Communists formed the National Liberation Front (EAM) and National Popular Liberation Army (ELAS) before the end of 1941. EAM/ELAS subsequently attacked other resistance factions as well as fought the Germans. The United Kingdom assaulted the Greek mainland in October 1944. Germany withdrew three weeks later. British troops and partisans loyal to King Georgios confronted communist factions within Athens who opposed plans to restore the King's government. Major violence ended by February 1945. Many ELAS fighters surrendered following the Varkiza Agreement and a plebiscite was promised to help determine future government. The plebiscite, eventually held September 1, 1946, affirmed popular support for return of the king.

Guerrilla warfare resumed in late September 1946 mere days after King Georgios' return. Radical socialist regimes had come to power at end of World War II within neighboring Albania, Bulgaria and Yugoslavia. Leftist Greek opposition groups rebuilt strength with their help. British troops remained until 1950 but took no direct role in renewed fighting. The United States began large-scale military assistance after the United Kingdom withdrew most forces in March 1947. American aid included military equipment, training and advisors attached down to battalion levels but did not involve direct military operations.

Conflict spilled over Balkan borders in 1947 as Greek forces began sporadic attacks upon the guerrillas' foreign sanctuaries and sources of supply. Greek aircraft attacked Albanian territory beginning in late May 1947 and raided Lake Doyran within Yugoslavia during June. Small ground units penetrated Bulgaria beginning in May 1947 and also Albania and Yugoslavia beginning in 1948. Low-intensity cross-border operations continued until August 1949. Neighbors also intervened in Greece occasionally. Yugoslav troops participated in a serious incident on the Greek side of the border in September 1948. Albanian soldiers were involved in a similar incident in August 1949.

Yugoslavia closed her borders to Greek insurgent forces in 1949 after being expelled from the Cominform in 1948. Moscow and Belgrade had disputed the proper direction of socialist development since 1944 when Josip Broz Tito seized power in Yugoslavia in the name of communism without direct assistance of the Red Army. Loss of Yugoslavian sanctuaries proved a fatal to the Greek insurgency. Some important guerrilla leaders capitulated in October 1949, ending serious fighting, and conflict as a whole dissipated in 1950.

The Greek civil war cost several hundred thousand lives, including civilians. Foreign military losses were minimal. Greece sustained no more than a few dozen fatalities during cross-border operations. Albania and Yugoslavia each suffered no more than a score of soldiers killed during regular military operations within Greece.

Butterworth, R. 1976. *Managing Interstate Conflict,* 76–77.
Campbell, J. 1972. "The Greek Civil War." In *The International Regulation of Civil Wars,* ed. E. Luard, 37–64.
Kousoulas, D. 1965. *Revolution and Defeat,* 236–288.
Matthews, K. 1972. *Memories of a Mountain War.*
O'Ballance, E. 1966. *The Greek Civil War, 1944–1949.*
Small, M., and J. Singer. 1982. *Resort to Arms,* 229.
Woodhouse, C. 1976. *The Struggle for Greece, 1941–1949,* 169–289.

5.2 East German Riots, 1953

The Soviet Union conquered eastern Germany in 1945 and helped to establish a radical socialist regime through the Socialist Unity party. The German Democratic Republic (East Germany) was proclaimed in 1949 but the Soviet Union retained formal supervisory authority until 1954. In June 1953 industrial workers who opposed a decree increasing production norms staged a strike and street demonstrations in East Berlin and other East German cities. The government declared an emergency June 17 and Soviet troops stationed within East Germany intervened to enforce martial law until July 17. Seventeen East German civilians were killed during the emergency but no Soviet military fatalities are reported.

Baring, A. 1972. *Uprising in East Germany; June 17, 1953.*
Brecher, M., J. Wilkenfeld, and S. Moser. 1988. *Crises in the Twentieth Century,* 1: 224–225.
Butterworth, R. 1976. *Managing Interstate Conflict,* 168–169.
Kecskemeti, P. 1961. *The Unexpected Revolution,* 125–134.
Schmid, A., and E. Berends. 1985. *Soviet Military Interventions Since 1945,* 23–25.

5.3 Trieste Riots, 1953

Trieste, part of the Austro-Hungarian Empire before World War I, was awarded to Italy in 1919 at the same time that adjoining territory along the Dalmatian Coast was assigned to Yugoslavia. Yugoslav guerrillas as well as U.S. and British troops helped to liberate the area from Italy during World War II. Italy and Yugoslavia both claimed the region. The United States and the United Kingdom constituted an Allied Military Government within their occupation zone in June 1945. Yugoslavia organized separate a administration occupied a contiguous zone. Pro-Yugoslav civilians provoked incidents within the Allied zone early in 1945 that called forth British and American troops to help maintain order. Further anti-Italian demonstrations and incidents in ensuing years were controlled by police, including riots during March 1952. Protracted negotiations among Italy, Yugoslavia and the Allied governors failed to define a permanent settlement. In October 1953 the United States and the United Kingdom announced their intention to withdraw garrison forces from the Allied zone and to hand administration over to Italy. More demonstrations followed including attacks directed at British servicemen. British and American troops were called out on November 6, 1953, in order to help police during an especially serious riot. Troops returned to barracks after one day's duty without casualty.

Blaxland, G. 1971. *The Regiments Depart*, 71–72.
Brecher, M., J. Wilkenfeld, and S. Moser. 1988. *Crises in the Twentieth Century*, 1: 225.
Butterworth, R. 1976. *Managing Interstate Conflict*, 81–83.
Duroselle, J. 1966. *Le Conflit de Trieste, 1943–1954*, 393–394.
M. K. G. 1954. "The Trieste Dispute." *World Today* 10 (January): 6–18.
Novak, B. 1970. *Trieste, 1941–1954*, 439–448.

5.4 Enosis Movement, 1955–1959

Cyprus was colonized by Greeks and Phoenicians by the beginning of the first millennium B.C. The island was subsequently absorbed within the Persian Empire and, following that, the Roman Empire. Turks eventually conquered the island in 1571 and ruled it until the late nineteenth century. The resulting multicultural population included a large Greek-speaking majority and a conspicuous Turkish-speaking minority, as well as minor representations of other ethnic groups. The United Kingdom administered Cyprus from 1878, annexed it in 1914 and made it a Crown Colony in 1925.

Greek Cypriot demands threatened British control after World War II. The leading Greek Orthodox prelate, Archbishop Markarios III, led a public movement to promote union of Cyprus and Greece (enosis). George Grivas, a retired Greek Army colonel, helped to form a surreptitious paramilitary band, the National Organization of Cypriot Fighters (EOKA), which planted bombs in public places beginning in April 1955 and attacked police stations beginning in June. In September 1955 British garrison troops and reinforcements deployed across the island in order to support police.

EOKA attacks increased in 1956–1958. Britain exiled Archbishop Makarios to the Seychelles in March 1956 and did not permit him to return until a year later. Turkish Cypriots practiced counterterror against Greeks. Protracted negotiations involving Makarios, the governments of Britain, Greece and Turkey, and the United Nations discussed various solutions including partition and union with Greece. In February 1959, the United Kingdom, Greece and Turkey agreed to complex arrangements under which Cyprus would obtain independence in 1960 under Greek, Turkish and British guarantees. British overt military intervention ceased following the February agreement. Approximately 600 persons died during Enosis movement violence, 100 British soldiers among them.

Bitsios, D. 1975. *Cyprus: The Vulnerable Republic*, 17–111.
Black, N. 1977. "The Cyprus Conflict." In *Ethnic Conflict in International Relations*, ed. A. Suhrke and L. Nobel, 43–92.
Butterworth, R. 1976. *Managing Interstate Conflict*, 181–182, 213.
Crawshaw, N. 1978. *The Cyprus Revolt.*
Day, A., ed. 1987. *Border and Territorial Disputes*, 16–26.
Denktash, R. 1982. *The Cyprus Triangle*, 22–25.
Dewar, M. 1984. *Brush Fire Wars*, 68–82.
Foley, C., and W. Scobie. 1975. *The Struggle for Cyprus.*
Grivas, G. 1965. *The Memoirs of General Grivas.*
Kosut, H., ed. 1970. *Cyprus, 1946–68*, 13–70.
Oberling, P. 1982. *The Road to Bellapais*, 87–121.
Paget, J. 1967. *Counter-Insurgency Operations*, 115–154.
Salih, H. 1968. *Cyprus: An Analysis of Cypriot Political Discord*, 83–162.
Stephens, R. 1966. *Cyprus, A Place of Arms*, 130–167.
Xydis, S. 1973. *Cyprus: Reluctant Republic.*

5.5 Budapest Uprising, 1956–1957

Hungary allied with Germany during World War II, was occupied by Germany in 1944, and was conquered by the Soviet Union in 1945. Moscow instituted a radical socialist regime which proclaimed the Hungarian Republic in 1946, later reformulated as the Communist People's Republic in 1949. Soviet military forces remained within Hungary after World War II. In 1955 Hungary joined the Warsaw Pact alliance with the Soviet Union and other eastern European socialist states.

Hungary's ruling circles divided following the death of Soviet leader Joseph Stalin in 1953. Premier Imre Nagy led a movement on behalf of "de-Stalinization," consistent with policies instituted by his Soviet counterpart, Georgi Malenkov. Matyas Rakosi, General Secretary of the Communist party, represented factions adhering to strict socialist principles such as pursued prior to Stalin's death. Nagy was forced from office in 1955 and was eventually expelled from the Communist party.

In October 1956, a time of economic difficulties within Hungary and of anti-Soviet agitation within neighboring Poland, massive street demonstrations in Budapest and other cities demanded return of Imre Nagy and reduction of Soviet influence. Soviet troops stationed within Hungary intervened October 23 to help suppress disorders. Nagy returned as premier. At the same time Janos Kadar, representing the Rakosi faction, took leadership of the Communist party. Soviet troops withdrew from Budapest following a cease-fire October 28. On November 1 Soviet reinforcements began to enter Hungary. Nagy announced Hungary's withdrawal from the Warsaw Pact the same day. Soviet troops promptly reentered Budapest and other cities with approval of anti-Nagy members of the Council of Ministers. Nagy was forcibly removed from office and Kadar appointed head of government on November 4. Soviet troops encountered serious resistance among civilians and some Hungarian military personnel until November 14. They continued to police sensitive areas until May 1957.

Recent estimates of the uprising's death toll suggest that as many as 3,000 Hungarians died, primarily within Budapest. The Soviet Union has not officially acknowledged losses but her military fatalities presumably amounted to several hundred.

Barber, N. 1974. *Seven Days of Freedom: The Hungarian Uprising.*
Berecz, J. 1986. *1956 Counter-Revolution in Hungary.*
Brecher, M., J. Wilkenfeld, and S. Moser. 1988. *Crises in the Twentieth Century,* 1: 233.
Butterworth, R. 1976. *Managing Interstate Conflict,* 217–219.
Irving, D. 1981. *Uprising.*
Kecskemeti, P. 1961. *The Unexpected Revolution.*
Kopacsi, S. 1987. *In the Name of the Working Class.*
Lomax, B. 1976. *Hungary 1956.*
Mikes, G. 1957. *The Hungarian Revolution.*
Molnar, M. 1971. *Budapest 1956.*
Remington, R. 1971. *The Warsaw Pact,* 28–40.
Schmid, A., and E. Berends. 1985. *Soviet Military Interventions Since 1945,* 26–29.
Small, M., and J. Singer. 1982. *Resort to Arms,* 93.
Tatu, M. 1981. "Intervention in Eastern Europe." In *Diplomacy of Power,* by S. Kaplan, 205–264.
Vali, F. 1961. *Rift and Revolt in Hungary,* 173–399.

5.6 Maltese Emergency, 1958

The United Kingdom annexed Malta as a Crown Colony in 1814. Malta obtained partial self-government in 1947 but Britain retained military bases on the island. The Malta Labor party under Dominic Mintoff agitated for British withdrawal during the 1950s. Mintoff became prime minister following the 1955 elections. A 1956 referendum nevertheless demonstrated substantial popular support for integration with Great Britain. Mintoff demanded increased financial aid from the United Kingdom in 1957–1958 and threatened to cut ties if more support were not provided. Anti-British demonstrations followed, including stoning of British Army headquarters at Valetta on April 7, 1958. The Labor party called a general strike. A few British troops deployed on

April 16 with approval of the British governor in order to help police to maintain order. A full state of emergency was declared April 30, calling forth additional troops. British forces continued to patrol the streets until May 1 when police assumed sole responsibility. The state of emergency was completely lifted in August. British military operations on Malta resulted in no reported fatalities.

Keesing's Contemporary Archives 11 (1958): 16362–16363.
New York Times 4/16/58, 17:3; 5/1/58, 5:2.

5.7 Cypriot Civil War, 1963–1964

The Republic of Cyprus became independent of the United Kingdom in 1960, after five years of conflict associated with the Enosis movement (5.4). Archbishop Makarios III, a leading figure among Greek Cypriots demanding union with Greece, became president. Treaties signed at time of independence among Greece, Turkey, the United Kingdom and Cyprus limited Cypriot sovereignty. Britain maintained military bases on the island and reserved right of intervention. Greece and Turkey each maintained military contingents upon Cyprus and officered separate segments of the Cypriot National Guard.

In 1963 Makarios proposed to amend the Cypriot constitution in order to limit rights of foreign powers. Turkey threatened to intervene if the constitution were altered. A December 21, 1963, incident involving Greek Cypriot police and Turkish Cypriot citizens sparked violence between the Greek and Turkish communities within Nicosia that continued for several days. On December 25 Turkey ordered garrisoned forces under its control to secure the road leading to the Turkish-populated town of Kyrenia. Greek troops left barracks the same day to join Greek Cypriots in Nicosia. The United Kingdom mobilized garrisoned soldiers on Cyprus December 26 in effort to help keep the peace. A formal cease-fire was obtained December 29 but incidents continued. British troops remained on patrol. Turkish soldiers remained in position on the Kyrenia road and Greek army units mounted sporadic forays from their camps.

In January 1964 the United Kingdom proposed that an international military force share peacekeeping duties with British soldiers. Makarios's government consented provided that the peace force operate under U.N. auspices. The U.N. Security Council agreed to accept responsibility and the United Nations Force in Cyprus (UNFICYP) formed with the arrival of Canadian and Danish military contingents on March 27, 1964. Finland, Ireland, and Sweden provided additional troops in April. Efforts to clarify neutral zones between Greek and Turkish Cypriot positions and to establish U.N. observation posts provoked occasional incidents during the spring and summer of 1964.

A further crisis erupted in August 1964. George Grivas, a leading terrorist within the Enosis movement during the 1950's, had by this time returned to Cyprus. At Grivas's prompting, Greek National Guard units and Greek Cypriot civilians renewed attacks upon Turkish Cypriot communities. The Turkish Air Force responded by bombing and strafing attacks August 7 and 8. Greece threatened major counterintervention. Turkey and Cyprus formally accepted a cease-fire August 10. British and other U.N. troops remained on duty as observers but suspended overt military operations after August 20, 1964. Turkish troops remained in static positions along the Kyrenia road. Greek troops returned to barracks.

Casualties during 1963–1964 fighting involved primarily civilians. Military losses included deaths of two Greek, one Turkish, one British, and one Finnish soldier.

Bitsios, D. 1975. *Cyprus: The Vulnerable Republic.*

Black, N. 1977. "The Cyprus Conflict." In *Ethnic Conflict in International Relations*, ed. A. Suhrke and L. Nobel, 43–92.

Blaxland, G. 1971. *The Regiments Depart*, 324–328.

Brecher, M., J. Wilkenfeld, and S. Moser. 1988. *Crises in the Twentieth Century*, 1: 265–266.

Butterworth, R. 1976. *Managing Interstate Conflict*, 375–376.

Crawshaw, N. 1978. *The Cyprus Revolt*, 366–370.

Day, A., ed. 1987. *Border and Territorial Disputes*, 16–26.

Denktash, R. 1982. *The Cyprus Triangle*, 26–47.

Dewar, M. 1984. *Brush Fire Wars*, 68–82.

Duncan-Jones, A. 1972. "The Civil War in Cyprus." In *The International Regulation of Civil Wars*, ed. E. Luard, 148–168.

Ehrlich, T. 1974. *Cyprus 1958–1967.*

Foley, C., and W. Scobie. 1975. *The Struggle for Cyprus*, 160–166.

Harbottle, M. 1971. *The Blue Berets*, 11–51.

Higgins, R. 1969–1981. *United Nations Peacekeeping*, vol 4.

Kosut, H., ed. 1970. *Cyprus, 1946–68*, 71–156.

Markides, K. 1977. *The Rise and Fall of the Cyprus Republic.*

Miller, L. 1967. *World Order and Local Disorder*, 116–118.

Oberling, P. 1982. *The Road to Bellapais*, 87–121.

Stephens, R. 1966. *Cyprus, A Place of Arms*, 181–204.

United Nations Department of Public Information. 1985. *The Blue Helmets*, 259–300.

Vanezis, P. 1977. *Cyprus: The Unfinished Agony*, 30–39.

Wainhouse, D. 1973. *International Peacekeeping at the Crossroads*, 345–413.

Yearbook of the United Nations 18 (1964): 150–173.

5.8 Kophinou Incident, 1967

The Enosis movement (5.4) led to international armed conflict on Cyprus during the late 1950s. Civil war between Greek and Turkish communities erupted in 1963–1964 (5.7). A fragile peace followed. The United Nations Force in Cyprus (UNFICYP) remained to events following the civil war but refrained from overt military operations after 1964. Greece, Turkey and the United Kingdom also separately garrisoned troops on the island under the 1960 Treaty of Guarantee that accompanied Cypriot independence. Cypriot police acting under authority of the government of President Makarios assumed primary responsibility for maintaining order.

George Grivas, former leader of EOKA terrorists during the 1950s and commander of Greek Cypriot National Guard contingents encouraged deployment of additional Greek troops on Cyprus during 1967. Serious violence resumed November 15, 1967, when Turkish Cypriots resisted Greek units of the National Guard and police attempting to enter the town of Kophinou. A battalion of Greek troops attacked and occupied Kophinou and a neighboring Turkish-populated town later that day. A company of British troops assigned to the Kophinou area under UNFICYP took no part in the fighting. Greek troops withdrew under diplomatic pressure without further military intervention. One Greek soldier and one Greek Cypriot policeman died. Twenty-five Turkish Cypriots were also killed.

Brecher, M., J. Wilkenfeld, and S. Moser. 1988. *Crises in the Twentieth Century,* 1: 280–281.

Butterworth, R. 1976. *Managing Interstate Conflict*, 375–376.

Crawshaw, N. 1978. *The Cyprus Revolt*, 378–379.

Denktash, R. 1982. *The Cyprus Triangle*, 50–52.

Dewar, M. 1984. *Brush Fire Wars*, 81–82.

Duncan-Jones, A. 1972. "The Civil War in Cyprus." In *The International Regulation of Civil Wars*, ed. E. Luard, 148–168.

Foley, C., and W. Scobie. 1975. *The Struggle for Cyprus*, 167–169.

Harbottle, M. 1971. *The Blue Berets*, 96–105, 145–160.

Hart, P. 1990. *Two NATO Allies at the Threshold of War*.

Kosut, H., ed. 1970. *Cyprus, 1946–68*, 157–185.

Markides, K. 1977. *The Rise and Fall of the Cyprus Republic*, 132–134.

Oberling, P. 1982. *The Road to Bellapais*, 123–145.

Polyviou, P. 1980. *Cyprus, Conflict and Negotiation*, 45–58.

United Nations Department of Public Information. 1985. *The Blue Helmets*, 279.

Vanezis, P. 1977. *Cyprus: The Unfinished Agony*, 43–44.

5.9 Prague Occupation, 1968

Germany occupied Czechoslovakia from 1939 until liberation, principally by Soviet Union military forces, in 1945. A coalition government representing communist and other factions took office in 1946. An orthodox radical socialist regime succeeded in 1948. Czechoslovak socialism subsequently developed similarly to that within other Eastern European states except for absence of a permanent Soviet military garrison. The Antonin Novotny regime enjoyed generally harmonious relations with other socialist states until 1968.

In January 1968 Alexander Dubcek replaced Novotny as first secretary of the Czechoslovak Communist party. General Ludvik Svoboda replaced Novotny as president of Czechoslovakia in March 1968. The Czechoslovak Party Central Committee approved an "Action Program" in early April 1968 that proposed numerous departures from orthodox practice, including abolition of censorship and reductions of government controls upon the economy. Additional suggestions to reduce Communist party influence surfaced from several quarters. The Soviet Union, Bulgaria, Hungary, Poland and the German Democratic Republic protested the drift of events. On August 18, 1968, an "Allied Socialist Force" comprising military units of these five states invaded Czechoslovakia, gained control within two days without serious opposition, and interned Dubcek, Svoboda and other Czech government leaders. Dubcek and others soon returned to office but were permanently replaced in 1969.

German troops withdrew from Czechoslovakia by the beginning of September 1968. Hungarian, Polish and Bulgarian troops withdrew October 18, 1968. Soviet troops stood down the same day after the Czech government signed an agreement in Moscow permitting continued stationing of Soviet military forces. No fatalities are reported among any intervening forces.

Brecher, M., J. Wilkenfeld, and S. Moser. 1988. *Crises in the Twentieth Century*, 1: 283–284.

Butterworth, R. 1976. *Managing Interstate Conflict*, 428–430.

Dawisha, K. 1984. *The Kremlin and the Prague Spring.*

Eidlin, F. 1980. *The Logic of "Normalization."*

Golan, G. 1971. *Czechoslovak Reform Movement*, 316–329.

Remington, R. 1969. *Winter in Prague.*

Remington, R. 1971. *The Warsaw Pact*, 94–112.

Schmid, A., and E. Berends. 1985. *Soviet Military Interventions Since 1945*, 30–34.

Schwartz, H. 1969. *Prague's 200 Days.*

Skilling, H. 1976. *Czechoslovakia's Interrupted Revolution*, 713–810.
Tatu, M. 1981. "Intervention in Eastern Europe." In *Diplomacy of Power*, by S. Kaplan, 205–264.
Tigrid, P. 1971. *Why Dubcek Fell*.
Valenta, J. 1979. *Soviet Intervention in Czechoslovakia, 1968*.

5.10 Turco-Cypriot War, 1974

Cyprus suffered repeated international conflict provoked by violence between Greek and Turkish Cypriot communities, including prior to independence in 1960 (5.4), in 1963–1964 (5.7) and 1967 (5.8). The United Nations Force in Cyprus (UNFICYP) remained to observe the peace after 1964 as did also permanent garrisons of Greek, Turkish and British troops. Renewed anti-Turkish violence arose during the early 1970s. The Cypriot government labelled the new terrorist movement "EOKA-B" due to its similarity to the National Organization of Cypriot Fighters (EOKA) which had fought Turkish Cypriots and British soldiers during the 1950s. In 1974 President Makarios of Cyprus condemned Greek officers who commanded the bulk of the National Guard for encouraging renewed terrorism and demanded that Greece remove them.

The Greek-led National Guard overthrew Makarios on July 15, 1974, and installed former EOKA terrorist Nikos Giorgiades Sampson as president. Turkish Cypriot civilians and Turkish elements of the National Guard resisted efforts of the new government to establish islandwide control. Garrisoned British soldiers intervened to assist evacuation of Turkish Cypriot civilians and foreign nationals but avoided direct engagement with the National Guard. UNFICYP refrained from overt action. On July 20, 1974, a Turkish invasion force landed on the northern coast of Cyprus, joined forces with Turkey's permanent garrison of 650 soldiers, and gained control over most of northern Cyprus by mid-August. Meanwhile, Greece committed an elite commando force of 200 soldiers the night of July 20–21. These, together with some members of Greece's permanent 950-man garrison, helped to resist Turkey's advance until Greece, Turkey, and the United Kingdom signed a formal cease-fire July 30, 1974. Turkey consolidated her position through sporadic additional military operations through October 1974. Makarios returned in December 1974 to head the recognized government of Cyprus which controlled merely the southern part of the island. Turkey established the Turkish Cypriot Federated State under Rauf Denktash within the northern sector in February 1975.

Several thousand Cypriot civilians and members of the National Guard died during 1974. Turkey lost as many as 1,000 troops. Greece admits no losses among regular soldiers although some may have been killed. The United Kingdom suffered no military fatalities.

Black, N. 1977. "The Cyprus Conflict." In *Ethnic Conflict in International Relations,* ed. A. Suhrke and L. Nobel, 43–92.

Brecher, M., J. Wilkenfeld, and S. Moser. 1988. *Crises in the Twentieth Century,* 1: 305–306.

Butterworth, R. 1976. *Managing Interstate Conflict,* 474–476.

Crawshaw, N. 1978. *The Cyprus Revolt,* 388–394,

Day, A., ed. 1987. *Border and Territorial Disputes,* 16–26.

Denktash, R. 1982. *The Cyprus Triangle,* 64–82.

Dewar, M. 1984. *Brush Fire Wars,* 68–82.

Foley, C., and W. Scobie. 1975. *The Struggle for Cyprus,* 173–177.

Harbottle, M. 1971. *The Blue Berets,* 145–167.

Keegan, J., ed. 1983. *World Armies,* 589–597.

Markides, K. 1977. *The Rise and Fall of the Cyprus Republic,* 147–193.

Polyviou, P. 1975. *Cyprus; the Tragedy and the Challenge.*

Small, M., and J. Singer. 1982. *Resort to Arms,* 94.

Stern, L. 1977. *The Wrong Horse.*

Vanezis, P. 1977. *Cyprus: The Unfinished Agony,* 43–104.

5.11 Larnaca Airport Raid, 1978

Egypt's government of Anwar Sadat took unilateral steps toward accommodation with Israel a few years after the costly Yom Kippur War of 1973 (13.27). In November 1977 President Sadat paid a state visit to Jerusalem. On December 5, 1977, Egypt suspended formal relations with the most fervent supporters of Palestinian national resistance against Israel, including Algeria, Iraq, Libya, Syria and the People's Democratic Republic of Yemen. On December 26 Israel's President Menachem Begin paid an official visit to Egypt. In February 1978 radical Palestinians assassinated Youssef al-Sibai, editor of Egypt's prestigious, semi–official newspaper, Al-Ahram, in Nicosia, Cyprus. The assassins hijacked an airliner and held passengers hostage at Larnaca Airport outside Nicosia. On February 19, 1978, an Egyptian commando team landed at Larnaca in an attempt to free the hostages and capture the assassins. Egypt failed to coordinate operations in advance with the Cypriot government, however, and the Cypriot National Guard resisted the Egyptian force. Fifteen Egyptian soldiers died during an ensuing gun battle and remaining members of the team were taken prisoner.

Keesing's Contemporary Archives 24 (1978): 29305.
New York Times 2/20/78, 1:4.
Times (London) 2/20/78, 1a.

5.12 Luqa Airport Raid, 1985

Violent Palestinian opposition to Egyptian accommodation with Israel provoked Egypt's Larnaca Airport raid in 1978 (5.11). President Anwar Sadat of Egypt was assassinated in 1981 and succeeded by Hosni Mubarak who continued most of his predecessor's policies. On November 23, 1985, five terrorists apparently associated with the militant Abu Nidal Palestinian resistance group seized a commercial airliner of Egypt Air en route from Cairo to Athens. The plane was forced to land at Luqa Airport on Malta. Maltese authorities sealed the airport but took no direct action against the terrorists. On November 24 seventy-five Egyptian soldiers accompanied by three American advisors arrived at the airport with Maltese approval. Part of this unit assaulted the plane later that day. Sixty persons died during the resulting melee but no Egyptian soldiers are reported killed.

Keesing's Contemporary Archives 32 (1986): 34326–34327.
New York Times 11/25/85, I, 1:6.

PART THREE

Africa

6

West Africa

Portugal's lengthy Guinea-Bissau War (6.5) represents West Africa's most violent recent conflict. France also intervened briefly within the Ivory Coast (6.2) and Dahomey (6.4) during colonial rule, as did similarly the United Kingdom within the Gold Coast (6.1) and Sierra Leone (6.3). Border troubles and internal instability incited Senegalese intervention within the Gambia upon several occasions between 1971 and 1981 (6.6, 6.8, 6.11, 6.12). During the same period Guinea committed forces to aid threatened governments within Sierra Leone (6.7) and Liberia (6.10). A persistent border dispute between Mali and Burkina Faso contributed to incidents in 1974–1975 (6.9) and to pitched battle in 1985 (4.13).

6.1 Accra Riots, 1948

Dutch and English settlements developed within the Gold Coast (Ghana) from the seventeenth century, primarily in association with the slave trade. The United Kingdom formally annexed the territory as a colony in 1871. Tribes associated with the Ashanti Union violently resisted British efforts to pacify them until 1901. In 1947 urban, professional-class nationalists led by J. B. Danquah formed the United Gold Coast Convention in order to advance the cause of self-government. Kwame Nkrumah became the organization's general secretary in January 1948. At the same time other groups formed separately to protest stores' high prices within Accra and other towns. The Anti-Inflation Campaign Committee and the Ashanti Boycott Committee began an organized boycott against imported goods on January 24, 1948. Danquah and Nkrumah spoke frequently before large gatherings and stressed the need for self-government in order to address prices and other grievances. On February 28 riots erupted within Accra. Disturbances spread to other towns the next day. The government declared a state of emergency and British garrison troops turned out to help maintain order. Soldiers continued patrols through the first week of March 1948. No British military fatalities are reported.

Apter, D. 1972. *Ghana in Transition*, 169–170.
Austin, D. 1966. *Politics in Ghana, 1946–1960*, 71–80.
Davidson, B. 1974. *Black Star*, 59–67.
Pedler, F. 1979. *Main Currents in West African History*, 14–16.
Milburn, J. 1977. *British Business and Ghanaian Independence*, 59–67.

6.2 Dimbokro Demonstration, 1950

France subjected West African coastal territory later identified as the Ivory Coast to protectorate status in the 1840s and to occupation after 1882. The Rassemblement Democratique Africain (RDA), a multinational political party, opposed continued French rule within West Africa after World War II but generally opposed the use of violence toward this end. Felix Houphouet-Boigny, a founder of the RDA and leader of its Ivory Coast affiliate, the Parti Democratique de la Cote d'Ivoire (PDCI), became a conspicuous spokesman for West African independence after acquiring a seat in the French National Assembly in 1946. France actively attempted to reduce PDCI influence beginning in 1949, including by discharging some supporters from government service and by organizing local groups to oppose the independence movement. PDCI demonstrations within Abidjan and other towns led to violence between its supporters and those of other groups at the end of January 1950. France employed regular troops from Senegal January 31–February 1 to help restore order. In succeeding months she employed police and paramilitary Alouite (Syrian mercenaries) to suppress the PDCI. No fatalities and few casualties occurred during the brief period of overt military intervention. Succeeding police and paramilitary operations, however, resulted in significant loss of life.

Morgenthau, R. 1964. *Political Parties in French-Speaking Africa*, 188–202.
Thompson, V., and R. Adloff. 1957. *French West Africa*, 126–130.
Zolberg, A. 1964. *One-Party Government in the Ivory Coast*, 131–135.

6.3 Sierra Leone Riots, 1955

The United Kingdom's colony and protectorate of Sierra Leone grew from settlements established on the western coast of Africa as early as 1788. The territory experienced little serious political violence in the early twentieth century except for an easily suppressed rebellion led by the self-styled Islamic prophet Idara in 1931. Sierra Leone moved gradually and generally peacefully toward self-government during the 1950s, led in part by the Sierra Leone People's party which was more closely tied to traditional elites than to radical nationalist sentiments. Riots that broke out following a labor demonstration within the capital Freetown during February 1955 represented an exception to general calm. Local police requested and received support from the British-officered Sierra Leone Regiment on February 11. More than one hundred casualties and eighteen deaths resulted during the brief upheaval but the regiment sustained no fatal losses before it returned to barracks on February 12.

Cox, T. 1976. *Civil-Military Relations in Sierra Leone*, 31.
Keesing's Contemporary Archives 10 (1955): 14342.

6.4 Dahomey Riots, 1959

French colonial authority penetrated coastal Dahomey as early as 1851. France conquered both the northern and southern kingdoms by 1894 and brought them under common administration in 1902. Elected local government was introduced after World War II. Justin Ahoumadegbe formed the Union Democratique Dahomeenne (UDD) in 1955 as a national political party with support from organized labor. Dahomey gained internal self-government within the French Community in 1958 and Sourou-Migan Apithy, who opposed the UDD, was elected head of the governing council. In preparation for and during the April 2, 1959, elections to the French National Assembly, Apithy manipulated electoral laws, district boundaries and the vote count itself in effort to minimize UDD successes. The UDD formally protested the results and riots occurred April 4 in the capital, Coutonou, among its labor and other supporters. France sent troops from Niger April 6, 1959, to reinforce local police in the face of continuing disturbances. These helped to enforce a curfew until April 11 and withdrew April 12. Apithy resigned as head of the government following the crisis. No French fatalities are reported.

Dugue, G. 1960. *Vers les Etats-Unis d'Afrique*, 239–240.
Thompson, V. 1972. *West Africa's Council of the Entente*, 22.

6.5 Guinea-Bissau War, 1963–1974

Portugal discovered the coast of Guinea in 1446, established settlements among the nearby Cape Verde Islands during the fifteenth century, but did not systematically develop the mainland until after

Portuguese Guinea (Guinea-Bissau) became a separate colony in 1879. Few Portuguese settled within Guinea even then. Europeans constituted less than five percent of the total population in the 1950s and most resided within a few urban centers.

In 1956 Amilcar Cabral and other expatriates from Cape Verde secretly founded the Party for the Independence of Guinea and Cape Verde (PAIGC) in the capital, Bissau. The militant PAIGC assumed leadership among clandestine nationalist groups within Guinea after a massacre at Pijiguiti in August 1959 where police killed fifty people during a strike. Portugal suppressed nationalist organizations on Cape Verde and within major Guinean towns. Amilcar Cabral was forced into exile in 1960. Nevertheless, the PAIGC developed extensive support within rural areas outside immediate Portuguese influence. PAIGC-directed guerrilla began systematic attacks upon Portuguese facilities in January 1963. Portugal committed regular army to assist the police in September that year. 30,000 Portuguese soldiers were deployed by the mid-1960s. Portugal fitfully attacked guerrilla sanctuaries within the Cassamance Province of neighboring Senegal, including an isolated air attack in April 1963 and intermittent air and small-unit ground actions from 1965 to 1972. Portuguese aircraft also raided guerrilla positions within the neighboring Republic of Guinea in 1969. Portuguese troops retained control of Cape Verde and of urban centers into the 1970s but the PAIGC effectively liberated most of the Guinean countryside by the late 1960s.

A military coup overthrew the Portuguese government in Lisbon on April 26, 1974. General Antonio Sebastiao Ribeirio de Spinola, former commander of forces within Portuguese Guinea, assumed the presidency. The new regime granted independence to Guinea-Bissau on September 10, 1974, and withdrew remaining forces by the end of October. The Cape Verde Islands, largely untouched by the war, gained independence separately as the Republic of Cape Verde in 1975. 2,000 or more Portuguese soldiers died during the eleven-year campaign, most due to mines and ambushes. Sporadic cross-border operations resulted in few if any Portuguese fatalities.

Beckett, I. 1985. "The Portuguese Army." In *Armed Forces and Modern Counter-Insurgency*, ed. I. Beckett and J. Pimlott, 136–162.
Bruce, N. 1975. *Portugal: The Last Empire*, 62–98.
Butterworth, R. 1976. *Managing Interstate Conflict*, 299–302, 355–357.
Davidson, B. 1984. *No Fist is Big Enough to Hide the Sky*.
Humbaraci, A., and N. Muchnik. 1974. *Portugal's African Wars*.
Kay, H. 1970. *Salazar and Modern Portugal*, 182–293.
Lopes, C. 1987. *Guinea-Bissau*, 27–74.
Venter, A. 1974. *Africa at War*, 47–58, 73–90.

6.6 Sene-Gambia Incident, 1971

Senegambia, the region of the Senegal and Gambia rivers in West Africa, contributed to the Euro-American slave trade from the sixteenth century. A British presence was established at the mouth of the Gambia River before 1700. France penetrated the Senegal by the seventeenth century. The United Kingdom proclaimed a colony within a narrow corridor along the lower Gambia and France took control of nearly all the rest of Senegambia by the end of the nineteenth century. French territories became independent as Senegal in 1960. The Gambia, surrounded by Senegal except on the Atlantic coast, became independent in its own right in 1965. The Gambia, which established a paramilitary Field Force but no regular army, signed cooperation agreements with Senegal at the time of independence including for military collaboration. Extensive cross-border smuggling, important to the Gambian economy, contributed to numerous minor border incidents. The Gambian government was unable or unwilling to suppress illegal trade. On January 14, 1971, Gambian police interned a Senegalese policeman and customs official caught pursuing a smuggler into the Gambia. On January 31, a small Senegalese army unit conducted reprisal raids upon two Gambian villages. No fatalities are reported in association with the incidents.

Africa Contemporary Record 4 (1971–72): B545–B547.
Africa Research Bulletin. Political, Social and Cultural Series 8 (1971): 2011.

6.7 Bangura Coup, 1971

Sierra Leone became independent of the United Kingdom in 1961. In 1967 a military coup d'etat led by Andrew Juxon-Smith overthrew the civilian government controlled by the Sierra Leone People's party since independence. Juxon-Smith's National Reformation Council was overthrown by a a military coup in 1968 that restored civilian government under Siaka P. Stevens, leader of the All People's Congress. On March 23, 1971, Major John Bangura attempted yet another military coup. Stevens escaped initial attempts to capture him and forces loyal to the government reestablished tenuous control of the capital, Freetown, by the end of the day. Stevens signed a mutual defense agreement with the government of Guinea March 26, a move in the offing before the attempted coup. On March 28, 1971, two hundred Guinean soldiers arrived in Freetown, established a guard at Stevens residence and helped police and loyal army units to patrol the city.

Guinean troops stood down at the end of the first week of April without
having suffered any casualties.

Africa Research Bulletin. Political, Social and Cultural Series 8 (1971): 2045.
Cox, T. 1976. *Civil-Military Relations in Sierra Leone*, 213–217.
David, S. 1987. *Third World Coups d'Etat and International Security*, 113–114.
Stevens, S. 1984. *What Life Has Taught Me*, 313–359.

6.8 Jokadu Raids, 1974

Senegal became independent from France in 1960 and the Gambian
enclave from the United Kingdom in 1965. Cross-border smuggling
provoked Senegalese military intervention in 1971 (6.6). Following this
incident, Senegal and the Gambia elaborated military cooperation
agreements under their 1965 alliance, but smuggling and minor border
incidents continued. During July 1974 Senegalese forces again raided
Gambian villages in Jokadu District upon more than one occasion and
seized seventeen local residents. Senegal accepted responsibility for
the actions some months later and offered compensation. No fatalities
are reported.

Africa Contemporary Record 7 (1974–75): B635–B636.
Africa Research Bulletin. Political, Social and Cultural Series 11 (1974): 3326.

6.9 Agacher Conflict, 1974–1975

Mali and Upper Volta (Burkina Faso) originated as colonial
administrative districts within French West Africa. France
established dominion within the region during the late nineteenth
century. She proclaimed the French Soudan (Mali) in 1904. Upper
Volta was formed in 1919, dissolved in 1932, and reestablished in 1948.
The territories became independent separately in 1960. They disputed
the location of their border in the Beli-Agacher region from the time of
independence. The area was largely populated by ethnic Mali but most
parts of it were administered by Upper Volta. A mixed commission
comprising representatives of both states attempted to demarcate the
border between 1961 and 1974. Violent incidents broke out along the
frontier in late November 1974. Small units of Mali troops attacked
Upper Volta positions in December while attempting to establish a
presence within the disputed region. Incidents ceased temporarily at
the end of December 1974 following mediation by President Senghor of
Senegal and President Eyadema of Togo. Further violence erupted
during the first week of June 1975 when Upper Volta artillery shelled
the disputed villages of Domo and Batou. Mediation by President

Sekou Toure of Guinea helped to produce an agreement signed by Guinea, Mali and Upper Volta July 11, 1975, under which the disputants renounced the use of force to settle the border question. A few civilians apparently died during these incidents but no fatalities are reported among regular military personnel.

Brownlie, I. 1979. *African Boundaries*, 427–430.
Day, A., ed. 1987. *Border and Territorial Disputes*, 105–110.
McFarland, D. 1978. *Historical Dictionary of Upper Volta*.
New York Times 12/28/74, 7:6; 6/8/75, 63:1; 7/14/75, 6:5.

6.10 Monrovia Rice Riots, 1979

Liberia was colonized by freed American slaves from 1822 and proclaimed itself an independent republic in 1847. The True Whig party controlled national politics from 1878. The government of President William Tolbert, inaugurated in 1972, practiced institutionalized corruption as had most of its predecessors. In 1978 the government announced its intention to raise the government-regulated price of rice, the staple cereal among Liberians. The ostensible reason for the price increase was to promote domestic economic self-sufficiency. Coincidentally, one of Tolbert's brothers was actively involved in the rice trade. The Progressive Alliance of Liberia led by Gabriel Baccus Mattews petitioned the government against the planned price increase. It also organized a protest demonstration in Monrovia April 14, 1979. The demonstration turned to riot. Liberian security forces reacted violently. Liberia appealed to Guinea for help and 100 Guinean troops arrived April 15, 1979, to help patrol the streets of Monrovia. The government relented and kept the regulated price of rice at the previous level. Guinean troops withdrew in mid-May 1979. Two hundred persons died during the riots of April 14. Guinea suffered no military fatalities during peacekeeping operations.

Boley, G. 1984. *Liberia: The Rise and Fall of the First Republic*, 101–119.
Liebenow, J. 1987. *Liberia: The Quest for Democracy*.

6.11 Banjul Occupation, 1980

The Gambia, bereft of a regular army, allied with surrounding Senegal in 1965 upon attaining independence from the United Kingdom. Smuggling across their artificial borders contributed to armed conflict in 1971 (6.6) and 1974 (6.8). Dawda Jawara served as head of government within the Gambia from 1962 and also served as head of state after being chosen as president in 1970. His liberal People's

Progressive party dominated electoral politics throughout the 1970s. In 1975 Pap Cheyassin Secka organized the National Liberation party as a vehicle to promote radical social reforms. Other radical groups, including the Movement for Justice in Africa—Gambia (MOJA-G), which was related to a similar organization within Liberia, and the Gambia Socialist Revolutionary Party (GSRP) appeared by 1980 and conducted propaganda campaigns against the Jawara government. Meanwhile, Libya established a presence within the Gambia through development aid programs and recruitment of Gambian workers, some of whom received military training while abroad. On October 27, 1980, Emmanuel Mahoney, second in command of the Gambia's paramilitary Field Force, was murdered by a another member of the unit. President Jawara charged that Libya encouraged the act in effort to subvert his government. The Gambian government banned MOJA-G and GSRP and also expelled some Libyans on October 30. At Jawara's request, 150 Senegalese troops deployed to the Gambia October 31 and patrolled the streets of the capital Banjul for the following week before withdrawing. No Senegalese fatalities are reported.

Africa Contemporary Record 13 (1980-81): B478–B480.

Africa Research Bulletin. Political, Social and Cultural Series 17 (1980): 5823.

Hughes, A. 1983. "From Colonialism to Confrontation." In *African Islands and Enclaves*, ed. R. Cohen, 57–80.

6.12 Sanyang Coup, 1981

Senegalese troops intervened within the Gambia to support President Dawda Jawara in 1980 at time of a suspected Libyan-backed plot (6.11). Senegal also raided Gambian territory during the 1970s in attempt to suppress cross-border smuggling (6.6, 6.8). On July 30, 1981, Kukoi Samba Sanyang led a mixed group of radical civilians and dissident members of the Gambia's paramilitary Field Force in an attempted coup d'etat while President Jawara was out of the country visiting London. Rebels seized control of the Banjul airport and other key facilities in the vicinity of the capital and proclaimed a Marxist-Leninist state under a Supreme Council of the Revolution. Jawara appealed for Senegalese assistance. Senegal dispatched more than 2,000 soldiers July 31 to help put down the rebellion and shortly took control of Banjul. President Jawara returned August 2. Senegalese forces continued operations until August 7 in effort to capture remaining dissidents. Some Senegalese troops remained within the Gambia thereafter but refrained from further direct action. On September 7, 1981, President Jawara and President Abdou Diouf of Senegal announced plan to form a Confederation of Senegambia as of 1982. Approximately ten Senegalese soldiers died during operations.

David, S. 1985. *Defending Third World Regimes from Coups d'Etat*, 55–57.
David, S. 1987. *Third World Coups d'Etat and International Security*, 126–128.
Hughes, A. 1983. "From Colonialism to Confrontation." In *African Islands and Enclaves*, ed. R. Cohen, 57–80.

6.13 Agacher Battle, 1985

Small military engagements occurred between Mali and Upper Volta (Burkina Faso) in 1974–1975 (6.9) growing out of a protracted border dispute regarding the Beli-Agacher region populated primarily by ethnic Mali under Upper Voltan administration. The two states pledged to renounce the use of force in 1975 and in 1979 agreed upon procedures to define a settlement to the border problem. In 1983 Thomas Sankara assumed the presidency of Upper Volta. The new administration renamed the state Burkina Faso in 1984 and also pursued more militant policies than had its predecessor. Incidents occurred within the disputed zone during December 1985 when Burkina Faso attempted to conduct a census under police guard. On December 25, 1985, Mali troops attacked towns within disputed Burkina Faso territory. Pitched battle followed. On December 26 Burkina aircraft bombed Sikasso, well inside Mali, and small units of Burkina soldiers also raided Mali territory. Algeria helped to arrange a cease-fire December 28 and Mali and Burkina Faso agreed to refer their dispute to the International Court of Justice. As many as 400 persons are reportedly killed during the four-day war, including 50 or more soldiers representing each side.

Africa Research Bulletin. Political Series 22 (1985): 7885.
Day, A., ed. 1987. *Border and Territorial Disputes*, 105–110.
Laffin, J. 1986. *War Annual 1*, 25–26.

7

Central Africa

Central Africa suffered frequent and wide-spread conflict from the mid-1950s. France's military forces intervened within colonial French Cameroon (7.1, 7.3) and French Congo (7.2, 7.4). The Congolese civil war (7.5) precipitated intervention by numerous states within Zaire (Belgian Congo) under auspices of the United Nations Operations in the Congo. Conflict occurred later on Zaire's border with the People's Republic of the Congo (7.11) and also that with Zambia (7.16). The Shaba I (7.12) and Shaba II (7.14) crises of 1977 and 1978 threatened the Zairean government. Chad experienced virtually continual strife from 1965 (7.9, 7.10, 7.13, 7.17, 7.18). France intervened within independent People's Republic of the Congo (7.6) in 1963, as did Cuba (7.8) in 1966, during domestic disorders. France intervened under similar circumstances within Gabon (7.7) in 1964 and the Central African Republic in 1979.

7.1 Cameroon Riots, 1955

British and French forces conquered Germany's Kamerun protectorate during World War I. France subsequently administered northern Cameroon under League of Nations mandate and continued to do so under U.N. trust following World War II. The Union des Populations du Cameroun (UPC) formed as a workers' party in 1948. It openly challenged continued French rule and demanded reintegration with the Southern Cameroons administered by the United Kingdom. French attempts to suppress the organization included actions by French troops and police to disperse an unauthorized gathering within Mbango on May 15, 1955, where several persons were wounded. Riots and demonstrations staged by UPC supporters in other towns and cities followed during the next two weeks. Serious incidents that led to the deaths of as many as twenty civilians took place within the capital, Douala. French troops actively assisted police in efforts to maintain order within the territory until the end of May but suffered no reported fatalities.

Butterworth, R. 1976. *Managing Interstate Conflict*, 193–194.
Clayton, A. 1988. *France, Soldiers and Africa*, 171–172.
Gardinier, D. 1963. *Cameroon, United Nations Challenge to French Policy*, 69–70.
Guillemin, J. 1982. "Les Campagnes Militaires Francaises de la Decolonisation en Afrique Sud-Saharienne." *Mois en Afrique* (June): 124–141.
Joseph, R. 1977. *Radical Nationalism in Cameroun*, 265–269.
Le Vine, V. 1964. *The Cameroons, from Mandate to Independence*, 155–156.
Le Vine, V., and R. Nye. 1974. *Historical Dictionary of Cameroon*.
Mortimer, E. 1969. *France and the Africans*, 217–218.
Nelson, H. 1974. *Area Handbook for the United Republic of Cameroon*, 294–297.

7.2 Brazzaville Riots, 1956

France occupied territory later designated as the colony of Middle Congo (People's Republic of the Congo) during the 1880s. The territory experienced little political violence after World War II until local elections in 1956. Youthful followers of the nationalist leader Fulbert Youlou, inspired in part by his identification with the legendary Lari leader Matsoua, disrupted elections within the capital, Brazzaville, on January 2, 1956. They and Youlou opponents continued street fighting through the next day. Local French military garrisons assisted police to restore order January 2–3, 1956. One Congolese was killed but no French military fatalities resulted.

Gauze, R. 1973. *The Politics of Congo-Brazzaville*, 22.
Thompson, V., and R. Adloff. 1960. *The Emerging States of French Equatorial Africa*, 484.

7.3 Bamileke Revolt, 1956–1960

Violent demonstrations within the French trusteeship of northern Cameroon in May 1955 led to French military intervention (7.1) and to banning of the nationalist Union des Populations du Cameroun (UPC). Underground UPC militants launched a sustained terrorist campaign within outlying areas beginning in December 1956. French troops deployed to affected areas and helped to institute violent repression. Revolt centered within the Bamileke region continued after Cameroon gained independence in 1960. French counterinsurgency action also persisted after independence.

France prepared to grant independence to northern Cameroon during 1959. Spokesmen for the UPC sought U.N. delay in order to unite northern and British-administered Cameroons. Nigeria, encouraged by the United Kingdom, proposed to annex the southern Cameroons. The United Nations authorized independence of the Republic of Cameroon in the north as of January 1, 1960. A plebiscite within British Cameroons in 1961 resulted in partition between Nigeria and the Republic of Cameroon in October 1961.

Violence within the Bamileke region continued until the mid-1960s. French military operations persisted until mid-June 1960 with approval of the new republic's government. French military assistance to Camerooni counterinsurgency operations continued until 1965. The Bamileke revolt resulted in hundreds or more civilian fatalities. At least thirty French soldiers were also killed.

Butterworth, R. 1976. *Managing Interstate Conflict*, 193–194.

Clayton, A. 1988. *France, Soldiers and Africa*, 195–196.

Gardinier, D. 1963. *Cameroon, United Nations Challenge to French Policy*, 103–104.

Guillemin, J. 1982. "Les Campagnes Militaires Francaises de la Decolonisation en Afrique Sud-Saharienne." *Mois en Afrique* (June): 124–141.

Joseph, R. 1977. *Radical Nationalism in Cameroun*, 346–349.

Le Vine, V. 1964. *The Cameroons, from Mandate to Independence*, 164–171, 180–182.

Le Vine, V. 1971. *The Cameroon Federal Republic*, 121–131, 180–181.

Le Vine, V., and R. Nye. 1974. *Historical Dictionary of Cameroon*.

Mortimer, E. 1969. *France and the Africans*, 242–218, 299–302, 336–340.

Nelson, H. 1974. *Area Handbook for the United Republic of Cameroon*, 294–297.

Prouzet, M. 1974. *Le Cameroun*, 252–254.

Rubin, N. 1971. *Cameroun: An African Federation*, 95–97.

7.4 French Congo Riots, 1958–1959

France intervened briefly within her Congo (People's Republic of the Congo) colony in 1956 during street violence perpetrated by supporters of nationalist leader Fulbert Youlou (7.2). The colony obtained limited self-government in 1958 and the territorial assembly selected Youlou as premier on November 28, 1958. Militant supporters and opponents of Youlou clashed in the capital, Brazzaville, and in other towns that day. French troops again intervened and order was temporarily restored by December 1. Serious rioting resumed within Brazzaville in February 1959 and was again suppressed. Violence resumed within Brazzaville and other towns during June and continued until August.

French military forces joined police to contain disorders until August 15, 1959. Violence abated after the territorial assembly granted extraordinary powers to police under a state of emergency August 16 and Youlou discouraged militants among his own followers. No French military fatalities are reported.

Gauze, R. 1973. *The Politics of Congo-Brazzaville*, 64–79.
Mortimer, E. 1969. *France and the Africans*, 358–359.
Thompson, V., and R. Adloff. 1960. *The Emerging States of French Equatorial Africa*, 489–492.

7.5 Congolese Civil War, 1959–1965

Belgium claimed central Congo (Zaire) in 1877 and formally annexed it in 1908 after suppressing an Arab rebellion in 1891–1894. Subsequent Belgian security policy relied primarily upon the Force Publique, a Belgian-officered and African-soldiered substitute for metropolitan troops and also territorial police. Belgium administered the Congo directly from Brussels and did little to encourage local self-government prior to independence.

Riots erupted within Leopoldville January 4–7, 1959, expressing both intertribal rivalry and anti-European sentiment. The Force Publique suppressed disorder with appreciable loss of life. It responded with similar violence during demonstrations within other towns and cities in following months. Death toll was especially high at Luluabourg in August 1959, at Matadi and Stanleyville in October, and again at Stanleyville in December 1959.

Belgium abruptly granted independence to the Congo on June 30, 1960. The new government included Prime Minister Patrice Lumumba, leader of the radical Congo National movement, and President Joseph Kasavubu, leader of the Abako party. Elements of the Force Publique mutinied against remaining Belgian officers July 5. Belgium deployed metropolitan troops to Katanga province at behest of European settlers without sanction of the new Congolese government. On July 11 Moise Tschombe, leader of Katanga's provincial government, declared an independent state with Belgian encouragement. Lumumba and Kasavubu called upon Ghana and the United Nations for assistance. Ghana dispatched troops to the Congo July 15. The United Nations called upon Belgium to withdraw and authorized an international peace force later designated as the United Nations Operations in the Congo (ONUC). ONUC absorbed Ghana's soldiers after they arrived. The United Arab Republic (Egypt, Ethiopia, Guinea, Ireland, Liberia, the Mali Federation (Mali), Morocco, Sudan, Sweden, and Tunisia contributed infantry units directly to ONUC during July and August. The United States provided logistical support, including transporting other states' forces to the Congo. ONUC assigned units to oversee most provinces, including Katanga, but took no immediate action against Tschombe's secession. Belgian troops withdrew by September 1, 1960.

The central Congolese government fractured in September 1960 after Lumumba and Kasavubu each attempted to remove one another from office. Joseph Mobutu, commander of the national army, dismissed both and declared himself national leader. Internecine warfare followed among factions loyal to each of these parties and also Katangan secessionists. Katanga tribesmen killed Lumumba in February 1961. Antoine Gizenga proclaimed a government at Stanleyville with support of former Lumumba followers. The United Nations steadfastly recognized Kasavubu as president and acknowledged Cyrille Adoula, supported by Kasavubu, as prime minister in August 1961.

Several African states withdrew from ONUC in late 1960 and early 1961, including Mali, following collapse of the Mali Federation, Egypt, Guinea, Morocco, and Sudan. Other states replaced them, including India, Malaya (Malaysia,) Nigeria and, briefly, Indonesia.

ONUC forcefully supported Kasavubu-Adoula government efforts to assert central control in 1961–1963. Irish and Ethiopian units helped to attack Katanga in September 1961. The Congolese government continued on the offensive within Katanga until agreeing to a cease-fire in December 1961 and also routed Gizenga's followers from Stanleyville in early 1962. Negotiations between the central government and Katanga broke down in 1962. Indian and Ethiopian troops helped to invade it in December. Tschombe fled after key areas were occupied in January 1963.

ONUC began to disband in March and April 1963, with departure of Tunisian, Malayan and Sierra Leone soldiers, the latter having arrived only in January 1962. An Indonesian unit returned briefly in February 1963 but withdrew in December as did Ghana's contingent the preceding month. Remaining units of Ethiopia, India, Ireland, Nigeria and Sweden left in June 1964.

Moise Tschombe returned as prime minister of the Congo in July 1964 at the invitation of President Kasavubu. He expanded mercenary forces serving the central government with covert assistance of the United States. Gizenga's faction, expelled from Stanleyville in 1962, captured Albertville in June 1964, retook Stanleyville in August and interned Europeans and others. A November 1964 counteroffensive involving mercenary ground forces and Belgian paratroops transported by the U.S. Air Force recaptured the two cities for the central government.

The central government attempted to destroy resistance elsewhere during 1964–1965. Mercenary commando units and aircraft attacked rebel bases within neighboring Sudan, Congo-Brazzaville (People's Republic of the Congo) and Uganda. Small Ugandan military units joined rebel bands within the Congo briefly during February 1965. Major fighting ended in 1965, as did foreign overt military intervention, but residual violence persisted throughout the 1960s.

As many as 100,000 persons died during the Congolese civil war. Belgium lost an estimated fifty regular soldiers killed. U.N. forces suffered 126 fatalities in all. Ghana alone lost thirty-eight and India a similar number. ONUC units of Ethiopia, Ireland, Morocco, Sudan, Sweden, and Tunisia also sustained fatal casualties. One Ugandan soldier is known killed within the Congo in 1965.

General

Brecher, M., J. Wilkenfeld, and S. Moser. 1988. *Crises in the Twentieth Century*, 1: 247–248, 272.
Butterworth, R. 1976. *Managing Interstate Conflict*, 281–293, 385–386, 387–388.
Small, M., and J. Singer. 1982. *Resort to Arms*, 230.

African States

Gauze, R. 1973. *The Politics of Congo-Brazzaville*, 115–134.
Mittelman, J. 1975. *Ideology and Politics in Uganda*, 104–105.
Thompson, W. 1969. *Ghana's Foreign Policy*, 119–161.

Belgium

Odom, T. 1988. *Dragon Operations: Hostage Rescues in the Congo.*
Wagoner, F. 1980. *Dragon Rouge: The Rescue of Hostages in the Congo.*

Congo

Epstein, H., ed. 1965. *Revolt in Congo, 1960–1964.*
Gerard-Libois, J. 1966. *Katanga Secession.*
Hoskyns, C. 1965. *The Congo Since Independence.*
Luard, E. 1972. "The Civil War in the Congo." In *The International Regulation of Civil Wars*, ed. E. Luard, 108–124.
Merriam, A. 1961. *Congo: Background to Conflict.*

Mercenaries

Clarke, S. 1968. *The Congo Mercenary.*
Hoare, M. 1967. *Congo Mercenary.*
Thomas, G. 1985. *Mercenary Troops in Modern Africa.*

United Nations

Harbottle, M. 1971. *The Blue Berets*, 32–57.
Higgins, R. 1969–1981. *United Nations Peacekeeping*. vol. 3.
Horn, C. von. 1967. *Soldiering for Peace*, 140–252.
Lefever, E. 1967. *Uncertain Mandate*.
Lefever, E. 1970. *Spear and Scepter*, 81–131.
Lefever, E. 1972. "Peacekeeping by Outsiders." In *Civil Wars in the Twentieth Century*, ed. R. Higham.
Miller, L. 1967. *World Order and Local Disorder*, 65–116.
Rikhye, I. 1984. *The Theory and Practice of Peacekeeping*, 81–89.
United Nations Department of Public Information. 1985. *The Blue Helmets*, 213–257.
Wainhouse, D. 1973. *International Peacekeeping at the Crossroads*, 267–344.

7.6 Anti-Youlou Riots, 1963

The Congo Republic (People's Republic of the Congo) became independent of France in 1960 under a government formed around the nationalist leader Fulbert Youlou. French troops previously intervened twice in the late 1950s (7.2, 7.4) during violent clashes between Youlou supporters and opponents. The Congo government signed security agreements at independence that provided base rights for French troops and included French security guarantees.

President Youlou moved toward one party rule in the early 1960s,. This provoked opposition within both the army and organized labor. On August 6, 1963, Youlou announced intention to prohibit opposition political parties as of August 15. Labor unions called a general strike August 13. Several thousand anti-Youlou demonstrators stormed the central jail in the capital, Brazzaville, that day and forced release of imprisoned labor leaders. The government declared a curfew which failed to prevent further demonstrations. Youlou requested and obtained deployment of French troops within Brazzaville on August 14. An estimated 7,000 demonstrators surrounded the presidential palace and demanded Youlou's resignation in the presence of French soldiers. French troops withdrew in favor of Congolese Army units at midday August 15 despite continuing unrest. Top-ranking officers of the Congolese Army forced Youlou to resign two hours later and interned him along with other members of his government. Demonstrations immediately abated and authority was quickly passed to a new civilian government. No French military casualties are reported.

Decalo, S. 1976. *Coups and Army Rule in Africa*, 136–148.
Gauze, R. 1973. *The Politics of Congo-Brazzaville*, 152–153, 223–224.

7.7 Aubame's Coup, 1964

Gabon gained independence from France in 1960. She signed agreements at that time which included French security guarantees. Leon Mba, leader of the Democratic Bloc party, became president of Gabon in 1960. Jean-Hillaire Aubame, leader of the rival Democratic and Social Union party and who opposed close ties to France, joined a coalition cabinet that survived until February 1963 when Mba assumed full powers. Mba took steps toward one-party rule, including certifying only Democratic party candidates prior to French national assembly elections scheduled for February 23, 1964. On February 17 junior Gabonese military officers and Gabonese police in Libreville staged a bloodless coup d'etat in the name of a Revolutionary Committee and took Mba into custody. Aubame was named head of a provisional government. France dispatched troops to Libreville from Congo-Brazzaville (People's Republic of the Congo) and Senegal, purportedly upon request of Mba government officials still at large. French forces secured the capital, forced release of Mba and reinstalled him as president by February 20. France continued a conspicuous military presence on behalf of the Mba regime until mid-April 1964 when most troops withdrew. Two French soldiers as well as twenty-five Gabonese died during restoration operations.

Chaigneau, P. 1984. *La Politique Militaire de la France en Afrique*, 94.
Darlington, C., and A. Darlington. 1968. *African Betrayal*, 126–141.
David, S. 1985. *Defending Third World Regimes from Coups d'Etat*, 34–38.
David, S. 1987. *Third World Coups d'Etat and International Security*, 120–122.
Gavshon, A. 1984. *Crisis in Africa*, 172–173.

7.8 Congo Mutiny, 1966

Political instability within the Congo (People's Republic of the Congo) led to French military intervention in 1963 (7.6) when senior Congolese military offices forced President Fulbert Youlou from office. Youlou's successor, Alphonse Massamba-Debat, proclaimed commitment to radical socialist principles and accepted a military assistance mission from Cuba in 1965. Cuban soldiers helped to reduce Congolese army influence by providing advanced training to the Civil Defense Corps, established in 1963, and by constituting a separate presidential guard. In April 1966 the Congolese government appointed political commissars to oversee all armed forces units. Elements of the regular army mutinied in late June 1966 while Massamba-Debat was out of the country. Cuban soldiers deployed within Brazzaville to guard key facilities and to help loyal Congolese security forces suppress the mutiny. Revolt subsided by June 30 and Cuban troops stood down. No Cuban fatalities are reported.

David, S. 1987. *Third World Coups d'Etat and International Security*, 122–124.
Decalo, S. 1976. *Coups and Army Rule in Africa*, 148–153.
Dominguez, J. 1989. *To Make a World Safe for Revolution*, 181.
Gauze, R. 1973. *The Politics of Congo-Brazzaville*, 162–163, 195, 225–226.
Leogrande, W. 1980. *Cuba's Policy in Africa, 1959–1980*, 10.
Keegan, J., ed. 1983. *World Armies*, 126–127.

7.9 Ouaddi Rebellion, 1966

Chad gained independence from France in 1960 as a deeply divided polity. France first penetrated the area in 1900 and incorporated it within French Equatorial Africa in 1910. French civil administration extended primarily within densely settled and black-peopled southern Chad. France established military administration within the Chad B.E.T., the Moslem, Arabic-speaking northern province of Borkou-Ennedi-Tibesti, in 1935. French military control of the north lasted through World War II under Free French forces and in effect until 1965, when troops finally withdrew. Chad was generally quiescent during the first two decades after World War II except for demonstrations at Babalem near Lake Chad in 1952 which were violently suppressed by police and territorial guards.

Northerners offered little support to the government of President Francois Tombolbaye established in 1960. In 1963 Tombolbaye dismissed Arab members of the government and banned all political parties but his own. The Front de Liberation Nationale de Tchad (FROLINAT) formed to oppose Tombolbaye as did other clandestine opposition bands. FROLINAT established its first headquarters at Khartoum, capital of the Sudan, and attracted support within the north and also culturally divided eastern provinces. Serious rebellion broke out within eastern Ouaddi Province in 1965. Minor incidents followed on the Sudanese-Chadian border. Small Chadian army raids attacked Sudan during August and September 1966. Although war continued within Chad during following years, Tombolbaye's government refrained from further overt cross border operations after 1966. An estimated 400 people died during the Ouaddi Rebellion to 1967. Seven or more Chadian soldiers are believed to have died during raids within Sudan.

Butterworth, R. 1976. *Managing Interstate Conflict*, 392–393.
Decalo, S. 1980. "Chad: The Roots of Centre-Periphery Strife." *African Affairs*

79 (October): 491–509.
Decalo, S. 1980. "Regionalism, Political Decay, and Civil Strife in Chad." *Journal of Modern African Studies* 18 (March): 23–56.
Decalo, S. 1987. *Historical Dictionary of Chad*, 302–303.
Thompson, V., and R. Adloff. 1981. *Conflict in Chad*, 116–117.

7.10 Chadian Civil War I, 1968–1972

Chad signed agreements with France at independence in 1960 that included base rights, military assistance and security guarantees. France also continued de facto military administration of northern Chad B.E.T. province. France withdrew most forces from Chad B.E.T. in 1965 at insistence of President Francois Tombolbaye's government and did not play an active role during the Ouaddi Rebellion (7.9). Rebellion begun in Ouaddi in 1965 subsequently spread to other regions, led in part by the Front de Liberation Nationale de Tchad (FROLINAT) which attracted support among Moslem and Arabic-speaking peoples, particularly in the north. France activated elements of her remaining garrisons in August 1968 upon request of Tombolbaye's government. She introduced additional troops in 1969 and deployed more than 3,500 air and ground personnel by 1970. Violence ebbed when President Tombolbaye agreed to incorporate Moslem politicians within a coalition government in May 1971. Most major opposition groups acceded except FROLINAT, some of whose members took refuge within Libya. Most French troops withdrew in June 1972.

Muammar Qaddafi's revolutionary regime within Libya commenced an indirect but important role within Chadian affairs after seizing power in 1969. Libya had long coveted the Aouzou strip in far northern Chad and provoked occasional incidents there from 1954. Qaddafi's government supported an attempted coup against President Tombolbaye in August 1971 and in September publicly recognized FROLINAT as the legitimate government of Chad. Tombolbaye ceded Aouzou to Libya in November 1972 and signed a treaty of friendship with her the following month. Libya assumed administration of Aouzou in 1973.

The Chadian civil war killed hundreds during 1968–1972. French losses may have included more than 50 military fatalities.

Brecher, M., J. Wilkenfeld, and S. Moser. 1988. *Crises in the Twentieth Century*, 1: 296.
Chaigneau, P. 1984. *La Politique Militaire de la France en Afrique*, 96.
Clayton, A. 1988. *France, Soldiers and Africa*, 384–385.
Day, A., ed. 1987. *Border and Territorial Disputes*, 113–116.
Decalo, S. 1980. "Chad: The Roots of Centre-Periphery Strife." *African Affairs* 79 (October): 491–509.

Decalo, S. 1980. "Regionalism, Political Decay, and Civil Strife in Chad." *Journal of Modern African Studies* 18 (March): 23–56.
Decalo, S. 1987. *Historical Dictionary of Chad*, 271–274.
Neuberger, B. 1982. *Involvement, Invasion and Withdrawal*, 9–30.
Pimlott, J. 1985 "The French Army." In *Armed Forces and Modern Counter-Insurgency*, ed. I. Beckett and J. Pimlott, 46–76.
Thompson, V., and R. Adloff. 1981. *Conflict in Chad*, 23–74.
Venter, A. 1974. *Africa at War*, 59–62.

7.11 Mbamou Incident, 1976

The Belgian Congo obtained independence in 1960 and immediately succumbed to civil war (7.5). She adopted the name Zaire in 1971. Neighboring French Congo also became independent in 1960 and proclaimed herself the People's Republic of the Congo in 1969. Zaire and the Congo pursued opposed foreign policies during the 1970s. Zaire intervened within Angola in 1975–1976 (10.2) against the Cuban-backed Popular Movement for the Liberation of Angola (MPLA) which seized power upon Portuguese withdrawal. The Congo cooperated closely with the MPLA regime. Zaire and the Congo generally avoided direct confrontation but smuggling across the Zaire (Congo) River boundary provoked occasional incidents. Some Zairean soldiers and gendarmes allegedly participated in illegal trade. In April 1976 a small number of Zairean troops attacked a village on the island of Mbamou in the Zaire River and captured several villagers. Villagers were returned to the Congo a few days later. Zaire's President Joseph Mobutu blamed the action upon "undisciplined elements" of his army. No fatalities are reported.

Africa Contemporary Record 9 (1976–77): B496.
Africa Research Bulletin. Political, Social and Cultural Series 13 (1976): 3988.

7.12 Shaba Crisis I, 1977

Remnants of Katanga rebel forces fled to Angola and Zambia after the Congolese civil war (7.5). They organized the Congo National Liberation Front (FNLC) in exile and received financial support and military training from the Soviet Union and Cuba. FNLC adherents periodically raided Zaire's Shaba (Katanga) Province during the 1970s, primarily from Angola. At the same time Zaire intervened within Angola against the Movement for the Liberation of Angola (MPLA) government which seized power in 1975 (10.2). She continued to support resistance by the rival National Front for the Liberation of Angola (FNLA) after withdrawing in 1976.

On March 8, 1977, several thousand FNLC irregulars invaded Shaba Province from Angola with apparent encouragement from the Angolan government. Zaire appealed for international assistance. Morocco dispatched 1,500 troops which arrived April 8 by French airlift. Egypt and the United States provided additional technical assistance. Moroccan and Zairean forces drove FNLC invaders out of Shaba into Angola and neighboring Zambia within a month. In the process, Zairean aircraft attacked Zambian territory during mid-April in pursuit of fleeing rebels. Moroccan troops departed May 22, 1977. No Moroccan fatalities are reported nor Zairean losses within Zambia.

Brecher, M., J. Wilkenfeld, and S. Moser. 1988. *Crises in the Twentieth Century*, 1: 320–321.

Chaigneau, P. 1984. *La Politique Militaire de la France en Afrique*, 95–96.

Coker, C. 1985. *NATO, the Warsaw Pact and Africa*, 122–124.

Hul, G. 1977. "Internationalizing the Shaba Conflict." *Africa Report* 22 (July–August): 4–9.

Lellouche, P., and D. Moisi. 1979. "French Policy in Africa." *International Security* 3 (#4): 108–133.

Keegan, J., ed. 1983. *World Armies*, 676–678.

Moose, G. 1985. "French Military Policy in Africa." In *Arms and the African*, ed. W. Foltz and H. Bienen, 59–97.

Schatzberg, M. 1989. "Military Intervention and the Myth of Collective Security." *Journal of Modern African Studies* 27 (June): 315–340.

Wolfers, M., and J. Bergerol. 1983. *Angola in the Frontline*, 217–223.

Zartman, I. 1989. *Ripe for Resolution*, 134–169.

7.13 Chadian Civil War II, 1978–1982

Chad suffered persistent political instability after 1965, including during the Ouaddi Rebellion (7.9) and general civil war from 1968 to 1972 (7.10). Conflict represented in part deep divisions between black southerners who dominated President Francois Tombolbaye's national government. and Moslem, Arabic-speaking northerners who supported the Front de Liberation Nationale de Tchad (FROLINAT).

The Chadian army overthrew Tombolbaye in April 1975 and installed a government under Felix Malloum. The Malloum government protested Libyan control of the Aouzou strip, quietly ceded by Tombolbaye in 1972. Libya helped to sponsor an attempted coup against Malloum in April 1976. FROLINAT, beneficiary of Libyan arms and money, resumed guerrilla attacks upon Chadian government installations. In January 1978 President Malloum and Hissene Habre, a FROLINAT leader, announced plans to form a unified government. Goukouni Ouddei, who controlled FROLINAT's northern military arm, the Conseil des Forces Armees du Nord (FAN), opposed accommodation as did Libya. FAN forces attacked and captured the north's most important town, Faya-Largeau, in February 1978 and approached the national capital of Ndjamena in the south in April. French troops intervened in the south at the end of April 1978 upon government request. Libya increased aid to FAN forces, including military advisors dispatched to northern battlegrounds. A July 1978 understanding between France and Libya effectively divided their respective spheres of influence within Chad at the 14th parallel. In August Malloum and Habre formed a coalition government and agreed to merge FROLINAT and government military forces.

The Habre-Malloum government collapsed in February 1979. Habre supporters rampaged in Ndjamena and FAN forces controlled by Goukouni Ouddei entered the capital at the end of the month. President Malloum resigned March 23. Urged by the Organization of African Unity (OAU), FROLINAT factions formed a Transitional Government of National Unity (GUNT) with Goukouni Ouddei as head of state and Habre as defense minister. Nigerian troops arrived at the end of March and remained until mid-June to constitute an OAU neutral force to help police Ndjamena. The GUNT resisted demands to include other important groups, including some favored by Libya. In late June more than 2,000 Libyan troops attacked in the vicinity of Faya-Largeau until French air and GUNT ground resistance encouraged retreat at the end of July. OAU mediation helped to form another, supposedly more broadly based national unity government under presidency of Goukouni Ouddei in November 1979. Troops of the People's Republic of the Congo arrived in January 1980 to form a reconstituted OAU neutral force. They withdrew in April 1980 in the face of continued fighting, including between Goukouni Ouddei and Habre factions. French troops withdrew a month later.

Libyan forces, including the multinational Islamic Legion, resumed operations within northern Chad in late April 1980. President Goukouni Ouddei belatedly sanctioned Libyan intervention after militia loyal to Habre captured Faya Largeau in June 1980. Libyan forces drove Habre supporters out of Faya Largeau and in December 1980 helped Goukouni Ouddei's GUNT to take full control of the capital Ndjamena in some of the bloodiest fighting of the war. Remnants of Habre's militia fled east toward the Sudan. Libyan pursuit provoked border incidents, including Libyan air raids upon Sudanese villages during September and October 1981. Most Libyan regular forces withdrew from Chad in November 1981 although some remained in the far north. Elements of an OAU peace force arrived later that month and in early December, including troops from Nigeria, Zaire and Senegal. In

June 1982 Habre's forces recaptured the capital and installed Habre as head of state. The OAU peace disbanded the same month.

More than a thousand soldiers and civilians died during the 1978–1982 Chadian civil war, many during the sack of Ndjamena in 1980. Libya lost more than 300 military personnel. Nine French soldiers and airmen were killed. So far as is known, neither the Congo, Nigeria, Senegal nor Zaire suffered any fatalities.

Amate, C. 1986. *Inside the OAU: Pan-Africanism in Practice*, 451–458.

Brecher, M., J. Wilkenfeld, and S. Moser. 1988. *Crises in the Twentieth Century*, 1: 327–328, 331–332, 340–341.

Bustin, E. 1983. "Chad." *The Middle East Annual* 3: 159–184.

Chaigneau, P. 1984. *La Politique Militaire de la France en Afrique*, 97.

Clayton, A. 1988. *France, Soldiers and Africa*, 385–386.

Coker, C. 1985. *NATO, the Warsaw Pact and Africa*, 116–122.

Cooley, J. 1982. *Libyan Sandstorm*, 195–213.

Day, A., ed. 1987. *Border and Territorial Disputes*, 113–116.

Decalo, S. 1980. "Chad: The Roots of Centre-Periphery Strife." *African Affairs* 79 (October): 491–509.

Decalo, S. 1980. "Regionalism, Political Decay, and Civil Strife in Chad." *Journal of Modern African Studies* 18 (March): 23–56.

Decalo, S. 1987. *Historical Dictionary of Chad*, 196–198.

Haley, P. 1984. *Qaddafi and the United States Since 1969*, 96–105, 198–218, 296–300.

Kelley, M. 1986. *A State in Disarray*.

Lemarchand, R. 1985. "The Crisis in Chad." In *African Crisis Areas and U.S. Foreign Policy*, ed. G. Bender, J. Coleman, and R. Sklar, 239–256.

Lemarchand, R. 1988. "The Case of Chad." In *The Green and the Black*, ed. R. Lemarchand, 106–124.

Moose, G. 1985. "French Military Policy in Africa." In *Arms and the African*, ed. W. Foltz and H. Bienen, 59–97.

Neuberger, B. 1982. *Involvement, Invasion and Withdrawal*.

Pimlott, J. 1985 "The French Army." In *Armed Forces and Modern Counter-Insurgency*, ed. I. Beckett and J. Pimlott, 46–76.

Rikhye, I. 1984. *The Theory and Practice of Peacekeeping*, 159–169.

Robinson, P. 1984. "Playing the Arab Card." In *African Security Issues*, ed. B. Arlinghaus, 171–184.

Thompson, V., and R. Adloff. 1981. *Conflict in Chad*, 74–128.

7.14 Shaba Crisis II, 1978–1979

Katangan exiles representing the Congo National Liberation Front (FNLC) invaded Zaire's Shaba (Katanga) Province from Angola in 1977 but were driven out with Moroccan assistance (7.12). Minor border incidents continued thereafter due both to continuing FNLC activities and Zairean support of exiled Angolan resistance groups operating from her territory (10.2).

Thousands of Katangan exiles invaded Shaba again on May 11, 1978. Command collapsed among invaders and also among some defending units of the Zairean Army. 1,200 French and 1,700 Belgian troops, brought in by American planes, arrived May 19–20 with approval of the Zairean government in order to evacuate foreign nationals from Kolwezi. French troops remained until mid-June and helped to reestablish government control in the area. Belgian troops stayed until mid-July. In the meantime, the Central African Republic, Morocco, Senegal and Togo contributed troops to an Interafrican Peace Force to help police the area. Advance parties began to arrive May 30. The Angolan government announced June 10 that it would halt further FNLC border crossings. Most rebels subsequently withdrew. The Interafrican force took to the field officially on June 30, 1978, and remained until August 14, 1979. Four French soldiers were killed but neither Belgium nor Interafrican Peace Force contributors suffered reported fatalities.

Brecher, M., J. Wilkenfeld, and S. Moser. 1988. *Crises in the Twentieth Century*, 1: 332–333.

Chaigneau, P. 1984. *La Politique Militaire de la France en Afrique*, 95–96.

Clayton, A. 1988. *France, Soldiers and Africa*, 383–384.

Coker, C. 1985. *NATO, the Warsaw Pact and Africa*, 122–129.

Depoorter, J. 1979. "Kolwezi." *Military Review* 54 (September): 29–35.

Keegan, J., ed. 1983. *World Armies*, 676–678.

Moose, G. 1985. "French Military Policy in Africa." In *Arms and the African*, ed. W. Foltz and H. Bienen, 59–97.

Schatzberg, M. 1989. "Military Intervention and the Myth of Collective Security." *Journal of Modern African Studies* 27 (June): 315–340.

Wolfers, M., and J. Bergerol. 1983. *Angola in the Frontline*, 217–223.

Zartman, I. 1989. *Ripe for Resolution*, 134–169.

7.15 Bokassa's Overthrow, 1979

The French territory of Oubangui Shari achieved independence in 1960 as the Central African Republic. Colonel Jean Bedel Bokassa, commander of armed forces, overthrew the original government of President David Dacko in 1966. Alleged antigovernment plots in November 1967 prompted President Bokassa to request French military assistance under a defense agreement signed at independence. French troops deployed to Bangui Airport where they stayed for a week but took no overt military action. The Bokassa regime became increasingly repressive during the 1970s. In 1977 Bokassa proclaimed himself emperor of the Central African Empire. The government also reacted violently following demonstrations in early 1979, including against schoolchildren. On the night of September 20–21, 1979, David Dacko seized power with army support while Bokassa was out of the country visiting Libya. Dacko restored the republic and reclaimed the presidency. At Dacko's request, 300 French troops flew in from Gabon on September 21, 1979, and an additional 600 soldiers arrived from France a few days later. French forces helped to patrol the streets of Bangui and to assist other police functions. Change of governments elicited little violent opposition and French troops retired in late October 1979 having suffered no fatal losses.

Chaigneau, P. 1984. *La Politique Militaire de la France en Afrique*, 94–95.
Clayton, A. 1988. *France, Soldiers and Africa*, 387.
Gavshon, A. 1984. *Crisis in Africa*, 169–171.
Moose, G. 1985. "French Military Policy in Africa." In *Arms and the African*, ed. W. Foltz and H. Bienen, 59–97.

7.16 Zaire-Zambia Border, 1982

Zaire achieved independence from Belgium in 1960. The former British protectorate of Northern Rhodesia became independent as Zambia in 1964. Relations were generally cordial in the early years of statehood but became more problematic beginning in the late 1970s. Zairean aircraft attacked Zambian territory during the Shaba crisis of 1977 (7.12). Zaire, Zambia and Angola signed a mutual nonaggression treaty after a second invasion of Shaba (7.14). In 1980 Zambia protested Zairean border posts within land it claimed as part of its Kaputa district and argued about Lake Mweru during ensuing years. Cross-border smuggling also contributed to numerous border incidents during the early 1980s. On February 28, 1982, a small party of Zairean soldiers raided Zambian territory and seized several Zambian soldiers as well as civilians. The two countries agreed to exchange prisoners in April. Minor border incidents continued during the next several years without further overt military intervention. Three Zairean soldiers are reported killed during the February 28 raid.

Africa Contemporary Record 14 (1981–1982): B421–B422, B864–B865.
Africa Research Bulletin. Political, Social and Cultural Series 19 (1982): 6378.
Day, A., ed. 1987. *Border and Territorial Disputes*, 193–194.

7.17 Lake Chad Skirmishes, 1983

Nigeria gained independence from the United Kingdom in 1960. France terminated colonial control of Chad the same year. Relations between the two new states were generally harmonious until 1982. Both generally accepted boundaries established during the colonial era but ambiguity surrounded ownership of islets within Lake Chad due to incomplete demarcation. Dispute concerning Lake Chad intensified during the late 1970s and early 1980s due in part to oil exploration within the region. Civil warfare within Chad also contributed to growing tensions. Nigerian soldiers constituted a peace force within Chad under Organization of African Unity (OAU) auspices in spring 1979 and returned again in 1981 at request of the government of Goukouni Ouddei (7.13). Hissen Habre toppled Goukouni Ouddei's government in 1982 and compelled Nigerian troops to withdraw. Minor incidents involving border guards in and around Lake Chad occurred in April 1983. Violence expanded at the end of the month when Chad began repeated small-unit assaults upon Nigerian-held islands. Nigeria began retaliatory small raids upon Chadian positions by the beginning of June. Fighting ended July 11, 1983. The scale of violence is subject to conflicting estimates but may have included several hundred military and civilian fatalities in all. As many as seventy-five Chadian soldiers perished during raids upon Nigeria. At least nine Nigerian military personnel died during raids upon Chadian positions.

African Recorder 22 (1983): 193, 225.
Africa Research Bulletin. Political, Social and Cultural Series 20 (1983): 6862.
Day, A., ed. 1987. *Border and Territorial Disputes*, 117.
Decalo, S. 1987. *Historical Dictionary of Chad*, 234–235.

7.18 Libyan-Chadian War, 1983–1987

Libya intervened within the Chadian civil war of 1978–1982 (7.13), primarily on behalf of Goukouni Ouddei whose Transitional Government of National Unity (GUNT) was eventually ousted from the capital Ndjamena by Hissen Habre in 1982. In June 1983 Libyan-backed insurgents operating in the name of GUNT attacked Faya Largeau, administrative center of the northern province of Chad-B.E.T. Habre's government appealed for international help. 1,800 Zairean paratroops deployed to Ndjamena to help police the city and to free government troops for other operations. Rebels were driven out of Faya Largeau in July but recaptured it again on August 10, 1983. Libya overtly intervened in support of GUNT insurgents by air strikes against government positions at the end of July 1983 and large-scale ground operations in August. France, which had intervened within Chad during previous conflicts (7.10, 7.13), deployed 1,500 troops south of Chad B.E.T. upon Habre's request in mid-August. French forces did not directly confront

Libyan troops on the ground but helped to establish fortifications dividing northern from southern Chad at the 14th Parallel. On September 16, 1984, Libya and France agreed to mutual withdrawal. French and Zairean troops left the country two months later, November 10. Contrary to agreement, some Libyan forces remained and quietly assisted GUNT forces to consolidate control.

Libya reinforced her military presence within northern Chad during 1985. The Chadian government attempted to consolidate control within the south at the same time, including by small raids upon alleged rebel camps within neighboring Central African Republic. In February 1986 France initiated Operation Epervier which included French air strikes and French and Zairean air logistical support of Chadian government forces. In late summer 1986 GUNT forces, openly supported by Libya, attacked remaining government positions in the north.

Suddenly, in October 1986, Goukouni Ouddei and GUNT forces loyal to him reversed stance and began to attack Libyans. France airlifted military supplies to turncoat rebels. In January 1987 Chadian government troops began an offensive against Libyan positions. France continued air strikes through the first days of January and logistical assistance to anti-Libyan forces for several months thereafter. Chadian government troops and defecting GUNT forces overran Libya's base at Faya Largeau by the end of March. Libyan units retreated toward the Aouzou strip, ceded to Libya by a previous Chadian government in 1972 and contested by successors. In August 1987 Chadian government and GUNT forces attacked the Aouzou strip without direct French assistance. During the first week of September Chadian armed forces also mounted a brief but devastating ground raid upon Libya's Maatan as Sarra air base sixty miles within Libya proper. Combatants accepted a cease-fire September 11, 1987, by which time Libyan troops had been expelled from nearly all of Chad, including Aouzou.

Thousands died during the Libyan-Chadian War, most during 1987. Libya suffered as many as 2,000 military fatalities within Chad plus many more at home during the Maatan as Sarra raid. Sixty-five soldiers controlled by the Chadian government died within Libya. France lost nine soldiers killed during overt military operations.

Bustin, E. 1983. "Chad." *The Middle East Annual* 3: 159–184.
Chaigneau, P. 1984. *La Politique Militaire de la France en Afrique*, 97.
Coker, C. 1985. *NATO, the Warsaw Pact and Africa*, 116–122.
Day, A., ed. 1987. *Border and Territorial Disputes*, 113–116.
Decalo, S. 1987. *Historical Dictionary of Chad*, 138–139, 274.
Foltz, W. 1988. "Libya's Military Power." In *The Green and the Black*, ed. R. Lemarchand, 52–69.
Haley, P. 1984. *Qaddafi and the United States Since 1969*, 317–321.

Kelley, M. 1986. *A State in Disarray*.

Laffin, J. 1986. *War Annual 1*, 30–33.

Laffin, J. 1987. *War Annual 2*, 51–56.

Laffin, J. 1989. *The World in Conflict 1989: War Annual 3*, 76–80.

Lemarchand, R. 1985. "The Crisis in Chad." In *African Crisis Areas and U.S. Foreign Policy*, ed. G. Bender, J. Coleman, and R. Sklar, 239–256.

Lemarchand, R. 1988. "The Case of Chad." In *The Green and the Black*, ed. R. Lemarchand, 106–124.

Moose, G. 1985. "French Military Policy in Africa." In *Arms and the African*, ed. W. Foltz and H. Bienen, 59–97.

Pimlott, J. 1985 "The French Army." In *Armed Forces and Modern Counter-Insurgency*, ed. I. Beckett and J. Pimlott, 46–76.

Rikhye, I. 1984. *The Theory and Practice of Peacekeeping*, 167–169.

Somerville, K. 1990. *Foreign Military Intervention in Africa.*, 61–83.

8

Horn of Africa

Ethiopian imperial aspirations, Somali irredentism and Eritrean nationalism contributed to recurrent conflict within the Horn of Africa. Eritreans agitating for union with Ethiopia provoked British military intervention in 1950 (8.2). Later, persistent Eritrean revolt against Ethiopian rule occasionally involved neighboring Sudan (8.6, 8.8, 8.11). The United Kingdom intervened within Italian Somaliland in 1948 to help suppress nationalist violence. Somalia claimed the Ogaden after gaining independence in 1960. This led to three decades of repeated conflict with Ethiopia (8.3, 8.4, 8.10), including the costly Ogaden War (8.9). Conflict between Somali and Afari tribesmen within French Somaliland also encouraged French military intervention (8.5, 8.7) during the 1960s and 1970s.

8.1 Mogadishu Riots, 1948

Italy established a protectorate within Somaliland on the Horn of Africa by agreement with local tribal leaders in 1893. She later expanded colonial control into adjoining territories including conquest of Ethiopia in 1935–1936. The United Kingdom seized Italian Somaliland (Somalia) in 1941 during the Second World War. She retained control through a military government until 1949 when a civilian British administration was established. The United Nations considered competing territorial claims to the area after World War II including that of Ethiopia. The nationalist Somali Youth League agitated on behalf of an independent state. In January 1948 Somali Youth League demonstrations led to riots which killed more than 50 Italians and a smaller number of Somali within the capital, Mogadishu. Britain committed units of the King's African Rifles to help police suppress violence. Order was restored within days with no reported losses among British troops.

Drysdale, J. 1964. *The Somali Dispute*, 70–71.
Lee, D. 1980. *Flight from the Middle East*, 40–41.
Lewis, I. 1980. *A Modern History of Somalia*, 126–127.

8.2 Eritrean Violence, 1950

Italy took control of Eritrea on the Red Sea coast of the Ethiopian Empire by 1894. The area included a preexisting Ottoman settlement at Massawa. She absorbed Eritrea within Italian East Africa in 1936 when she conquered Ethiopia. The United Kingdom occupied Italian East Africa in 1941, restored emperor Haile Selassie to the Ethiopian throne, but retained military authority over Eritrea. Ethiopia claimed Eritrea from 1942 and helped to form the Eritrea-Ethiopia Union party in 1946. Other organizations formed on behalf of Eritrean independence, including the Muslim League in 1946 and the Liberal Progressive party in 1947 after Italy abandoned claim and Europeans joined the antiunion cause. Antiunion groups combined in 1949 as the Independence bloc. Unionists began terrorist attacks during 1949 and conducted systematic violence against Italian residents of Asmara by the end of the year. The United Kingdom called out garrison troops to help keep order during the first days of January 1950 and again in February. Sporadic military patrols continued until the end of July 1950. No British military fatalities are reported.

Butterworth, R. 1976. *Managing Interstate Conflict*, 68–69.
Markakis, J. 1987. *National and Class Conflict in the Horn of Africa*, 66–67.
Trevaskis, G. 1960. *Eritrea: A Colony in Transition*, 103–113.

8.3 Ogaden Conflict, 1960–1961

France, Italy and the United Kingdom divided coastal territory on the Horn of Africa inhabited by Somali peoples during the late nineteenth century, primarily through protectorate agreements with individual tribal leaders. At the same time Ethiopia conquered inland Somali areas including the Haud and Ogaden. Italy occupied Ethiopia in 1936. The United Kingdom defeated Italy in the Horn in 1941. She immediately restored Emperor Haile Selassie to the Ethiopian throne but continued to occupy the Haud and Ogaden until 1948 as well as former Italian Somaliland and her own British Somaliland protectorate. Riots led by the Somali Youth League within Mogadishu, capital of Italian Somaliland in 1948 (8.1) demonstrated resurgent Somali nationalism as did demonstrations that year at Jigjiga in the Haud after transfer to Ethiopian authority.

Ethiopia retained control of the Ogaden when British and Italian Somaliland obtained independence in June 1960. The two former protectorates combined to form the Republic of Somalia on July 1, 1960. The new Somali government promptly asserted claim to all areas inhabited by Somali peoples, including within Ethiopia, Kenya and French Somaliland (Djibouti). Somali nationalist organizations had by this time sprung up within the Ogaden region, including Nassir Allah. Rebellion broke out among Somali tribesmen of the Ogaden. Ethiopian armed forces responded aggressively, including by air and small-unit ground raids upon Somali territory between August 1960 and January 1961. At least 100 Somali tribesmen died during the 1960 rebellion as did at least twenty Ethiopian soldiers. Most fatalities occurred upon Ethiopian territory.

Brown, D. 1961. "Recent Developments in the Ethiopia-Somaliland Frontier Dispute." *International and Comparative Law Quarterly* 10 (January): 167–178.
Brownlie, I. 1979. *African Boundaries*, 827–851.
Butterworth, R. 1976. *Managing Interstate Conflict*, 143–144.
Drysdale, J. 1964. *The Somali Dispute.*
Touval, S. 1963. *Somali Nationalism*, 132–136.

8.4 Ogaden Battle, 1963–1964

Territorial dispute between Somalia and Ethiopia regarding the Ogaden Desert and adjacent regions under Ethiopian control contributed to international armed conflict in 1960 (8.3). Somalia claimed all areas inhabited by Somali peoples from the first days of her independence in 1960. Nationalist Somali leaders within the Ogaden formed the Nassir Allah political organization and the commercial Company for Trade and Industry in the 1950s and accumulated arms and followers during the early 1960s with encouragement of the Somali government. In February 1963 the Ethiopian administrator of the Ogaden announced intention to collect taxes from nomadic Somali herdsmen in the area. Nassir Allah launched a guerrilla campaign against outlying Ethiopian police posts in June 1963. Small units of Somali soldiers joined the Ogaden rebels beginning in November 1963. Both Ethiopia and Somalia also moved major units to their border. Ethiopia launched air attacks upon Somalia beginning in mid-January 1964. In early February Ethiopia invaded border areas of Somalia from Tug Wajale in the north to Ferfer and Dolo in the south. Skirmishes between Ethiopian and Somali military forces continued, primarily on the Somali side of the border, as did guerrilla warfare within Ethiopian Ogaden until early April 1964. Fighting ended ten days after a formal cease-fire between Ethiopia and Somalia was agreed March 30, 1964, with Sudanese mediation. Thirty or more Ethiopian soldiers died during attacks upon Somalia. As many as fifty Somali military personnel were killed within Ethiopia.

Brecher, M., J. Wilkenfeld, and S. Moser. 1988. *Crises in the Twentieth Century,* 1: 269–270.
Brownlie, I. 1979. *African Boundaries,* 827–851.
Butterworth, R. 1976. *Managing Interstate Conflict,* 327–329.
Day, A., ed. 1987. *Border and Territorial Disputes,* 126–132.
Farer, T. 1979. *War Clouds on the Horn of Africa,* 100.
Gorman, R. 1981. *Political Conflict on the Horn of Africa,* 36–37.
Hoskyns, C., ed. 1969. *The Ethiopia-Somalia-Kenya Dispute,* 48–68.
Lefever, E. 1970. *Spear and Scepter,* 154–156.
Markakis, J. 1987. *National and Class Conflict in the Horn of Africa,* 169–181.
Ottaway, M., and D. Ottaway. 1978. *Ethiopia: Empire in Revolution,* 163.
Spencer, J. 1984. *Ethiopia at Bay,* 320.

8.5 Djibouti Riots, 1966–1967

France maintained a presence on the Somali coast from the mid-nineteenth century. The colonial territory of French Somaliland (Djibouti) was formally demarcated in 1897 by agreement with Ethiopia and other European powers. France granted local self-government in 1956. A 1958 referendum reaffirmed popular preference to remain a French territory. Somalia claimed French Somaliland as she did other neighboring territories upon gaining independence in 1960 despite the fact that a majority represented Afari rather than Somali peoples. Somali residents staged demonstrations during a visit of French president Charles de Gaulle in August 1967. French troops garrisoned in the territory deployed within the capital Djibouti during the last week of August. France called out soldiers repeatedly in later months to help deal with further incidents. A local plebiscite held in March 1967, policed by French troops, again confirmed majority support for continuing association with France. French troops returned to barracks at the end of March shortly after the election. No French military fatalities are reported.

Butterworth, R. 1976. *Managing Interstate Conflict,* 364–365.
Farer, T. 1979. *War Clouds on the Horn of Africa,* 104.
Shehim, K., and J. Searing. 1980. "Djibouti and the Question of Afar Nationalism." *African Affairs* 79 (April): 209–226.
Saint Veran, R. 1981. *Djibouti, Pawn of the Horn of Africa,* 17–22.
Thompson, V., and R. Adloff. 1968. *Djibouti and the Horn of Africa,* 59–60.

8.6 Eritrean War I, 1967–1968

Rival claims between Ethiopia and local nationalists within Eritrea led to violence during 1949–1950 (8.2) while the area was still under British administration. The territory was federated to Ethiopia in 1952 by decision of the United Nations. Ethiopia abrogated the federation agreement in 1962 and declared Eritrea a province. The Eritrean Democratic Front (EDF) formed in 1956 to champion independence from Ethiopian rule. It drew support primarily among Moslems and especially from Beni Amer tribesmen inhabiting the Eritrean-Sudanese frontier. Organized armed resistance began in the early 1960s after the EDF was reconstituted as the Eritrean Liberation Front (ELF). Fighting increased in 1965. By 1967 pitched battles occurred between Eritrean separatists and Ethiopian military forces. The ELF attracted arms and money from Egypt. Cuba and the People's Republic of China also declared support for the secessionist movement. In March 1967 Ethiopia instituted harsh military measures that drove thousands of ELF adherents into Sudan. Small units of Ethiopian soldiers also attacked border villages and police posts within Sudan on several occasions between March 1967 and March 1968. At least four Ethiopian military personnel died during cross-border operations.

Abir, M. 1974. Oil, *Power and Politics*, 168–173.
Butterworth, R. 1976. *Managing Interstate Conflict*, 411–413.
Erlich, H. 1984. *The Struggle Over Eritrea*, 65.
Ethiopiawi. 1977. "The Eritrean-Ethiopian Conflict." In *Ethnic Conflict in International Relations*, ed. A. Suhrke and L. Nobel, 127–145.
Farer, T. 1979. *War Clouds on the Horn of Africa*, 35–36.
Gilkes, P. 1975. *The Dying Lion*, 197–199.
Lefever, E. 1970. *Spear and Scepter*, 151–154.
Markakis, J. 1987. *National and Class Conflict in the Horn of Africa*, 104–145, 191–201.
Sherman, R. 1980. *Eritrea, the Unfinished Revolution*, 73–78.
Small, M., and J. Singer. 1982. *Resort to Arms*, 99.

8.7 Djibouti Conflict, 1976–1977

France's colony of French Somaliland (Djibouti), renamed the Territory of the Afars and the Issas in 1967, experienced repeated political disturbances during the late 1960s and 1970s. Conflict was due partly to tensions among indigenous Somali (Issa) and Afari nationalities and partly to Somalia's efforts to incorporate the territory. French troops intervened in 1966–1967 to help suppress disorders (8.5). Further incidents occurred in 1970–1971 but were suppressed by local police. Prolonged violence began in 1973. In February 1976 Somali guerrillas representing the Front for the Liberation of the Somali Coast (FLCS) seized a bus carrying schoolchildren and fled to Loyoda at the border of Somalia. French soldiers and gendarmes surrounded the bus and eventually freed the hostages. In the process a party of French troops crossed into Somalia and exchanged fire with Somali police. French troops were called out repeatedly during further local incidents in 1976–1977. The territory gained independence as Djibouti in June 1977 following May elections policed by French troops. French forces temporarily stood down but were called upon by the Djibouti government in December 1977 in response to violence by Afari nationalists opposed to policies favoring Somali. No French military fatalities are reported.

Brownlie, I. 1979. *African Boundaries*, 767–774.
Clayton, A. 1988. *France, Soldiers and Africa*, 388.
Lewis, I. 1980. *A Modern History of Somalia*, 229–231.
Moose, G. 1985. "French Military Policy in Africa." In *Arms and the African*, ed. W. Foltz and H. Bienen, 59–97.
Saint Veran, R. 1981. *Djibouti, Pawn of the Horn of Africa*.
Shehim, K., and J. Searing. 1980. "Djibouti and the Question of Afar Nationalism." *African Affairs* 79 (April): 209–226.
Spencer, J. 1977. *Ethiopia, the Horn of Africa and U.S. Policy*, 27–30.

8.8 Eritrean War II, 1976–1980

The Eritrean Liberation Front (ELF) waged armed struggle against Ethiopian control from the early 1960s, aided by sanctuaries and limited military assistance from neighboring Sudan. Ethiopian counterinsurgency operations included sporadic raids upon Sudanese territory in 1967–1968 (8.6). The Marxist-oriented Popular Liberation Front (PLF) broke from the ELF by 1970 to fight separately for independence. The secessionist movement suffered additional factional splits in later years. Sudan restricted Eritrean dissident activities within border areas during the early 1970s but Sudanese-Ethiopian relations deteriorated after overthrow of Haile Selassie's government in Ethiopia in 1974. Sudan gradually increased support to the ELF and PLF as Ethiopia's Dergue pursued increasingly radical policies at home and abroad. The Ethiopian air force, in turn, began to attack border villages and other installations within Sudan in February 1976 and continued to do so until January 1980. In January 1977 President Jafar Muhammad Nimeiri openly endorsed the Eritrean independence movement. On at least one occasion in April 1977 Sudanese artillery provided covering fire to Eritrean guerrillas crossing the Ethiopian-Sudanese border. Neither Ethiopia nor Sudan is reported to have suffered military fatalities upon the other's territory.

Erlich, H. 1984. *The Struggle Over Eritrea,* 77, 81–82.
Ethiopiawi. 1977. "The Eritrean-Ethiopian Conflict." In *Ethnic Conflict in International Relations,* ed. A. Suhrke and L. Nobel, 127–145.
Farer, T. 1979. *War Clouds on the Horn of Africa,* 45–49.
Halliday, F., and M. Molyneux. 1981. *The Ethiopian Revolution,* 223.
Legum, C. 1981. "Angola and the Horn of Africa." In *Diplomacy of Power,* by S. Kaplan, 570–637.
Markakis, J. 1987. *National and Class Conflict in the Horn of Africa,* 104–145.
Ottaway, M., and D. Ottaway. 1978. *Ethiopia: Empire in Revolution,* 170.
Sherman, R. 1980. *Eritrea, the Unfinished Revolution,* 87–89.
Small, M., and J. Singer. 1982. *Resort to Arms,* 99.
Spencer, J. 1977. *Ethiopia, the Horn of Africa and U.S. Policy,* 36–39.

8.9 Ogaden War, 1977–1985

Somalia claimed the Ogaden in 1960 upon attaining independence. The area was populated primarily by Somali but had been assigned to Ethiopia by the United Nations in 1952. Armed conflict followed in 1960–1961 (8.3) and 1963–1964 (8.4). Somali tribesmen resumed revolt against the Ethiopian government in the early 1970s. Resistance increased after the Dergue overthrew the Ethiopian monarchy in 1974 and attempted to impose strong central control within the region. Arms and money from Somalia helped to support insurgent forces. Somalia also committed small army units wearing regular uniforms with insignia removed to assist rebels directly at the end of June 1977. One such unit transiting the corner of Kenya engaged in a skirmish with Kenyan police. A major guerrilla offensive stalled in mid-July. On July 28, 1977, the Somali army launched a full-scale invasion. Ethiopia counterattacked by air against Somali territory but was unable to hold back invaders. Somalia captured nearly all the Ogaden by October.

Ethiopia's Mengistu regime appealed to the Soviet Union for help. Somalia had previously benefitted from substantial Soviet military assistance. Ethiopia relied upon assistance from the United States, especially prior to 1974. The Soviet Union immediately provided military advisors and armaments to Ethiopia. At the end of December 1977, she also brought in Cuban troops from bases in Angola. Cuban and Ethiopian troops, aided by infantrymen and tank crews from the People's Democratic Republic of Yemen which arrived in January, drove Somali forces from the Ogaden by March 14, 1978. Cuban troops remained on guard within the Ogaden until October 1979.

Low-intensity conflict persisted near the Somalian-Ethiopian border after major battles ceased. Sporadic Ethiopian air attacks upon Somalia continued until the beginning of January 1985. Irregular Somali tribal formations conducted repeated attacks within the Ogaden. Regular Somali soldiers participated in some raids during summer 1980. Ethiopian ground forces invaded a strip of Somali territory near Balemballe at the end of June 1982 and subdued the area by mid-September. Ethiopian troops also participated in a raid upon the Somali village of Lawale in August 1984. Minor border incidents continued during the late 1980s.

The Ogaden War killed as many as 30,000 civilians and military personnel, including 8,000 Somali troops. Ethiopian troops suffered comparable fatalities, almost entirely upon Ethiopian soil. An estimated 1,000 Cubans died. A handful of Yemeni were also killed.

General

Brecher, M., J. Wilkenfeld, and S. Moser. 1988. *Crises in the Twentieth Century,* 1: 323.
Day, A., ed. 1987. *Border and Territorial Disputes,* 126–132.
Keegan, J., ed. 1983. *World Armies,* 175–180, 522–524.
Small, M., and J. Singer. 1982. *Resort to Arms,* 99.

Cuba

Dominguez, J. 1989. *To Make a World Safe for Revolution,* 157–162.
Legum, C. 1981. "Angola and the Horn of Africa." In *Diplomacy of Power,* by S. Kaplan, 570–637.
Leogrande, W. 1980. *Cuba's Policy in Africa, 1959–1980,* 35–51.
Leogrande, W. 1982. "Cuban-Soviet Relations and Cuban Policy in Africa." In *Cuba in Africa,* ed. C. Mesa-Lago and J. Belkin, 13–50.
McCormick, G. 1984. "Proxies, Small Wars, and Soviet Foreign Policy." In *Military Intervention in the Third World,* ed. J. Maurer and R. Porth, 37–55.
Porter, B. 1984. *The USSR in Third World Conflict.*
Valdes, N. 1982. "Cuba's Involvement in the Horn of Africa." In *Cuba in Africa,* ed. C. Mesa-Lago and J. Belkin, 63–94.

Ethiopia

Brownlie, I. 1979. *African Boundaries,* 827–851.
Erlich, H. 1984. *The Struggle Over Eritrea,* 77–78.
Gorman, R. 1981. *Political Conflict on the Horn of Africa.*
Halliday, F., and M. Molyneux. 1981. *The Ethiopian Revolution.*
Selassie, B. 1980. *Conflict and Intervention in the Horn of Africa,* 97–165.

Somalia

Farer, T. 1979. *War Clouds on the Horn of Africa*, 120–127.
Fitzgibbon, L. 1982. *The Betrayal of the Somalis*, 52–61, 72–84.
Laitin, D., and S. Samatar. 1987. *Somalia: Nation in Search of a State*, 140–145.
Lewis, I. 1980. *A Modern History of Somalia*, 231–242.
Markakis, J. 1987. *National and Class Conflict in the Horn of Africa*, 222–236.
Zartman, I. 1989. *Ripe for Resolution*, 82–133.

Yemen PDR

Bidwell, R. 1983. *The Two Yemens*, 292.
Halliday, F. 1990. *Revolution and Foreign Policy*, 172.
Ismael, T., and J. Ismael. 1986. *The People's Democratic Republic of Yemen*, 149–150.
Lackner, H. 1985. *P.D.R. Yemen: Outpost of Socialist Development*, 103.

8.10 Todghere Battle, 1987

Low–intensity warfare between Ethiopia and Somalia associated with the Ogaden War continued until 1985 (8.10). Violence persisted after 1985 due primarily to irregular forces representing, on the one hand, the Western Somali Liberation Front supported by Somalia and, on the other, the Somali National Movement (SNM) and the Somali Salvation Democratic Front (SSDF) supported by Ethiopia. In mid-February 1987, following several minor border incidents, SNM irregulars backed by Ethiopian aircraft and tanks manned by regular Ethiopian soldiers attacked Somali border villages in the vicinity of Todghere. Somali forces repulsed the attack after suffering 25 reported fatalities in defense and inflicting at least equivalent casualties upon invaders. Further incidents involving irregular forces continued until Ethiopia and Somalia agreed April 3, 1988, to demilitarize the border and to restore normal diplomatic relations. No fatalities are reported among regular Ethiopian military units during the Todghere incident.

Africa Contemporary Record 20 (1987–88): B392–B405.
Day, A., ed. 1987. *Border and Territorial Disputes*, 126–132.
Laffin, J. 1989. *The World in Conflict 1989: War Annual 3*, 89–101.
Zartman, I. 1989. *Ripe for Resolution*, 123.

8.11 Eritrean War III, 1987

Protracted war for Eritrean independence from Ethiopia, active from the 1960s, led to low-intensity armed conflict involving Ethiopia and the Sudan in 1967–1968 (8.6) and again in 1977–1980 (8.8). The Sudanese government publicly endorsed the Eritrean resistance movement in 1977 and permitted the Eritrean Liberation Front (ELF) to maintain headquarters within Sudan. It tended to restrict activities of rival secessionist groups, however, including the Eritrean People's Liberation Front. The Eritrean war continued throughout the 1980s. At the same time the Sudan People's Liberation Movement (SPLM) waged guerrilla war against the government in Khartoum. Sudan complained that Ethiopia's Dergue helped to support the SPLM. Border incidents and diplomatic tensions increased during the mid-1980s. In August 1987 Ethiopian aircraft once more attacked Sudanese territory harboring Eritrean rebels. No Ethiopian fatalities are reported.

Africa Research Bulletin. Political Series 24 (1987): 8708–8709; 25 (1988): 8719–8720.
Keesing's Record of World Events 33 (1987): 35173, 35368–35369; 34 (1988): 35882.

9

East Africa

Intertribal and ethnic disputes frequently precipitated international armed conflict within East Africa. Anya-Nya resistance to northern Sudanese rule spilled across international boundaries between 1964 and 1971 (9.8, 9.10, 9.12, 9.14). Recurring Hutu-Tutsi conflict within Rwanda and Burundi (9.4, 9.6, 9.15, 9.17) also led to international engagements. Britain intervened during Moslem-Creole conflict on Mauritius during the 1960s (9.9, 9.11). and during disturbances on Zanzibar in 1961 (9.5). 1947 uprisings on Madagascar (9.1), suppressed by France, and Mau Mau violence within Kenya (9.3), contained by the United Kingdom, represented in part anti-European sentiments as well as intertribal differences. Britain also intervened within Uganda during the Kampala riots of 1949 (9.2) and in Kenya, Tanganyika and Uganda during the East African mutinies of 1964 (9.7). Idi Amin's government within Uganda provoked a storm of conflicts during the 1970s (9.13, 9.16, 9.18, 9.19) which culminated in the Kagara War (9.20).

9.1 Madagascan War, 1947–1948

France formally claimed Madagascar and associated islands from 1642 but established effective dominion only after a major military campaign in 1895–1896. Serious anti-French rebellion resumed by 1898 and continued until 1904. United Kingdom forces captured the islands from Vichy France in 1942 and later handed them over to Free French administration. The Movement Democratique de la Renovation Malagache (MDRM), initially a political party, demanded independence immediately after World War II. Some French Malagasy military units also mutinied briefly in 1946 but were contained without overt military action. On March 29, 1947, rebel bands claiming to represent the MDRM attacked French military installations at several places on the main island of Madagascar. French troops responded violently against nationalists and suspected nationalists during the following months. Additional French Senegalese and Foreign Legion units aided the counterinsurgency effort beginning in August 1947. France crushed main elements of the rebellion by December 1947. Sporadic resistance, contained by local police, continued until 1949. More than 10,000 Malagasy are said to have died during the revolt, including many civilians who perished from starvation after being driven from their villages. Approximately 350 French soldiers were killed.

Brown, Mervyn. 1979. *Madagascar Rediscovered*, 265–269.
Butterworth, R. 1976. *Managing Interstate Conflict*, 86–88.
Clayton, A. 1988. *France, Soldiers and Africa*, 172–173.
Deschamps, H. 1961. *Histoire de Madagascar*, 268–271.
Heseltine, N. 1971. *Madagascar*, 176–183.
Kent, R. 1962. *From Madagascar to the Malagasy Republic*, 95–112.
Small, M., and J. Singer. 1982. *Resort to Arms*, 98.
Stratton, A. 1964. *The Great Red Island*, 239–261.
Thompson, V., and R. Adloff. 1965. *The Malagasy Republic*, 54–69.
Tronchon, J. 1974. *L'Insurrection Malagache de 1947*.

9.2 Kampala Riots, 1949

The United Kingdom established a Ugandan protectorate over the kingdom of Buganda and related territories in 1894. The Kabaka (king) ruled internal affairs within Buganda Province from Kampala with aid of three native ministers. British administrators governed the remainder of Uganda indirectly through local chiefs. The Bataka party and the African Farmers Union voiced opposition to the Kabaka and to British influence after World War II. On April 25, 1949, demonstrations in Kampala demanded resignation of the Kabaka's ministers and abolition of British export controls. Demonstrators rioted after police attempted to disperse them and violence continued for several days. The United Kingdom brought in units of the King's African Rifles from Kenya on April 28, 1949, and Royal Air Force units from Aden. Troops and police restored order within Kampala and also pursued dissidents within outlying areas. Resistance ceased by May 3 and troops stood down. No British military fatalities are reported.

Lee, D. 1980. *Flight from the Middle East*, 46–47.
Times (London) 4/27/49, 3e; 4/28/49, 3b; 4/29/49, 4e; 4/30/49, 3a; 5/4/49, 3b.

9.3 Mau Mau Violence, 1952–1956

British Kenya was originally acquired as a protectorate from the sultan of Zanzibar in 1895. Part of it was annexed to the Crown in 1920.

Numerous British settlers established prosperous farms, including within and adjoining highland territories formally designated as the Kikuyu Tribal Reserve. Friction over land ownership increased after World War II. Kikuyu opponents of settler practices and British government policies formed loose associations that later became known colloquially as "Mau Mau ". Attacks upon European farms and upon Africans cooperating with European settlers occurred beginning in September 1952. The governor of Kenya declared a state of emergency and British troops took the field in late October. Terrorism increased in 1953 and continued at a serious level until 1956 when British military units withdrew. The emergency was formally declared ended only in 1960. Throughout the emergency, British counterterrorist strategy relied heavily upon paramilitary units comprising primarily of locally recruited Kikuyu. Partly for this reason and also due to the terrorists' lack of modern arms, fewer than sixty British soldiers died while more than 8,000 known and suspected Mau Mau were killed.

Blaxland, G. 1971. *The Regiments Depart*, 269–291.
Clayton, A. 1984. *Counter-Insurgency in Kenya*.
Dewar, M. 1984. *Brush Fire Wars*, 50–62.
Edgerton, R. 1989. *Mau Mau: An African Crucible*.
Gordon, D. 1986. *Decolonization and the State in Kenya*, 113–135.
Lee, D. 1980. *Flight from the Middle East*, 58–77.
Majdalany, F. 1963. *State of Emergency*.
Paget, J. 1967. *Counter-Insurgency Operations*, 81–113.
Rosberg, C., and J. Nottingham. 1966. *The Myth of the 'Mau Mau'*.
Throup, D. 1985. "The Origins of Mau Mau." *African Affairs* 84 (July): 399–433.

9.4 Hutu Terrorism, 1959–1962

Belgium acquired Ruanda-Urundi, formerly German East Africa, under League of Nations mandate following World War I. She continued to administer the territory under League of Nations trust after World War II. The area suffered from long-standing intertribal enmity. A Tutsi monarchy and aristocracy dominated the more numerous Hutu (Kiga) before Germans arrived in the nineteenth century. Belgium, and before her, Germany, administered the territory indirectly, preserving the Tutsi king (Mwami) and disproportionate Tutsi control of cattle, land and local power. Hutu nationalists published the so-called Bahutu Manifesto in March 1957 opposing continued Tutsi caste privileges but took no other major action at that time. Mwami Mutara died unexpectedly in July 1959. Tutsi chieftains passed kingship to Mutara's twenty-one-year-old half-brother, Kigeri, who proved unable to establish his authority. Dissension arose among

Tutsi chiefs as well as between Hutu and Tutsi. On November 3, 1959 a Hutu peasant uprising began by attack upon a Tutsi subchief in Ndiza. Violence quickly spread throughout Rwanda, mostly involving roving bands of Hutu who attacked Tutsi without quarter and Tutsi counterterrorism. Belgian security forces including two companies of paratroops from the Congo intervened during the second week of November. Calm was temporarily restored by November 14 but terrorism involving small Hutu and Tutsi groups resumed in 1960. Many Tutsi fled, including Mwami Kigeri, contributing to partial collapse of traditional Tutsi aristocracy. Intermittent violence continued and Belgian forces undertook sporadic counteractions until withdrawn during July 1962 following the granting of independence to Rwanda. During 1961–1962 Belgian troops within Rwanda also occasionally skirmished with Congolese rebels seeking sanctuary during the Congolese Civil War (7.5). At least three Belgian soldiers are known killed within Rwanda.

Butterworth, R. 1976. *Managing Interstate Conflict*, 247–248.
Lemarchand, R. 1970. *Rwanda and Burundi*, 93–196.
Melady, T. 1974. *Burundi, The Tragic Years*, 46–48.
Nyrop, R. 1969. *Area Handbook for Rwanda*, 20.
Segal, A. 1964. *Massacre in Rwanda*, 8–11.

9.5 Zanzibar Riots, 1961

Multicultural tensions within Zanzibar have a long history. Arabic and Moslem settlement of Zanzibar dates from the first millennium a.d. Sayyid Said, Sultan of Muscat, moved his capital to the island in 1828 and ruled extensive holdings on the East African mainland as well as among other Indian Ocean territories. Zanzibar, in association with the island of Pemba, became a British protectorate in 1890. The United Kingdom freed slaves and encouraged immigration of farm laborers from the mainland during the twentieth century. A minority of Arabs and a few East Indians continued to occupy positions of relative privilege after World War II compared to the majority who represented either native Africans or recent mainland immigrants. Riots in 1948 growing out of a dockworkers' strike that reflected in part African immigrant antagonisms were quelled with the aid of police reinforcements from Tanganyika and without military intervention. Political parties formed along racial and cultural lines. The Zanzibar National party (ZNP), a primarily Arab grouping, formed in 1955. The Afro-Shirazi Union emerged in 1957 primarily to represent black native interests; it was renamed the Afro-Shirazi party (ASP) in 1959.

National legislature elections held in January 1961 denied either ASP or ZNP a majority. New elections were scheduled for June 1961 and riots and general anti-Arab violence erupted at that time. A state of emergency was declared and British troops were brought in from Kenya to enforce a curfew during the first week of June. Military forces retired in favor of police June 8. Sixty-eight persons died during disturbances but no British soldiers were killed.

Blaxland, G. 1971. *The Regiments Depart*, 412–413.
Clayton, A. 1981. *The Zanzibar Revolution and Its Aftermath*, 44.

9.6 Tutsi War, 1964

Violence between a privileged Tutsi minority and majority Hutu within Ruanda-Urundi led to Belgian military intervention during 1959–1962 (9.4). Rwanda and Burundi became separate independent states in July 1962. Hutu assumed control of most Rwandan national institutions, including the army and policy, in part because many traditional Tutsi aristocrats fled to Uganda, Tanzania, the Congo, and especially to Burundi after 1959. Tutsi continued to dominate Burundi government and society after independence. The Union Nationale Rwandaise (UNAR), originally founded within Rwanda in 1959 to promote Tutsi political power, claimed to represent all Tutsi's in exile but exercised little direct control. Tutsi-led guerrilla bands raided Rwanda without overall coordination and came to be known colloquially as "inyenzi" (cockroaches).

UNAR factions in exile attempted a general offensive in 1963. On November 25, 1,500 lightly armed refugees in Burundi attempted to march upon Rwanda but were turned back at the border by Burundi police and soldiers. Tutsi exiles mounted a second attack on December 21. This time Burundi authorities did not intercede. Some bands infiltrated also from the Congo and Uganda. Rwandan army and police exterminated most of the invaders, arrested leading Tutsi residents of Rwanda, and tolerated Hutu vengeance against Tutsi lasting until February 1964. Rwandan troops also raided Tutsi refugee camps within Burundi during January. Further incidents involving small groups of "inyenzi" continued until 1966. At least 10,000 Tutsi were massacred within Rwanda during the first months of 1964. No Rwandan soldiers are known to have died during raids upon Burundi.

Brecher, M., J. Wilkenfeld, and S. Moser. 1988. *Crises in the Twentieth Century*, 1: 267–268.
Butterworth, R. 1976. *Managing Interstate Conflict*, 373–374.

Lemarchand, R. 1970. *Rwanda and Burundi.*
Melady, T. 1974. *Burundi: The Tragic Years,* 46–48.
Segal, A. 1964. *Massacre in Rwanda,* 16–19.
Small, M., and J. Singer. 1982. *Resort to Arms,* 230.

9.7 East African Mutinies, 1964

The United Kingdom ruled the Kenya colony and protectorate, the Uganda protectorate and the Tanganyika (Tanzania) trusteeship until the early 1960s. British troops helped to suppress disorders within Uganda in 1949 (9.2) and assisted locally recruited paramilitary forces to suppress the Mau Mau rebellion within Kenya in 1952–1956. Tanganyika achieved independence in 1961, Uganda in 1962, and Kenya in 1963. On January 19, 1964, elements of the Tanganyikan army mutinied and interned European officers. Similar mutinies occurred within Uganda January 23 and within Kenya January 24. British troops stationed in Kenya and reinforcements drawn from Aden intervened in each of the three former colonial territories January 25 at the request of their governments. Mutineers were quickly subdued in each case. British troops remained in Tanganyika until mid-February. Two months after their departure Tanganyika and Zanzibar united to form Tanzania. British forces continued operations within Kenya until mid-April, and withdrew from Uganda by the beginning of August 1964. The United Kingdom suffered no military fatalities.

Brecher, M., J. Wilkenfeld, and S. Moser. 1988. *Crises in the Twentieth Century,* 1: 269.
Blaxland, G. 1971. *The Regiments Depart,* 414–418.
Decalo, S. 1976. *Coups and Army Rule in Africa,* 202–203.
Listowel, J. 1965. *The Making of Tanganyika,* 430–440.
Mazrui, A., and D. Rothchild. 1967. "The Soldier and the State in East Africa." *Western Political Quarterly* 20 (March): 82–96.
Nnoli, O. 1978. *Self-Reliance and Foreign Policy in Tanzania,* 107–113.
Venter, A. 1974. *Africa at War,* 147–159.

9.8 Anya-Nya War I, 1964

Egypt subjected the politically fragmented Sudan during several military expeditions beginning in 1821. She conquered most of northern Sudan by 1881 as far south as previously penetrated by Arabic trade, culture and language. The Mahdi revolt which started in 1881 expelled Egypt by 1885. Mahdists attempted unsuccessfully to extend control to southern equatorial regions beyond the Arabic cultural frontier. In 1896–1899 combined British and Egyptian forces reconquered northern Sudan and established an Anglo-Egyptian condominium under British administration. The United Kingdom also claimed unorganized southern territory for the Sudan. British administration of the south relied upon indirect rule through local chiefs as late as 1930. Repeated southern uprisings led to punitive military expeditions as late as 1928. The United Kingdom permitted local self-government to the Sudan in 1954 under an administration largely dominated by northern Sudanese.

In 1955 demonstrations protesting northern domination occurred within the southern towns of Nazra and Juba. Two companies of the Equatoria Corps, southern Sudanese territorial forces, mutinied when ordered to take action against demonstrators. Sudanese national administrators in Khartoum initially requested British and Egyptian help but eventually suppressed the mutiny without foreign assistance. Sudan gained independence in 1956, a step supported by most recognized southern political leaders. Survivors of the 1955 mutiny and other former Equatoria Corps members organized small guerrilla bands. Many bandits calling themselves "Anya-Nya" helped to proclaim the Land Freedom Army in 1963 under leadership of Emilio Tafeng. Anya-Nya began organized attacks upon central government installations within the south in September 1963, relying in part upon bases within neighboring Uganda and Zaire. The Khartoum government sent additional military units to the south a few months later and also conducted a small raid against a rebel camp near Abo, Zaire, in May 1964. The Anya-Nya War continued until 1972 and eventually entailed hundreds of thousands of fatalities. No Sudanese government soldiers are reported killed during the Abo raid.

Albino, O. 1970. *The Sudan: A Southern Viewpoint*, 47–56.
Alier, A. 1973. "The Southern Sudan Question." In *The Southern Sudan*, ed. D. Wai, 11–27.
Assefa, H. 1987. *Mediation of Civil Wars*, 153–185.
Beshir, M. 1968. *The Southern Sudan: Background to Conflict*.
Butterworth, R. 1976. *Managing Interstate Conflict*, 357–360.
Markakis, J. 1987. *National and Class Conflict in the Horn of Africa*, 146–168.
O'Ballance, E. 1977. *The Secret War in the Sudan: 1955–1972*, 62–63.
Small, M., and J. Singer. 1982. *Resort to Arms*, 230.
Wai, D. 1981. *The African-Arab Conflict in the Sudan*, 136–137.

9.9 Mauritius Riots I, 1965

The Indian Ocean island of Mauritius was settled by the Dutch at the end of the sixteenth century. It was taken over by the French in the eighteenth century and ceded to the United Kingdom in 1814. British colonial policy promoted extensive sugar plantations whose exports formed the basis of the economy. Immigrant laborers swelled the population and contributed to communal and class conflict between minority Moslem and majority Creole communities. The latter comprised mostly Hindus and Roman Catholics. Serious intercommunal riots occurred as early as 1937. Political parties also developed along class and ethnic lines, exacerbating social tensions during the 1960s. Communal violence in May 1965 provoked the declaration of an emergency. British troops deployed for the first time in the twentieth century and quelled rioting within a day. No British fatalities are reported.

Blaxland, G. 1971. *The Regiments Depart,* 449, 465.
Mannick, A. 1979. *Mauritius: The Development of a Plural Society,* 58.
Simmons, A. 1982. *Modern Mauritius,* 157–163.

9.10 Anya-Nya War II, 1966

The Anya-Nya War began within southern Sudan in 1963 and led to international armed conflict as early as 1964 (9.8) due in part to rebel reliance upon bases within neighboring countries. Violent repression by the central government in Khartoum contributed to flight of tens of thousands of southern refugees to neighboring countries, including to Uganda and Ethiopia. In December 1964 a civilian government replaced the Sudanese military regime controlled by Ibrahim Abboud since 1958. A Round-Table Conference began in Khartoum in March 1965 among representatives of recognized northern and southern political factions. Spokesmen for the banned Sudan African National Union (SANU), which operated from exile in Zaire, and observers from Egypt and Uganda were also present. The conference adjourned without finding a stable solution and the war continued to expand. In 1966 the Sudanese government of Premier Sadik al-Mahdi obtained limited commitment from the Ugandan government of Milton Obote to help suppress rebel activities on the Ugandan-Sudanese border. During the brief period of October and early November 1966 small Sudanese army units attacked Anya-Nya bases within Uganda with approval of the Ugandan government. No Sudanese soldiers are reported killed during 1966 cross-border raids.

Albino, O. 1970. *The Sudan: A Southern Viewpoint,* 56–66.
Alier, A. 1973. "The Southern Sudan Question." In *The Southern Sudan,* ed. D. Wai, 11–27.
Assefa, H. 1987. *Mediation of Civil Wars,* 153–185.
Beshir, M. 1975. *The Southern Sudan: From Conflict to Peace,* 24–44.
Butterworth, R. 1976. *Managing Interstate Conflict,* 357–360.

Mahgoub, M. 1974. *Democracy on Trial.*
Markakis, J. 1987. *National and Class Conflict in the Horn of Africa*, 146–168.
O'Ballance, E. 1977. *The Secret War in the Sudan: 1955–1972*, 92.
Small, M., and J. Singer. 1982. *Resort to Arms*, 230.
Wai, D. 1981. *The African-Arab Conflict in the Sudan*, 130–132.

9.11 Mauritius Riots II, 1968

The British Army intervened on Mauritius in 1965 to help suppress violence between Moslem and Creole communities (9.9). In January 1968, six weeks before scheduled independence, serious intercommunal violence erupted again. Another state of emergency was declared. The United Kingdom deployed 150 soldiers from Singapore during the last week of January to help suppress disorders. British troops remained on duty until after formal independence was granted March 12, 1968. They withdrew March 19. No British fatalities are reported.

Blaxland, G. 1971. *The Regiments Depart*, 465.
Mannick, A. 1979. *Mauritius: The Development of a Plural Society*, 58.
Simmons, A. 1982. *Modern Mauritius*, 186–189.

9.12 Anya-Nya War III, 1968

The Anya-Nya War in southern Sudan, begun in 1963, spilled over international borders in 1964 (9.8) and 1966 (9.10). The Anya-Nya relied in part upon support among exiles within neighboring countries. Milton Obote's government of Uganda sanctioned Sudanese government raids upon its territory in 1966 but cooperated less freely thereafter. In May 1968 Sudanese government troops again raided Ugandan border villages believed to support the Anya-Nya. The Ugandan government protested and Sudan later offered compensation for its actions. No Sudanese government soldiers are reported killed within Uganda during 1968.

Albino, O. 1970. *The Sudan: A Southern Viewpoint*, 66–76.
Alier, A. 1973. "The Southern Sudan Question." In *The Southern Sudan*, ed. D. Wai, 11–27.
Assefa, H. 1987. *Mediation of Civil Wars*, 153–185.
Beshir, M. 1975. *The Southern Sudan: From Conflict to Peace*, 24–44.
Butterworth, R. 1976. *Managing Interstate Conflict*, 357–360.
Markakis, J. 1987. *National and Class Conflict in the Horn of Africa*, 146–168.
O'Ballance, E. 1977. *The Secret War in the Sudan: 1955–1972*, 96–102.
Small, M., and J. Singer. 1982. *Resort to Arms*, 230.
Wai, D. 1981. *The African-Arab Conflict in the Sudan*, 130–132.

9.13 Obote's Resistance, 1971

The United Kingdom terminated her protectorate within Uganda in 1962. She ended trusteeship of Tanganyika in 1961. In 1963 Tanganyika and Zanzibar united to form Tanzania. In January 1971 disaffected elements of the Ugandan military displaced the government of Milton Obote and installed a regime under Idi Amin. Obote and a large number of followers, including some former Ugandan soldiers, took sanctuary within neighboring Tanzania. A few Obote supporters also fled to Sudan (9.14). Tanzania refused to recognize the Amin regime and permitted exiled Obote partisans to infiltrate Uganda in an attempt to undermine the new government. Uganda formally closed its border with Tanzania July 7, 1971. Small units of Tanzanian military forces accompanied Obote partisan raiders beginning in late August. Uganda retaliated by conducting repeated small raids into Tanzania. Raids and air strikes conducted by both Tanzania and Uganda continued until early November 1971. Kenya mediated a temporary settlement and on November 21, 1971, Uganda restored communications with Tanzania. As many as 100 Ugandan and fifty Tanzanian military personnel are reported to have died in border clashes.

Avirgan, T., and M. Honey. 1982. *War in Uganda*, 33–42.
Brecher, M., J. Wilkenfeld, and S. Moser. 1988. *Crises in the Twentieth Century*, 1: 297.
Butterworth, R. 1976. *Managing Interstate Conflict*, 459–460.
Decalo, S. 1976. *Coups and Army Rule in Africa*, 211–230.
Keegan, J., ed. 1983. *World Armies*, 574–576.
Martin, D. 1974. *General Amin*, 130–157.
Mittelman, J. 1975. *Ideology and Politics in Uganda*, 199–214.
Nnoli, O. 1978. *Self-Reliance and Foreign Policy in Tanzania*, 259–266.

9.14 Anya-Nya War IV, 1971

The Anya-Nya War within southern Sudan began in 1963 and continued until 1972. Southern opposition to the central government at Khartoum lacked cohesive political representation until 1969 when Joseph Lagu formed the Anya-Nya Eastern Organisation, later renamed the Southern Sudanese Liberation Movement. Even then, the Anya-Nya failed to obtain concerted support from neighboring states although Israel provided aid from 1969. The war drove tens of thousands of southern Sudanese to take refuge abroad and the Anya-Nya relied upon support among exiles. These conditions contributed to numerous minor border incidents and also encouraged occasional raids by the Sudanese government upon foreign sanctuaries, including within Zaire in 1964 (9.8) and within Uganda in 1966 and 1968 (9.10, 9.12). In 1969 Idi Amin overthrew the Milton Obote's government within Uganda. Obote supporters fled to Tanzania and Sudan. In April 1971 the Amin's government protested raids by Obote partisans out of Sudan—a prelude to more serious confrontation with Tanzania later that year (9.13).

Fighting within Sudan peaked during late 1971 and early 1972. Sudanese government units raided Ugandan territory again in mid-December 1971. The Anya-Nya War ended officially on March 12, 1972, when the Sudanese government and the Southern Sudanese Liberation Movement agreed to a cease-fire mediated in part by Ethiopia. Several hundred thousand civilians and military personnel died between 1963 and 1972. No Sudanese government fatalities are reported during 1971 engagements within Uganda.

Assefa, H. 1987. *Mediation of Civil Wars*, 153–185.
Butterworth, R. 1976. *Managing Interstate Conflict*, 357–360.
Eprile, C. 1974. *War and Peace in the Sudan*, 142–143.
Markakis, J. 1987. *National and Class Conflict in the Horn of Africa*, 146–168.
O'Ballance, E. 1977. *The Secret War in the Sudan: 1955–1972*, 140–141.
Small, M., and J. Singer. 1982. *Resort to Arms*, 230.

9.15 Hutu Resistance, 1972

Violent strife between a traditional Tutsi aristocracy and majority Hutu (Kiga) within Rwanda and Burundi contributed to repeated international armed conflict from 1959. A Hutu peasant uprising in 1959 (9.4) deprived Tutsi of predominant power within Rwanda and put many to flight. Efforts of Tutsi exiles to reclaim power within Rwanda led to further massacre in 1964 (9.6). Tutsi exiles continued sporadic raids upon Rwanda until the late 1960s.

Hutu resistance eventually emerged within Burundi and included organized attacks upon Tutsi beginning early in 1972. The Burundi government mounted a countercampaign against Hutu dissidents beginning in April 1972. In early May 1972, upon request of the Burundi government, Zaire deployed a company of regular soldiers to help guard the palace and airport within the capital, Bujumbura. Zairean soldiers withdrew two weeks later without serious incident and without casualty. Ensuing Tutsi repression within Burundi during 1972–1973 may have killed as many as 100,000 persons, mostly Hutu.

Butterworth, R. 1976. *Managing Interstate Conflict*, 462–463.
Lemarchand, R. 1975. "Ethnic Genocide." *Society* 12 (January–February): 50–60.

Melady, T. 1974. *Burundi: The Tragic Years*, 3–34.
Small, M., and J. Singer. 1982. *Resort to Arms*, 231.

9.16 Obote's Invasion, 1972

Idi Amin overthrew the government of Milton Obote within Uganda in 1971. Subsequent efforts to reclaim power by Obote and loyal followers who took refuge within neighboring Tanzania led to armed conflict between Tanzania and Uganda later that year (9.13). Serious fighting between the two states ceased temporarily in November 1971 but minor border incidents continued due to continued raids by Obote's exile partisans. In September 1972 1,000 Obote loyalists invaded Uganda. The Tanzanian government tolerated the invasion but provided no direct military support. Ugandan aircraft retaliated by bombing Bukoba and Mwanze within Tanzania on September 18 and September 22, 1972. Libya airlifted troops to Uganda but withheld them from battle or other overt operations. Obote's invaders failed to stimulate uprisings within Uganda as they had hoped and withdrew to Tanzania within weeks. Somalia helped to mediate a Tanzanian-Ugandan agreement to enforce a cease-fire October 5, 1972. No Ugandan fatalities are reported during air raids upon Tanzania.

Avirgan, T., and M. Honey. 1982. *War in Uganda*, 33–42.
Brecher, M., J. Wilkenfeld, and S. Moser. 1988. *Crises in the Twentieth Century*, 1: 298.
Butterworth, R. 1976. *Managing Interstate Conflict*, 459–460.
Decalo, S. 1976. *Coups and Army Rule in Africa*, 211–230.
Martin, D. 1974. *General Amin*, 170–197.
Mittelman, J. 1975. *Ideology and Politics in Uganda*, 225–226.
Nnoli, O. 1978. *Self-Reliance and Foreign Policy in Tanzania*, 264–265.
Smith, G. 1980. *Ghosts of Kampala*, 164.

9.17 Tutsi-Hutu Violence, 1973

Violence and counterterror among majority Hutu (Kiga) and traditionally privileged Tutsi within Rwanda and Burundi resulted in repeated genocide from the late 1950s (9.4, 9.6, 9.15). Many Hutu fled Burundi to Rwanda and Tanzania during Tutsi repression in 1972–1973. Exiles conducted frequent raids upon Burundi. Small units of Burundi military forces attacked refugee camps within Tanzania from March through June 1973. Tanzania protested and closed its border. In addition, a small unit of Tanzanian soldiers participated directly in at least one raid upon Burundi territory during mid-July 1973. Burundi ceased cross-border raids after reaching an agreement with Tanzania

July 21, 1973, mediated by Zaire but fighting continued within Burundi. The Burundi civil war of 1972–1973 resulted in deaths of as many as 100,000 persons, mostly Hutu. Neither Burundi nor Tanzania reportedly suffered military fatalities upon one another's territory.

Butterworth, R. 1976. *Managing Interstate Conflict*, 462–463.
Lemarchand, R. 1975. "Ethnic Genocide." *Society* 12 (January–February): 50–60.
Melady, T. 1974. *Burundi: The Tragic Years*.

9.18 Mombassa Port Boycott, 1976

The United Kingdom established protectorates within Uganda in 1894 and Kenya in 1895. She transferred some lands originally considered part of Uganda to Kenya through a series of administrative decisions between 1902 and 1926. Uganda became independent in 1962 within 1926 boundaries as did Kenya in 1963. President Idi Amin of Uganda complained about colonial territorial transfers during a speech to the Ugandan Defense Council reported by Radio Kampala February 15, 1976. President Jomo Kenyatta and other Kenya government spokesmen voiced vociferous objection to Amin's statement and demanded an apology. Dockworkers at the port of Mombassa, Kenya, imposed a boycott upon transshipment of goods to and from Uganda February 19. On March 19 Amin publicly denied making land claims against Kenya. Accusations of mistreatment of one another's citizens delayed resolution of the dispute. Cattle rustling on the Ugandan-Kenyan border, a problem throughout the 1970s, helped to increase tensions. Ugandan soldiers participated in an April 1, 1976, cattle raid which resulted in deaths of several Kenyans. Seventeen Ugandan soldiers also landed by helicopter within Kenya on April 18 and were captured by Kenyan forces. Diplomatic confrontation continued until August 1976 without further major incidents. No Ugandan military fatalities are reported.

Africa Research Bulletin. Political, Social and Cultural Series 13 (1976): 3988.
Brownlie, I. 1979. *African Boundaries*, 940–955.

9.19 Entebbe Airport Raid, 1976

On June 27, 1976, terrorists associated with the Popular Front for the Liberation of Palestine (PFLP) hijacked an Air France airliner en route from Tel Aviv, Israel, to Paris. The hijackers forced the plane to fly to Libya and then to Entebbe Airport within Uganda where Idi Amin's government permitted it to remain. The hijackers released most passengers except Jews and Israeli but demanded Israeli concessions regarding Palestine in return for remaining hostages. On July 3, 1976, an Israeli commando team landed at Entebbe and secured release of the remaining passengers after a gun battle involving both hijackers and Ugandan soldiers. Two Israeli soldiers died during the raid.

Brecher, M., J. Wilkenfeld, and S. Moser. 1988. *Crises in the Twentieth Century*, 1: 316–317.
Herzog, C. 1984. *The Arab-Israeli Wars*, 327–336.
Kyemba, H. 1977. *A State of Blood: The Inside Story of Idi Amin*, 166–178.
Ofer, Y. 1976. *Operation Thunder: The Entebbe Raid*.
Smith, G. 1980. *Ghosts of Kampala*, 121–122.
Stevenson, W. 1976. *90 Minutes at Entebbe*.

9.20 Kagara War, 1978–1981

Relations between Tanzania and Uganda were troubled throughout the 1970s. Tanzania gave sanctuary to Uganda's former president Milton Obote after he was overthrown by Idi Amin in 1971. Obote partisans subsequently used Tanzanian territory to attack the Amin government, contributing to armed conflict between the two states in 1971 (9.13) and in 1972 (9.16). The Tanzanian-Ugandan border in the vicinity of Lake Victoria was also subject to dispute. President Amin publicized a claim to the Kagara salient in September 1972 although his government did not vigorously prosecute the issue at that time. The Kagara salient includes territory south of the 1st Parallel and north of the Kagara River traditionally inhabited by Buganda and Ankole tribes. It was allocated to German East Africa (predecessor of Tanzania) under Anglo-German agreements of 1890 and 1914.

Ugandan military forces initiated small raids within the Kagara salient in early October 1978. Tanzanian artillery and commando immediately began counterattacks upon Ugandan territory. Uganda invaded the Kagara October 30 and announced its annexation November 1. Tanzania counterattacked within the salient November 11 and drove Ugandan troops out by November 13. Ten days later, large Tanzanian units crossed the 1st Parallel into Uganda. Sporadic battles occurred on both sides of the border until late January 1979 when Tanzania launched a major offensive deep into Uganda. Ugandan air attacks and commando raids upon Tanzania ceased by the end of March as fighting focused about Entebbe and the capital, Kampala. Libya dispatched an expeditionary force of several hundred soldiers which arrived in early March in time to participate in an unsuccessful defense of Entebbe. Tanzania conquered Entebbe on April 7. Kampala fell April 10, 1979, and Amin fled. Tanzania helped to establish the National

Consultative Council as governing body under titular leadership of the Ugandan National Liberation Front. In effect, however, Tanzania maintained military occupation of Uganda until the end of June 1981 when most of her forces withdrew.

An estimated 2,000 Ugandan troops were killed during the Kagara War, mostly within Uganda. Tanzania suffered approximately 1,000 military fatalities. At least 200 Libyan soldiers died.

Avirgan, T., and M. Honey. 1982. *War in Uganda.*
Brecher, M., J. Wilkenfeld, and S. Moser. 1988. *Crises in the Twentieth Century,* 1: 336–337.
Brownlie, I. 1979. *African Boundaries,* 1011–1016.
Foltz, W. 1988. "Libya's Military Power." In *The Green and the Black,* ed. R. Lemarchand, 52–69.
Keegan, J., ed. 1983. *World Armies,* 574–576, 598–600.
Small, M., and J. Singer. 1982. *Resort to Arms,* 95.
Smith, G. 1980. *Ghosts of Kampala,* 8, 175–187.

10

Southern Africa

Resistance to European rule developed late in Southern Africa. Minor events involved Nyasaland in 1959 (10.1) and Swaziland in 1963 (10.4). The Southwest African War, begun against Portuguese rule within Angola in 1960, later engulfed Namibia and continued throughout most of the 1980s (10.2). Insurrection commenced within the Portuguese colony of Mozambique in 1964 (10.4). Black nationalist rebellion within Rhodesia, which started in the 1960s, assumed serious international proportions during the late 1970s (10.5). Renamo Insurgency within Mozambique (10.7) and disorder within Zimbabwe (10.10) contributed to international armed conflict during the 1980s. At the same time, South Africa conducted repeated foreign raids against the African National Congress (10.8, 10.9, 10.11, 10.12, 10.13, 10.14).

10.1 Nyasaland Emergency, 1959

The United Kingdom's Nyasaland Protectorate (Malawi) was constituted in 1891 and federated with Northern Rhodesia (Zambia) and Southern Rhodesia (Zimbabwe) in 1953. The Rhodesian Federation, headquartered within Southern Rhodesia, enjoyed broad self-governing powers but Britain retained a governor-general for the federation and governors within each territory. Nationalists within Nyasaland and Northern Rhodesia resisted efforts to impose federal economic policies thought to serve primarily Southern Rhodesian interests. Strikes and demonstrations encouraged by Hastings Banda's Malawi Congress party led to violence within Nyasaland during February 1959. Units of the Royal Rhodesian Regiment, a European-officered regular force stationed within Southern Rhodesia, intervened on February 20 with approval of the British governor. "Operation Sunrise" continued to police disturbed areas of Nyasaland until March 24, 1959. No fatalities are reported during military operations.

Butterworth, R. 1976. *Managing Interstate Conflict*, 256–258.
Jones, G. 1964. *Britain and Nyasaland*, 231–243.
Rotberg, R. 1965. *The Rise of Nationalism in Central Africa*, 294–297.
Short, P. 1974. *Banda*, 89–116.
Wood, J. 1983. *The Wilensky Papers*, 629–659.

10.2 Southwest African War, 1960–1988

Thirty years of warfare beset Southwest Africa from 1960. War began within the Portuguese colony of Angola. Portuguese settled coastal lands south of the Congo River Delta as early as 1491 and founded Luanda, the future capital of Angola, in 1575. Insurrections in 1913–1915 represented the last serious resistance to Portuguese rule until 1960.

Nationalist opposition began to organize in the 1950s. It was divided from the start. The Popular Movement for the Liberation of Angola (MPLA) formed in 1956 but did not become a significant armed force until almost a decade later. The Union of Angolan Peoples (UPA), representing primarily Bakongo peoples who resided within the Congo as well as Angola, appeared in 1958 and made its presence felt by 1960. UPA established headquarters within Zaire and became the core of the later National Front for the Liberation of Angola (FNLA).

Portugal employed garrison troops sporadically to help control demonstrations and to hunt down suspected dissidents from June 1960. War began in earnest on February 4, 1961, when UPA and other rebels attacked Luanda's central prison. During the next month Bakongo tribesmen massacred hundreds of European civilians and thousands of Africans within northern Angola who had refused to cooperate with the UPA. Portugal deployed additional forces, eventually including more than 50,000 soldiers, and put FNLA/UPA guerrillas on the defensive by the mid-1960s.

Division among Angolan nationalists deepened during the 1960s. Joseph Savimbi split from FNLA to establish the Union for the Total Independence of Angola (UNITA) in 1964, supported primarily among Bandu peoples of southern Angola. UNITA become a major fighting force only in the mid-1970s. The MPLA became more visible in 1965–1966 after moving headquarters to Brazzaville, Congo, in 1964 and expanding bases within Zambia. Its leader, Agostinho Neto, a committed Marxist, obtained financial support from the Soviet Union and as well as help from East German and Algerian military advisors.

Portugal periodically conducted commando and air raids against MPLA bases within Zambia from July 1966 until 1974 and attacked border villages of Congo-Brazzaville (People's Republic of the Congo) upon at least one occasion in June 1966. She also occasionally raided Zairean villages sympathetic to the FNLA but refrained from undertaking concerted ground assaults against any foreign sanctuaries.

War in Angola represented a bloody stalemate by April 25, 1974., when the Armed Forces Movement overthrew the civilian government within Portugal. Portugal's new regime announced its intention to grant independence to African colonies and quickly reached cease-fire agreements with the FNLA and UNITA. The MPLA also agreed to a cease-fire in November but continued to provoke incidents thereafter. The Alvor Agreement of January 1975 proposed independence as of November 10, 1975. Rival opposition organizations failed to form an effective coalition government, however. Portugal reimposed martial law in May 1975 but subsequently did little to enforce it.

South Africa was embroiled in war within neighboring Namibia by this time. South African forces under British command captured German Southwest Africa in 1915. South Africa administered the territory under League of Nations mandate after World War I and under U.N. trust following World War II. Protest by the South West Africa People's Organization (SWAPO) supported by Afro-Asian states encouraged the U.N. General Assembly to condemn the South African administration in 1966. South Africa refused to accept a 1971 opinion of the International Court of Justice obliging her to leave Namibia. South African police contained sporadic SWAPO-inspired disturbances until 1972. Serious violence followed a general strike within Ovambaland near the Angolan border in December 1971. Portuguese troops sent from Angola in late January 1972 helped South African police until the first week of February when regular South African Defense Forces took over. South Africa instituted what amounted to martial law within Namibia. She also undertook regular surveillance of southern Angola where SWAPO based some operations and shared intelligence with Portuguese authorities. Moreover, South Africa reached accommodation with UNITA to deny support to SWAPO.

Several parties poised for action by mid-1975 as Portugal prepared to withdraw from Angola. Zaire, encouraged by the United States, dispatched small army units to assist FNLA forces within northern Angola beginning in July 1975 and committed battalion-size units in August. Meanwhile, MPLA forces drove UNITA from some positions within southern Angola. South Africa deployed military forces immediately north of the Namibian border in early June and occupied Angola's Calueque Dam in early August. She also organized composite units that included regular South African troops, UNITA guerrillas and former Portuguese soldiers which began an armored offensive against the MPLA in September 1975. Forces under South African command advanced hundreds of miles before halting at Angola's Queve River in early November.

The Zairean-FNLA offensive in the north begun in August attempted to capture the capital Luanda in October 1975 where the MPLA already held sway. The MPLA appealed for outside help. Cuban troops transported by the Soviet Union began to arrive in Luanda in early October. Thousands more arrived after Portugal formally abandoned power on November 10 and the MPLA declared itself the national government. MPLA and Cuban forces counterattacked and Zairean troops were forced to withdraw from Angola by February 1976 despite last minute help from South African military advisors. Battles near the border during January included Cuban artillery attacks upon Zairean territory. Cuba and the MPLA also mounted a counteroffensive in the south beginning in January that impelled South African withdrawal by the end of March 1976. Cuban troops remained within Angola to help the new MPLA-based government control continuing challenges posed by UNITA and FNLA forces, which enjoyed material support from South Africa and the United States.

South Africa fought continuing insurgency within Namibia in part by frequent cross-border attacks after Angola joined Zambia and other African state in declaring official support for SWAPO in 1976. In July that year and again in 1978–1980 regular South African troops raided suspected SWAPO positions within Zambia. South African police and paramilitary units also repeatedly violated Zambia's border during the 1980s as they did Botswana's as well. Regular South African commandos and aircraft raided Angolan territory continuously from 1976. South Africa resumed armored attacks in May 1980 and engaged in periodic pitched battles within Angola until February 1984. She also established military positions north of the Namibian border in support of UNITA from which she was not finally expelled until 1988 despite her promise to withdraw under the 1984 Lusaka accords.

War climaxed in 1987–1988. Cuba expanded her Angolan garrison to nearly 50,000 troops. South Africa deployed similar numbers within northern Namibia and southern Angola. Cuban and Angolan forces launched an offensive against UNITA and South African positions in June 1967. They surrounded an exposed South African field force north of the Namibian border by mid-1988. U.N. representatives helped mediate a cease-fire among Cuba, South Africa and Angola, agreed to on August 22, 1988. South Africa withdrew forces from Angola by the end of the month. The same parties signed a further agreement at U.N. headquarters in New York December 22, 1988, that included South African commitment to withdraw troops from Namibia and to grant independence and Cuban commitment to phased withdrawal from Angola. South African military forces withdrew from Namibia by November 23, 1989.

200,000 or more persons died during the Southwest African War. The majority represented civilians killed within Angola after 1975. Portuguese soldiers suffered 3,000–5,000 fatalities, mostly due to mines, ambushes and accidents. Cuba sustained an estimated 2,000 military fatalities as well as three to four times that number injured or missing. Regular South African Defense Forces may have suffered only 1,000 deaths, including approximately equal numbers within Angola and Namibia, excluding losses among paramilitary units and other irregular formations. A few hundred Zairean soldiers were killed.

General

Brecher, M., J. Wilkenfeld, and S. Moser. 1988: *Crises in the Twentieth Century*, 1: 307–30-8, 331–332, 337, 340, 344–345.
Butterworth, R. 1976. *Managing Interstate Conflict*, 78–80, 299–302, 363–364, 476–478.
Day, A., ed. 1987. *Border and Territorial Disputes*, 166–171.
Hartman, T. 1984. *A World Atlas of Military History*, 40–41.
Keegan, J., ed. 1983. *World Armies*, 522–532.
Laffin, J. 1986. *War Annual 1*, 17–21.
Laffin, J. 1987. *War Annual 2*, 20–34 , 190–193.
Laffin, J. 1989. *The World in Conflict 1989: War Annual 3*, 26–41, 198–204.
Small, M., and J. Singer. 1982. *Resort to Arms*, 232.

Angola

Alberts, D. 1980. "Armed Struggle in Angola." *In Insurgency in the Modern World*, ed. B. O'Neill, W. Heaton, and D. Alberts, 234–267.
Burchett, W. 1978. *Southern Africa Stands Up*, 1–202, 276–303.
Davidson, B. 1972. *In the Eye of the Storm*, 133–347.
Davies, N. 1978. "The Angola Decision of 1975." *Foreign Affairs* 57 (Fall): 109–124.
Gauze, R. 1973. *The Politics of Congo-Brazzaville*, 193, 205–206.
Legum, C. 1981. "Angola and the Horn of Africa." In *Diplomacy of Power*, by S. Kaplan, 570–637.
Legum, C., and T. Hodges. 1978. *After Angola*.
Marcum, J. 1969–1978. *The Angolan Revolution*.
Pettman, J. 1974. *Zambia: Security and Conflict*, 164–167.
Stockwell, J. 1978. *In Search of Enemies*.
Thomas, G. 1985. *Mercenary Troops in Modern Africa*.
Wolfers, M., and J. Bergerol. 1983. *Angola in the Frontline*, 1–84, 224–234.

Cuba

Dominguez, J. 1989. *To Make a World Safe for Revolution*, 152–159.
Greig, I. 1977. *The Communist Challenge to Africa*, 211–236.
Halperin, M. 1980. "The Cuban Role in Southern Africa." In *Southern Africa since the Portuguese Coup*, ed. J. Seiler, 25–43.
Leogrande, W. 1980. *Cuba's Policy in Africa*, 13–34.
Leogrande, W. 1982. "Cuban-Soviet Relations and Cuban Policy in Africa." In *Cuba in Africa*, ed. C. Mesa-Lago and J. Belkin, 13–50.
Porter, B. 1984. *The USSR in Third World Conflict*.
Washington Post 1/10/77, A14:1; 1/11/77, A11:1; 1/12/77, A12:1.

Namibia

Brownlie, I. 1979. *African Boundaries*, 1025–1040.
Dugard, C. 1973 *The South West Africa/Namibia Dispute*, 216–238, 516–524.
Katjavivi, P. 1988. *A History of Resistance in Namibia*.
Kiljunen, K. 1981. "National Resistance and the Liberation Struggle." In *Namibia: The Last Colony*, ed. R. Green, K. Kiljunen, and M. Kiljunen, 145–171.
Landis, E., and M. Davis. 1982. "Namibia." In *Southern Africa: The Continuing Crisis*, ed. G. Carter and P. O'Meara, 141–174.
Soggot, D. 1986. *Namibia: The Violent Heritage*.
SWAPO of Namibia. 1981. *To Be Born a Nation*.
Zartman, I. 1989. *Ripe for Resolution*, 170–254.

Portugal

Beckett, I. 1985. "The Portuguese Army." In *Armed Forces and Modern Counter-Insurgency*, ed. I. Beckett and J. Pimlott, 136–162.
Bruce, N. 1975. *Portugal: The Last Empire*, 62–98.
Gauze, R. 1973. *The Politics of Congo-Brazzaville*, 193, 205–206.
Humbaraci, A., and N. Muchnik. 1974. *Portugal's African Wars*, 166–175.
Kay, H. 1970. *Salazar and Modern Portugal*, 182–293.
Wheeler, D. 1969. "The Portuguese Army in Angola." *Journal of Modern African Studies* 7 (October): 425–439.

South Africa

Cawthra, G. 1986. *Brutal Force*, 144–159, 176–215.
Coker, C. 1985. *NATO, the Warsaw Pact and Africa*, 143–153.
Coker, C. 1985. "South Africa." In *Southern Africa: Regional Security Problems and Prospects*, ed. R. Jaster, 142–150.
Coker, C. 1987. *South Africa's Security Dilemmas*, 27–47.
Gavshon, A. 1984. *Crisis in Africa*, 224–257.

Hallett, R. 1978. "The South African Intervention in Angola." *African Affairs* 77 (July): 347–386.

Heitman, H. 1985. *South African War Machine*, 134–175.

Jaster, R. 1985. "A Regional Security Role for Africa's Front-Line States." In *Southern Africa: Regional Security Problems and Prospects*, ed. R. Jaster, 88–132.

Jaster, R. 1985. *South Africa in Namibia*.

Jaster, R. 1985. "South Africa's Narrowing Security Options." In *Southern Africa: Regional Security Problems and Prospects*, ed. R. Jaster, 37–84.

Jaster, R. 1989. *The Defence of White Power*, 59–140.

Leonard, R. 1983. *South Africa at War*, 54–97.

Toase, F. 1985 "The South African Army." In *Armed Forces and Modern Counter-Insurgency*, ed. I. Beckett and J. Pimlott, 190–221.

Venter, A. 1974. *Africa at War*, 73–90, 133–146.

Venter, A. 1974. *The Zambesi Salient*, 141–155.

Young, C. 1980. "The Portuguese Coup and Zaire's Southern Africa Policy." In *Southern Africa since the Portuguese Coup*, ed. J. Seiler, 195–212.

10.3 Swaziland Strikes, 1963

The United Kingdom and the Republic of South Africa guaranteed Swaziland as a homeland for Swazi peoples in the 1880s. The territory became a protectorate of South Africa in 1894. The United Kingdom supervised South African administration of Swaziland through a High Commissioner from 1903, following the Boer War. Nationalist labor leaders promoted a protracted general strike that turned violent within the Swazi mining district in May 1963. British troops flown in from Kenya helped police to quell disorder for a few days during mid-June 1963. Troops remained on station for two weeks without further overt activity while police suppressed the strike and arrested labor leaders. No British military fatalities are reported.

Barker, D. 1965. *Swaziland*, 131–133.

Blaxland, G. 1971. *The Regiments Depart*, 413–414.

Butterworth, R. 1976. *Managing Interstate Conflict*, 285–286.

Halpern, J. 1965. *South Africa's Hostages*, 369–378.

Potholm, C. 1972. *Swaziland: The Dynamics of Political Modernization*, 89–98.

Stevens, R. 1967. *Lesotho, Botswana, and Swaziland*, 232–236.

10.4 Mozambican War, 1964–1975

Portuguese first colonized coastal territory of Mozambique in 1506 but began to pacify the interior only at the end of the nineteenth century. The last serious tribal revolt occurred in Tete Province in 1918. Nationalist and labor disturbances arose after World War II. Police violently suppressed demonstrations within the capital, Lorenco Marques, in 1948 and dealt similarly with a dock strike there in 1956. Action by police against demonstrators at Mueda in 1960 is believed to have resulted in as many as 500 deaths. Nationalist resistance to Portuguese rule gained strength after the Mueda massacre. Portuguese authorities employed special police units representing the Policia Internationale Defensa do Estado to suppress demonstrations and opposition organizations. In June 1962 several nationalist organizations merged to form the Mozambique Liberation Front (FRELIMO). Eduardo Mondlane was elected president of the organization in September 1962. Mondlane was eventually assassinated by Portuguese agents in 1969. Between 1962 and 1964 FRELIMO built political apparatus in the countryside. Newly independent Algeria helped to train guerrilla fighters.

FRELIMO called publicly for armed insurrection against the Portuguese on September 25, 1964, and attacks promptly began at scattered locations throughout Mozambique. Portugal deployed regular military forces in October 1964 to help suppress the rebellion. She eventually committed 60,000 soldiers. Tanzania, Zambia and Malawi provided sanctuary to guerrillas and were subject to frequent Portuguese retaliation short of major ground assault. Portuguese aircraft and commandos repeatedly attacked Malawi territory from 1966 until 1974 and also raided eastern Zambia, especially during 1968–1969, at the same time that Portuguese forces attacked Western Zambia out of Angola during the Southwest African War (10.2). In April 1972 Portuguese aircraft also attacked Tanzania on Mozambique's northern border.

The Mozambican War was complicated in the early 1970s by association with black nationalist insurgency (10.5) within neighboring Rhodesia (Zimbabwe). FRELIMO assisted the Zimbabwe African National Union (ZANU) by providing it passage through liberated areas of Mozambique. With Portuguese approval, Rhodesian paramilitary security forces entered Mozambique in "hot pursuit" of ZANU as early as 1970. From April 1971 to at least April 1974 regular Rhodesian army units also participated in border patrols and deep penetration raids within Mozambique. Rhodesian attacks included occasional contact with FRELIMO guerrillas.

Portugal entered negotiations with FRELIMO at the same time as she sued for peace with insurgents in Angola (10.2) and Guinea–Bissau (6.5) following the April 1974 overthrow of Portugal's government by the Armed Forces Movement. She granted independence to a government formed by Samora Moises Machel representing FRELIMO on June 25, 1975.

An estimated 3,000–4,000 Portuguese soldiers died during the war. Most were killed by mines and ambushes within Mozambique. Rhodesia sustained only a handful of reported fatalities within Mozambique prior to Portuguese withdrawal.

General

Butterworth, R. 1976. *Managing Interstate Conflict*, 299–302, 369–371, 407–408.
Hartman, T. 1984. *A World Atlas of Military History*, 40–41.

Portugal

Beckett, I. 1985. "The Portuguese Army." In *Armed Forces and Modern Counter-Insurgency*, ed. I. Beckett and J. Pimlott, 136–162.
Bruce, N. 1975. *Portugal: The Last Empire*, 62–98.
Burchett, W. 1978. *Southern Africa Stands Up*, 125–203.
Hanlon, J. 1984. *Mozambique: The Revolution Under Fire*, 23–45.
Henderson, R. 1977. "Relations of Neighbourliness." *Journal of Modern African Studies* 15 (September): 425–455.
Henriksen, T. 1978. *Mozambique: A History*, 154–232.
Henriksen, T. 1983. *Revolution and Counterrevolution*.
Hodges, T. 1982. "Mozambique." In *Southern Africa: The Continuing Crisis*, ed. G. Carter and P. O'Meara, 175–198.
Humbaraci, A., and N. Muchnik. 1974. *Portugal's African Wars*, 144–153.
Isaacman, A., and B. Isaacman. 1983. *Mozambique: From Colonialism to Revolution*, 79–107.
Kay, H. 1970. *Salazar and Modern Portugal*, 182–293.
Middlemas, K. 1975. *Cabora Bassa*, 131–159, 281–307.
Mondlane, E. 1983. *The Struggle for Mozambique*.
Munslow, B. 1983. *Mozambique: The Revolution and Its Origins*.
Pettman, J. 1974. *Zambia: Security and Conflict*, 164–167.
Venter, A. 1974. *Africa at War*, 73–105.
Venter, A. 1974. *The Zambesi Salient*, 43–53, 90–140.

Rhodesia

Arbuckle, T. 1979. "Rhodesian Bush War Strategies and Tactics." *R.U.S.I.* 124 (December): 27–33.
Beckett, I. 1985. "The Rhodesian Army." In *Armed Forces and Modern Counter-Insurgency*, ed. I. Beckett and J. Pimlott, 163–189.
Cilliers, J. 1985. *Counter-insurgency in Rhodesia*, 14.
Middlemas, K. 1975. *Cabora Bassa*, 283–287.
Wilkinson, A. 1976. "From Rhodesia to Zimbabwe." In *Southern Africa: The New Politics of Revolution*, by B. Davidson, by B. Davidson, J. Slovo, and A. Wilkinson, 211–344.
Wilkinson, A. 1978. "Introduction." In *Black Fire*, by M. Raeburn, 1–52.

10.5 Rhodesian War, 1976–1980

The British South Africa Company obtained royal charter to Rhodesia in 1889. Southern Rhodesia (Zimbabwe) became a British crown colony with rights of self-government in 1923. A minority of white settlers resisted demands to extend political franchise to the majority of black Rhodesians. In November 1965 the Ian Smith's regime unilaterally declared independence from the United Kingdom. The United Kingdom imposed economic sanctions but refrained from military intervention. Black nationalists forcibly resisted the Smith government from 1966. The Zimbabwe African People's Union (ZAPU) and the Zimbabwe African National Union (ZANU) organized separate challenges, both at first primarily within northeastern Rhodesia near the Zambian and Mozambican borders. South Africa provided military assistance to the Smith government from 1967, including commitment of as many as 2,000 paramilitary police. Rhodesian police occasionally intruded upon neighbor states' territories from the early 1970s. In addition, regular Rhodesian military personnel operated openly within Mozambique from 1971 to 1974 (10.4).

Resistance spread throughout Rhodesia in 1975–1976. In 1976 ZANU and ZAPU combined with the African National Congress (ANC) to form the Patriotic Front. Botswana, Tanzania, Zambia and newly independent Mozambique combined strategy against her as opposition "Front Lines States" in August 1977. Rhodesia carried war to her neighbors, including frequent air and commando raids upon Mozambique and Botswana beginning in 1976 and Zambia beginning in 1977. She also mounted repeated ground offensives within Mozambique and Zambia. Mozambican and Zambian artillery shelled Rhodesian territory occasionally in 1976 and 1977 but not thereafter. In addition, Rhodesian air forces attacked Angolan territory on at least one occasion in February 1979.

Bishop Abel Muzorewa replaced Ian Smith as prime minister on May 31, 1979, after April elections in which some blacks participated. Lancaster House conference began in London in September including the Muzorewa government and the Patriotic Front representing black nationalist organizations. South African troops deployed at the end of November to protect southern rail lines with approval of the Muzorewa government. On December 5 the Rhodesian government and the Patriotic Front agreed to a cease-fire and to interim reversion to British rule preparatory to independence. The Rhodesian government terminated cross-border operations against Zambia and Mozambique on

December 9, 1979, having previously ceased actions within Botswana in August. Settlement was signed December 23 and Britain resumed official responsibility for the territory. South African troops withdrew January 30, 1980.

Approximately 1,000 members of Rhodesian security forces were killed during the war, including both regular and paramilitary personnel. No more than a few hundred died during foreign operations. Insurgents suffered an estimated 8,000 fatalities. No South African soldiers are reported killed within Rhodesia and no Mozambican or Zambian fatalities are reported during their artillery attacks.

Arbuckle, T. 1979. "Rhodesian Bush War Strategies and Tactics." *R.U.S.I.* 124 (December): 27–33.

Beckett, I. 1985. "The Rhodesian Army." In *Armed Forces and Modern Counter-Insurgency*, ed. I. Beckett and J. Pimlott, 163–189.

Brecher, M., J. Wilkenfeld, and S. Moser. 1988. *Crises in the Twentieth Century*, 1: 314–315, 318–321; 323–324; 326–327, 333–334, 338–339, 343–344.

Cilliers, J. 1985. *Counter-insurgency in Rhodesia*, 172–201.

Gann, L., and T. Henriksen. 1981. *The Struggle for Zimbabwe*.

Hodges, T. 1982. "Mozambique." In *Southern Africa: The Continuing Crisis*, ed. G. Carter and P. O'Meara, 175–198.

Leonard, R. 1983. *South Africa at War*, 82–86.

Moriarty, J. 1983. "Rhodesia (Zimbabwe)." In *Nonaligned, Third World, and Other Ground Armies*, ed. R. Gabriel, 191–207.

O'Meara, P. 1982. "Zimbabwe." In *Southern Africa: The Continuing Crisis*, ed. G. Carter and P. O'Meara, 18–56.

Small, M., and J. Singer. 1982, *Resort to Arms*, 232.

Wilkinson, A. 1978. "Introduction." In *Black Fire*, by M. Raeburn, 1–52.

Wiseman, H., and A. Taylor. 1981. *From Rhodesia to Zimbabwe*.

10.6 Matola Raid, 1981

The National party dominated South African national politics for decades beginning in 1948, primarily due to support among Dutch-speaking Afrikaners and disenfranchisement of black residents who constituted the great majority of the population. The National party pursued apartheid until the end of the 1980s, segregating blacks from whites in most aspects of life. Clandestine black nationalist organizations formed to oppose government policies from the 1950s, including the African National Congress (ANC). The government banned the ANC in 1960 and incarcerated Nelson Mandela, one of its leaders, for almost thirty years. The ANC established branches within several African states and came to symbolize black resistance to colonial and white minority rule throughout southern Africa.

The South African government became increasingly isolated after collapse of Portuguese rule within Angola and Mozambique in 1975 (10.2, 10.4) and inauguration of black majority government within Zimbabwe (Rhodesia) in 1980 (10.5). Most of South Africa's neighbors permitted the ANC to operate openly within their territories. South Africa began a series of raids against foreign ANC facilities in 1981 at the same time that she waged continuing war within Namibia and Angola (10.2) and covertly supported Renamo within Mozambique (10.7).

The first overt anti-ANC raid occurred January 30, 1981, when regular South African commandos attacked and destroyed several houses within Matola, a suburb of Maputo, Mozambique, which allegedly served as an operational headquarters for the ANC. Fifteen or more persons were killed, including two South African soldiers.

Africa Research Bulletin. Political, Social and Cultural Series 18 (1981): 5921.
Cawthra, G. 1986. *Brutal Force*, 163.
Heitman, H. 1985. *South African War Machine*, 178.
Jaster, R. 1989. *The Defence of White Power*, 119.

10.7 Renamo Insurgency, 1982–continuing

Mozambique gained independence from Portugal in June 1975 following a bloody eleven-year war (10.4). The Mozambique Liberation Front (FRELIMO) established an avowedly Marxist government under President Samora Moises Machel. In 1976 Mozambique signed a mutual defense agreement with Angola, Tanzania and Zambia representing other "Front Line" states opposing white-dominated Rhodesian and South African governments. Rhodesia repeatedly attacked rebel sanctuaries within her territory during the Rhodesian War (10.5). In May 1980, Mozambique signed a security agreement with newly independent Zimbabwe, successor to Rhodesia.

The opposition Resistencia Nacional Moçambicana (Renamo), represented by the Movimento Nacional da Resistencia de Mozambique (MNRM), began attacks upon economically important targets within Mozambique in 1979. Renamo followers included former Portuguese and Rhodesian security personnel as well as other dissidents and the organization received clandestine financial support from the South African government. By 1982 it numbered thousands of guerrillas engaged in widespread pillage. Zimbabwe committed an army battalion to help the Machel government suppress Renamo in July 1982. She eventually committed more than 10,000 soldiers. Tanzania also contributed troops in March 1987, as did Malawi the next month.

Tanzanian troops withdrew by the beginning of 1988. Conflict carried over to Zambia where Renamo maintained bases in border areas. Urged by Mozambique, Tanzania and Zimbabwe, the government of Zambia moved belatedly to expel Renamo during the latter half of 1988. Upon at least one occasion in November 1988 Zambian soldiers pursued Renamo guerrillas into Mozambique. The Renamo war continued in 1989 at which time several thousand Zimbabwe soldiers and a few hundred Malawi troops remained within Mozambique.

Renamo insurgency cost thousands of lives directly and contributed to widespread famine by disrupting normal economic activity. Zimbabwe military fatalities amounted to at least 100 by 1989. Tanzania lost 30 or more troops killed. Four Malawi soldiers are known to have died. Zambia reported no fatalities during cross-border operations.

Cawthra, G. 1986. *Brutal Force*, 160–168.
Coker, C. 1987. *South Africa's Security Dilemmas*, 36–41.
Hanlon, J. 1984. *Mozambique: The Revolution Under Fire*, 219–233.
Jaster, R. 1989. *The Defence of White Power*, 51–59.
Keegan, J., ed. 1983. *World Armies*, 681–684.
Laffin, J. 1986. *War Annual 1*, 104–107.
Laffin, J. 1987. *War Annual 2*, 150–155.
Laffin, J. 1989. *The World in Conflict 1989: War Annual 3*, 167–173.
Metz, S. 1986. "The Mozambique National Resistance and South African Foreign Policy." *African Affairs* 85 (October): 491–507.

10.8 Maseru Raid, 1982

South African Defense Forces raided African National Congress (ANC) facilities within Matola, Mozambique, in January 1981 (10.6). On December 9, 1982, South African commandos attacked homes of alleged ANC members within Maseru, Lesotho. Forty-two persons were killed during the attack but no South African losses are reported.

Bardill, J., and J. Cobbe. 1985. *Lesotho*, 141, 169–170.
Cawthra, G. 1986. *Brutal Force*, 172.
Day, A., ed. 1987. *Border and Territorial Disputes*, 151–154.
Heitman, H. 1985. *South African War Machine*, 178–179.
Jaster, R. 1989. *The Defence of White Power*, 119–120.
Leonard, R. 1983. *South Africa at War*, 90–91, 93.

10.9 Maputo Raids, 1983

South African commandos raided houses harboring African National Congress (ANC) members within Matola, Mozambique, a suburb of

Maputo, in January 1981 (10.6). A similar attack took place within Maseru, Lesotho, in December 1982 (10.8). On May 25, 1983, South African aircraft again attacked houses allegedly used by the ANC within suburbs of Maputo, Mozambique. On October 17, 1983, South African commandos destroyed an alleged ANC office within Maputo. No South African military personnel are reported killed during the two raids.

Africa Research Bulletin. Political, Social and Cultural Series 20 (1983): 6828-6829, 6997–6998.

Cawthra, G. 1986. *Brutal Force*, 163–164.

Heitman, H. 1985. *South African War Machine*, 179–181.

Jaster, R. 1989. *The Defence of White Power*, 120.

10.10 Maitengwe Disorders, 1983

Separate black nationalist organizations struggled against the white-dominated Rhodesian government during the 1960s and early 1970s. These included the Zimbabwe African People's Union (ZAPU) and the Zimbabwe African National Union (ZANU) each of which depended primarily upon different regions and tribes for support. In 1976 ZANU and ZAPU combined with the African National Congress (ANC) to form the Patriotic Front which succeeded in forcing temporary restoration of British rule in 1979 at end of the Rhodesian War (10.5). The Patriotic Front fractured prior to scheduled February 1980 national elections. Robert Mugabe campaigned under the name of ZANU-Patriotic Front. Joshua Nkomo campaigned against him under banner of the Patriotic Front-ZAPU. Mugabe's faction won a substantial majority of seats in the lower legislative body. On April 18, 1980, the United Kingdom transferred authority to an independent government of Zimbabwe of which Robert Mugabe was prime minister and Canaan Sodindo Banana, a Mugabe supporter, was president. ZAPU obtained only four of twenty-two cabinet positions within the new government.

Conflict occurred between ZAPU and ZANU forces during 1980 as Mugabe's government attempted to extend central government authority within Metabeleland, base of Nkomo's ZAPU. In November 1981 an integrated national army was finally formed that included main units of both ZANU and ZAPU forces. Sporadic resistance continued within Metabeleland, nevertheless, aided in part by sanctuaries within neighboring Botswana. The Zimbabwe National Army attempted to impose order within the province beginning in 1982. On November 8, 1983, a small unit of Zimbabwe national troops entered Botswana in pursuit of rebel guerrillas and clashed with Botswana border guards

near Maitengwe. Another similar incident occurred December 20. One
Zimbabwean soldier is reported killed within Botswana.

Times (London) 11/10/ 83, 5d; 11/12/83, 5h.
Washington Post 12/25/83, A19:1.

10.11 Gabarone Raid I, 1985

South African Defense Forces openly attacked facilities of the
African National Congress (ANC) within Mozambique in 1981 (10.6)
and did so again upon two occasions in 1983 (10.9). South Africa also
attacked Lesotho in 1982 (10.8). On June 14, 1985, seventy South African
commandos attacked ten houses and offices within Gabarone,
Botswana, that were allegedly used by the ANC. No South African
losses are reported.

Africa Research Bulletin. Political Series 22 (1985): 7668.
Cawthra, G. 1986. *Brutal Force*, 172.
Dale, R. 1987. "Not Always So Placid a Place." *African Affairs* 86 (January): 73–
    91.
Jaster, R. 1989. *The Defence of White Power*, 122.

10.12 Anti-ANC Raids, 1986

South African Defense Forces repeatedly attacked foreign facilities
of the African National Congress (ANC) within Mozambique, Lesotho
and Botswana beginning in 1981 (10.6, 10.8, 10.9, 10.11). On May 19,
1986, South African Defense Forces carried out three additional attacks
in quick succession against alleged ANC targets. Shortly after
midnight South African commandos attacked an office building and a
house in Harare, Zimbabwe. At dawn South African commandos
attacked houses in Mogaditsane, Botswana. Later that day South
African aircraft bombed targets near Lusaka, Zambia, including a
refugee camp. No South African military fatalities are reported.

Africa Research Bulletin. Political Series 23 (1986): 8073–8079.
Dale, R. 1987. "Not Always So Placid a Place." *African Affairs* 86 (January): 73–
    91.
Jaster, R. 1989. *The Defence of White Power*, 122.

10.13 Livingstone Raid, 1987

South African Defense Forces conducted raids upon foreign facilities
of the African National Congress (ANC) within most of her neighbors

beginning in 1981, including within Botswana, Lesotho, Mozambique, Zambia and Zimbabwe (10.6, 10.8, 10.9, 10.11, 10.12). On April 25, 1987, South Africa mounted a helicopter-borne raid upon two buildings in Livingstone, Zambia, that allegedly housed African National Congress operations. No South African military fatalities are reported.

Africa Research Bulletin. Political Series 24 (1987): 8458–8459.
Jaster, R. 1989. *The Defence of White Power*, 123.

10.14 Gabarone Raid II, 1988

South African Defense Forces repeatedly attacked foreign facilities that allegedly supported the African National Congress (ANC) beginning in 1981 (10.6, 10.8, 10.9, 10.11, 10.12, 10.13). South African Defence Force commandos again raided a house within Gabarone, Botswana, that allegedly housed African National Congress operations on March 28, 1988. No South African military fatalities are reported.

Africa Contemporary Record 20 (1987–88): B592–B593.
Africa Research Bulletin. Political Series 25 (1988): 8801.
Jaster, R. 1989. *The Defence of White Power*, 123.

11

North Africa

Demonstrations against foreign rule led the United Kingdom to intervene within Libya (11.1, 11.4, 11.6), France within Morocco (11.2, 11.5, 11.7) and Spain within Spanish Morocco (11.3) between 1945 and 1951. The North African War (11.8) engulfed the entire Maghreb, including Tunisia, Algeria, Morocco and the Western Sahara beginning in 1952 and ending upon Algerian independence in 1962. Morocco and Algeria quarrelled over their border during the early 1960s (11.9, 11.10). Sustained warfare also came to Western Sahara beginning in 1974 (11.11) and lasting through the 1980s. Other international armed conflicts included the Egyptian-Libyan clash of 1977 (11.12), strife on the Libyan-Tunisian border in 1984 (11.13), Israel's raid upon Palestine Liberation Organization bases within Tunisia in 1985 (11.14), and U.S. air attacks upon Libya in 1986 (11.15).

11.1 Tripoli Riots I, 1945

Italy seized Tripoli by force from the Ottoman Empire in 1912 and annexed it to Italian Libya. British and Free French forces captured Italy's Libyan colonies by the end of 1942. British military occupation of Tripolitania during and for several years after World War II relied primarily upon previously established Italian administrative machinery. A variety of local resentments, including anti-Italian and anti-Jewish sentiments, provoked incidents as early as 1944. In November 1945 major riots within Tripoli killed more than 100 Jews. British troops called out of garrison suppressed the disturbances in less than a week without incurring any fatalities.

Rennell, F. 1948. *British Military Administration of Occupied Territories in Africa*, 466.
New York Times 11/8/45, 1:2; 11/9/45, 5:5; 11/10/45, 6:1; 11/11/45, 18:3; 11/13/45, 7:1; 11/17/45, 8:6.

11.2 Moroccan Incidents, 1947

The Sultanate of Morocco, independent for more than a thousand years including against Ottoman encroachment, conceded a protectorate to France in 1912. France, in turn, allowed Spain a protectorate within northern Morocco. French attempts to pacify the territory met resistance, especially within remote areas. A fierce revolt within the Rif Mountains challenged both Spanish and French control during the 1920s. Further violent incidents occurred during the 1930s. The nationalist Istiqlal party was founded in 1943 to advance demands for Moroccan autonomy. It gained some favor with Sultan Mohammed V and was promptly outlawed. French Senegalese troops helped to suppress Istiqlal-aided riots within Casablanca in April 1947. French forces also took action at Khuraybiqah during labor strikes later the same month. No French casualties are reported.

Al-Fasi, A. 1970. *The Independence Movements in Arab North Africa*, 263–265.
Butterworth, R. 1976. *Managing Interstate Conflict*, 32–38.
Julien, C. 1952. *L'Afrique du Nord en Marche*, 362.
Landau, R. 1956. *Moroccan Drama*, 1900–1955, 255–257.

11.3 Tetuan Demonstration, 1948

Spain established small enclaves on Morocco's Mediterranean Coast beginning in 1497. She obtained a protectorate within northern Morocco by agreement with France in 1912 after France gained a protectorate over most of the remainder of Morocco. Violent resistance to Spanish rule, and later also French control, erupted within the Rif War during the 1920s. The Moroccan independence movement after World War II primarily affected the French zone except for a few notable incidents. February 8, 1948, demonstrations within the capital, Tetuan, prompted Spain to call out regular army units. Spanish soldiers inflicted injury upon some civilians but suffered no casualties of their own and retired to barracks the next day.

Al-Fasi, A. 1970. *The Independence Movements in Arab North Africa*, 355.
Barbour, N. 1962. *A Survey of North West Africa*, 160.
New York Times 2/9/48, 10:5; 2/10/48, 19:8.

11.4 Tripoli Riots II, 1948

The United Kingdom captured Italian colonies within Libya during World War II and continued to administer them until 1951. Local disturbances provoked military action in November 1945 (11.1). She deployed regular troops again during rioting in February 1948 and even more serious violence between Jews and Arabs within Tripoli in June. British soldiers killed several Libyans in the course of operations but reported no casualties of their own.

Facts on File 8 (1948): 58.
New York Times 2/18/48, 11:3; 6/14/48, 1:7

11.5 Oudja Riots, 1948

Violent disturbances repeatedly afflicted France's protectorate within Morocco after World War II. Some incidents represented efforts of the underground Istiqlal independence movement; others owed primarily to local grievances. Police alone restrained violence most of the time but French soldiers also intervened upon several occasions beginning with the Casablanca riots of 1947 (11.2). Garrison troops were called upon again to patrol the streets of Oudja in mid-June 1948 during riots involving Moslem and Jewish communities. French military forces suffered no casualties.

Butterworth, R. 1976. *Managing Interstate Conflict,* 32–38.
Keesing's Contemporary Archives 6 (1948): 9357.
New York Times 6/14/48, 1:7.

11.6 Tripoli Riots III, 1949

British troops intervened within Libya in 1945 and 1948 (11.1, 11.4) during riots challenging continued United Kingdom administration. Further demonstrations within Tripoli against American use of Libyan air bases became violent during May 1949. British garrison troops suppressed disorder within a few days without suffering fatalities.

Keesing's Contemporary Archives 7 (1949): 10029.
New York Times 5/12/49, 1:2; 5/15/49, 33:6; 5/16/49, 7:5; 5/20/49, 5:1.

11.7 Casablanca Riots, 1951

Nationalist demonstrations within France's Moroccan protectorate elicited French military intervention in 1947 and 1948 (11.3, 11.5). The independence movement gained political strength during following years. France scheduled local elections for November 1, 1951, under arrangements designed to minimize effectiveness of popular nationalist parties. Nationalists attempted to boycott the elections and riots encouraged by the Istiqlal broke out within Casablanca and other towns. France employed Senegalese troops and metropolitan French army units on November 2–3 to assist police in controlling disturbances. French military forces reported no fatalities.

Butterworth, R. 1976. *Managing Interstate Conflict*, 32–38.
Bernard, S. 1969. *The Franco-Moroccan Conflict, 1943–1956*, 95–97.
New York Times 11/3/51, 3:1; 11/4/51, 26:5.

11.8 North African War, 1952–1962

International armed conflict began within Tunisia in January 1952 and engulfed nearly all of French and Spanish North Africa. France obtained a protectorate within Tunisia in 1881. The Neo-Destour party led by Habib Bourgiba vocally opposed French rule beginning in 1934. French policy toward Tunisian nationalists vacillated between accommodation and repression during the 1930s and 1940s. Nationalists began guerrilla resistance in January 1952. France mobilized locally stationed army units later that month. Tunisian violence continued until December 1954 when France conceded independence in principle. Tunisia gained internal autonomy under a Bourgiba government in September 1955 and full independence in March 1956.

France retained large military installations within Tunisia after independence, including along the Algerian border and at Bizerte. A radical nationalist faction led by Salah ben Youssef opposed continued French presence and initiated attacks against Bourgiba's government in 1955. French troops and units of Tunisia's fledgling army conducted joint operations during the first half of 1956, before and after independence, and largely eradicated the Youssefist rebellion by midyear.

Meanwhile, sustained conflict began within the French protectorate of Morocco in December 1952. Demonstrations by Moroccan nationalists provoked brief French military interventions in 1947, 1948 and 1951 (11.2, 11.5, 11.7). Riots broke out again on December 7, 1952. France established de facto military occupation. In 1953 France deposed Sultan Mohammed who supported the nationalist cause. French settlers organized paramilitary "ultras" with governmental assistance. Nationalists organized the Moroccan Liberation Army (AOL), further contributing to widespread bloodshed by 1954. The AOL engaged French army units in full-scale battles by 1955, including within the Rif Mountains, scene of savage anti-French resistance during the 1920s. France eventually acceded to Moroccan independence March 2, 1956.

Resistance spread immediately to Spanish Morocco when France capitulated. Spain administered a region within and north of the Rif

Mountains under a 1912 agreement with France. She tolerated guerrilla operations launched from her zone into French-administered territory during 1954–1956. Violent demonstrations erupted within Tetuan on March 2, 1956. Spain mobilized troops to suppress disorders as she had previously in 1948 (11.3). She withdrew claims to Moroccan territory in April except for a few coastal enclaves. Spanish and French zones reunited under Sultan Mohammed in October 1956.

The North African War continued until 1962 primarily due to conflict within the French colony of Algeria. France conquered Algiers from the Ottoman Empire in 1830. She annexed the territory in 1842 and gradually extended domains southward and westward. Hundreds of thousands of French citizens settled within Algeria and obtained control of fully one-third of arable land by the early twentieth century. Algeria experienced little disquiet after World War II until rebellion erupted suddenly on November 1, 1954, led by Ahmed Ben Bella's National Liberation Front (FLN). France committed major military forces during fierce fighting that followed.

War within Algeria affected neighboring states and territories. Algerian rebels employed sanctuaries within Tunisia and Morocco. France mounted ground operations within both, before and after independence, until she completed electrified fences along key portions of Algeria's borders in summer 1958. French cross-border air and commando operations resumed later and continued nearly to the end of the war. In July–September 1961 French ground forces intervened within Tunisia against demonstrators and supporting Tunisian Army units protesting continued French military presence at Bizerte and other bases. Incidents occurred on the Algerian-Libyan border. FLN supplies from Egypt often traversed Libya. A French ground sweep in October 1957 intercepted FLN supply columns within Libyan Sahara.

War also spread to the western Sahara. Morocco claimed French and Spanish Saharan territories, including Ifni, Spanish Sahara (Western Sahara), and Mauritania. Moroccan Liberation Army (AOL) elements not incorporated among regular Moroccan military forces following independence moved into unoccupied areas of Spanish Sahara by the end of 1956 and began incursions within French Mauritania by the beginning of 1957. French troops defended Mauritania and periodically pursued assailants into Spanish Sahara. AOL units attacked Spain's Ifni enclave in August 1957 and Spanish Saharan military positions in December. Spain retaliated by air strikes against Moroccan territory during late-November 1957. France and Spain conducted joint ground operations during February 1958 which cleared AOL forces from Spanish Sahara and ended serious attacks upon Ifni and Mauritania by the first of March.

Continuing war within Algeria aggravated French political instability leading to collapse of the Fourth Republic in 1958. Charles de Gaulle became president of the Fifth Republic and discussed accommodation with Algerian nationalists beginning in 1959. Mutinous elements of the French Army in Algeria formed the Secret Army Organization (OAS). The OAS attempted an unsuccessful coup in 1961 and sponsored terrorism on behalf of French Algerian settlers. A formal cease-fire was obtained within Algeria in March 1962 after the OAS was suppressed. French military operations ceased entirely at the end of June when France recognized Algerian independence under a government formed by Ahmed Ben Bella.

Fighting within Algeria represented the most brutal aspect of the North African War, involving deaths of tens of thousands of civilians and approximately 15,000 French soldiers. French military fatalities during the war as a whole amounted to as many as 17,000. Spanish military losses included about 100 killed.

General

Brecher, M., J. Wilkenfeld, and S. Moser. 1988. *Crises in the Twentieth Century,* 1: 235–237, 239–240, 252–253.

Butterworth, R. 1976. *Managing Interstate Conflict,* 32–38, 137–138, 187–190, 222–223, 228–229, 233–235, 314–316.

Small, M., and J. Singer. 1982. *Resort to Arms,* 99.

Algeria

Barbour, N. 1962. *A Survey of North West Africa.*

Clark, M. 1960. *Algeria in Turmoil.*

Clayton, A. 1988. *France, Soldiers and Africa,* 162–196.

Gillespie, J. 1960. *Algeria, Rebellion and Revolution.*

Guillemin, J. 1982. "Les Campagnes Militaires Francaises de la Decolonisation en Afrique Sud-Saharienne." *Mois en Afrique* (June): 124–141.

Harrison, A. 1989. *Challenging De Gaulle.*

Heggoy, A. 1972. *Insurgency and Counterinsurgency in Algeria.*

Henissart, P. 1970. *Wolves in the City.*

Horne, A. 1987. *A Savage War of Peace.*

Humbaraci, A. 1966. *Algeria: A Revolution That Failed,* 32–80, 128–135.

Hutchinson, M. 1978. *Revolutionary Terrorism: The FLN in Algeria.*

Kelly, G. 1965. *Lost Soldiers,* 143–358.

Nutting, A. 1958. *I Saw for Myself,* 1–17.

O'Ballance, E. 1967. *The Algerian Insurrection, 1954–62.*

Talbott, J. 1980. *The War Without a Name: France in Algeria.*

Wright, J. 1969. *Libya,* 234.

Morocco

Ashford, D. 1961. *Political Change in Morocco.*
Bernard, S. 1963. *Le Conflit Franco-Marocain.*
Bernard, S. 1969. *The Franco-Moroccan Conflict, 1943–1956.*
Cohen, M., and L. Hahn. 1966. *Morocco: Old Land, New Nation,* 51–110, 216–220.
Landau, R. 1956. *Moroccan Drama, 1900–1955,* 249–384.
Maxwell, G. 1966. *Lords of the Atlas,* 206–265.
Touval, S. 1972. *The Boundary Politics of Independent Africa.*
Trout, F. 1969. *Morocco's Saharan Frontiers,* 407–430.
Zartman, I. 1964. *Morocco: Problems of New Power,* 3–116.
Zartman, I. 1966. *International Relations in the New Africa,* 1–8, 100–101.

Tunisia

Bourgiba, H. 1963. "Tunisia." In *Foreign Policies in a World of Change,* ed. J. Black and K. Thompson, 351–375.
Julien, C. 1952. *L'Afrique du Nord en Marche,* 217–394.
Ling, D. 1967. *Tunisia: From Protectorate to Republic,* 146–201.

Western Sahara

Curran, B., and J. Schrock. 1972. *Area Handbook for Mauritania,* 152.
Dugue, G. 1960. *Vers les Etats-Unis d'Afrique,* 55–68.
Gerteiny, A. 1967. *Mauritania,* 127–130.
Gerteiny, A. 1981. *Historical Dictionary of Mauritania.*
Hodges, T. 1982. *Historical Dictionary of Western Sahara.*
Hodges, T. 1983. *Western Sahara: Roots of a Desert War,* 73–84.
Mercer, J. 1976. *Spanish Sahara,* 218–236.
Thompson, V., and R. Adloff. 1980. *The Western Saharans,* 107–108, 117–118.
Welles, B. 1965. *Spain: The Gentle Anarchy,* 238–244.

11.9 Tindouf Conflict, 1962

Morocco's southern boundary within the lightly-populated Sahara was not precisely defined prior to French penetration of the Maghreb in the nineteenth century. Ambiguity persisted after France established a colony within Algeria and a protectorate over Morocco. French administrative review of the Algerian-Moroccan border in 1952 assigned a mineral–rich zone including Bechar and Tindouf to Algeria. Morocco gained independence in 1956 in the midst of Algeria's war for independence (11.8) and sought to reclaim the territory. In July 1961 the exiled Provisional Government of the Algerian Republic (GPRA) recognized by Morocco and other Arab states agreed to cede the disputed area to Morocco. This agreement became moot when the GPRA collapsed in early 1962 and France passed authority to a government formed by Ahmed Ben Bella. France formally recognized Algerian independence on July 3, 1962. Moroccan auxiliaries established police posts within the Tindouf area during the last weeks of June. Morocco's association with dissident elements of the National Liberation Front forcibly resisted Ben Bella's regime prior to and immediately after Algerian independence exacerbated tensions. In mid–July Algerian government military forces reclaimed Tindouf and also engaged in small attacks upon other Moroccan border posts. Small Moroccan army units attempted unsuccessfully to recapture the disputed area during mid-October 1962. No regular military fatalities are reported.

Brownlie, I. 1979. *African Boundaries*, 55–83.
Butterworth, R. 1976. *Managing Interstate Conflict*, 337–339.
Cohen, M., and L. Hahn. 1966. *Morocco: Old Land, New Nation*, 231.
Farsoun, K., and J. Paul. 1976. "War in the Sahara." In *The Struggle for Sahara*, 13–16.
Hodges, T. 1983. *Western Sahara: Roots of a Desert War*, 92.
Humbaraci, A. 1966. *Algeria; A Revolution That Failed*, 141–147.
Keegan, J., ed. 1983. *World Armies*, 399–406.
Thompson, V., and R. Adloff. 1980. *The Western Saharans*, 230.

11.10 Moroccan-Algerian War, 1963

Border dispute between Morocco and Algeria provoked low-intensity armed conflict in 1962 which resulted in Algerian control of a disputed area in the Sahara including Hassi-Beida and Tindouf (11.9). Moroccan auxiliary paramilitary units again occupied Hassi-Beida and Tindouf in September 1963. Algerian army units forcibly expelled Moroccan presence October 8. Regular Moroccan troops replaced auxiliaries at the frontier on October 14 and recaptured the towns. Fighting spread elsewhere along the border. On October 27, 1963, Cuban tanks and soldiers arrived in Algeria under prior arrangement and were immediately dispatched to the front, arriving in time to participate in a few final battles before cease-fire was achieved on November 4 through Ethiopian mediation. Approximately 100 Moroccan soldiers and 100 Algerian soldiers died during the course of fighting. No fatalities are reported among Cuban troops.

Brecher, M., J. Wilkenfeld, and S. Moser. 1988. *Crises in the Twentieth Century*, 1: 263.
Brownlie, I. 1979. *African Boundaries*, 55–83.
Butterworth, R. 1976. *Managing Interstate Conflict*, 337–339.

Cohen, M., and L. Hahn. 1966. *Morocco: Old Land, New Nation*, 232–233.
Dominguez, J. 1989. *To Make a World Safe for Revolution*, 175.
Erisman, H. 1985. *Cuba's International Relations*, 31–32.
Farsoun, K., and J. Paul. 1976. "War in the Sahara." In *The Struggle for Sahara*, 13–16.
Hassouna, H. 1975. *The League of Arab States and Regional Disputes*, 211–240.
Hodges, T. 1983. *Western Sahara: Roots of a Desert War*, 92–96.
Humbaraci, A. 1966. *Algeria; A Revolution That Failed*, 141–147.
Keegan, J., ed. 1983. *World Armies*, 399–406.
Maghreb Labor Digest. 1963. "Algerian-Moroccan Border Conflict Flares into Open Conflict." 1 (December): 3–9.
Thompson, V., and R. Adloff. 1980. *The Western Saharans*, 230–232.
Trout, F. 1969. *Morocco's Saharan Frontiers*, 426–427.
Wild, P. 1966. "The Organization of African Unity and the Algerian-Moroccan Border Conflict." *International Organization* 20 (Winter): 18–36.
Zartman, I. 1966. *International Relations in the New Africa*, 88–89.

11.11 Western Saharan War, 1974–continuing

Spain established imperial holdings within the Sahara at the end of the nineteenth century, including Ifni and also districts of Rio de Oro and Sekia el Hamra constituting Spanish Sahara (Western Sahara. Spain abandoned most territories within neighboring Morocco in 1956 but resisted encroachment by the Moroccan Liberation Army within Ifni and Spanish Sahara during 1956–1958 (11.8).

Morocco publicly claimed Spanish North African territories in 1963. Mauritania, which became independent of France in 1960, claimed Rio de Oro in 1965. Spain abandoned Ifni to Morocco in 1969. Meanwhile, indigenous Saharan nationalists formed resistance organizations, including the Polisario Front. Spanish police killed numerous Sahrawi during nationalist-inspired riots within El Aaiun in 1970. Polisario waged sustained guerrilla war against Spanish authority from 1973 and enjoyed Algerian support from 1974. Spanish police contained initial disturbances; regular Spanish troops deployed in January 1974. Later that year, Spain announced plans to grant independence.

Morocco and Mauritania appealed to the International Court of Justice in 1975. The two states also agreed secretly to partition Spanish Sahara. On October 16, 1975, the Court ruled that neither Morocco nor Mauritania possessed an enforceable claim to the territory. Despite this decision, Moroccan Army units entered Spanish Sahara and attempted to occupy the border town of Farsia on October 31, 1975. On November 6–9 Morocco directed a "Green March" involving as many as several hundred thousand civilians within the Spanish Sahara area. Spain conceded to partition on November 14. Moroccan military forces promptly occupied most northern urban centers. Mauritanian military units, assisted by Morocco, entered Rio de Oro on December 10. Spanish military forces stood down on January 8, 1976, and withdrew a few days later. Spain formally abandoned control on February 26, 1976.

Polisario resistance continued, now directed primarily against Morocco and Mauritania. Algerian army units intervened briefly in January 1976 to help evacuate Polisario supporters and clashed with Moroccan troops. Polisario began attacks within Mauritania in June 1976. Morocco deployed several thousand troops to Mauritania in July 1977 in order to assist defense. France increased military aid. Her air forces attacked Polisario concentrations within Mauritania in December 1977 and May 1978. Polisario declared a cease-fire within Mauritania in July 1978. In August 1979 Mauritania withdrew from Rio de Oro. Morocco then attempted to secure control of all Western Sahara.

Serious fighting continued within Western Sahara throughout the following decade. Morocco constructed physical barriers in attempt to prevent infiltration across the Algerian frontier. Conflict occasionally spilled into neighboring states. In 1980 and again in 1981 the Moroccan air force attacked Polisario concentrations within Mauritania. In 1981 and 1984 Moroccan patrols pursued Polisario guerrillas into Algeria.

The death toll of the Western Saharan War presumably numbers in the tens of thousands. Morocco apparently sustained between 5,000 and 10,000 military fatalities by 1989. Mauritania lost as many as 1,000 soldiers killed within the Western Sahara. A score of Spanish troops died prior to 1976. Algeria's 1976 incursion is believed to have cost her thirty soldiers. No French fatalities are reported.

Brecher, M., J. Wilkenfeld, and S. Moser. 1988. *Crises in the Twentieth Century,* 1: 309–311, 315–316, 32, 325–326, 337–338, 341–342.
Brownlie, I. 1979. *African Boundaries,* 149–158, 437–444.
Butterworth, R. 1976. *Managing Interstate Conflict,* 388–390.
Coker, C. 1985. *NATO, the Warsaw Pact and Africa,* 115–116.
Damis, J. 1983. *Conflict in Northwest Africa.*
Day, A., ed. 1987. *Border and Territorial Disputes,* 172–183.
Franck, T. 1976. "The Stealing of the Sahara." *American Journal of International Law* 70 (October): 694–721.
Hodges, T. 1982. *Historical Dictionary of Western Sahara.*
Hodges, T. 1983. *Western Sahara: Roots of a Desert War.*
Keegan, J., ed. 1983. *World Armies,* 389–392, 399–406.
Laffin, J. 1986. *War Annual 1,* 164–167.
Laffin, J. 1987. *War Annual 2,* 145–149.
Laffin, J. 1989. *The World in Conflict 1989: War Annual 3,* 162–166.
Lellouche, P., and D. Moisi. 1979. "French Policy in Africa." *International Security* 3 (4): 108–133.

Mercer, J. 1976. *Spanish Sahara*, 225–247.

Mercer, J. 1988. "The Cycle of Invasion and Unification in the Western Sahara." *African Affairs* 75 (October): 598–510.

Moose, G. 1985. "French Military Policy in Africa." In *Arms and the African*, ed. W. Foltz and H. Bienen, 59–97.

Seddon, D. 1987. "Morocco at War." In *War and Refugees*, ed. R. Lawless and L. Monahan, 98–136.

Small, M., and J. Singer. 1982. *Resort to Arms*, 99.

Thompson, V., and R. Adloff. 1980. *The Western Saharans*.

Zartman, I. 1989. *Ripe for Resolution*, 19–81.

11.12 Egyptian-Libyan Clash, 1977

Egyptian-Libyan relations became troubled during the 1970s. Muammar Qaddafi's regime within Libya pursued an avowedly revolutionary course, including aid to dissent against Egyptian-supported governments within Sudan and Chad. Egypt's government of Anwar Sadat drifted toward accommodation with Israel despite vehement Libyan objection. Libya allegedly supported plots against Sadat, including rioting within Cairo in January 1977. Egypt allegedly aided Libyans opposed to Qaddafi. In addition, an undemarcated border, although not actively disputed prior to 1977, encouraged troublesome incidents.

On April 10, 1977, Libyan and Egyptian demonstrators attacked one another state's missions within Alexandria and Benghazi. Egypt intercepted Libyan saboteurs attempting to poison an Egyptian water source during the second week of July. An exchange of fire involving Libyan border police followed. On July 16, 1977, regular Libyan soldiers began commando and artillery attacks upon Egyptian border positions. Egypt responded in kind the same day. On July 21 Egypt launched an armored assault across Libya's border. Her aircraft also attacked interior Libyan villages and air bases. Egypt's main offensive halted July 24 but small-unit operations continued on both sides of the border the next day until a cease-fire encouraged by Yassir Arafat, chairman of the Palestine Liberation Organization, took effect. Minor incidents persisted throughout August. Egypt and Libya disengaged troops from the border on September 10, 1977. Combined losses numbered one to a few hundred killed, including at least 30 Libyan military fatalities upon Egyptian soil and at least fifty Egyptian dead within Libya.

Africa Research Bulletin. Political, Social and Cultural Series 14 (1977): 4493–4494.

Brecher, M., J. Wilkenfeld, and S. Moser. 1988. *Crises in the Twentieth Century*, 1: 322.

Cooley, J. 1982. *Libyan Sandstorm*, 118–124.
Foltz, W. 1988. "Libya's Military Power." In *The Green and the Black*, ed. R. Lemarchand, 52–69.
Keegan, J., ed. 1983. *World Armies*, 162–173, 366–375.
Wright, J. 1982. *Libya: A Modern History*, 201.
Times (London) 7/22/77, 1a; 7/23/77, 1e; 7/24/77, 1d.

11.13 Libyan-Tunisian Strife, 1984

Muammar Qaddafi seized power within Libya in 1969. His ruling Revolutionary Committee pursued confrontational policies toward most neighboring states during the 1970s and 1980s. Among other incidents, Libya helped to arm and train Tunisian émigrés who attacked Gafsa, Tunisia, in January 1980 in unsuccessful effort to stimulate an uprising against President Habib Bourgiba. Qaddafi's government suffered sporadic violent opposition from several quarters, including among Libyan exiles residing within Tunisia. On May 8, 1984, opposition militants attacked military barracks within Tripoli, including one that served as headquarters of the Revolutionary Committee. Attacks were beaten off within a few hours, after as many as eighty Libyan soldiers had been killed. Qaddafi condemned the Bourgiba government for allowing use of Tunisian territory to organize the raids. In apparent retaliation, a small unit of Libyan troops entered Tunisia and kidnapped three Tunisian border guards the evening of May 8. Additional Libyan border forays took place during the following week. No fatalities are reported during border incidents.

Africa Research Bulletin. Political, Social and Cultural Series 21 (1984): 7248.
Keesing's Contemporary Archives 30 (1984): 33249.
Tessler, M. 1988. "Libya in the Maghreb." In *The Green and the Black*, ed. R. Lemarchand, 73–105.

11.14 Bori Cedria Raid, 1985

The Palestine Liberation Organization (PLO) gained recognition from the Arab League and the United Nations as the international representative of the Palestinian peoples in the 1970s. It also developed a substantial military presence within Lebanon. Palestinian terrorist groups associated directly or indirectly with the PLO repeatedly attacked Israeli citizens at home and abroad. Israel compelled most PLO leaders and armed forces to withdraw from Lebanon after invading that country in 1982. Yassir Arafat, chairman of the PLO, moved headquarters to Tunisia. On September 25, 1985, Palestinian terrorists killed several Israeli tourists on Cyprus. On

October 1 Israeli aircraft bombed PLO headquarters within Bori Cedria on the outskirts of Tunis in retaliation. The raid killed more than fifty people but no Israeli losses are reported.

Hart, A. 1989. *Arafat, a Political Biography*, 484–515.
Keesing's Contemporary Archives 31 (1985): 34077.
New York Times 10/2/85, 1:6.

11.15 Libya Raids, 1986

The United States and Libya engaged in sustained diplomatic confrontation after Muammar Qaddafi seized power within Tripoli in 1969. Qaddafi's regime publicly opposed American and other Western imperialism and patronized diverse revolutionary groups, including radical Palestinian factions. Libya also claimed all of the Gulf of Sidra as territorial waters, contrary to international convention. American officials publicly vilified the Libyan government, especially during the early and mid-1980s. The United States conducted naval and air exercises within the Mediterranean off Libya during January–March 1986, including movements within the Gulf of Sidra. Libya fired missiles upon U.S. warplanes in the area March 24. U.S. aircraft counterattacked a Libyan missile site on shore and two Libyan patrol boats the same day. On April 5 terrorists bombed a West German nightclub, injuring numerous American military personnel. The United States blamed Libya for encouraging the assault. On April 15 U.S. aircraft attacked targets within Tripoli and Bengazi, Libya, including one of Qaddafi's personal residences. Two American airmen were killed during the April 15 raids.

Africa Research Bulletin. Political Series 23 (1986): 8023–8028, 8059–8068.
Foltz, W. 1988. "Libya's Military Power." In *The Green and the Black*, ed. R. Lemarchand, 52–69.
Laffin, J. 1987. *War Annual 2*, 221–227.

PART FOUR

Middle East

12

Persian Gulf

International strife within the Persian Gulf region represents a congeries of conflicts. In 1945–1946 the Soviet Union encouraged secession of Azerbaijan from Iran (12.1). Iraq's Mosul Rebellion of 1959 carried over into Syria (12.2). Kurdish separatism within Iraq during the 1960s affected neighboring territories (12.3, 12.4, 12.5). Iran's Gulf aspirations led it to seize Tunbs and other islands in 1971 (12.6). Iraq attacked Kuwait in 1973 (19.8). Border conflict between Iran and Iraq brought them to blows in 1972–1975 (12.7) and to major war during the 1980s (12.9). Resurgence of Kurdish separatism encouraged Turkish intervention within Iraq during the 1980s (12.12, 12.13). Other incidents included an abortive U.S. raid upon Iran in 1980 (12.10), Israel's attack upon Iraq's nuclear reactor in 1982 (12.11) and border conflict between Qatar and Bahrain in 1986 (12.14).

12.1 Azerbaijani Secession, 1945–1946

The United Kingdom and the Soviet Union stationed soldiers within Iran (Persia) during World War II, later joined by the United States, after forcing Reza Shah to abdicate in favor of his son in 1941. The United States withdrew military forces by the end of 1945 as did the United Kingdom by February 1946. Soviet troops remained and encouraged separatist and communist movements within Iranian Kurdistan and Azerbaijan. Under watch of Russian soldiers, radical Tudeh party elements seized public buildings within Azerbaijan in August 1945. The Soviet Union committed more troops in November 1945 and deployed some of them to impede Iranian military intercession within Azerbaijan. The Democratic party of Azerbaijan declared independence in December 1945. The Democratic party of Kurdistan, led by Mullah Mustafa Barzani and followers expelled from Iraq in 1943, proclaimed the Republic of Mahabad with aid of Soviet-supplied arms in January 1946. The United States protested to Moscow against continued Soviet military presence and assisting Iran to place the issue on the U.N. Security Council agenda. In early April the Soviet Union agreed to leave in return for Iranian oil concessions. Soviet troops withdrew May 9, 1946, without fatality. Iran then quickly suppressed both rebellions.

Arfa, H. 1966. *The Kurds*, 81–95.
Brecher, M., J. Wilkenfeld, and S. Moser. 1988. *Crises in the Twentieth Century*, 1: 202–203.
Butterworth, R. 1976. *Managing Interstate Conflict*, 59–65.
Eagleton, W. 1963. *The Kurdish Republic of 1946*.
Kirk, G. 1954. *The Middle East 1945–1950*, 56–90.
Kuniholm, B. 1980. *The Origins of the Cold War in the Near East*.
Lenczowski, G. 1968. *Russia and the West in Iran*, 284–300.
Lenczowski, G. 1980. *The Middle East in World Affairs*, 182–184.
Ramazani, R. 1975. *Iran's Foreign Policy, 1941–1973*, 107–153.
Roosevelt, A. 1947. "The Kurdish Republic of Mahabad." *Middle East Journal* 1 (July): 247–269.
Rossow, R. 1956. "The Battle of Azerbaijan, 1946." *Middle East Journal* 10 (Winter): 17–32.
Schmid, A., and E. Berends. 1985. *Soviet Military Interventions Since 1945*, 54–58.
Zabih, S. 1966. *The Communist Movement in Iran*, 95–100.

12.2 Mosul Rebellion, 1959

A coup d'etat led by Abdul Karim Kassem overthrew King Faisal II and Prime Minister Nuri es-Said of Iraq on July 14, 1958, and proclaimed a republic. The unexpected event helped to precipitate U.S. intervention within Lebanon's ongoing civil war (13.14). Kassem's regime subsequently attracted support among radical Iraqi factions. Egypt's President Gamel Abdel Nasser had previously induced Iraq's neighbor Syria to accede to the United Arab Republic, partly in order to constrain growing influence of radical socialists within Syria. The United Arab Republic encouraged opposition to Kassem among Iraqi military officers. Rebellious army units combined with Shammar tribesmen seized the Iraqi town of Mosul near the Syrian border during the first week of March 1959. Loyal air and army units attacked rebels mercilessly with help of some Iraqi Kurds and Iraqi Communist party irregulars. Iraqi air forces also bombed and strafed rebel sanctuaries within Syria March 10–14. As many as 2,000 persons died by end of rebellion in mid-March. Iraqi government forces reportedly suffered no fatalities within Syria.

Arfa, H. 1966. *The Kurds*, 129–134.
Butterworth, R. 1976. *Managing Interstate Conflict*, 253–254.
Dann, U. 1969. *Iraq Under Qassem*, 156–177.
Ghareeb, E. 1981. *The Kurdish Question in Iraq*, 37–39.
Harris, G. 1977. "The Kurdish Conflict in Iraq" In *Ethnic Conflict in International Relations*, ed. A. Suhrke and L. Nobel, 68–92.
Hofstadter, D. 1973. *Egypt and Nasser*, 2: 54–55.
Jawad, S. 1981. *Iraq and the Kurdish Question*, 42–43.
O'Ballance, E. 1973. *The Kurdish Revolt: 1961–1970*, 66–68.
Pellitiere, S. 1984. *The Kurds: An Unstable Element in the Gulf*, 115–126.
Petran, T. 1972. *Syria*, 132–133.
Shwardran, B. 1960. *The Power Struggle in Iraq*, 41–51.
Small, M., and J. Singer. 1982. *Resort to Arms*, 230.

12.3 Iraqi-Kurd War I, 1962

Kurdish separatism provoked repeated strife since collapse of the Ottoman Empire. Post-World War I arrangements denied Kurdish peoples a separate homeland within mountainous domains extending from Iran through Iraq and Turkey and into the Soviet Union. Kurdish tribes of northern Iraq, especially the Barzani, resisted British efforts to pacify them under League of Nations mandate. The Royal Air Force repeatedly attacked them even after Iraq became independent in 1932. Mullah Mustafa Barzani and followers fled to Iran in 1943 where they helped to proclaim the abortive Mahabad Kurdish Republic during the Azerbaijani crisis of 1945–1946 (12.1). Mullah Barzani then took refuge within the Soviet Union. He returned to Iraq in 1958 after pardon by the new government of Abdul Karim Kassem.

Barzani helped to found the Democratic party of Kurdistan which claimed to represent the Kurdish nation. Barzani forces attacked other Kurdish tribes and took control of substantial territory within northern Iraq, including near Turkey's border, beginning in 1961. The Iraqi government counterattacked Barzani positions late that year and continued to do so until 1970. Iraqi air forces also raided Kurdish villages and border posts within Turkey in July–August 1962. The Iraqi-Kurd war killed tens of thousands, primarily civilians, by 1970. No Iraqi fatalities are reported during 1962 raids upon Turkey.

Butterworth, R. 1976. *Managing Interstate Conflict*, 310–312.
Chubin, S., and S. Zabih. 1974. *The Foreign Relations of Iran*, 179.
Ghareeb, E. 1981. *The Kurdish Question in Iraq*, 42–43.
Harris, G. 1977. "The Kurdish Conflict in Iraq." In *Ethnic Conflict in International Relations*, ed. A. Suhrke and L. Nobel, 68–92.
Jawad, S. 1981. *Iraq and the Kurdish Question*, 288–300.
Khadduri, M. 1969. *Republican Iraq*, 173–181.

O'Ballance, E. 1973. *The Kurdish Revolt: 1961–1970*, 93.
Pellitiere, S. 1984. *The Kurds: An Unstable Element in the Gulf*, 126–178.
Schmidt, D. 1964. *Journey Among Brave Men.*

12.4 Iraqi-Kurd War II, 1963

The Iraqi-Kurd War, begun in 1961 and continuing to 1970, involved Iraqi air attacks upon Turkey in 1962 (12.3). Iraq's revolutionary regime of Karim Kassem was overthrown in February 1963 and replaced by a military government under Abdul Salam Aref. Syrian ground and air forces intervened against Kurdish separatists within Iraq at behest of the new government beginning the end of June 1963. Syrian aircraft attacked Kurdish positions from bases within Syria and Syrian Army units established a presence within secured areas in order to free Iraqi troops to conduct offensive operations. Syrian intervention, officially denied but generally aknowledged, continued until the end of November 1963 . Tens of thousands of soldiers and civilians died during the Iraqi-Kurd war between 1961 and 1970. No Syrian military fatalities are reported.

Arfa, H. 1966. *The Kurds*, 147–148.
Butterworth, R. 1976. *Managing Interstate Conflict*, 310–312.
Cheriff Vanly, I. 1965. *The Revolution of Iraki Kurdistan*, 44–47.
Ghareeb, E. 1981. *The Kurdish Question in Iraq*, 66–67.
Harris, G. 1977. "The Kurdish Conflict in Iraq" In *Ethnic Conflict in International Relations*, ed. A. Suhrke and L. Nobel, 68–92.
Jawad, S. 1981. *Iraq and the Kurdish Question*, 284.
Khadduri, M. 1969. *Republican Iraq*, 173–181, 207.
O'Ballance, E. 1973. *The Kurdish Revolt: 1961–1970*, 99–115.
Pellitiere, S. 1984. *The Kurds: An Unstable Element in the Gulf*, 126–178.
Petran, T. 1972. *Syria*, 236.
Vernier, B. 1965. "La Question Kurde." *Revue de Defense Nationale* 20 (January): 102–122.

12.5 Iraqi-Kurd War III, 1965–1966

Attempt by Kurdish peoples, led primarily by Mullah Mustafa Barzani, to establish a separate state within northern Iraq contributed to bloody warfare between 1961 and 1970. Iraqi military operations carried into Turkey in 1962 (12.3) and attracted Syrian intervention in 1963 (12.4). Iraq's anti-Kurdish offensives also spilled over her borders in 1965–1966. Iraqi aircraft attacked a Turkish border village at the end of June 1965, allegedly by mistake. Iraqi aircraft also bombed and strafed Iranian border villages between December 1965 and May 1966.

The Iraqi-Kurd war killed thousands by 1970. No Iraqi military fatalities are reported during 1965–1966 cross-border operations.

Butterworth, R. 1976. *Managing Interstate Conflict*, 310–312.
Jawad, S. 1981. *Iraq and the Kurdish Question*, 288–300.
Khadduri, M. 1969. *Republican Iraq*, 268–278.
O'Ballance, E. 1973. *The Kurdish Revolt: 1961–1970*, 138.
Pellitiere, S. 1984. *The Kurds: An Unstable Element in the Gulf*, 126–178.

12.6 Tunbs Island Seizure, 1971

The United Kingdom established protectorates within Bahrain and Trucial Oman (United Arab Emirates) in the nineteenth century. British colonial control continued until 1971. Both Iraq and Iran claimed Bahrain and Persian Gulf islands associated with the Trucial states as independence neared. Bahrain became independent without incident in August 1971. On November 30, 1971, the day before the Trucial states were scheduled to become the independent United Arab Emirates, Iran forcibly seized disputed islands of Abu Musa and Greater and Lesser Tunbs. Britain refrained from direct counteraction. Three Iranian soldiers died as did four policeman of the Trucial sheikdom of Ras Al Khaimah upon Greater Tunbs.

Abdullah, M. 1978. *The United Arab Emirates*, 273–284.
Butterworth, R. 1976. *Managing Interstate Conflict*, 436–438.
Chubin, S., and S. Zabih. 1974. *The Foreign Relations of Iran*, 214–234.
Cordesman, A. 1984. *The Gulf and the Search for Strategic Stability*, 416–417.
Day, A., ed. 1987. *Border and Territorial Disputes*, 242–244.
El-Hakim, A. 1979. *The Middle Eastern States and the Law of the Sea*, 122–130.
Halliday, F. 1979. *Iran: Dictatorship and Development*, 270–271.
Kelly, J. 1980. *Arabia, the Gulf and the West*, 87–97.
Litwak, R. 1981. *Sources of Inter-State Conflict*, 56–59.
Martin, L. 1984. *The Unstable Gulf*, 48–50.
Ramazani, R. 1972 *The Persian Gulf: Iran's Role*, 56–68.
Ramazani, R. 1975. *Iran's Foreign Policy, 1941–1973*, 408–427.
Taryam, A. 1987. *The Establishment of the United Arab Emirates*, 177–189.

12.7 Shatt-al-Arab Conflict, 1972–1975

Iran's (Persia's) boundary with Iraq(Mesopotamia) has been disputed for millennia, including after the Ottoman Empire assumed control of Mesopotamia in the sixteenth century. The southern border, including the Shatt-al-Arab estuary leading to the Persian Gulf, became more important after nearby oil discoveries in 1908. A 1913 agreement signed by Persia and the Ottoman Empire reaffirmed Ottoman sovereignty within the Shatt-al-Arab waterway. The United Kingdom ruled Mesopotamia after World War I under League of Nations mandate, including the Shatt-al-Arab. Iraq claimed Ottoman rights upon attaining independence in 1932. Persian protests led to compromise with Iraq in 1937 which accorded each state partial control within the waterway.

Iran abrogated 1937 treaties with Iraq in 1969. She seized Tunbs and other islands from the United Arab Emirates at the end of November 1971 (12.6). Iranian artillery and raiding parties attacked Iraqi positions near the Shatt-al-Arab beginning in mid-January 1972 following numerous minor border incidents. Iraq responded in kind starting in June 1972. Low-intensity border conflict continued for several years. Iraq launched a ground offensive in February 1974 that attempted to seize full control of disputed areas. An Iranian counteroffensive commenced March 4, 1974. Serious battles ended March 7 under a United Nations special arranged cease-fire but sporadic artillery exchanges and small-unit raids persisted to 1975

Renewed Kurdish resistance within Iraq compounded border conflict in 1974. Mullah Mustafa Barzani led rebellion among tribal Kurds against the Iraqi government during the 1960s (12.3, 12.4, 12.5). The Iraqi-Kurd War ended by cease-fire in March 1970. Baghdad recognized Kurdish autonomy in principle at that time but subsequent negotiations failed to reach a formal settlement due in part to dispute about allocation of oil revenues. Mullah Barzani rejected a March 11, 1974, ultimatum which offered limited self-rule. Kurdish forces resumed attacks upon government positions with aid of arms from Iran and allegedly also the United States. Government counteroffensives included artillery and commando assaults upon Kurdish sanctuaries within Iran during the next year and also artillery attacks upon Kurdish settlements within Turkey in late April and early May 1974.

Fighting ceased on the Iran-Iraq border in February 1975. Iraq formally acceded to most Iranian border demands on March 6, 1975. In return, Iran halted support of Kurdish rebels within Iraq. Mullah Barzani and some of his followers fled to exile within Iran. 1972-1975 border strife resulted in as many as 50–100 Iraqi and Iranian military fatalities. Many additional soldiers and civilians died during exchanges involving Kurds elsewhere within Iraq.

Abdulghani, J. 1984. *Iraq and Iran: The Years of Crisis*, 106–151.
Butterworth, R. 1976. *Managing Interstate Conflict*, 436–438, 472–474.
Cheriff Vanly, I. 1980. "Kurdistan in Iraq." In *People Without a Country*, ed. G. Chaliand, 153–210.

Cotrell, A. 1978. "Iran's Armed Forces Under the Pahlavi Dynasty." In *Iran under the Pahlavis*, ed. G. Lenczowski, 389–431.

Day, A., ed. 1987. *Border and Territorial Disputes*, 234–241.

Ghareeb, E. 1981. *The Kurdish Question in Iraq*, 160–174.

Halliday, F. 1979. *Iran: Dictatorship and Development*, 272.

Harris, G. 1977. "The Kurdish Conflict in Iraq" In *Ethnic Conflict in International Relations*, ed. A. Suhrke and L. Nobel, 68–92.

Helms, C. 1984. *Iraq: Eastern Flank of the Arab World*, 144–151.

Ismael, T. 1982. *Iraq and Iran: Roots of Conflict*, 19–22.

Jawad, S. 1981. *Iraq and the Kurdish Question*, 288–300.

Jawad, S. 1984. "Recent Developments in the Kurdish Issue." In *Iraq, the Contemporary State*, ed. T. Niblock, 47–61.

Khadduri, M. 1978. *Socialist Iraq*, 148–153.

Litwak, R. 1981. *Sources of Inter-State Conflict*, 5–6.

Martin, L. 1984. *The Unstable Gulf*, 38–40.

Pellitiere, S. 1984. *The Kurds: An Unstable Element in the Gulf*, 178–187.

Ramazani, R. 1979. *The Persian Gulf and the Straits of Hormuz*, 104–107.

Viotti, P. 1980. "Iraq: The Kurdish Rebellion." In *Insurgency in the Modern World*, ed. B. O'Neill, W. Heaton, and D. Alberts, 190–210.

12.8 Sametah Seizure, 1973

Kuwait represented part of the Ottoman Empire until 1914 when the United Kingdom recognized her independence and extended a treaty of protection. The United Kingdom administered other Mesopotamian territories of the former Ottoman Empire under League of Nations mandate following World War I until granting independence to Iraq in 1932. The British protectorate of Kuwait terminated in June 1961 and Iraq immediately claimed the territory as her own. United Kingdom and Saudi Arabian troops deployed to Kuwait in order to deter Iraqi military action. An Arab League force replaced them in September 1961. Iraq refrained from attack and formally recognized Kuwaiti independence in 1963. Sporadic minor incidents occurred along their unmarked border in following years, most notably in 1967. On March 20, 1973, Iraqi troops seized Kuwaiti border posts at Sametah near disputed islands in the Persian Gulf. Saudi Arabia again deployed troops to Kuwait but refrained from direct counteraction. Kuwait and Iraq accepted mediation by Yassir Arafat of the Palestine Liberation Organization in early April and Iraqi troops withdrew. Two Iraqi soldiers reportedly died at Sametah.

Abdulghani, J. 1984. *Iraq and Iran: The Years of Crisis*, 96–98.

Assiri, A 1990. *Kuwait's Foreign Policy: City-State in World Politics.*, 54–55.

Brecher, M., J. Wilkenfeld, and S. Moser. 1988. *Crises in the Twentieth Century*, 1: 301.

Butterworth, R. 1976. *Managing Interstate Conflict*, 466–468.
Day, A., ed. 1987. *Border and Territorial Disputes*, 244–247.
Kelly, J. 1980. *Arabia, the Gulf and the West*, 282–284.
Khadduri, M. 1978. *Socialist Iraq*, 153–159.
Litwak, R. 1981. *Sources of Inter-State Conflict*, 29–30.
Martin, L. 1984. *The Unstable Gulf*, 46–47.

12.9 Persian Gulf War, 1979–1988

Iran and Iraq waged a minor war involving the disputed Shatt-al-Arab waterway leading to the Persian Gulf and also involving Kurdish separatist resistance within Iraq during 1972-1975 (12.7). Iraq's government of Ahmad Hasan al-Bakr accepted most of the border claims pressed by Iran's Muhammad Reza Shah Pahlavi in March 1975 at the end of fighting. Kurdish leader Mullah Mustafa Barzani fled to Iran.

Domestic revolt drove the Shah out of Iran by December 6, 1978. Ayatollah Ruhollah Khomeini, who orchestrated revolution from abroad, dominated the succeeding government. An Islamic Republic was proclaimed following a March 28–April 1, 1979, referendum.

Kurdish separatist ambitions rekindled during 1978–1979. Kurds demonstrated against the Shah in 1978. They fomented serious uprising within the Sanandaj area against the Khomeini regime during spring 1979. Similar Kurdish restiveness within Iraq provoked Iraqi retaliation at home and air and artillery attacks upon Kurdish villages within Iran beginning in June 1979. Iraq apologized and offered compensation following the first cross-border assault; but attacks increased after Saddam Huseyn succeeded al-Bakr as head of the Baath Socialist party and the Revolutionary Command Council. Iraqi artillery bombarded Iran as far south as the Shatt-al-Arab by December 1979.

Iraq began commando raids upon Iranian territory in March 1980. Saddam Hussein repudiated the 1975 border agreement on September 17, 1980, and invaded the Shatt-al-Arab region in force within the week. Iran retaliated by deep air strikes, including upon airfields near Baghdad, beginning September 23. Iranian aircraft also attacked Kuwaiti customs posts and other sites near the battle zone several times between November 1980 and October 1981. Iranian counteroffensives penetrated Iraqi territory at a few points by the end of March 1981. Iran's Operation Ramadan launched in July 1982 captured additional Iraqi territory but failed to drive Iraq entirely from Iranian soil.

A lengthy war of attrition followed. Iran employed lightly trained Revolutionary Guards as well as regular soldiers. Iraq allegedly used poison gas to blunt some Iranian attacks. Fighting spread to Gulf waters by 1984. Iraq repeatedly attacked Iranian oil facilities at Kharg Island and tankers servicing Iranian ports. Iran threatened to close the Straits of Hormuz and also attacked Gulf shipping. The United States deployed a naval task force within the Gulf but refrained from military action ashore despite repeated air and naval incidents. Between September 1987 and April 1988 Iran also occasionally attacked Kuwaiti territory, primarily by Silkworm missiles. U.N. representatives helped to bring about a cease-fire August 20, 1988, and a UN observation group helped to monitor troop withdrawals. Nearly a half million soldiers died during the Gulf War, including 300,000 or more Iranians and 100,000 to 150,000 Iraqis.

Abdulghani, J. 1984. *Iraq and Iran: The Years of Crisis*, 178–228.
Cordesman, A. 1984. *The Gulf and the Search for Strategic Stability*, 642–724.
Cordesman, A. 1987. *The Iran-Iraq War and Western Security*.
Cordesman, A. 1988. *The Gulf and the West*, 309–455.
Cotrell, A. 1978. "Iran's Armed Forces Under the Pahlavi Dynasty." In *Iran under the Pahlavis*, ed. G. Lenczowski, 389–431.
Day, A., ed. 1987. *Border and Territorial Disputes*, 234–241.
Dupuy, R., and T. Dupuy. 1986. *The Encyclopedia of Military History*, 1368–1369.
Helms, C. 1984. *Iraq: Eastern Flank of the Arab World*, 153–154.
Khadduri, M. 1988. *The Gulf War*.
Laffin, J. 1986. *War Annual 1*, 72–87.
Laffin, J. 1987. *War Annual 2*, 105–118.
Laffin, J. 1989. *The World in Conflict 1989: War Annual 3*, 102–115.
Marr, P. 1985. *The Modern History of Iraq*, 234–236, 292.
Martin, L. 1984. *The Unstable Gulf*, 26–27, 40–42.
Mylroie, L. 1989. "After the Guns Fell Silent." *Middle East Journal* 43 (Winter): 51–67.
O'Ballance, E. 1988. *The Gulf War*.
Pellitiere, S. 1984. *The Kurds: An Unstable Element in the Gulf*, 178–187.
Ramazani, R. 1986. *Revolutionary Iran*, 57–113.
Small, M., and J. Singer. 1982. *Resort to Arms*, 95.
Staudenmaier, W. 1983. "A Strategic Analysis." In *The Iran-Iraq War*, ed. S. Tahir-Kheli and S. Ayubi, 27–50.
Zabih, S. 1988. *The Iranian Military in Revolution and War*.

12.10 Tehran Hostage Crisis, 1980

The United States cooperated closely with Mohammad Reza Shah Pahlavi of Iran after covertly assisting him to seize full power in 1953. Domestic rebellion overthrew the Shah's repressive regime and forced him to flee the country in December 1978. Iran's new government, dominated by the Ayatollah Ruhollah Khomeini, pursued social revolution at home and anti-American policies abroad, including expulsion of most American personnel. The Shah entered the United States for medical treatment on October 22, 1979. On November 4, persons identifying themselves as students seized the U.S. embassy compound in Tehran, took dozens of Americans hostage and demanded that the Shah return to Iran for trial. The United States protested and froze Iranian assets within the United States. A December 15 International Court of Justice ruling called upon Iran to restore the embassy to U.S. control. The Shah departed the United States for Panama in December. U.N. Secretary General Kurt Waldheim attempted to mediate the continuing dispute without success. On April 24, 1980, a U.S. commando strike force landed within Iran as the first stage of a raid planned to free the hostages. The mission aborted the next day, short of battle and before reaching Tehran, due in part to accidents that killed eight American soldiers.

Beckwith, C., and D. Knox. 1983. *Delta Force.*
Brecher, M., J. Wilkenfeld, and S. Moser. 1988. *Crises in the Twentieth Century,*
    1: 345–346.

12.11 Osirak Reactor Raid, 1981

Iraq participated in the Palestine War against Israel's newly proclaimed government in 1948–1949 (13.1). She openly supported Palestinian causes in following years, especially after a republican regime replaced the Iraqi monarchy in 1958. Israel attacked Iraqi airfields during the Six Day War in 1967 (13.18). Iraqi forces fought Israeli forces again during the Yom Kippur War in 1973 (13.27). On June 7, 1981, at a time of increasing Israeli-Palestinian conflict within southern Lebanon, Israeli aircraft bombed and severely damaged Iraq's Osirak nuclear reactor outside Baghdad. Israel alleged that the reactor and associated laboratories contributed to Iraqi efforts to develop nuclear weapons. No Israeli fatalities are reported.

Dupuy, T. 1986. *Flawed Victory,* 67–73.
Nakdimon, S. 1987. *First Strike.*
O'Ballance, E. 1988. *The Gulf War,* 76–77.
Weissman, S., and H. Krosney. 1981. *The Islamic Bomb,* 3–10.

12.12 Turco-Kurd Expedition, 1983

Kurdish separatism fueled international armed conflict among most states where large numbers of Kurds resided after World War II. Iran was affected in 1945–1946 (12.1) and 1979 (12.9), as was Iraq from the 1960s to the 1980s (12.3, 12.4, 12.5, 12.7, 12.9). Kurdish separatist activity eventually spead to Turkey, which possesed the region's largest population of Kurds. Increasing Kurdish violence within Turkey during the early 1980s was stimulated in part by Kurdish rebellion within Iraq. Kurds supported by Iran resumed guerrilla activity against the Iraqi government during the Persian Gulf War and sometimes also attacked Turkish territory, including a May 1983 raid that killed three Turkish soldiers. Turkey dispatched an army division to Iraq with Iraqi government approval in late May 1983 in an attempt to eradicate Kurdish rebel camps. The expedition failed in its main mission because most Kurdish guerrilla bands eluded it. Turkish troops withdrew by mid-June after sustaining one fatality.

Cordesman, A. 1984. *The Gulf and the Search for Strategic Stability*, 690.
Gunter, M. 1988. "The Kurdish Problem in Turkey." *Middle East Journal* 42 (Summer): 289–406.
McDowell, D. 1985. *The Kurds*, 24.
O'Ballance, E. 1988. *The Gulf War*, 136–137, 141.
Yapp, M. 1989. "'The Mice Will Play'." In *The Gulf War*, ed. H. Maull and O. Pick, 103–118.

12.13 Turco-Kurd Raids, 1984–1987

Kurdish separatist activity within Iraq during the Persian Gulf War, aided in part by Iran, spilled over into Turkey and threatened to ignite nationalist sentiment within Turkey's large Kurdish minority. A division-sized Turkish military expedition attempted unsuccessfully to destroy Kurdish rebel camps within Iraq in 1983 (12.12). Between October 1984 and March 1987 Turkish aircraft repeatedly attacked Kurds within Iraq with Baghdad's approval. On at least one occasion in August 1987 Iraqi aircraft also attacked Turkish territory while pursuing Kurdish dissidents. Incidents abated as the Gulf War drew to a close and Kurds lost Iranian patronage. No regular military fatalities are reported during 1984–1987 cross-border operations.

Gunter, M. 1988. "The Kurdish Problem in Turkey." *Middle East Journal* 42 (Summer): 289–406.
Laffin, J. 1986. *War Annual 1*, 88–91.
Laffin, J. 1987. *War Annual 2*, 129–134.
Laffin, J. 1989. *The World in Conflict 1989: War Annual 3*, 136–142.
O'Ballance, E. 1988. *The Gulf War*, 136–141, 202.
Yapp, M. 1989. "'The Mice Will Play'." In *The Gulf War*, ed. H. Maull and O. Pick, 103–118.

12.14 Al-Dibal Incident, 1986

Traditional sheikdoms governing the Persian Gulf island of Bahrain and nearby Qatar Peninsula each signed treaties of protection with the United Kingdom in 1861 and 1916, respectively. Britain terminated both protectorates in 1971. Bahrain and Qatar disputed ownership of the Hawar Islands controlled by Bahrain immediately off Qatar's coast as early as the 1930s and continued to do so after independence. In 1985 Bahrain began to construct a coast guard station on Al-Dibal shoal within the disputed area. On April 26, 1986, a contingent of Qatari soldiers landed by helicopter on Al-Dibal and arrested Bahraini personnel. Bahrain protested but did not retaliate militarily. No fatalities are reported.

Day, A., ed. 1987. *Border and Territorial Disputes*, 229–231.
Middle East Contemporary Survey (1986): 294–298.

13

Levant

The territorial dispute between Israel and her neighbors regarding the status of Palestine has been the major source of conflict among Levantine states of the eastern Mediterranean since World War II. Several major wars resulted, including the Palestine War (13.1), the Sinai War (13.8), the Six Day War (13.80), the War of Attrition (13.21), the Yom Kippur War (13.27), and the Lebanese War (13.22). Other conflicts over Palestine ended less violently, including those involving Israel and Egypt (13.4, 13.24), Israel and Jordan (13.3, 13.10, 13.12, 13.13), Israel and Syria (13.5, 13.9, 13.11, 13.16, 13,17, 13.26), and Israel and Lebanon (13.20). Jordanian efforts to suppress the Palestine Liberation Organization led to international engagements (13.23, 13.25). Israeli-Palestinian conflict involved other world regions as well, including Israel's Entebbe Airport Raid (9.19) within Uganda (9.19), her Osirak Reactor raid against Iraq (12.11), and her attack upon PLO headquarters at Bori Cedria, Tunisia (11.14). Other issues contributing to international armed conflict within the Levant include Egyptian efforts to expel the United Kingdom from Suez (13.6, 13.7), Lebanese political instability (13.2, 13.14, 13.19, 13.22), and Jordanian friction with the Arab nationalist movement (13.15).

13.1 Palestine War, 1945–1949

The United Kingdom seized Palestine from the Ottoman Empire during World War I and subsequently administered it under League of Nations mandate. The territory's population traditionally included an Arab majority and significant Jewish and Christian minorities. Rival Arab and Jewish nationalists disputed who should inherit Palestine from the Turks and the British. The United Kingdom encouraged Arab revolt against the Turks in 1916. She also promulgated the Balfour Declaration in 1917 endorsing Zionist proposals for a Jewish national home. Jewish immigration increased after World War I. Arab nationalists promoted anti-British and anti-Jewish disturbances during the 1920s and 1930s.

Violence abated during World War II but resumed at war's end. The United Kingdom reinforced her garrisons in late September 1945 during mounting unrest, including Jewish-sponsored terrorism. In September 1947 she announced her intention to terminate responsibilities and later set May 15, 1948, as the date for separation. The U.N. General Assembly endorsed the principle of partition for Palestine in November 1947, which satisfied neither Zionists nor Arab nationalists. Member states of the Arab League subsidized an irregular Arab Liberation Army which took the field in January 1948. British forces ceased direct action on May 15 and withdrew by June 30, 1948.

The United Kingdom employed elements of the Jordanian Arab Legion to help garrison Palestine during World War II. Jordan continued to maintain some soldiers on station after gaining her own independence in 1946, but did not commit them to overt operations until April 1948. All Jordanian troops withdrew early the next month at British insistence.

Jewish leaders unilaterally proclaimed the State of Israel on May 14, 1948. The United States promptly recognized the regime. Arab states, including Egypt, Iraq, Jordan, Lebanon and Syria, which had massed regular forces on Palestine's borders, invaded on May 15. War proceeded by fits and starts. Prior to the first truce, June 11, former Jewish resistance forces constituting the new Israeli Army reacted primarily defensively except for air raids against Egyptian and Syrian territory and air and commando attacks against Lebanon. Israeli forces assumed the offensive from July 9, 1948, until the second truce July 18 but did not break out of Palestine at that time. New Israeli offensives begun in October penetrated Lebanon by the end of the month, breached Egyptian Sinai by the end of December and included small-unit operations within Jordan. A Saudi Arabian contingent appeared briefly during October in the company of Egyptian forces resisting Israel's southern offensive.

War ended in staggered truce on different fronts from January 6, 1949, with Egypt to April 13 with Syria. Israel controlled most of Palestine except the Gaza Strip held by Egypt, disputed lands near Syria's Golan Heights, and territories on the West Bank of the Jordan River and part of Jerusalem occupied by Jordan.

Total military fatalities approached 10,000 including former Jewish terrorists and Arab irregulars converted to regular soldiers in May 1948. Israeli forces suffered nearly 3,000 killed. Egypt and Lebanon are estimated to have lost 2,000 soldiers each. Syria and Jordan may each have sustained 1,000 fatalities and Iraq several hundred. More than

200 British troops died as result of 1945–1948 terrorism. No Saudi deaths are reported.

General

Bailey, S. 1990. *Four Arab-Israeli Wars and the Peace Process*, 1-106.
Brecher, M., J. Wilkenfeld, and S. Moser. 1988. *Crises in the Twentieth Century*, 1: 210–213, 216–217.
Butterworth, R. 1976. *Managing Interstate Conflict*, 66–69.
Day, A., ed. 1987. *Border and Territorial Disputes*, 197–226.
Dupuy, R., and T. Dupuy. 1986. *The Encyclopedia of Military History*, 1221–1227.
Kirk, G. 1954. *The Middle East 1945–1950*, 187–319.
Small, M., and J. Singer. 1982. *Resort to Arms*, 92.

Arab States

Glubb, J. 1957. *A Soldier with the Arabs*, 71–237.
Hof, F. 1985. *Galilee Divided*, 51–59.
Khouri, F. 1985. *The Arab-Israeli Dilemma*, 43–101.
O'Ballance, E. 1957. *The Arab-Israeli War*, 1948.
Safran, N. 1985. *Saudi Arabia: The Ceaseless Quest for Security*, 130.
Shlaim, A. 1988. *Collusion Across the Jordan*.
Wilson, M. 1987. *King Abdullah, Britain, and the Making of Jordan*, 151–186.

Israel

Bar-Joseph, U. 1987. *The Best of Enemies*.
Bar-Yaacov, N. 1967. *The Israel-Syrian Armistice*, 13–36.
Bell, J. B. 1969. *The Long War*, 19–236.
Bell, J. B. 1977. *Terror out of Zion*.
Cordesman, A. 1987. *The Arab-Israeli Military Balance and the Art of Operations*, 9–10, 19.
Dupuy, T. 1978. *Elusive Victory*, 1–125.
Herzog, C. 1984. *The Arab-Israeli Wars*, 17–108.
Kurzman, D. 1970. *Genesis 1948: The First Arab-Israeli War*.
Lorch, N. 1968. *Israel's War of Independence, 1947–1949*.
Luttwak, E., and D. Horowitz. 1983. *The Israeli Army*, 22–70.
Rothenberg, G. 1979. *The Anatomy of the Israeli Army*, 39–67, 197.
Sachar, H. 1976. *A History of Israel: From the Rise of Zionism*, 279–353.

United Kingdom

Blaxland, G. 1971. *The Regiments Depart*, 26–59.
Charters, D. 1989. *The British Army and Jewish Insurgency in Palestine*.
Dewar, M. 1984. *Brush Fire Wars*, 17–26.

13.2 Saadeh's Rebellion, 1949

France administered several *villayet* (provinces) of the former Ottoman Empire designated as Syria and Lebanon under League of Nations mandate following World War I. Rival nationalists advanced conflicting demands, including Maronite leaders who proposed a separate Christian homeland within Lebanon and the Parti Populaire Syrien (PPS, or Syrian National party), founded by Antoun Saadeh in Beirut, which championed pan-Syrian unity. France suppressed the PPS and forced Saadeh to flee to exile in 1938. She granted internal self-government to Lebanon and Syria separately in 1943. PPS and other Syrian nationalist guerrillas attacked French garrisons during 1944 and early 1945. France withdrew fully in 1946 upon terminating the mandate.

Saadeh returned to Beirut in 1947. Husni al-Za'im seized power within Syria by military coup d'etat on March 30, 1949. Incidents occurred near the Lebanese-Syrian border in April involving opponents of the new regime operating out of Lebanon. A small unit of Syrian troops attacked opposition forces upon Lebanese territory in early May. Za'im also encouraged Saadeh and provided him small arms with which to attack the Lebanese government. Saadeh's forces assaulted Lebanese police posts near the Syrian border during the first days of July. Za'im then reversed position and on July 6, 1949, Syrian troops helped to capture Saadeh at his border redoubt and turned him over to Lebanese authorities who later executed him. One Syrian soldier is reported killed within Lebanon.

Butterworth, R. 1976. *Managing Interstate Conflict*, 131–132.
Meo, L. 1965. *Lebanon, Improbable Nation*, 93–94.
Seale, P. 1965. *The Struggle for Syria*, 64–72.

13.3 West Bank Conflict, 1950–1954

Jordan occupied part of Palestine at the end of the Palestine War in 1949 (13.1). She annexed occupied territory on the West Bank of the Jordan River that housed large numbers of Arab Palestinian war refugees in December 1949. Border incidents commenced almost immediately after armistice despite presence of the United Nations Truce Supervision Organization, mostly due to Palestinian infiltration into Israel. Israeli commando units conducted frequent reprisals, including raids against Jordanian police stations, army positions and villages beginning in March 1950 and continuing until 1954. An especially controversial Israeli raid upon the Jordanian village of Qibya in October 1953 killed more than sixty civilians. Incidents became less frequent in spring 1954 after Jordan took additional measures to inhibit infiltration. Israeli raids ceased temporarily after an attack upon the Jordanian village of Beit Liqya in early September 1954. Jordan refrained from military action within Israel during the early 1950s except at Battir in November 1954 where a Jordanian patrol stumbled into a small skirmish. Approximately thirty Israeli soldiers were killed within Jordan during 1950–1954. Four Jordanians died during the Battir incident.

Bell, J. B. 1969. *The Long War*, 260–261.
Blechman, B. 1972. "The Impact of Israel's Reprisals." *Journal of Conflict Resolution* 16 (June): 155–181.
Brecher, M., J. Wilkenfeld, and S. Moser. 1988. *Crises in the Twentieth Century*, 1: 225.
Burns, E. 1963. *Between Arab and Israeli*, 33–57.
Butterworth, R. 1976. *Managing Interstate Conflict*, 124–125.
Glubb, J. 1957. *A Soldier with the Arabs*, 241–343.
Hutchison, E. 1956. *Violent Truce*, 10–106.
Khouri, F. 1985. *The Arab-Israeli Dilemma*, 187–188, 197–198.
Luttwak, E., and D. Horowitz. 1983. *The Israeli Army*, 104–118.
O'Ballance, E. 1959. *The Sinai Campaign, 1956*, 13–31.
Plascov, A. 1981. *The Palestinian Refugees in Jordan*, 73–91.
Rothenberg, G. 1979. *The Anatomy of the Israeli Army*, 88–89.
Sachar, H. 1976. *A History of Israel: From the Rise of Zionism*, 444–445.
Shimshoni, J. 1988. *Israel and Conventional Deterrence*, 34–68.
Snow, P. 1972. *Hussein: A Biography*.
Stock, E. 1967. *Israel on the Road to Sinai*, 67–70.

13.4 Rafah Incident, 1950

Two hundred thousand Palestinian refugees crowded the Egyptian-occupied Gaza Strip when armistice ended the Palestine War in 1949 (13.1). Subsequent Palestinian infiltration into Israel provoked occasional incidents, although not so many, at first, as on the Jordanian-Israeli border (13.3). On June 30, 1950, an Israeli patrol attacked Egyptian-controlled Rafah, killing three Arabs but suffering no fatalities of its own. Israeli authorities attributed the incident to error among field commanders.

Blechman, B. 1972. "The Impact of Israel's Reprisals." *Journal of Conflict Resolution* 16 (June): 155–181.
Butterworth, R. 1976. *Managing Interstate Conflict*, 124–125.
New York Times 7/3/50, 3:6.

13.5 Tel Mutillah Battle, 1951

The Israeli-Syrian armistice in 1949 ending the Palestine War (13.1) left opposing forces facing one another around the Sea of Galilee (Lake Tiberias). Disputes respecting rights within the watershed and on the lake itself contributed to ensuing mutual hostilities. In 1951 Israel determined to reclaim nearby Hula Swamp. Syria protested the plan. Israeli and Syrian soldiers exchanged rifle fire across the border on several occasions beginning in March. On April 4 a Syrian unit raided the town of El-Hammu. Israeli aircraft attacked Syrian border posts the next day. Cross-border fire and occasional small-unit raids continued throughout April. On May 2, 1951, a Syrian offensive captured Israel's Tel Mutillah outpost. Israel counterattacked this and other Syrian positions later the same day. Serious fighting continued until May 5 and ended inconclusively. Further incidents involving small arms fire continued until May 9. Approximately twenty regular Syrian soldiers died in the vicinity of Tel Mutillah as did also numerous Syrian irregulars. Israel suffered nearly thirty military fatalities.

Bar-Yaacov, N. 1967. *The Israel-Syrian Armistice*, 66–113.
Blechman, B. 1972. "The Impact of Israel's Reprisals." *Journal of Conflict Resolution* 16 (June): 155–181.
Brecher, M., J. Wilkenfeld, and S. Moser. 1988. *Crises in the Twentieth Century*, 1: 220.
Butterworth, R. 1976. *Managing Interstate Conflict*, 124–125.
Khouri, F. 1985. *The Arab-Israeli Dilemma*, 194.
Luttwak, E., and D. Horowitz. 1983. *The Israeli Army*, 106–107.
Rothenberg, G. 1979. *The Anatomy of the Israeli Army*, 88.
Sachar, H. 1976. *A History of Israel: From the Rise of Zionism*, 445–446.
Seale, P. 1965. *The Struggle for Syria*, 106–109.
Yaniv, A. 1986. "Syria and Israel." In *Syria under Assad*, ed. M. Maoz and A. Yaniv, 157–178.

13.6 Suez Riots I, 1951–1952

In 1869 Egypt granted a ninety-nine year concession to construct and operate the Suez Canal to the Suez Canal Company, partly owned by the British and French governments. The United Kingdom stationed forces within Egypt under various arrangements, including British protectorate from 1914 to 1922, and by provision of the 1936 Anglo-Egyptian Treaty of Alliance, set to expire in 1956. Dispute arose over control of the Canal after World War II. Police contained anti-British rioting and attacks upon British servicemen in February–March 1946.

The Egyptian government introduced draft legislation to abrogate the 1936 alliance and to reassert Egyptian sovereignty over the Canal in October 1951. It also encouraged repeated riots and irregular attacks upon British installations beginning later that month. Incidents continued until March 1952 when the United Kingdom announced her intention to withdraw from Ismailia where some of the most serious disturbances took place. Hundreds of Egyptian civilians were killed or injured and approximately forty British soldiers died during 1951–1952.

Blaxland, G. 1971. *The Regiments Depart*, 215–232.
Brecher, M., J. Wilkenfeld, and S. Moser. 1988. *Crises in the Twentieth Century*, 1: 221–222.
Butterworth, R. 1976. *Managing Interstate Conflict*, 156–158.
Farnie, D. 1969. *East and West of Suez*, 691–717.
Hofstadter, D. 1973. *Egypt and Nasser*, 1: 17–23.
Marlowe, J. 1965. *Anglo-Egyptian Relations, 1800–1956*, 381–404.
Moussa, F. 1955. *Les Negotiations Anglo-Egyptiennes de 1950–1951 sur Suez et la Sudan*.
Royal Institute of International Affairs. 1952. *Great Britian and Egypt, 1914–1951*, 115–151, 184–185.
Schonfield, H. 1969. *The Suez Canal in Peace and War*, 124–134.

13.7 Suez Riots II, 1953–1954

The United Kingdom stationed troops in the vicinity of the Suez Canal from the nineteenth century, including under provision of a twenty-year alliance signed with Egypt in 1936. Egyptian opposition to British military presence contributed to conflict in 1951–1952 (13.6). Egypt's King Farouk was overthrown in July 1952. An aggressively nationalist government arose under Gamal Abdel Nasser. The United Kingdom agreed to reduce her garrisons during subsequent negotiations but refused to withdraw troops completely. On February 24, 1953, President Nasser threatened to attack the Canal if any British forces remained. Talks suspended. Beginning at the end of March and continuing for more than a year Egypt encouraged sporadic riots and irregular terrorist attacks in the vicinity of the Canal. Violence ceased after the United Kingdom agreed July 28, 1954, to withdraw all military forces from Egypt as of 1956. Approximately twenty British soldiers died during 1953–1954.

Blaxland, G. 1971. *The Regiments Depart*, 232–236.
Butterworth, R. 1976. *Managing Interstate Conflict*, 156–158.
Farnie, D. 1969. *East and West of Suez*, 691–717.
Hofstadter, D. 1973. *Egypt and Nasser*, 1: 53–57, 61–63.

Marlowe, J. 1965. *Anglo-Egyptian Relations, 1800–1956*, 381–404.
Schonfield, H. 1969. *The Suez Canal in Peace and War*, 135–148.

13.8 Sinai War, 1953–1957

Minor incidents troubled the Egyptian-Israeli border from shortly after the Palestine War in 1949 (13.1) despite presence of the United Nations Truce Supervision Organization. An Israeli military patrol also attacked Rafah in 1950 (13.4). Most incidents involved the large community of Palestinian refugees concentrated within the Egyptian-occupied Gaza Strip. Egypt encouraged Palestinian infiltration into Israel after Gamel Abdel Nasser took power in 1952. Israel began reprisal commando raids upon Gaza border posts and towns in August 1953. Small units of Egyptian forces occasionally counterattacked Israeli territory, including in March 1954 and in January 1955. In November 1955 an Israeli battalion attacked Sabha, killing as many as fifty Egyptian soldiers. Further terrorist incidents and Israeli reprisals continued into 1956. Egypt employed artillery against Israeli territory in April 1956 following another damaging Israeli raid.

Other issues also contributed to full-scale warfare in October 1956. Egypt barred Israeli shipping from the Suez Canal after the Palestine War and attempted to prevent Israeli access to the Red Sea through the Gulf of Aqaba. Egypt also opposed British military presence on her territory after World War II, encouraged serious rioting in 1951–1952 and 1953–1954 (13.6, 13.7), and forced British military withdrawal in June 1956 on expiration of the Anglo-Egyptian treaty of alliance. On July 26, 1956, Egypt nationalized the Suez Canal, owned primarily by British and French investors. The United Kingdom, France and Israel secretly planned joint action. Israel invaded Egyptian Gaza and Sinai on October 29, 1956, and approached the eastern bank of the Suez Canal within a few days. British and French aircraft attacked Egyptian airfields and other military installations on October 31. On November 5 British and French paratroops landed within Egypt and began to take control of the Suez Canal.

The United States and the Soviet Union protested the invasions and a cease-fire was obtained. The U.N. Security Council authorized a United Nations Emergency Force (UNEF) to police the Israeli-Egyptian border. First UNEF contingents arrived November 15, 1956. British and French forces withdrew the following day. Israel withdrew to the 1949 armistice line in March 1957 and UNEF units deployed as observers on the Egyptian side of the border.

Approximately 1,000 Egyptian soldiers died during major fighting in the Sinai in 1956. Israel lost almost 200 troops killed during her Sinai offensive, the United Kingdom twenty and France ten. A handful of Egyptian and Israeli regulars died upon one another's territory during three preceding years of low-intensity conflict.

General

Brecher, M., J. Wilkenfeld, and S. Moser. 1988. *Crises in the Twentieth Century*, 1: 229–234.
Butterworth, R. 1976. *Managing Interstate Conflict*, 124–125, 219–221.
Day, A., ed. 1987. *Border and Territorial Disputes*, 197–226.
Dupuy, R., and T. Dupuy. 1986. *The Encyclopedia of Military History*, 1227–1230.
Small, M., and J. Singer. 1982. *Resort to Arms*, 93.

Egypt

Barker, A. 1965. *Suez: The Seven Day War.*
Fullick, R., and G. Powell. 1979. *Suez: The Double War.*
Hofstadter, D. 1973. *Egypt and Nasser*, vol. 1.
Khouri, F. 1985. *The Arab-Israeli Dilemma*, 182–221.
Love, K. 1969. *Suez: The Twice-Fought War.*
O'Ballance, E. 1959. *The Sinai Campaign, 1956.*

France

Beaufre, A. 1969. *The Suez Expedition 1956.*

Israel

Alon, H. 1980. *Countering Palestinian Terrorism in Israel*, 14–20.
Bar-Siman-Tov, Y. 1987. *Israel, the Superpowers, and the War in the Middle East*, 27–83.
Bell, J. B. 1969. *The Long War*, 305–358.
Blechman, B. 1972. "The Impact of Israel's Reprisals." *Journal of Conflict Resolution* 16 (June): 155–181.
Brecher, M. 1975. *Decisions in Israel's Foreign Policy*, 225–317.
Cordesman, A. 1987. *The Arab-Israeli Military Balance and the Art of Operations*, 17–23.
Dayan, M. 1966. *Diary of the Sinai Campaign.*
Dayan, M. 1976. *Story of My Life*, 171–259.
Dupuy, T. 1978. *Elusive Victory*, 127–218.
Herzog, C. 1984. *The Arab-Israeli Wars*, 112–141.
Luttwak, E., and D. Horowitz. 1983. *The Israeli Army*, 104–164.
Rothenberg, G. 1979. *The Anatomy of the Israeli Army*, 91–113.
Sachar, H. 1976. *A History of Israel: From the Rise of Zionism*, 447–450, 472–514.

Shimshoni, J. 1988. *Israel and Conventional Deterrence*, 69–122.
Stock, E. 1967. *Israel on the Road to Sinai.*

United Kingdom

Blaxland, G. 1971. *The Regiments Depart*, 215–267.
Farnie, D. 1969. *East and West of Suez*, 718–745.
Nutting, A. 1967. *No End of a Lesson.*
Robertson, T. 1965. *Crisis: The Inside Story of the Suez Conspiracy.*
Thomas, H. 1967. *The Suez Affair.*

United Nations

Bailey, S. 1990. *Four Arab-Israeli Wars and the Peace Process*, 107–186.
Burns, E. 1963. *Between Arab and Israeli.*
Hutchison, E. 1956. *Violent Truce*, 111–123.

13.9 Kinneret Conflict I, 1954–1955

Border dispute contributed to fighting between Syria and Israel at Tel Mutillah in 1951 (13.5). Lake Kinneret (Lake Tiberias) represented another locus of continuing friction. The lake was included within Palestine under British rule. Israel claimed it as a matter of right but Syria occupied commanding positions near the eastern shore following the armistice ending the Palestine War in 1949 (13.1). Incidents provoked by Syrian fishermen using the lake without Israeli permit occurred frequently during the early 1950s. Syrian and Israeli shore batteries engaged in a brief artillery duel in March 1954. Syria continued to shell Israeli positions from time to time until nearly the end of 1955. Israeli commandos attacked Syrian border positions in October 1955. She mounted a larger and more destructive raid in mid-December that silenced further Syrian artillery fire. Six Israeli soldiers died during raids upon Syria. Syria lost at least twenty military personnel.

Bar-Yaacov, N. 1967. *The Israel-Syrian Armistice*, 214–226.
Blechman, B. 1972. "The Impact of Israel's Reprisals." *Journal of Conflict Resolution* 16 (June): 155–181.
Burns, E. 1963. *Between Arab and Israeli*, 107–122.
Butterworth, R. 1976. *Managing Interstate Conflict*, 124–125.
Horn, C. von. 1967. *Soldiering for Peace*, 269–270.
Hutchison, E. 1956. *Violent Truce*, 107–110.
Khouri, F. 1985. *The Arab-Israeli Dilemma*, 194–197.
O'Ballance, E. 1959. *The Sinai Campaign, 1956*, 13–31.
Sachar, H. 1976. *A History of Israel: From the Rise of Zionism*, 447.

Yaniv, A. 1986. "Syria and Israel." In *Syria under Assad,* ed. M. Maoz and A. Yaniv, 157–178.

13.10 Qalqilya Raid, 1956

Palestinian infiltration into Israel from the Jordanian-controlled West Bank after the Palestine War (13.1) provoked repeated Israeli military reprisals between 1950 and 1954 (13.3). On July 24, 1956, a small detachment of Jordanian soldiers briefly seized a house within the demilitarized zone of Jerusalem's disputed Mt. Scopus area and from it fired upon Israeli border guards. Three days later Israeli artillery shelled Jordanian positions elsewhere on the border. Israel undertook small ground probes against Jordanian positions on August 2. On September 10 a Jordanian patrol killed several Israeli soldiers near Idna, Israel. Israel launched a series of retaliatory raids that climaxed with an attack upon Qalqilya October 10, 1956. The Qalqilya raid went awry when Arab Legion units interdicted the commandos' escape route. Israel dispatched an armored rescue column. The battle continued through the night of October 10–11. Quiet returned to the border after this debacle. Israel suffered approximately forty fatalities during attacks upon Jordan, twenty-seven of them at Qalqilya. Jordan suffered comparable losses although none within Israel.

Alon, H. 1980. *Countering Palestinian Terrorism in Israel,* 14–40.
Bell, J. B. 1969. *The Long War,* 260–261.
Blechman, B. 1972. "The Impact of Israel's Reprisals." *Journal of Conflict Resolution* 16 (June): 155–181.
Brecher, M., J. Wilkenfeld, and S. Moser. 1988. *Crises in the Twentieth Century,* 1: 232.
Burns, E. 1963. *Between Arab and Israeli,* 47, 123–176.
Butterworth, R. 1976. *Managing Interstate Conflict,* 124–125.
Luttwak, E., and D. Horowitz. 1983. *The Israeli Army,* 139–40.
O'Ballance, E. 1959. *The Sinai Campaign, 1956,* 13–31.
Plascov, A. 1981. *The Palestinian Refugees in Jordan,* 73–91.
Rothenberg, G. 1979. *The Anatomy of the Israeli Army,* 94–95.
Snow, P. 1972. *Hussein: A Biography.*
Stock, E. 1967. *Israel on the Road to Sinai,* 195–198.

13.11 Israeli-Syrian Border, 1957–1958

Syrian-Israeli border tensions following the Palestine War (13.1) contributed to occasional direct conflict (13.5, 13.9) and numerous minor incidents. Syrian soldiers attacked Israeli border positions with small arms and mortars in early July 1957. Israel immediately responded in kind. A ten-hour firefight from fixed positions on each side of the border resulted. Further such incidents continued until early December 1958. No Israeli or Syrian fatalities are reported as a direct result of these engagements.

Bar-Yaacov, N. 1967. *The Israel-Syrian Armistice*, 196–197.
Butterworth, R. 1976. *Managing Interstate Conflict*, 226–227.
Horn, C. von. 1967. *Soldiering for Peace*, 86–89.
Khouri, F. 1985. *The Arab-Israeli Dilemma*, 222–223.

13.12 Mount Scopus Incident, 1957

The disputed Jordanian-Israeli armistice line within the Mount Scopus section of Jerusalem, established at end of the Palestine War (13.1), provoked repeated incidents beginning in 1956 (13.10). In July 1957 regular Israeli soldiers dressed as border guards posted watch while Israeli citizens cultivated disputed land within the demilitarized zone. Jordan protested to the U.N. truce observation team but Israel continued to encourage intrusions. On August 22, 1957, Jordanian soldiers attacked a party of Israeli soldiers and civilians within the demilitarized zone, killing three and suffering one fatality of their own.

Butterworth, R. 1976. *Managing Interstate Conflict*, 226–227.
Day, A., ed. 1987. *Border and Territorial Disputes*, 195.
Keesing's Publications Limited. 1968. *The Arab-Israeli Conflict*, 8.
Khouri, F. 1985. *The Arab-Israeli Dilemma*, 221–222.
Sachar, H. 1976. *A History of Israel: From the Rise of Zionism*, 445.

13.13 Mount Scopus Clash, 1958

Serious incidents occurred between Jordanian and Israeli forces within the disputed Mount Scopus area of Jerusalem in 1956 (13.10) and 1957 (13.12). Minor incidents followed, including kidnapping of a Jordanian border guard and exchange of small arms fire across the border in November 1957. Israel initiated provocative patrols by regular soldiers wearing border guard uniforms during spring 1958. On May 26, 1958, an Israeli patrol intruded within Jordanian territory and clashed with Jordanian forces. Four Israeli soldiers died.

Butterworth, R. 1976. *Managing Interstate Conflict*, 226–227.
Day, A., ed. 1987. *Border and Territorial Disputes*, 195.
Horn, C. von. 1967. *Soldiering for Peace*, 93–95.
Keesing's Publications Limited. 1968. *The Arab-Israeli Conflict*, 8.

Khouri, F. 1985. *The Arab-Israeli Dilemma*, 221–222.
Sachar, H. 1976. *A History of Israel: From the Rise of Zionism*, 445.

13.14 Lebanese Civil War, 1958

Lebanon, home of ancient Phoenician centers of Tyre and Sidon, was ruled by one or another foreign power from 700 B.C. until after World War II, beginning with the Assyrians and ending with the Ottoman and finally French administration of Lebanon and Syria under League of Nations mandate. France separated Lebanon from Syria before departing in 1946, so contributing to later conflict between the two (13.2). Lebanese society represented diverse ethnic, religious and other loyalties and lacked a cohesive sense of nationalism. Understandings reached prior to independence among the largest religious groups allocated important political posts among Maronite and Greek Orthodox Christians, Sunni and Shi'a Moslems. The president, for example, was expected to be a Maronite. Other communal groups, including Druze, and an overlay of political parties crossing ethnic lines further complicated the political landscape.

In June 1957, President Camille Chamoun, the only Middle Eastern leader to embrace the Eisenhower Doctrine that year, manipulated legislative elections in order to assure continued hold on power. Diverse opponents of Chamoun and of Premier Sami Solh, a Sunni, staged demonstrations in 1957 but did not pose a serious challenge until after the editor of the left-leaning newspaper, the *Telegraph*, was assassinated May 8, 1958. A several-sided civil war broke out in which the Lebanese Army avoided taking direct part. The government alleged that Syria supported opposition violence. Lebanon closed its Syrian border May 13 and the United States prepared plans for military intervention.

On July 14, 1958, a nationalist military coup d'etat overthrew King Faisal II and Premier Nuri es-Said of Iraq. On July 15 the United States landed a Marine battalion in Beirut at Chamoun's request. Additional U.S. forces followed and took up positions to protect points of entry to the capital, including the airport and the highway leading to Damascus, Syria. Conflict quickly abated. Troops withdrew in late October 1958 after General Fuad Shehab, commander of the Lebanese Army, established a caretaker government. Two U.S. soldiers died as rthe esult of apparent accidents.

Brecher, M., J. Wilkenfeld, and S. Moser. 1988. *Crises in the Twentieth Century*, 1: 241–242.
Bull, O. 1976. *War and Peace in the Middle East*, 1–27.

Butterworth, R. 1976. *Managing Interstate Conflict,* 229–233.
Dowty, A. 1984. *Middle East Crisis,* 21–108.
Kerr, M. 1972. "The Lebanese Civil War." In *The International Regulation of Civil Wars,* ed. E. Luard, 65–90.
Meo, L. 1965. *Lebanon, Improbable Nation,* 165–203.
Quandt, W. 1978. "Lebanon, 1958, and Jordan, 1970." In *Force Without War,* by B. Blechman and S. Kaplan, 222–288.
Qubain, F. 1961. *Crisis in Lebanon.*
Salibi, K. 1976. *Crossroads to Civil War.*
Shulimson, J. 1966. *Marines in Lebanon 1958.*
Small, M., and J. Singer. 1982. *Resort to Arms,* 228.
Spiller, R. 1981. *"Not War But Like War."*
Tillema, H. 1973. *Appeal to Force.*

13.15 UAR Union Conflict, 1959

Gamel Abdel Nasser established an avowedly nationalist regime within Egypt in 1952 and represented himself as leader of the Arab world thereafter. He proclaimed a new constitution in January 1958 and also Syrian accession to the United Arab Republic (UAR) in February as first steps toward universal Arab unity. Policy differences divided Jordan's government from the UAR, including Jordan's greater cooperation with the United States and Israel. King Hussein ibn Talal also suffered numerous domestic attempts to assassinate or dethrone him after taking the crown in 1953, including among Palestinians incorporated within Jordan upon annexation of the West Bank in 1949. Anti-Hussein elements supported by the UAR infiltrated Jordan from Syrian territory during 1958–1959 and attempted to promote further discord. Small units of Jordanian soldiers attacked Syrian villages thought to harbor UAR agents and other dissidents during mid-April 1959. Following a Jordanian assault upon the Syrian village of Gharoyah, a small unit of regular Syrian troops entered Jordan briefly and fired upon civilians near the border town of Mafraq. No military fatalities are reported.

Butterworth, R. 1976. *Managing Interstate Conflict,* 272–274.
Nevo, J. 1986. "Syria and Jordan." In *Syria under Assad,* ed. M. Maoz and A. Yaniv, 140–156.
New York Times 4/24/59, 3:1; 4/25/59, 4:7.

13.16 Tawafiq Raid, 1960

Syria joined other members of the Arab League in refusing to recognize Israel as rightful heir to Palestine during and after the

Palestine War (13.1). Armed conflict erupted periodically along the Syrian-Israeli armistice line during the 1950s (13.5, 13.9, 13.11) due to border disputes and Arab Palestinian infiltration. Infiltration into Israel increased after Syria joined Egypt to form the United Arab Republic (UAR) in 1958, contributing to further minor border incidents including Syrian-Israeli small arms fire across the border in 1959. Israeli commandos attacked the Syrian village of Tawafiq on January 31, 1960. Syrian artillery shelled Israeli territory in retaliation. Further clashes involving Israeli patrols and Syrian artillery continued until February 12, 1960. Five Israeli soldiers are known killed as well as four Syrian military personnel.

Bar-Yaacov, N. 1967. *The Israel-Syrian Armistice*, 182–189.
Blechman, B. 1972. "The Impact of Israel's Reprisals." *Journal of Conflict Resolution* 16 (June): 155–181.
Brecher, M., J. Wilkenfeld, and S. Moser. 1988. *Crises in the Twentieth Century*, 1: 245–256.
Butterworth, R. 1976. *Managing Interstate Conflict*, 226–227.
Horn, C. von. 1967. *Soldiering for Peace*, 127–138.
Yaniv, A. 1986. "Syria and Israel." In *Syria under Assad*, ed. M. Maoz and A. Yaniv, 157–178.

13.17 Kinneret Conflict II, 1962

Repeated armed conflict between Syria and Israel followed the armistice ending the Palestine War in 1949 (13.5, 13.11, 13.16), including at disputed Lake Kinneret (Lake Tiberias) in 1954–1955 (13.9). Israel claimed the right to control access to Lake Kinneret based upon prior British maps of Palestine despite Syrian occupation of commanding positions near the eastern shore following the Palestine War. Syrian fishermen provoked frequent incidents by operating without Israeli permit. Syrian artillery again shelled Israeli positions and patrol boats upon Lake Kinneret during February and early March 1962, including from positions within the demilitarized zone. Israeli patrol boats responded by small arms fire upon occasion. Israeli commandos attacked Syria's forward gun emplacements the night of March 16–17, 1962. A small battle ensued in and about the demilitarized zone. Five Israeli and approximately thirty Syrian soldiers died.

Bar-Yaacov, N. 1967. *The Israel-Syrian Armistice*, 226–242.
Blechman, B. 1972. "The Impact of Israel's Reprisals." *Journal of Conflict Resolution* 16 (June): 155–181.
Butterworth, R. 1976. *Managing Interstate Conflict*, 226–227.

Horn, C. von. 1967. *Soldiering for Peace*, 269–290.
Keesing's Publications Limited. 1968. *The Arab-Israeli Conflict*.

13.18 Six Day War, 1963–1967

Armed conflict smoldered on Israel's borders beginning with Syria in 1963 until major warfare erupted in June 1967. Palestinian terrorists repeatedly infiltrated Israel following the Palestine War (13.1), including from the Egyptian-occupied Gaza Strip, Syrian-held territory near the Golan Heights, and territory on the West Bank of the Jordan River annexed by Jordan in 1949. Israel invaded and occupied Gaza and Egyptian Sinai in 1956 but withdrew under international pressure (13.8). Quiet reigned on the Israeli-Egyptian border during the following decade due in part to presence of United Nations Emergency Force (UNEF) observers who operated solely upon Egyptian territory.

Israeli and Syrian troops became embroiled in violent exchanges in 1960 (13.16) and again in 1962 (13.17). In June 1963 Syrian artillery began to shell Israeli border settlements and continued to do so frequently until 1967. Israel retaliated a few days after the first attack by air strikes upon the Syrian town of El Douga. In July 1964 Israeli artillery began to shell Syrian border positions in counterpoint to Syrian attacks.

The Israeli-Jordanian border was frequently troubled by Palestinian infiltration and other incidents following the Palestine War. Israeli forces raided Jordan repeatedly during 1950–1954 (13.3). Sporadic border incidents occurred during the late 1950s (13.10, 13.12, 13.13). Palestinian infiltration into Israel out of Jordan increased early in 1965 and Israel resumed commando reprisals against Jordanian territory in May.

Low-intensity conflict continued on the Israeli-Jordanian and Israeli-Syrian borders to spring 1967, including an Israeli-Syrian air battle in April 1967. Egypt and Syria each declared a state of emergency May 14 after reports that Israel was massing forces on the Syrian border. Egypt moved army divisions into the Sinai the next day and called upon the United Nations to withdraw UNEF observers. UNEF withdrew on May 18. Egypt announced closure of the Straits of Tiran on May 23, preventing Israeli access to the Red Sea.

On June 5, 1967, Israel launched preemptive air strikes upon military airfields of Egypt, Jordan, Iraq, and Syria, destroying much of each air force on the ground. She invaded Sinai the same day and also Jordan after Jordanian artillery opened fire upon Israeli positions. Israel secured control of Gaza and most Jordanian territory west of the Jordan River by June 9. On June 10 Israel attacked Syria and quickly occupied the Golan Heights. Cease-fire was achieved on all fronts by June 10. Military contingents sent to Egypt and Syria by other Arab League members arrived too late to participate in fighting.

Nearly 800 Israeli soldiers were killed during the Six Day War, primarily on the Egyptian and Syrian fronts. Egypt may have lost as many as 10,000 troops; Jordan, 2,000; and Syria, 700; all primarily upon their own territories.

General

Brecher, M., J. Wilkenfeld, and S. Moser. 1988. *Crises in the Twentieth Century,* 1: 278–280.

Butterworth, R. 1976. *Managing Interstate Conflict,* 226–227, 417–419.

Day, A., ed. 1987. *Border and Territorial Disputes,* 197–226.

Dupuy, R., and T. Dupuy. 1986. *The Encyclopedia of Military History,* 1230–1234.

Small, M., and J. Singer. 1982. *Resort to Arms,* 93.

Arab States

Bar-Yaacov, N. 1967. *The Israel-Syrian Armistice,* 243–280.

Cordesman, A. 1987. *The Arab-Israeli Military Balance and the Art of Operations,* 24–30.

Hofstadter, D. 1973. *Egypt and Nasser,* 3: 9–22, 29–38.

Khouri, F. 1985. *The Arab-Israeli Dilemma,* 242–292.

Keesing's Publications Limited. 1968. *The Arab-Israeli Conflict.*

Kosut, H., ed. 1968. *Israel and the Arabs: The June 1967 War.*

Mansfield, P. 1973. *The Middle East; a Political and Economic Survey.*

Mutawi, S. 1987. *Jordan in the 1967 War.*

O'Ballance, E. 1972. *The Third Arab-Israeli War.*

Petran, T. 1972. *Syria,* 187–204.

Quandt, W., F. Jabber, and A. Lesch. 1973. *The Politics of Palestinian Nationalism,* 168–175.

Snow, P. 1972. *Hussein: A Biography,* 170–193.

Stephens, R. 1972. *Nasser: A Political Biography,* 435–509.

Yaniv, A. 1986. "Syria and Israel." In *Syria under Assad,* ed. M. Maoz and A. Yaniv, 157–178.

Israel

Alon, H. 1980. *Countering Palestinian Terrorism in Israel,* 37–40.

Barker, A. 1980. *Arab-Israeli Wars,* 41–96.

Bar-Siman-Tov, Y. 1987. *Israel, the Superpowers, and the War in the Middle East,* 85–145.

Bell, J. B. 1969. *The Long War,* 359–430.

Blechman, B. 1972. "The Impact of Israel's Reprisals." *Journal of Conflict Resolution* 16 (June): 155–181.
Brecher, M. 1975. *Decisions in Israel's Foreign Policy*, 318–453.
Brecher, M., with B. Geist. 1980. *Decisions in Crisis*.
Dayan, M. 1976. *Story of My Life*, 287–381.
Dupuy, T. 1978. *Elusive Victory*, 219–340.
Hastings, Michael. 1970. *Embassies in Crisis*.
Herzog, C. 1984. *The Arab-Israeli Wars*, 147–191.
Laqueur, W. 1968. *The Road to Jerusalem*.
Luttwak, E., and D. Horowitz. 1983. *The Israeli Army*, 209–298.
Rothenberg, G. 1979. *The Anatomy of the Israeli Army*, 130–152.
Sachar, H. 1976. *A History of Israel: From the Rise of Zionism*, 615–666.
Safran, N. 1969. *From War to War*, 266–420.
Stein, J., and R. Tanter. 1980. *Rational Decision-Making*.
Weissman, S., and H. Krosney. 1981. *The Islamic Bomb*, 6–7.

United Nations

Bailey, S. 1990. *Four Arab-Israeli Wars and the Peace Process*, 187–284.
Bull, O. 1976. *War and Peace in the Middle East*, 38–131.
Lall, A. 1967. *The UN and the Middle East Crisis*.
Rikhye, I. 1980. *The Sinai Blunder*.

13.19 UAR Agents Crisis, 1963

Syria and Lebanon represented a congeries of villayet (provinces) within the Ottoman Empire until World War I. France established separate states when it abandoned the League of Nations mandate in 1946. Their border remained porous to political movements within one another's territory, contributing to later civil and international conflicts (13.2, 13.14). In February 1958 President Gamal Abdel Nasser of Egypt induced the government of Syria to accede to the United Arab Republic (UAR) under his leadership. Syrian-Egyptian union lasted three years. On September 1961 right-wing Syrian military officers deposed the Cairo-backed administration within Damascus. A quickly formed provisional government seceded from the UAR. Egyptian troops resisted separation until Nasser acknowledged dissolution on October 5, 1961, and withdrew Egyptian administrators and military forces.

Pro- and anti-Nasserite factions vied for political influence within Syria after secession. On March 8, 1963, the National Council on Revolution seized power within Syria with support of left-leaning nationalist military officers and the Arab Socialist Renaissance (Baath) party. A military regime dominated by General Amin al-Hafez emerged. Pro-Nasserite elements attempted an abortive coup d'etat on July 18, 1963. Incidents involving opposition mounted from within Lebanon provoked border incidents from July to October 1963, including an October 18 raid by thirty Syrian soldiers upon Lebanese territory. Three Lebanese policemen died October 18 but no Syrian military fatalities are reported.

New York Times 10/20/63, 13:1; 10/21/63, 9:1.

13.20 Houle Raids, 1965

Lebanon joined other members of the Arab League in fighting the newly proclaimed government of Israel during the Palestine War (13.1). The Israeli-Lebanese frontier remained generally quiet during the 1950s and early 1960s despite serious violence involving Israel and most of her other neighbors. Border incidents increased during the mid-1960s after Arab resistance groups associated with the Palestine Liberation Organization (PLO) began to support raids into Israel from southern Lebanon. The Lebanese government did not directly support PLO activities but neither did it decisively impede them. On October 29, 1965, Israeli commandos raided the Lebanese villages of Houle and Meiss aj Jebel in retaliation for Palestinian attacks within Israel. No Israeli military fatalities are reported.

Alon, H. 1980. *Countering Palestinian Terrorism in Israel*, 37.
Blechman, B. 1972. "The Impact of Israel's Reprisals." *Journal of Conflict Resolution* 16 (June): 155–181.
New York Times 10/29/65, 7:3.

13.21 War of Attrition, 1967–1970

Upon the cease-fire ending the Six Day War in June 1967 (13.18), Israel occupied Egyptian Sinai to the banks of the Suez Canal, Jordanian territory on the West Bank of the Jordan River, and Syria's Golan Heights. Low-intensity warfare resumed almost at once and grew by stages to constitute another major war among Israel and most of her neighbors.

Israeli and Egyptian artillery began to duel across the Suez Canal as early as July 14, 1967, a few days after formal cease-fire ending the Six Day War. Similar, albeit smaller artillery exchanges began on the Jordanian-Israeli border in early November 1967. Palestinian guerrillas also commenced attacks within Israeli-occupied territory, particularly the West Bank. Egyptian commando raids against Israeli positions east of the Suez Canal started in late October 1968. Israel immediately initiated air and commando counterattacks upon Egypt. She also commenced commando raids against Jordan in early December 1968. Iraqi artillery deployed within Jordan began to provide artillery support to Palestinian guerrillas infiltrating Israel beginning in December 1968 and continuing until the end of 1969.

1969 and early 1970 witnessed a war of attrition along the Suez Canal conducted primarily by heavy artillery barrages, commando raids, and aerial operations involving both sides. Soviet Union military personnel assisted Egyptian defense short of overt military intervention by manning antiaircraft missile batteries and by piloting reconnaissance planes within Egyptian air space. On September 9, 1969, Israel undertook a one-day combined arms assault intended to destroy Egyptian artillery emplacements. She commenced deep-penetration air attacks against Egypt in January 1970.

Israeli aircraft began attacks upon Syria in February 1969. Syrian artillery began to shell Israeli-occupied territory by December 1969. Israeli launched commando raids against Syria starting in March 1970 and launched a ground offensive at the beginning of April that secured control of additional Syrian territory. On January 20, 1970, armored Israeli ground forces swept Jordanian border territory before withdrawing the next day. Jordanian artillery attacks upon Israeli-occupied territory ceased at this time. On March 19, 1970, Israeli armored units crossed into Jordan, destroyed bases Palestine Liberation Organization bases at Karameh on March 21, and battled with Jordanian troops.

War finally halted in summer 1970. Hostilities ceased on the Syrian-Israeli frontier at the end of June after a largely unsuccessful Syrian ground offensive aimed to drive Israel from the Golan. Israel suspended attacks upon Jordan in early July. On August 7, 1970, Egypt and Israel accepted a cease-fire under urging of the United Nations and U.S. Secretary of State William Rogers.

The War of Attrition involved at least 3,000 military fatalities in all encounters, mostly on the Egyptian-Israeli front. As many as 2,000 Egyptian military personnel are estimated killed. More than 500 Israeli soldiers and airmen died as did a few hundred Jordanians, similar numbers of Syrians, and a score or more of Iraqi troops.

General

Brecher, M., J. Wilkenfeld, and S. Moser. 1988. *Crises in the Twentieth Century*, 1: 282–283, 285, 287–288, 290–291.
Butterworth, R. 1976. *Managing Interstate Conflict*, 422–424.
Small, M., and J. Singer. 1982. *Resort to Arms*, 94.

Arab States

Bailey, C. 1984. *Jordan's Palestinian Challenge*, 30–56.
Brown, N. 1971. "Jordanian Civil War." *Military Review* 51 (September): 38–58.
Bull, O. 1976. *War and Peace in the Middle East*, 132–175.
Cordesman, A. 1987. *The Arab-Israeli Military Balance and the Art of Operations*, 31–36.
Haykal, M. 1975. *The Road to Ramadan.*
Hofstadter, D. 1973. *Egypt and Nasser*, 3: 66–257.
Keesing's Publications Limited. 1968. *The Arab-Israeli Conflict*, 44–47.
Khouri, F. 1985. *The Arab-Israeli Dilemma*, 356–366.
Kosut, H., ed. 1968. *Israel and the Arabs: The June 1967 War*, 171–199.
O'Neill, B. 1978. *Armed Struggle in Palestine.*
Snow, P. 1972. *Hussein: A Biography*, 194–220.
Stephens, R. 1972. *Nasser: A Political Biography.*
Whetten, L. 1974. *The Canal War*, 39–128.

Israel

Alon, H. 1980. *Countering Palestinian Terrorism in Israel*, 41–81.
Bar-Siman-Tov, Y. 1980. *The Israeli-Egyptian War of Attrition.*
Bar-Siman-Tov, Y. 1987. *Israel, the Superpowers, and the War in the Middle East*, 147–185.
Blechman, B. 1972. "The Impact of Israel's Reprisals." *Journal of Conflict Resolution* 16 (June): 155–181.
Brecher, M. 1975. *Decisions in Israel's Foreign Policy*, 454–517.
Dupuy, T. 1978. *Elusive Victory*, 341–383.
Herzog, C. 1984. *The Arab-Israeli Wars*, 195–223.
Luttwak, E., and D. Horowitz. 1983. *The Israeli Army*, 299–336.
Rothenberg, G. 1979. *The Anatomy of the Israeli Army*, 165–176.
Sachar, H. 1976. *A History of Israel: From the Rise of Zionism*, 667–713.
Shimshoni, J. 1988. *Israel and Conventional Deterrence*, 123–211.
Sicker, M. 1989. *Between Hashemites and Zionists*, 130.

13.22 Lebanese War, 1968–continuing

Lebanon fought Israel during the Palestine War (13.1). Peace generally prevailed on their border for two decades thereafter except for Israeli retaliatory attacks upon Houle and Meiss aj Jebel in 1965 (13.20). Lebanon experienced civil war in 1958 (13.14) but enjoyed a fragile domestic truce until the 1970s. Beginning in the mid-1960s the Palestine Liberation Organization (PLO) established major bases within Lebanon from it raided Israel. This development foreshadowed heightened conflict with Israel starting in 1968 and renewed civil warfare in the 1970s.

Israeli artillery shelled the Houle area beginning in May 1968. On December 28, 1968, Israeli commandos destroyed aircraft at the Beirut airport after a Palestinian attack at the Athens airport two days before. For the next twenty years, Israeli conducted air, artillery, and commando attacks and occasional ground offensives against Lebanese territory at least every few months. In May 1970 and again in February 1972, Israeli armored units swept southern Lebanon in efforts to destroy PLO bases. Lebanon generally refrained from direct counteraction against Israel except for brief artillery barrages in January 1969 and again in January 1975.

Civil warfare returned to Lebanon in April 1975 when Phalange party militia, representing primarily Lebanese Maronites, attacked Palestinians within Beirut. Fighting soon spread among other factions and the Lebanese Army proved ineffective in containing violence. In March 1976 Moslem army officers attempted to overthrow President Sulaiman Franjiyah. Syria, united with Lebanon until 1946 and having intervened previously in 1949 (13.2) and 1963 (13.19) committed large army units April 9, 1976, upon Franjiyah's request. Syria occupied part of eastern Lebanon and Beirut by the beginning of June against Palestinian and other radical resistance. Libya, Sudan, and Saudi Arabia deployed military units within northern Lebanon outside the main arena of battle in late June at the behest of the Franjiyah government.

A cease-fire involving Syrian forces was arranged in October 1976. The Arab League authorized an Arab Deterrent Force (ADF). The ADF originally comprised troops previously deployed by Syria and other League members. Libya, which supported radical Lebanese causes, withdrew at the end of November 1976 and was replaced by the People's Democratic Republic of Yemen (South Yemen) and the United Arab Emirates the next month. South Yemen withdrew in January 1978. Other ADF contingents withdrew in early 1979, except for Syrian troops which remained into the 1990s.

Meanwhile, Palestinian terrorist raids continued against Israel and Israel repeatedly retaliated, primarily within southern Lebanon. In March 1978 Israel invaded as far north as the Litani River and installed private Lebanese militia under Saad Haddad within the border region before leaving in June.

The U.N. Security Council condemned Israel's invasion on March 19, 1978, and authorized a United Nations Interim Force in Lebanon (UNIFIL) to be deployed primarily within southern Lebanon. Contingents arrived from Iran, France and Norway during the last week of March 1978, from Nigeria and Senegal in April and from Fiji, Ireland and Nepal in May. UNIFIL remained into the 1990s although its composition changed several times. Other participating states included Finland, Ghana and the Netherlands. UNIFIL units suffered repeated assaults but generally refrained from offensive operations.

Israeli armored forces again swept briefly through southern Lebanon in April 1980. In June 1982 Israel invaded southern Lebanon in her largest operation to date, proceeding to the outskirts of Beirut. Israel bypassed UNIFIL positions, which put up no resistance, but routed Syrian, Palestinian and other Lebanese armed factions from most of southern Lebanon. Her air force also attacked Syria proper during the first week of the invasion. Israel demanded that paramilitary forces associated with the PLO leave Lebanon. The United States, France and Italy constituted a Multilateral Force in August 1982 which oversaw evacuation of several thousand Syrians and Palestinians from the Beirut area by the first week of September. PLO leaders repaired to Tunis, Tunisia. American, French and Italian forces retired temporarily but returned later that month to occupy key transit facilities including the Beirut airport after Phalange party militia massacred hundreds of Palestinian refugees at camps south of Beirut. Phalange party leader Amin Gemayel was shortly inaugurated as president of Lebanon.

The Multilateral Force, joined by the United Kingdom, remained throughout 1983. On October 23, 1983, suicide attacks upon French and U.S. military facilities resulted in the deaths of more than fifty French servicemen and more than 240 Americans. The United States immediately initiated air and naval rocket attacks upon Lebanese opposition enclaves. The Multilateral Force disbanded in early 1984; the last contingents representing the United States departed in March.

Israel remained within southern Lebanon until June 1985 against increasing resistance, including from Shi'a nationalists, supported in part by Iran. Israel reinstalled Haddad's militia near the border before leaving. She continued air and commando raids into the 1990s and during May 1988 briefly committed armored units to help strengthen Haddad's positions.

Lebanese fatalities during the 1970s and 1980s may have amounted to more than 100,000. More than 2,000 Syrian soldiers reportedly died, mostly in 1976 and 1982. Other contributors to the Arab Deterrent Force suffered no known fatalities. As many as 800 Israeli military personnel were killed, prmarily during the invasion in 1982 and the subsequent occupation. The United States suffered more than 260 fatalities. Approximately ninety French soldiers died. One Italian soldier assigned to the Multilateral Forces was killed, but the United Kingdom suffered no fatal losses. Most UNIFIL contingents suffered some fatal losses by 1989, including almost 20 Fijians.

General

Brecher, M., J. Wilkenfeld, and S. Moser. 1988. *Crises in the Twentieth Century,* 1: 285–286, 313–314, 319, 328–331.

Cordesman, A., and A. Wagner. 1990. The Lessons of Modern War. 1: 117–348.

Day, A., ed. 1987. *Border and Territorial Disputes,* 197–226.

Laffin, J. 1986. *War Annual 1,* 92–99.

Laffin, J. 1987. *War Annual 2,* 135–144.

Laffin, J. 1989. *The World in Conflict 1989: War Annual 3,* 154–161.

Small, M., and J. Singer. 1982. *Resort to Arms,* 232.

Israel

Alon, H. 1980. *Countering Palestinian Terrorism in Israel,* 78–81.

Blechman, B. 1972. "The Impact of Israel's Reprisals." *Journal of Conflict Resolution* 16 (June): 155–181.

Cordesman, A. 1987. *The Arab-Israeli Military Balance and the Art of Operations,* 54–90.

Dupuy, T. 1986. *Flawed Victory.*

Evron, Y. 1987. *War and Intervention in Lebanon.*

Gabriel, R. 1984. *Operation Peace for Galilee.*

Haddad, W. 1985. "Israeli Occupation Policy in Lebanon, the West Bank, and Gaza." In *The Regionalization of Warfare,* ed. J. Brown and W. Snyder, 96–116.

Herzog, C. 1984. *The Arab-Israeli Wars,* 339–369.

Luttwak, E., and D. Horowitz. 1983. *The Israeli Army,* 310–313.

Posner, S. 1987. *Israel Undercover.*

Rothenberg, G. 1979. *The Anatomy of the Israeli Army,* 168–169, 245–247.

Sachar, H. 1987. *A History of Israel: From the Aftermath of the Yom Kippur War.*

Safran, N. 1985. *Saudi Arabia: The Ceaseless Quest for Security,* 245–251, 277–278.

Schiff, Z., and E. Yaari. 1984. *Israel's Lebanon War.*

Yaniv, A. 1987. *Dilemmas of Security.*

Lebanon

Cobban, H. 1985. *The Making of Modern Lebanon.*

Deeb, M. 1980. *The Lebanese Civil War.*

Hamizrachi, B. 1988. *The Emergence of the South Lebanon Security Belt.*

Hof, F. 1985. *Galilee Divided,* 71–116.

Khalidi, W. 1979. *Conflict and Violence in Lebanon.*

Khouri, F. 1985. *The Arab-Israeli Dilemma,* 386–389, 405–406, 422–467.

Meo, L. 1977. "The War in Lebanon." In *Ethnic Conflict in International Relations,* ed. A. Suhrke and L. Nobel, 93–126.

Rabinovich, I. 1985. *The War for Lebanon, 1970–1985.*

Salibi, K. 1976. *Crossroads to Civil War.*
Whetten, L. 1979. "The Military Dimension." In *Lebanon in Crisis*, ed. P. Haley and L. Snider, 75–90.

Palestine Liberation Organization

Becker, J. 1984. *The PLO.*
Cooley, J. 1979. "The Palestinians." In *Lebanon in Crisis*, ed. P. E. Haley and L. Snider, 21–54.
Hart, A. 1989. *Arafat, a Political Biography*, 337–474.
Khalidi, R. 1986. *Under Siege.*
O'Neill, B. 1978. *Armed Struggle in Palestine.*
Quandt, W., F. Jabber, and A. Lesch. 1973. *The Politics of Palestinian Nationalism*, 188–194.

Syria

Abd-Allah, U. 1983. *The Islamic Struggle in Syria*, 68–80.
Dawisha, A. 1980. *Syria and the Lebanese Crisis.*
Pogany, I. 1987. *The Arab League and Peacekeeping in the Lebanon.*
Rabinovich, I. 1986. "The Changing Prism." In *Syria under Assad*, ed. M. Maoz and A. Yaniv, 179–190.
Weinberger, N. 1986. *Syrian Intervention in Lebanon.*

United Nations

Pelcovits, N. 1984. *Peacekeeping on Arab-Israeli Fronts.*
Rikhye, I. 1984. *The Theory and Practice of Peacekeeping*, 134–136, 100–113.
Skogmo, B. 1989. *UNIFIL: International Peacekeeping in Lebanon, 1978–1988.*
Thakur, R. 1987. *International Peacekeeping in Lebanon.*
United Nations Department of Public Information. 1985. *The Blue Helmets*, 108–156.

United States

Frank, B. 1987. *U.S. Marines in Lebanon 1982-1984.*
Hammel, E. 1985. *The Root: The Marines in Beirut.*
Tanter, R. 1990. *Who's at the Helm?*

13.23 PLO-Jordanian War, 1970

Jordan lost control of the West Bank of the Jordan River during the Six Day War in 1967 (13.18). She had captured the land during the Palestine War (13.1) and annexed it in 1949. Palestinian guerrillas associated with the Palestine Liberation Organization (PLO) used

Jordanian territory as base to attack the Israeli-occupied West Bank during the War of Attrition (13.21). Jordan's government of King Hussein ibn Talal attempted to suppress the PLO during spring and summer 1970 at the same time that it reduced direct hostilities with Israel.

Palestinians attempted to assassinate King Hussein on September 1, 1970. On September 16 Hussein's government demanded that guerrillas surrender their arms; PLO leader Yassir Arafat, apparently encouraged by Syria, called for Hussein's overthrow. The Jordanian Legion attacked Palestinians near Amman on September 17. On September 19 three brigades of Syrian infantry and armor intervened on behalf of the PLO. Small Jordanian units raided Syria the next day. Iraqi troops stationed within Jordan remained neutral. Syria's expeditionary force, repulsed by Jordanian forces, withdrew by September 23. On September 27, 1970, Yassir Arafat agreed to remove Palestinian forces from urban areas of Jordan. An Arab Observer Cease-Fire Mission representing the Arab League arrived September 30 to oversee withdrawals. 1,000 to 2,000 persons are believed to have died during September fighting, including approximately 100 Syrian soldiers. No Jordanian fatalities are reported within Syria.

Bailey, C. 1984. *Jordan's Palestinian Challenge*, 49–59.
Becker, J. 1984. *The PLO*, 74–77.
Brecher, M., J. Wilkenfeld, and S. Moser. 1988. *Crises in the Twentieth Century*, 1: 292–293.
Brown, N. 1971. "Jordanian Civil War." *Military Review* 51 (September): 38–58.
Butterworth, R. 1976. *Managing Interstate Conflict*, 445–448.
Cooley, J. 1973. *Green March, Black September*, 87–132.
Hart, A. 1989. *Arafat, a Political Biography*, 284–336.
Nevo, J. 1986. "Syria and Jordan." In *Syria under Assad*, ed. M. Maoz and A. Yaniv, 140–156.
O'Neill, B. 1978. *Armed Struggle in Palestine*, 139–144.
Petran, T. 1972. *Syria*, 247–248.
Quandt, W., F. Jabber, and A. Lesch. 1973. *The Politics of Palestinian Nationalism*, 124–128, 195–211.
Quandt, W. 1978. "Lebanon, 1958, and Jordan, 1970." In *Force Without War*, by B. Blechman and S. Kaplan, 222–288.
Sicker, M. 1989. *Between Hashemites and Zionists*, 133–138.
Small, M., and J. Singer. 1982. *Resort to Arms*, 231.
Snow, P. 1972. *Hussein: A Biography*, 203–236.

13.24 Suez Canal Incidents, 1971

Israel and Egypt confronted one another from military positions on opposite sides of the Suez Canal after the Six Day War in 1967 (13.18).

They occupied the same positions following the cease-fire terminating the War of Attrition in August 1970 (13.21). Numerous minor incidents involving small arms and antiaircraft fire occurred during the following year as did also two potentially more serious actions in 1971. On March 29, 1971, Egyptian artillery fired upon Israeli positions without provoking like response. On September 18 Israeli artillery attacked Egyptian positions without provoking comparable Egyptian retaliation. No fatalities are reported during the March or September incidents.

Butterworth, R. 1976. *Managing Interstate Conflict*, 422–424.
Whetten, L. 1974. *The Canal War*, 216.
New York Times 9/19/71, 1:8.

13.25 PLO Suppression, 1971

Palestine Liberation Organization (PLO) leader Yassir Arafat agreed in September 1970 to withdraw Palestinian guerrilla forces from urban areas of Jordan following a bloody war with the Jordanian Legion (13.21). Implementation of the agreement progressed slowly and was accompanied by numerous incidents in late 1970 and early 1971, especially within northern Jordan. In early July 1971 the Jordanian Legion attacked Palestinian guerrilla bases within northern Jordan. Most remaining guerrillas were forced to withdraw to Syria by midmonth. On July 19, the government announced that all guerrilla bases within Jordan had been destroyed. Palestinian guerrillas continued to attack government positions from sanctuaries within Syria. Jordanian artillery retaliated against Syrian territory during late July and early August. On August 11 Jordanian commandos attacked PLO bases within Syria. Palestinian infiltration abated and in September Jordan and Syria, encouraged by Egypt, restored diplomatic relations severed the previous year. No Jordanian fatalities are reported within Syria.

Bailey, C. 1984. *Jordan's Palestinian Challenge*, 59–62.
Butterworth, R. 1976. *Managing Interstate Conflict*, 444–448.
Cooley, J. 1973. *Green March, Black September*, 87–132.
Hart, A. 1989. *Arafat, a Political Biography*, 274–336.
Nevo, J. 1986. "Syria and Jordan." In *Syria under Assad*, ed. M. Maoz and A. Yaniv, 140–156.
O'Neill, B. 1978. *Armed Struggle in Palestine*, 144–150.
Quandt, W., F. Jabber, and A. Lesch. 1973. *The Politics of Palestinian Nationalism*, 128–145, 195–211.
Snow, P. 1972. *Hussein: A Biography*, 237–245.

13.26 Golan Conflict, 1972–1973

Israel captured the Golan Heights from Syria during the Six Day War in 1967 (13.18) and retained control after the War of Attrition (13.21). Conflict resumed in 1972. Some Palestinian guerrillas driven out of Jordan in 1970 and 1971 (13.23, 13.25) attacked Israel from Syria. Israel retaliated by air attacks upon Syria in early March 1972. Syrian aircraft simultaneously attacked Israeli territory. Further Israeli air raids occurred in early September and intermittently until early January 1973. In addition, Israeli and Syrian artillery dueled repeatedly along the Golan Heights from November 1972 until January 1973. A half-dozen Syrian soldiers died as did a similar number of Israeli military personnel.

Butterworth, R. 1976. *Managing Interstate Conflict*, 422–424.
Hart, A. 1989. *Arafat, a Political Biography*, 352–353.
Herzog, C. 1975. *The War of Atonement, October 1973*, 57–60.
O'Neill, B. 1978. *Armed Struggle in Palestine*, 176.

13.27 Yom Kippur War, 1973–1974

Israel captured the Sinai Peninsula from Egypt, the Golan Heights from Syria, and the West Bank from Jordan during the Six Day War in 1967 (13.18). She retained all these disputed territories during the War of Attrition from 1967 to 1970 (13.21). Additional small military engagements involved Israel and Egypt in 1971 (13.24) and Israel and Syria in 1972–1973 (13.26).

On Yom Kippur, October 6, 1973, Egypt launched a major ground offensive across the Suez Canal into Israeli-occupied Sinai. Syria mounted a major offensive against Israeli positions in the Golan Heights the same day. Israel immediately retaliated by air attacks against Egyptian and Syrian troop concentrations and airfields. Iraqi aircraft joined fighting on the Egyptian front two days later. The attackers initially enjoyed advantage on both fronts but both offensives soon stalled. An Israeli counteroffensive pushed Syrian troops off the Golan Heights and by October 11 penetrated undisputed Syrian territory. Moroccan and Kuwaiti troops immediately came to Syria's support as did army units from Saudi Arabia October 12 and Jordan October 13.

Egypt reinforced its Sinai offensive October 14, prompting Israel to redirect forces from the Syrian front. On October 16 Israel began a counteroffensive on Egypt's side of the Suez Canal. Kuwaiti troops assisted immediately in defense of Egyptian territory. Algerian air and ground forces joined battle October 17 as did Tunisian troops October 18. By October 20 Israel established a major presence on the western bank of the canal and surrounded part of the Egyptian Army on the east bank.

The U.N. Security Council, urged by both the United States and the Soviet Union, called for cessation of hostilities. Participants accepted a formal cease-fire on October 22 but serious fighting continued on the Syrian front until October 24 and on the Egyptian front until October 28. Additional maneuvers involving Egyptian and Israeli ground forces continued until final disengagement in February 1974. Israeli troops withdrew from Syria to the 1967 line in June 1974.

The Yom Kippur War cost more than 10,000 soldiers' lives, two-thirds of them on foreign territory. Total fatalities, including losses in home defense, included 5,000 Egyptian troops, nearly 3,000 Israeli, 3,000 Syrian soldiers, 200 Iraqi and more than 100 military personnel representing other Arab states.

General

Bailey, S. 1990. *Four Arab-Israeli Wars and the Peace Process*, 285–393.

Brecher, M., J. Wilkenfeld, and S. Moser. 1988. *Crises in the Twentieth Century*, 1: 302–303.

Butterworth, R. 1976. *Managing Interstate Conflict*, 468–470.

Cordesman, A., and A. Wagner. 1990. The Lessons of Modern War. 1: 14–116.

Day, A., ed. 1987. *Border and Territorial Disputes*, 197–226.

Dupuy, R., and T. Dupuy. 1986. *The Encyclopedia of Military History*, 1235–1240.

Keegan, J., ed. 1983. *World Armies*, 561–571.

Small, M., and J. Singer. 1982. *Resort to Arms*, 94.

Arab States

Al-Ayoubi, Al-H. 1975. "The Strategies of the Fourth Campaign." In *Middle East Crucible*, ed. N. Aruri, 65–96.

El-Badri, H., T. El-Magdoub, and M. Zohdy. 1973. *The Ramadan War.*

Cordesman, A. 1987. *The Arab-Israeli Military Balance and the Art of Operations*, 37–53.

Haykal, M. 1975. *The Road to Ramadan.*

Insight Team of the London Sunday Times. 1974. *The Yom Kippur War.*

Khalidi, A. 1975. "The Military Balance, 1967–1973." In *Middle East Crucible*, ed. N. Aruri, 21–63.

Khouri, F. 1985. *The Arab-Israeli Dilemma*, 370–371.

O'Neill, B. 1978. *Armed Struggle in Palestine.*

Shazly, S. el. 1980. *The Crossing of the Suez.*

Israel

Barker, A. 1980. *Arab-Israeli Wars*, 109–172.

Bar-Siman-Tov, Y. 1987. *Israel, the Superpowers, and the War in the Middle East*, 187–237.

Brecher, M., with B. Geist. 1980. *Decisions in Crisis*.

Dayan, M. 1976. *Story of My Life*, 459–539.

Dupuy, T. 1978. *Elusive Victory*, 385–622.

Flint, R., P. Kozumplik, and T. Waraksa. 1987. *The Arab-Israeli Wars, the Chinese Civil War, and the Korean War*, 28.

Herzog, C. 1975. *The War of Atonement, October 1973*.

Laqueur, W. 1974. *Confrontation: The Middle East and World Politics*.

O'Ballance, E. 1978. *No Victor, No Vanquished: The Yom Kippur War*.

Rothenberg, G. 1979. *The Anatomy of the Israeli Army*, 177–202.

Sachar, H. 1976. *A History of Israel: From the Rise of Zionism*, 740–835.

Sobel, L., ed. 1980. *Peace-Making in the Middle East*, 7–33.

Whetten, L. 1974. *The Canal War*, 233–300.

14

Southern Arabia

Political instability within Southern Arabia contributed to frequent international armed conflict from the 1940s through the 1970s. The United Kingdom intervened within her South Arabian protectorates in 1947–1950 (14.1) and again in 1953–1959 (14.3) as well as within Aden in 1947 (14.2) and within Oman during the late 1950s (14.5). She also helped to seize the Buraimi Oasis from Saudi Arabia in 1955 (14.4). The Yemen-Aden War of the 1960s (14.6) represented the region's most serious conflict; at the end the United Kingdom abandoned Aden and the South Arabian protectorates in favor of the new state of South Yemen. The Dhofar rebellion followed within Oman (14.9). Conflict among North Yemen, South Yemen and Saudi Arabia punctuated the period from 1969 to 1979 (14.7, 14.8, 14.10, 14.11, 14.12, 14.13).

14.1 South Arabian Disorders, 1947–1950

The United Kingdom acquired Aden Protectorates within South Arabia (People's Democratic Republic of Yemen) through agreements signed with individual tribal leaders after she colonized the port of Aden in 1839. Protectorates were administered indirectly and many were never fully pacified. Local levies and, after World War I, the Royal Air Force (RAF) assumed primary responsibility for maintaining order within the hinterlands. Outbreaks of intertribal violence prompted RAF bombing missions beginning in April 1947. Intermittent air strikes against various tribes continued until August 1950. Some incidents involved the Arab Republic of Yemen. Yemen and the United Kingdom disputed the culturally and geographically indistinct South Arabian border after World War II. In 1949 and 1950 the RAF attacked Yemeni within territory claimed part of Aden Beihan. In March 1949 the United Kingdom also strafed positions clearly inside Yemen. One British pilot is known killed.

Butterworth, R. 1976. *Managing Interstate Conflict*, 113–115.
Gavin, R. 1975. *Aden Under British Rule*, 336.
Ingrams, W. 1964. *The Yemen: Imams, Rulers and Revolutions*, 78–83.
Lee, D. 1980. *Flight from the Middle East*, 36–40.
O'Ballance, E. 1971. *The War in the Yemen*, 49–50.
Peterson, J. 1986. *Defending Arabia*, 78–83.
Reilly, B. 1960. *Aden and the Yemen*, 20–35.

14.2 Aden Riots, 1947

The United Kingdom assumed control of the port of Aden in 1839 and later annexed it to the Crown. She administered the Aden colony separately from the Aden protectorates of South Arabia, which she later acquired to surrounded the colony. Unlike the often-troubled protectorates, Aden colony experienced little domestic turmoil during the early twentieth century until the first days of December 1947 when rioting broke out between Arabs and Jews. Royal Marines and regular British troops from Egypt were called out December 5 and restored order within a few days. 122 persons died during the December unrest, a majority of them Jews, but no regular British military personnel were killed.

Blaxland, G. 1971. *The Regiments Depart*, 422.
Gavin, R. 1975. *Aden Under British Rule*, 323.
Lee, D. 1980. *Flight from the Middle East*, 39.

14.3 South Arabian Revolt, 1953–1959

The United Kingdom intervened within her Aden Protectorates of South Arabia (People's Democratic Republic of Yemen) during the 1947–1950 disturbances (14.1). The Arab Republic of Yemen claimed sovereignty over many of the protectorates and encouraged renewed intertribal fighting in 1952. The Royal Air Force (RAF) resumed bombing and strafing missions within South Arabia in May 1953. Raiding parties attacked South Arabia out of the Arab Republic of Yemen and Yemeni soldiers participated in some such attacks during 1954. Tribal auxiliaries representing the Aden Protectorate Levies entered Yemen occasionally while pursuing dissidents. In at least one instance in March 1955 a few RAF personnel accompanied Levies into Yemen.

The United Kingdom committed regular army in mid-June 1955 following serious incidents within the sultanate of Upper Aulaqi near the Yemeni border. Various British Army units brought in from abroad undertook sporadic offensives within the protectorates during the next few years. The RAF extended air operations into Yemen during 1956–1958 at the same time that small groups of Yemeni troops openly participated in cross-border raids into South Arabia. A Yemeni attack upon a South Arabian border fort in January 1957 provoked British Army and auxiliary pursuit to Yemen's military barracks at Qataba. Dissident activity declined during 1958 except among the Bubakr bin Farid tribe in the Upper Aulaqi protectorate. The British Army ceased overt operations in February 1959 and the RAF suspended action by the end of the year. Protectorate auxiliaries continued pacification efforts in 1960. Approximately forty British soldiers and airmen were killed during the South Arabian Revolt. A similar number of Yemeni soldiers died within South Arabia.

Bidwell, R. 1983. *The Two Yemens*, 95–103.
Blaxland, G. 1971. *The Regiments Depart*, 421–428.
Butterworth, R. 1976. *Managing Interstate Conflict*, 113–115.
Gavin, R. 1975. *Aden Under British Rule*, 325–342.
Halliday, F. 1974. *Arabia without Sultans*, 190–201.
Ingrams, W. 1964. *The Yemen: Imams, Rulers and Revolutions*, 84–103.
Lee, D. 1980. *Flight from the Middle East*, 139–155, 162–164.
Little, T. 1968. *South Arabia: Arena of Conflict*, 45–59.
Peterson, J. 1986. *Defending Arabia*, 78–83.
Reilly, B. 1960. *Aden and the Yemen*, 36–61.

14.4 Buraimi Oasis Crisis, 1955

Desert borders among Saudi Arabia, the Sultanate of Muscat and Oman (Oman) and British-protected Trucial Oman (United Arab Emirates) were not fully demarcated when these territories became recognized as distinct political entities during the nineteenth and early twentieth centuries. Saudi Arabia, Oman and the trucial state of Abu Dhabi disputed control of small villages representing the Buraimi Oasis, especially after oil exploration began in the region. Saudi Arabia occupied the oasis in 1952 with the assistance of armed irregulars. Oman arrayed tribal forces near Buraimi at the request of the Sheik of Abu Dhabi but did not counterattack. A standstill agreement was obtained on October 26, 1952. The issue was submitted to formal arbitration in 1954 and Saudi Arabia and Oman withdrew except for small police detachments. Arbitration broke down in 1955, due in part to Omani protests against Saudi transfers of arms and money, partly through Buraimi, to support of Imam Ghalib bin Ali's bid for power within Oman (14.5). On October 26, 1955, elements of the Trucial Oman Scouts, a regular military formation commanded by British officers, and of the Sultan of Muscat and Oman's personal guard forcibly occupied Buraimi. Two Scouts died as did several civilians. No Omani fatalities are reported.

Abdullah, M. 1978. *The United Arab Emirates*, 204–210.
Allfree, P. 1967. *Warlords of Oman*, 11–51.
Blaxland, G. 1971. *The Regiments Depart*, 352–353.
Butterworth, R. 1976. *Managing Interstate Conflict*, 127–131.
Halliday, F. 1974. *Arabia without Sultans*, 292–295.
Hawley, D. 1970. *The Trucial States*, 186–194.
Heard-Bey, F. 1982. *From Trucial States to United Arab Emirates*, 302–314.
Kelly, J. 1964. *Eastern Arabian Frontiers*, 204–206.
Kelly, J. 1980. *Arabia, the Gulf and the West*, 60–74.
Landen, R. 1967. *Oman Since 1856*, 414–420.
Lee, D. 1980. *Flight from the Middle East*, 110–122.
Litwak, R. 1981. *Sources of Inter-State Conflict*, 52–55.
Phillips, W. 1967. *Oman: A History*, 163–185.

14.5 Imam's Rebellion, 1957–1959

The Sultan of Muscat and Oman (Oman) attempted to extend central control throughout Omani territory during the mid-1950s, including against the Imamate of Oman with which the Sultan traditionally shared power. The Sultan's efforts conflicted with aspirations of Ghalib bin Ali who claimed the Imamate in 1954 upon death of the previously acknowledged Imam. Ghalib asserted independence and applied unsuccessfully for membership within the Arab League. Saudi Arabia supplied him arms and money, transferred in part through Buraimi Oasis. Sultan's forces seized Buraimi with British help in November 1955 (14.4) and also established a presence within Nizwa and other towns near the Saudi border. An unofficial truce followed.

Ghalib temporarily resigned the Imamate. His younger brother, Talib, fled to Saudi Arabia, organized an irregular military force, and invaded Oman in early 1957. Ghalib reclaimed the Imamate in June. The Sultan appealed to the United Kingdom for help and the Royal Air Force began attacks upon the Imam's position within Oman in late July 1957. Trucial Oman Scouts and a few British Army units drawn from Aden deployed in August and drove the Imam into hiding within the Jebel Akhdar massif.

The United Kingdom withdrew regular ground forces in mid-August 1957 but continued RAF sorties against rebel positions. She also helped to reorganize the Sultan's Armed Forces (SAF) under contract officers seconded from the British Army. The SAF contained the Imam but failed to eradicate his forces. In November 1958 regular British troops returned and attacked rebel strongholds within the Jebel. RAF and

British Army forces continued to assist the SAF until February 1959. The SAF dealt with residual resistance thereafter. Regular British forces suffered seven fatalities during the Imam's rebellion, including five soldiers killed during 1958–1959.

Allfree, P. 1967. *Warlords of Oman.*
Blaxland, G. 1971. *The Regiments Depart,* 354–358.
Butterworth, R. 1976. *Managing Interstate Conflict,* 184–186.
Cordesman, A. 1984. *The Gulf and the Search for Strategic Stability,* 428–431.
Dewar, M. 1984. *Brush Fire Wars,* 83–93.
Halliday, F. 1974. *Arabia without Sultans,* 294–297.
Kelly, J. 1972. "A Prevalence of Furies." In *The Arabian Peninsula,* ed. D. Hopwood, 107–141.
Kelly, J. 1980. *Arabia, the Gulf and the West,* 104–117.
Landen, R. 1967. *Oman Since 1856,* 414–422.
Lee, D. 1980. *Flight from the Middle East,* 122–136.
Peterson, J. 1986. *Defending Arabia,* 83–88.
Phillips, W. 1967. *Oman: A History,* 186–222.
Peterson, J. 1978. *Oman in the Twentieth Century,* 180–187.

14.6 Yemen-Aden War, 1961–1967

Turmoil with the United Kingdom's Aden Protectorates of South Arabia (VPeople's Democratic Republic of Yemen) surrounding Aden colony led to British military intervention in 1947–1950 (14.1) and again in 1953–1959 (14.3). The Arab Republic of Yemen also disputed control of the area and encouraged local rebellion. The United Kingdom resumed air attacks within the Hadhramaut in July 1961 after a tribal assault upon protectorate levies. She also conducted air actions within Western protectorates in late 1961 and early 1962. Trouble spread after civil war broke out within neighboring Yemen in September 1962.

Yemen (Arab Republic of Yemen) was nominally part of the Ottoman Empire from 1517 although ruling imam's of the Zaidi sect enjoyed substantial local autonomy. Yemen became formally independent in 1918, by which time the United Kingdom had established protectorates among southern Zaidi domains. In February 1948 Imam Yahya was assassinated and a rival, Abdulla al Wazir, seized power. A brief civil war broke out in which Yahya's sons prevailed and Saif al Islam Ahmad became Imam in March 1948. Yemen joined the Union of Arab States in March 1958 associated with the United Arab Republic of Egypt and Syria under direction of Gamal Abdel Nasser. Imam Ahmad died September 18, 1962. His son Mohammed al-Badr claimed power. On September 26, 1962, army officers led by Colonel Abdullah Sallal staged a coup d'etat and declared a republic with apparent encouragement from Egypt. Badr and his family escaped to northern Yemen. Civil war ensued between Royalist forces loyal to the Imamate in control of the north and the Republican government which controlled the south. Egyptian troops aided Republicans beginning in early October 1962 and remained until 1967. Jordan and Saudi Arabia provided arms, money and irregular personnel to help support the Royalists. Egypt periodically attacked Saudi territory by air from November 1962 until May 1967. The United Nations Observation Mission in Yemen (UNYOM) arrived in July 1963 following one of many cease-fires but left by September 1964.

Meanwhile, the United Kingdom refused to recognize Yemen's Republican government. Sallal's regime openly encouraged revolt within the Aden protectorates, which it referred to as the "occupied south," and, with Egypt, supported the National Front for Liberation of South Yemen (FLOSY) based in Yemen. FLOSY irregulars intruded frequently and Yemeni government forces also sporadically attacked South Arabian positions from October 1962. Republican forces also attempted to occupy disputed border valleys in spring 1963 until forced to withdraw. The United Kingdom relied primarily upon the Royal Air Force (RAF) and auxiliary protectorate levies to maintain border security. The RAF generally confined activity south of the Yemeni border except during a retaliatory raid in March 1964.

The United Kingdom formally united her colony at Aden port with the Aden protectorates to form the South Arabian Federation under British administration in January 1963. Major rebellion erupted within the Radfan, midway between Aden port and the Yemeni border in 1964. British Royal Marines and regular Army joined the struggle beginning April 30, 1964. Violence spread to Aden colony and regular British soldiers took the field there beginning in October 1965.

Within Yemen, Republican and Egyptian forces confined Royalists to northern and eastern territory near the Saudi border by 1964 but were unable to eradicate opposition. Egyptian troops began to withdraw in 1965–1966. In August 1967, shortly after the Six Day War with Israel (13.8), Saudi Arabia and Egypt agreed to cease support of fighting factions. Egyptian troops withdrew fully by October 16, 1967. Royalists continued to occupy a few positions but no longer posed a serious threat.

Fighting within South Arabia also ended in 1967. In February 1966 the United Kingdom announced intention to withdraw military forces from east of Suez. South Arabian nationalists split between FLOSY, based within Yemen, and the more radical National Liberation Front (NLF), based within South Arabia. British troops withdrew to Aden colony at the end of June 1967 after a final offensive that included artillery exchanges on the Yemen-South Arabian border. British air actions ceased within the protectorates in early September. The NLF routed both FLOSY and protectorate levies representing South Arabia's Federal Regular Army and captured nearly all protectorates by October. British forces abandoned all of South Arabia on November 29, 1967. The NLF proclaimed the Southern Yemen People's Republic (later renamed the People's Democratic Republic of Yemen) the next day.

Civil warfare within Yemen is estimated to have killed 100,000 persons, primarily civilians. Death toll within South Arabia probably amounted only to less than 1,000. Approximately 1,000 Egyptian troops died within Yemen. The United Kingdom suffered ninety military fatalities within South Arabia.

General

Brecher, M., J. Wilkenfeld, and S. Moser. 1988. *Crises in the Twentieth Century*, 1: 259–260, 270, 273, 277–278.
Butterworth, R. 1976. *Managing Interstate Conflict*, 113–115, 341–344, 351–355.
Small, M., and J. Singer. 1982. *Resort to Arms*, 230.

South Arabia

Blaxland, G. 1971. *The Regiments Depart*, 429–464.
Cordesman, A. 1984. *The Gulf and the Search for Strategic Stability*, 455–467.
Dewar, M. 1984. *Brush Fire Wars*, 113–136.
Gavin, R. 1975. *Aden Under British Rule*, 318–350.
Halliday, F. 1974. *Arabia without Sultans*, 113–142.
Kelly, J. 1980. *Arabia, the Gulf and the West*, 1–46.
Kostiner, J. 1984. *The Struggle for South Yemen*.
Lackner, H. 1985. *P.D.R. Yemen: Outpost of Socialist Development*, 26–50.
Lee, D. 1980. *Flight from the Middle East*, 196–231.
Little, T. 1968. *South Arabia: Arena of Conflict*, 100–186.
Martin, L. 1984. *The Unstable Gulf*, 55, 58–59.
Paget, J. 1969. *Last Post; Aden 1964–67*.
Peterson, J. 1986. *Defending Arabia*, 92–98.

Yemen

Babeeb, S. 1986. *The Saudi-Egyptian Conflict Over North Yemen*.
Bidwell, R. 1983. *The Two Yemens*, 130–261.
Dawisha, A. 1975. "Intervention in Yemen." *Middle East Journal* 29 (Winter): 47–64.
Gause, F. 1990. *Saudi-Yemeni Relations*, 57–74.
Hasou, T. 1985. *The Struggle for the Arab World*, 136–161.
Hofstadter, D. 1973. *Egypt and Nasser*, 2: 171–213.
Ingrams, W. 1964. *The Yemen: Imams, Rulers and Revolutions*, 117–151.

O'Ballance, E. 1971. *The War in the Yemen.*
Safran, N. 1985. *Saudi Arabia: The Ceaseless Quest for Security,* 96–97, 99, 121, 199–201.
Schmidt, D. 1968. *Yemen: The Unknown War.*
Schmidt, D. 1972. "The Civil War in Yemen." In *The International Regulation of Civil Wars,* ed. E. Luard, 125–147.
Stephens, R. 1972. *Nasser: A Political Biography,* 378–431.
Stookey, R. 1978. *Yemen: The Politics of the Yemen Arab Republic,* 225–249.
Wenner, M. 1967. *Modern Yemen, 1918–1966,* 193–228.

14.7 Najran Air Raids, 1969–1970

Saudi Arabia supported Royalists seeking to restore the Imamate within the Arab Republic of Yemen during major warfare until 1967 (14.6). Subsequently, Royalists continued to resist the Republican government on a smaller scale from small areas held near the Saudi Arabian border. In September 1969 government troops captured Sada, previously held by Royalists. Royalists, supplied by Saudi Arabia, attempted to recapture the town in November. Yemeni aircraft attacked Saudi territory during fighting that followed that month and continued to do so sporadically until October 1970, primarily near Najran. On at least one occasion in January 1970 Saudi aircraft reportedly attacked Yemeni territory. No regular military fatalities are reported during cross-border raids.

ARR: Arab Report and Record (1970): 50.
Gause, F. 1990. *Saudi-Yemeni Relations,* 75–92.

14.8 Al-Wadiah Battle, 1969

The border between Saudi Arabia, which achieved unified status only in 1932, and Britain's Aden Protectorates of South Arabia was not clearly defined. South Arabia (South Yemen) experienced protracted civil war prior to independence in 1967 that included, at the end, violence between rival nationalist groups (14.6). The radical National Liberation Front established the People's Democratic Republic of Yemen (South Yemen) upon British withdrawal. Elements of the rival Front for the Liberation of Occupied South Yemen (FLOSY) fled to exile within neighboring Saudi Arabia and the Yemen Arab Republic. FLOSY exiles mounted repeated incursions into South Yemen during the next few years. On November 26, 1969, Regular South Yemeni forces conquered the disputed Saudi border oasis of Al-Wadiah. Saudi air and ground forces drove the invaders out by December 3, 1969, but stopped short of the South Yemen border. Reports of the battle disagree about its scale but it appears that South Yemen suffered 5–10 military fatalities and that Saudi Arabia suffered similar losses.

ARR: Arab Report and Record (1969): 492–493.
Bell, J. B. 1970. "South Yemen." *World Today* 26 (February): 76–82.
Bidwell, R. 1983. *The Two Yemens*, 242.
Butterworth, R. 1976. *Managing Interstate Conflict*, 434–436.
Cordesman, A. 1984. *The Gulf and the Search for Strategic Stability*, 137–140.
Gause, F. 1990. *Saudi-Yemeni Relations*, 88–89.
Halliday, F. 1974. *Arabia without Sultans*, 268.
Halliday, F. 1990. *Revolution and Foreign Policy*, 159–160.
Holden, D., and R. Johns. 1982. *The House of Saud*, 281–282.
Lackner, H. 1978. *A House Built on Sand*, 125.
Lackner, H. 1985. *P.D.R. Yemen: Outpost of Socialist Development*, 68.
Martin, L. 1984. *The Unstable Gulf*, 57.
Safran, N. 1985. *Saudi Arabia: The Ceaseless Quest for Security*, 129–130.

14.9 Dhofar Rebellion, 1970–1977

The United Kingdom intervened within independent Oman in 1957–1959 to help suppress the Imam's rebellion (14.5) which primarily involved conflict between traditional religious and secular authorities. In the early 1960s dissidents within the western province of Dhofar established links to foreign Arab nationalist groups, including within neighboring British-ruled South Arabia. Serious incidents between Omani government forces and resistance groups occurred as early as 1963. In June 1965 rebels attacked government installations throughout Dhofar. Several resistance factions, including the Dhofar Liberation Front (DLF) and the National Democratic Front for the Liberation of the Occupied Arabian Gulf (NDF), gained effective control of much of Dhofar by 1970. On June 11, 1970 Dhofari tribesmen attacked garrisons of the Sultan's Armed Forces within central Oman and also the British Royal Air Force base at Sallalah. Small units of British Special Air Services (SAS) counterinsurgency personnel helped to defeat the attacks. On July 23 Qabus Ibn Said deposed his father, Sultan Said bin Taimur, in a bloodless coup d'etat apparently encouraged by the United Kingdom. The United Kingdom promptly committed additional SAS units to assist combat operations of the Sultan's Armed Forces, which were largely officered by British contract personnel. Shortly after he took power, Sultan Qabus invited Dhofari rebels to join in an ambitious plan to promote Omani economic and social development. Some DLF elements did so. Other rebels, including most of the NDF, rejected the offer and in February 1972 formed the Popular Front for the Liberation of Oman and the Arabian Gulf (PFLOAG).

PFLOAG obtained sanctuary, arms and irregular military personnel from South Yemen (People's Democratic Republic of Yemen). Regular South Yemeni artillery sporadically attacked Omani government positions from across the border beginning in May 1972 and continued to do so for the next four years. The Omani government retaliated in early May 1972 by air strikes upon artillery positions and PFLOAG training bases within South Yemen. On May 24 an Omani commando team raided South Yemeni artillery positions near Hauf. In December 1973 Iran deployed large ground forces at the invitation of the Sultan and helped to drive the rebels out of most of Oman by the end of 1974. In January 1975 Jordan contributed infantry units assigned primarily to static defense until leaving in September that year.

PFLOAG was reduced to a few small pockets, primarily near the South Yemen border, by October 1975. On October 17, 1975, Iranian naval artillery and Omani aircraft attacked support facilities near Hauf within South Yemen. PFLOAG withdrew from the last towns under its control. Britain ceased direct support of the Sultan's Armed Forces. The Sultan declared the war over December 11, 1975. Small-scale resistance continued and South Yemeni artillery fired from time to time upon Oman as late as March 1976. Iranian troops continued patrols until departing at the end of January 1977. In March 1977 the United Kingdom withdrew her last SAS personnel and also abandoned bases at Sallalah and Masirah.

The Dhofar rebellion is believed to have cost between one and a few thousand lives. Iran alone lost as many as 500 troops. More than twenty British soldiers died. The People's Democratic Republic of Yemen sustained a half dozen or more fatalities among regular military personnel. No fatal casualties are reported among Jordanian troops.

Bidwell, R. 1983. *The Two Yemens*, 301.

Brecher, M., J. Wilkenfeld, and S. Moser. 1988. *Crises in the Twentieth Century*, 1: 304–305.

Butterworth, R. 1976. *Managing Interstate Conflict*, 367–369.

Cordesman, A. 1984. *The Gulf and the Search for Strategic Stability*, 431–439.

Cotrell, A. 1978. "Iran's Armed Forces Under the Pahlavi Dynasty." In *Iran under the Pahlavis*, ed. G. Lenczowski, 389–431.

Dewar, M. 1984. *Brush Fire Wars*, 165–179.

Halliday, F. 1974. *Arabia without Sultans*, 316–403.

Halliday, F. 1979. *Iran: Dictatorship and Development*, 271.

Halliday, F. 1990. *Revolution and Foreign Policy*, 142–147.

Keegan, J., ed. 1983. *World Armies*, 438–440, 666–671.

Kelly, J. 1980. *Arabia, the Gulf and the West*, 120–150.

Litwak, R. 1981. *Sources of Inter-State Conflict*, 73–77.

Martin, L. 1984. *The Unstable Gulf*, 60.

O'Neill, B. 1980. "Revolutionary War in Oman." In *Insurgency in the Modern World*, ed. B. O'Neill, W. Heaton, and D. Alberts, 213–233.
Peterson, J. 1978. *Oman in the Twentieth Century*, 187–199.
Peterson, J. 1986. *Defending Arabia*, 99–105.
Pimlott, J. 1985. "The British Army." In *Armed Forces and Modern Counter-Insurgency*, ed. I. Beckett and J. Pimlott, 16–45.
Price, D. 1975. *Oman: Insurgency and Development*.
Stookey, R. 1982. *South Yemen: Marxist Republic in Arabia*, 99.
Townsend, J. 1977. *Oman: The Making of a Modern State*, 95–111.

14.10 Yemeni Conflict, 1971–1972

The government of the Arab Republic of Yemen (North Yemen) effectively defeated Royalists seeking to restore the Imamate at end of civil war in 1967 (14.6). The National Liberation (NLF) defeated both British forces and the Front for the Liberation of Occupied South Yemen (FLOSY) to establish the People's Democratic Republic of Yemen (South Yemen) a few months later. Defeated FLOSY partisans retreated to Saudi Arabia and North Yemen. With Saudi Arabian financial support and North Yemeni tolerance, FLOSY exiles established positions of strength on both sides of the North Yemen-South Yemen border near Saudi Arabia and frequently attacked South Yemeni government positions during 1969–1971. North and South Yemen also disputed parts of their border, including Kamaran Island. Nevertheless, in November 1970, the two governments agreed to procedures toward unification.

In October 1971 the South Yemeni government began an offensive against dissidents upon its own territory and initiated small raids upon guerrilla camps within North Yemen. Exile attacks increased in 1972 out of both North Yemen and Saudi Arabia. North Yemeni army units intervened within South Yemen in support of exiles in late September 1972. At the beginning of October South Yemeni troops invaded border regions of North Yemen. Later that month North and South Yemen agreed to a cease-fire encouraged by Kuwait and other Arab League members. In November the two governments jointly proclaimed their intention to unite. Ten or more regular South Yemeni soldiers apparently died within North Yemen in 1971–1972 as did a similar number of North Yemeni troops within South Yemen.

Abir, M. 1974. *Oil, Power and Politics*, 109–113.
Bidwell, R. 1983. *The Two Yemens*, 255–261.
Brecher, M., J. Wilkenfeld, and S. Moser. 1988. *Crises in the Twentieth Century*, 1: 298–299.
Butterworth, R. 1976. *Managing Interstate Conflict*, 434–436.

Cordesman, A. 1984. *The Gulf and the Search for Strategic Stability*, 443–449.
El-Hakim, A. 1979. *The Middle Eastern States and the Law of the Sea*, 17–20.
Gause, F. 1990. *Saudi-Yemeni Relations*, 93–111.
Halliday, F. 1974. *Arabia without Sultans*, 268–269.
Halliday, F. 1990. *Revolution and Foreign Policy*, 116–117.
Ismael, T., and J. Ismael. 1986. *The People's Democratic Republic of Yemen*, 141–142.
Keegan, J., ed. 1983. *World Armies*, 659–671.
Lackner, H. 1978. *A House Built on Sand*, 125.
Lackner, H. 1985. *P.D.R. Yemen: Outpost of Socialist Development*, 68–70.
Litwak, R. 1981. *Sources of Inter-State Conflict*, 81–82.
Martin, L. 1984. *The Unstable Gulf*, 58.
Stookey, R. 1982. *South Yemen: Marxist Republic in Arabia*, 95.

14.11 Al-Wadiah Incident, 1973

Saudi Arabia and South Yemen (People's Democratic Republic of Yemen) battled at Al-Wadiah in 1969 in dispute over their border (14.8). Saudi Arabian arms and money also supported groups opposed to the National Liberation Front government which took over South Yemen from the British in 1967. Saudi-financed South Yemeni exiles contributed to border warfare involving North and South Yemen in 1971–1972 (14.10). Saudi Arabia continued to support dissidents in 1973 although less generously than she had during previous years. In March 1973, following incidents in the border area, South Yemeni aircraft strafed the Saudi post at Al-Wadiah. South Yemen publicly denied taking military action although her attack was amply demonstrated. No fatalities are reported.

ARR: Arab Report and Record (1973): 137.
Butterworth, R. 1976. *Managing Interstate Conflict*, 434–436.
Gause, F. 1990. *Saudi-Yemeni Relations*, 93–111.
Halliday, F. 1990. *Revolution and Foreign Policy*, 160.

14.12 Ismail's Coup, 1978

The National Liberation Front (NLF) established the People's Democratic Republic of Yemen upon British withdrawal from South Arabia (South Yemen) at the end of the Yemen–Aden War in 1967 (14.6). Conflict followed with neighbors, including with Saudi Arabia in 1969 and 1973 (14.8, 14.11) and with North Yemen (Arab Republic of Yemen) in 1971–1972 (14.10). Rival factions within the NLF vied for power during the 1970s. Abd al-Fattah Ismail, Secretary-General of the NLF, and Salim Rubayyi Ali, President of South Yemen, were personal rivals as well as spokesmen for differing foreign and domestic policies. Ismail generally advanced socialist principles and favored alignment with the Soviet Union. Ali tended to favor a pragmatic course, including accommodation with Saudi Arabia.

On June 24, 1978, President Ahmad al-Ghashmi of North Yemen was assassinated by an envoy from South Yemen. Ismail's faction, in control of the Politburo and Central Committee, condemned President Ali for allegedly engineering the assassination. Ali and approximately 700 followers attacked Central Committee headquarters June 26 but were driven off and forced to flee. Ethiopia provided a contingent of troops June 26 to help the newly proclaimed Ismail government. Ethiopia intervened partly in recognition of Yemeni aid to Ethiopia during the Ogaden War (8.9). Soviet Union naval gunfire also helped to defeat Ali's attack upon the Central Committee June 26. Ali was captured and executed later that day. Fighting ceased by July 3 after most of Ali's followers were captured. No Ethiopian or Soviet fatalities are reported.

Cordesman, A. 1984. *The Gulf and the Search for Strategic Stability*, 448–449, 467–471.
David, S. 1985. *Defending Third World Regimes from Coups d'Etat*, 51–55.
David, S. 1987. *Third World Coups d'Etat and International Security*, 89–92.
Gause, F. 1990. *Saudi-Yemeni Relations*, 119–129.
Halliday, F. 1990. *Revolution and Foreign Policy*, 123–124, 190–191.
Keegan, J., ed. 1983. *World Armies*, 659–671.
Kelly, J. 1980. *Arabia, the Gulf and the West*, 470–477.
Martin, L. 1984. *The Unstable Gulf*, 59.
Page, S. 1985. *The Soviet Union and the Yemens*, 70–80.
Peterson, J. 1981. *Conflict in the Yemens and Superpower Involvement*, 17–21.

14.13 NDF Invasion, 1979

The Arab Republic of Yemen (North Yemen) and the People's Democratic Republic of Yemen (South Yemen) fought a small border war in 1972 (14.10). Minor incidents involving primarily irregular forces occurred sporadically thereafter despite public commitment by both governments to promote unification. In June 1978 an envoy from South Yemen assassinated President Ahmad al-Ghashmi of North Yemen (14.12). Ali Abdallah Salih replaced Ghashmi. President Salim Rubayyi Ali of South Yemen was deposed and executed by Abd al-Fattah Ismail in the wake of Ghashmi's assassination. Ismail's South Yemeni government supported armed resistance to the Salih regime through the left-leaning National Democratic Front (NDF). NDF irregulars invaded North Yemen from South Yemen in February 1979 and captured border territory near the cities of Ibb and Taiz. Regular North Yemeni soldiers counterattacked within South Yemen in late February. South Yemen immediately committed regular troops on both sides of the border in support of NDF irregulars. Syria and Iraq helped to mediate a cease-fire which took effect March 19, 1979. On March 29 the two presidents reaffirmed their intention to promote Yemeni unity. 1979 border battles resulted in at least a dozen fatalities among regular soldiers on each side.

Brecher, M., J. Wilkenfeld, and S. Moser. 1988. *Crises in the Twentieth Century,* 1: 339–340.
Burrowes, R. 1985. "The Yemen Arab Republic and the Ali Abdallah Salih Regime." *Middle East Journal* 39 (Summer): 287–316.
Cordesman, A. 1984. *The Gulf and the Search for Strategic Stability,* 449–453, 467–471.
Gause, F. 1988. "Yemeni Unity." *Middle East Journal* 42 (Winter): 33–47.
Gause, F. 1990. *Saudi-Yemeni Relations,* 130–136.
Halliday, F. 1990. *Revolution and Foreign Policy,* 124–125.
Lackner, H. 1985. *P.D.R. Yemen: Outpost of Socialist Development,* 85–86.
Leogrande, W. 1980. *Cuba's Policy in Africa,* 57–59.
Litwak, R. 1981. *Sources of Inter-State Conflict,* 83–84.
Martin, L. 1984. *The Unstable Gulf,* 59.
Peterson, J. 1981. *Conflict in the Yemens and Superpower Involvement,* 23–25.
Stookey, R. 1982. *South Yemen: Marxist Republic in Arabia,* 97–98.

PART FIVE

Asia and Oceania

15

Southwest Asia

Pushtun insurgency within Pakistan, encouraged by Afghanistan, provoked international in 1949 (15.1) and 1950 (15.2). Domestic revolt within Afghanistan spilled into Pakistan in early 1979 (15.3) and led to the Russo–Afghan War (15.4) when the Soviet Union intervened later that year.

15.1 Moghulgai Raid, 1949

The United Kingdom imposed the Durand Line between Afghanistan and northwest India at the end of the nineteenth century. India acquired territory traditionally inhabited by Pushtun (Pathan), a major Afghan tribe, as a result. King Mohammed Zahir Shah of Afghanistan denounced the Durand Line boundary after World War II. He publicly proclaimed affinity with all Pushtun and attempted to promote separatist sentiment within Pakistan following Indian partition and independence in 1947. Afghanistan also deployed ground and air units near the Pakistan border during heightened tensions in spring 1949. In June 1949 a Pakistani plane bombed the town of Moghulgai inside Afghanistan. Pakistan later claimed that the incident, which inflicted some casualties but suffered none, represented a pilot's error.

Anwar, R. 1988. *The Tragedy of Afghanistan*, 30–32.
Brecher, M., J. Wilkenfeld, and S. Moser. 1988. *Crises in the Twentieth Century*, 1: 217.
Burke, S. 1973. *Pakistan's Foreign Policy*, 74.
Butterworth, R. 1976. *Managing Interstate Conflict*, 94–96.
Day, A., ed. 1987. *Border and Territorial Disputes*, 263–277.
Fletcher, A. 1965. *Afghanistan: Highway of Conquest*, 256.
Franck, D. 1952. "Pathanistan—Disputed Disposition of a Tribal Land." *Middle East Journal* 6 (Winter): 49–68.
Ghaus, A. 1988. *The Fall of Afghanistan*, 66–74.

15.2 Pushtun Conflict, 1950

Afghanistan promoted separatist sentiments among Pushtun (Pathan) tribesmen within Pakistan after the British withdrew from the Indian subcontinent in 1947. Pakistan bombed an Afghan border town during heightened tensions in 1949 (15.1). On September 30, 1950, Pushtun tribesmen invaded border areas of Pakistan from Afghanistan. Small units of regular Afghan soldiers supported the initial invasion. Pakistan protested Afghan involvement. Afghanistan denied direct participation and apparently ceased overt military operations after the first day. Pakistani military forces drove all invaders out by October 5. No fatalities are reported among regular Afghan troops.

Anwar, R. 1988. *The Tragedy of Afghanistan*, 30–32.
Brecher, M., J. Wilkenfeld, and S. Moser. 1988. *Crises in the Twentieth Century*, 1: 217.
Butterworth, R. 1976. *Managing Interstate Conflict*, 94–96.
Day, A., ed. 1987. *Border and Territorial Disputes*, 263–277.
Dupree, L. 1973. *Afghanistan*, 492–493.
Ghaus, A. 1988. *The Fall of Afghanistan*, 66–74.
Razvi, M. 1971. *The Frontiers of Pakistan*, 153.

15.3 Afghan Revolt, 1979

Afghanistan separated from Persia in the eighteenth century. A traditional monarchy survived until 1973 when a military coup d'etat deposed King Mohammad Zahir Shah. Prince Sardar Mohammad Daoud, who had been prime minister from 1953 to 1963, became president of the new republic. Radical Afghan military officers staged another coup d'etat in April 1978 that overthrew Daoud's regime. Nur Mohammad Taraki, leader of the radical Khalq movement from which later emanated the People's Democratic Party of Afghanistan, became head of state and prime minister of the newly declared Democratic Republic of Afghanistan. The Taraki regime, encouraged by the Soviet Union, attempted to centralize state institutions. Violent resistance to the new government arose immediately among traditional tribal and other authorities, particularly within eastern provinces near the Pakistan border.

Pakistan's relations with Afghanistan were frequently strained after World War II. Armed incidents occurred in 1949 (15.1) and 1950 (15.2) associated with Afghan efforts to promote Pushtun separatism within Pakistan. Irregular Afghan tribal levies also invaded Pakistan in 1961 on behalf of the Pushtun cause. Baluchi separatist resistance within Pakistan, encouraged by Afghanistan as well as Iran, also contributed to Afghan-Pakistani tensions during the 1970s.

Civil war broke out within Afghanistan in 1978. Government counterinsurgency operations helped to drive thousands of refugees into Pakistan. Resistance to the Afghan government relied in part upon sanctuaries within Pakistan. Numerous minor border incidents occurred in 1978–1979. In mid-March 1979 Afghan soldiers fired artillery shells upon a refugee camp immediately across the Pakistan border. No military fatalities are reported during the incident.

Anwar, R. 1988. *The Tragedy of Afghanistan*, 155–159.
Bhasin, V. 1984. *Soviet Intervention in Afghanistan*, 172–174.
Bradsher, H. 1985. *Afghanistan and the Soviet Union*, 100–101.
Day, A., ed. 1987. *Border and Territorial Disputes*, 263–277.
Hyman, A. 1984. *Afghanistan Under Soviet Domination*, 99–120.
Newell, N., and R. Newell. 1981. *The Struggle for Afghanistan*, 85–106.
Schmid, A., and E. Berends. 1985. *Soviet Military Interventions Since 1945*, 127–132.
Small, M., and J. Singer. 1982. *Resort to Arms*, 232.
Urban, M. 1989. *War in Afghanistan*, 7–28.

15.4 Russo-Afghan War, 1979–continuing

Civil war broke out within Afghanistan in 1978 after Nur Mohammad Taraki became head of state and prime minister of the newly proclaimed Democratic Republic of Afghanistan following a military coup d'etat. Traditional tribal and other elements resisted the new centralized regime and relied partly upon sanctuaries within neighboring Pakistan from an early date and Afghanistan shelled refugee camps across the border in mid-March 1979 (15.3). On March 27, 1979, Hafizullah Amin replaced Taraki as prime minister. Taraki remained head of state. Civil war spread despite military assistance from the Soviet Union intended to help shore up the regime.

The Soviet Union had long shown interest in Afghanistan. During the nineteenth century Russia and the United Kingdom, which then ruled India, competed for allegiance among Afghan tribal and other leaders. The Soviet Union and Afghanistan signed a nonaggression treaty in the 1920s that was never formally terminated. The Soviet Union and the United States competed for influence within Kabul from the 1950s through such means as rival economic assistance programs. The Soviet Union initiated a military assistance program after the fall of the monarchy in 1973. Khalq's rise to power in 1978 facilitated closer Soviet-Afghan relations and increased aid. The two states signed a friendship and cooperation treaty in December 1978.

Prime Minister Amin proved unable to end the civil war. In September 1979 Soviet personnel allegedly participated in an anti-Amin plot that went awry, resulting in the death of President Taraki. Amin became president on September 16, 1979. The Soviet Union increased its military presence within Afghanistan during November. A division of Soviet troops deployed to Kabul by air between December 24 and 26, apparently with approval of the Amin government. On December 27, 1979, Babrak Karmal, a rival of Amin within the official People's Democratic Party of Afghanistan (PDPA), declared himself president. Soviet troops in Kabul moved immediately to support him. Additional Soviet divisions crossed the Russo-Afghan border at the same time. President Amin died during fighting around the presidential palace.

War continued and Soviet forces remained for almost ten years. The United States provided military equipment and other assistance to various rebel factions, channelled principally through Pakistan. Low-intensity conflict raged along the Afghan-Pakistan border for most of the war, especially during late 1981 and from September 1983 to March 1987 when Afghan aircraft repeatedly bombed and strafed Pakistani territory. It has been alleged, but not officially admitted, that Soviet pilots flew some cross-border missions. Pakistani troops regularly facilitated Afghan rebel transit across the border. Upon at least one occasion in September 1985 a few Pakistani regular soldiers joined a raiding party that operated for a week upon Afghan soil. Trouble also occurred occasionally on the Afghan-Iranian border. In early April 1982 a small Afghan unit raided Iranian territory in pursuit of fleeing rebels.

Resistance groups controlling a majority of the Afghan countryside formed the Islamic Alliance of Afghan Holy Warriors in May 1985. The Alliance elicited financial support and volunteer fighters from other Moslem nations, including Iran. In July 1986 negotiations involving the Soviet Union, Afghanistan and Pakistan began in Geneva under U.N. sponsorship. On April 14, 1988, the Soviet Union agreed to remove its forces from Afghanistan in stages. The last Soviet ground combat contingents withdrew in February 1989. Afghan resistance groups continued to fight against the Kabul after Soviet forces withdrew, albeit with less international assistance. The Soviet Union continued to provide military assistance to the Afghan government and attacked rebels by air from bases within the Soviet Union throughout 1989.

Hundreds of thousands of persons, mostly civilians, died within Afghanistan by 1989. Soviet military fatalities are usually estimated at approximately 15,000. Two to three times as many Afghan government soldiers were killed. Military losses during cross-border operations were minimal, although at least one Afghan soldier died within Iran and another within Pakistan.

Anwar, R. 1988. *The Tragedy of Afghanistan,* 182–253.

Arnold, A. 1985. *Afghanistan, the Soviet Invasion in Perspective,* 85–142.

Bhasin, V. 1984. *Soviet Intervention in Afghanistan.*

Bodansky, Y. 1987. "Soviet Military Involvement in Afghanistan." In *Afghanistan, the Great Game Revisited,* ed. R. Klass, 229–285.

Bradsher, H. 1985. *Afghanistan and the Soviet Union,* 110–297.

Collins, J. 1986. *The Soviet Invasion of Afghanistan.*

Cordesman, A., and A. Wagner. 1990. The Lessons of Modern War. 3: 3–237.

Day, A., ed. 1987. *Border and Territorial Disputes,* 263–277.

Girardet, E. 1985. *Afghanistan: The Soviet War.*

Hammond, T. 1984. *Red Flag Over Afghanistan,* 95–180.

Hyman, A. 1984. *Afghanistan Under Soviet Domination,* 121–221.

Laffin, J. 1986. *War Annual 1,* 1–16.

Laffin, J. 1987. *War Annual 2,* 2–19.

Laffin, J. 1989. *The World in Conflict 1989: War Annual 3,* 3–25.

Malley, M. 1989. "The Geneva Accords of April 1988." In *The Soviet Withdrawal from Afghanistan,* eds. A. Saikal and W. Haley, 12–28.

Merriam, J. 1987. "Arms Shipments to the Afghan Resistance." In *Afghan Resistance,* ed. G. Farr and J. Merriam, 71–101.

Newell, N., and R. Newell. 1981. *The Struggle for Afghanistan,* 107–220.

Schmid, A., and E. Berends. 1985. *Soviet Military Interventions Since 1945,* 127–132.

Sena, C. 1986. *Afghanistan: Politics, Economics, and Society,* 85–174.

Urban, M. 1989. *War in Afghanistan.*

16

East Asia

International armed conflict affected several parts of East Asia. The United States occupied southern Korea following World War II (16.1), as did the Soviet Union northern Korea before the war's end. The Korean War (16.5) followed shortly after U.S. and Soviet withdrawal. The Korean truce was marred by serious raids during the 1960s (16.10, 16.11) and further incidents in 1976 (16.16).The United States also occupied part of northern China following World War II (16.2). China restored rule over Taiwan (16.3). Taiwan became host to the Republic of China government which fled the mainland in 1949 and thereafter fought a twenty-year war for control of offshore islands (16.6). China invaded Tibet in 1950, eventually pacified it and incorporated it as a Chinese province (16.7). Resistance to Chinese rule within Tibet contributed indirectly to conflict with India (17.10, 17.12) and Burma (18.7, 18.12, 18.17). The Sino-Mongolian border was also troubled during 1947–1948 (16.4). Sino-Soviet disagreements eventually led to serious violence in 1969 (16.15) and a minor incident in 1978 (16.17). Britain intervened during disturbances within its Hong Kong colony on several occasions including 1956 (16.9), 1966 (16.12), and 16.14). Portugal intervened within Macao in 1952 (16.8) and 1966 (16.13).

16.1 Korean Occupation, 1945–1948

Japan controlled Korea following the Russo-Japanese War of 1904–1905. The United Nations allies did not directly challenge Japan's position during World War II except by naval and air bombardment during the summer of 1945. The United States and the Soviet Union agreed to divide the peninsula at the 38th Parallel for the purpose of accepting Japanese surrender. Russian forces entered northern Korea in late August 1945 before the formal armistice. American troops arrived in the south September 8. Two separate states eventually resulted from these actions: the Republic of Korea in the south; and the Democratic

People's Republic of Korea in the north. The United States administered southern Korea under military government until independence in August 1948. U.S. military forces assumed various police duties. Violence marred the occupation upon occasion, particularly in 1948; but no American military personnel are known to have been killed in action.

Butterworth, R. 1976. *Managing Interstate Conflict*, 96–98.
Cumings, B. 1981. *The Origins of the Korean War*.
Cumings, B. 1983. "Introduction." In *Child of Conflict*, ed. B. Cumings, 3–55.
Gallicchio, M. 1988. *The Cold War Begins in Asia*.
Henderson, G. 1968. *Korea: The Politics of the Vortex*, 113–162.
Meade, E. 1951. *American Military Government in Korea*.
Sawyer, R. 1962. *Military Advisors in Korea*.

16.2 Chinese Occupation, 1945–1946

Japan acquired spheres of influence within Manchuria and coastal China during the late nineteenth and early twentieth centuries. She forcibly occupied Manchuria in 1931–1932. In 1937 she began a full-scale invasion of northern and central China. Chinese Nationalist (Kuomintang) government and Communist insurgent forces which had fought one another since the 1920s both resisted Japan's advance. Fighting between Japanese and Chinese forces continued until the end of World War II. U.S. Marines deployed within Tientsin in northern China, where were several foreign enclaves, on September 30, 1945, a few weeks after Japanese surrender. They helped to perform police and guard duties there and elsewhere within northern China until September 1946. A few American units remained in garrison until 1947. U.S. troops did not directly engage Communist insurgent forces who resumed warfare against the Nationalist government in 1946. No American fatalities are reported.

Frank, B., and H. Shaw. 1968. "North China Marines." In *History of U.S. Marine Corps Operations in World War II*, by U.S. Marine Corps, 5: 521–650.
Gallicchio, M. 1988. *The Cold War Begins in Asia*.

16.3 Taiwanese Occupation, 1945

China ceded Taiwan to Japan at the end of the Sino-Japanese War in 1895. It served as an important base for Japanese operations against China in the 1930s and during World War II. Chinese troops arrived on Taiwan to accept the surrender of Japanese forces in mid-October 1945, six weeks after the armistice ending World War II. Military operations concluded within ten days without serious incident. Taiwan was thereafter reintegrated with the Republic of China.

Kerr, G. 1965. *Formosa Betrayed*, 61–79.
New York Times 9/10/45, 29:1; 10/8/45, 6:5; 10/22/45, 2:6.

16.4 Peitashan Affair, 1947–1948

The ambiguous border between China and Mongolia has long been a locus of conflict. Most of what is generally regarded as Mongolia was subject to Chinese suzerainty from the sixteenth century. Influence over and possession of Mongolian territory was actively disputed by Russia from the eighteenth century, and by the Japanese also after the Sino-Japanese War of 1894–1895. A Mongolian People's Government came to power within Outer Mongolia in 1921 with Moscow's assistance, after Japan attempted to establish a puppet government in the area. The new government proclaimed Mongolian autonomy. The Republic of China declined to recognize the regime.

Insurrection within Sinkiang against Republican Chinese rule during the mid-1940s exacerbated the Sino-Mongolian dispute. The Sinkiang rebellion benefitted from Soviet patronage although it represented primarily Uighur nationalism and was not directly connected with Mao Tse-tung's radical insurgency movement. In 1946 local Chinese leader Uthman Batur, who generally supported the Republican government, established a military presence in the remote mountains of Peitashan on Mongolia's border. Mongolian armed forces attacked Uthman's positions from June 1947 until July 1948 when Uthman withdrew. Mongolia suffered approximately thirty fatalities.

Barnett, A. 1963. *China on the Eve of the Communist Takeover*, 266–267.
Butterworth, R. 1976. *Managing Interstate Conflict*, 39–40.
Chen, J. 1977. *The Sinkiang Story*, 260–263.
Forbes, A. 1986. *Warlords and Muslims in Chinese Central Asia*, 206–215.
Friters, G. 1949. *Outer Mongolia and Its International Position*, 291.
Rupen, R. 1964. *Mongols of the Twentieth Century*, 258–259.
Watson, F. 1966. *The Frontiers of China*, 34–46.
Whiting, A., and Sheng Shih-Tsai. 1958. *Sinkiang: Pawn or Pivot?* 98–123.

16.5 Korean War, 1949–1953

International armed conflict leading to major warfare within Korea began in 1949. The United States and the Soviet Union each accepted the surrender of Japanese forces on either side of Korea's 38th Parallel at the end of World War II (16.1). Negotiations aimed at reunification failed. The Democratic People's Republic of Korea in the north and the Republic of Korea in the south emerged in 1948 as separate regimes under Soviet and American tutelage. Minor border incidents began almost as soon as North Korea and South Korea began to assume responsibility for boundary security in fall 1948. North Korean and South Korean soldiers openly raided one another's positions near the 38th Parallel from January 1949, shortly after Soviet troops withdrew from North Korea. Raids continued until spring 1950. North Korea also encouraged civil disturbances within the south.

Border conflict expanded during summer 1949 as the United States withdrew its remaining infantry units from Korea. A South Korean offensive in early May captured disputed territory in the Onjin area on the western frontier. North Korean forces counterattacked in July and drove across the original boundary by early August. Seesaw battles continued near Onjin until October while frequent small-unit raids took place at other border points.

On June 24, 1950, after a two-month lull in border incidents, North Korea launched full-scale invasion and quickly approached the South Korean capital at Seoul. The United States began air and naval action within South Korea at her request June 27. That day the U.N. Security Council approved a resolution calling upon U.N. members to assist the Republic of Korea. United Kingdom air action began in the south June 28. The United States extended air and naval operations into North Korea on June 30 as did the United Kingdom on July 6. Australian aircraft joined action within South Korea on July 4.

On July 1, 1950, U.S. ground units landed in South Korea from bases in Japan. American and South Korean soldiers formed the core of an evolving United Nations Command directed by the United States. British troops deployed in August. Other nations contributed combat forces under the U.N. flag between September 1950 and June 1951, including infantry and artillery from Australia and New Zealand, Belgium and Luxembourg, Canada, Colombia, Ethiopia, France, Greece, the Netherlands, the Philippines, Thailand, and Turkey, as well as South African air forces.

U.N. forces landed at Inchon behind North Korean lines in September 1950 following loss of Seoul and bitter defensive battles around the far southern port of Pusan. Seoul was recaptured. South Korean units crossed into North Korea on September 30. U.S. units followed suit on October 7. U.N. forces rushed toward the North Korean-Chinese border. The People's Republic of China quietly deployed large numbers of experienced troops within mountainous areas of North Korea. The first brief engagement with Chinese forces occurred October 25, 1950. In November China mounted a major counterattack that eventually crossed the 38th Parallel at the end of December and overran Seoul once more.

Taking the offensive again, U.N. forces recaptured the capital and by March 1951 established a battle line across the peninsula diagonally intersecting the 38th Parallel. A war of attrition involving minor changes of position continued until truce was finally established July 27, 1953. The United Nations Command remained for the next several decades in order to help police the truce line.

By most accounts, the Korean War represents the most deadly international conflict since 1945. Three million persons were killed, including nearly two million soldiers. Half of the latter were Chinese. North Korean and South Korean military fatalities approached a half million each. More than 50,000 American military personnel died, as did 3,000 other U.N. soldiers, including especially large losses among Turkish and British Commonwealth troops.

General

Brecher, M., J. Wilkenfeld, and S. Moser. 1988. *Crises in the Twentieth Century*, 1: 218–220, 223–224.
Butterworth, R. 1976. *Managing Interstate Conflict*, 96–98, 145–148.
Day, A., ed. 1987. *Border and Territorial Disputes*, 356–365.
Dupuy, R., and T. Dupuy. 1986. *The Encyclopedia of Military History*, 1240–1253.
Small, M., and J. Singer. 1982. *Resort to Arms*, 92.

China

Gurtov, M., and B. Hwang. 1980. *China under Threat*, 25–62.
Hinton, H. 1966. *Communist China in World Politics*, 205–234.
Segal, G. 1985. *Defending China*, 92–113.
Whiting, A. 1960. *China Crosses the Yalu*.

Korea

Cho, S. 1967. *Korea in World Politics*.
Henderson, G. 1968. *Korea: The Politics of the Vortex*, 148–168.
Korea (Democratic People's Republic) Academy of Sciences. 1961. *History of the Just Fatherland Liberation War of the Korean People*.
Lowe, P. 1986. *The Origins of the Korean War*.
Merrill, J. 1983. "Internal Warfare in Korea, 1948–1950." In *Child of Conflict*, ed. B. Cumings, 133–162.
Oliver, R. 1978. *Syngman Rhee and American Involvement in Korea*, 238–431.
Simmons, R. 1975. *The Strained Alliance*, 111–112.

United Nations

Blaxland, G. 1971. *The Regiments Depart*, 132–206.
Gordenker, L. 1959. *The United Nations and the Peaceful Unification of Korea*, 186–210.
Heitman, H. 1985. *South African War Machine*, 58.
Higgins, R. 1970. *United Nations Peacekeeping*, 2: 151–312.
King, M. 1981. *New Zealanders at War*, 277.
O'Ballance, E. 1969. *Korea: 1950–1953*.

United States

Appleman, R. 1961. *South to the Naktong, North to the Yalu*.
Collins, J. 1969. *War in Peacetime*.
Cumings, B. 1983. "Introduction." In *Child of Conflict*, ed. B. Cumings, 3–55.
Futrell, R., L. Moseley, and A. Simpson 1961. *The United States Air Force in Korea*.
Hermes, W. 1966. *Truce Tent and Fighting Front*.
Meade, E. 1951. *American Military Government in Korea*.
Paige, G. 1968. *The Korean Decision*.
Rees, D. 1964. *Korea: The Limited War*.
Sawyer, R. 1962. *Military Advisors in Korea*, 73–75.
Schnabel, J. 1971. *Policy and Direction: The First Year*.
Stone, I. 1952. *The Hidden History of the Korean War*.
Stueck, W. 1983. "The March to the Yalu." In *Child of Conflict*, ed. B. Cumings, 195–237.
Tillema, H. 1973. *Appeal to Force*.
U.S. Department of State. 1951. *The Conflict in Korea*.
U.S. Marine Corps. 1954–1972. *U.S. Marine Operations in Korea*.

16.6 Chinese Islands Conflict, 1949–1969

Mao Tse-tung led the revolt against the Kuomintang (Nationalist) government of Chiang Kai-shek for control of the Republic of China from the late 1920s until Japan invaded China in 1937, and again after World War II. Mao defeated Nationalist armies in the north and proclaimed the People's Republic of China in Peking on October 2, 1949. Nationalists fought on, including from bases on Taiwan, restored to China after World War II (16.2), other offshore islands and pockets on the mainland. The Soviet Union immediately recognized the People's Republic. The United States continued to recognize the Republic of China government headquartered on Taiwan.

China attempted to eradicate remaining Nationalist positions after seizing Peking, including shelling islands in Amoy Harbor starting October 9, 1949. Amphibious assaults upon Nationalist-held islands followed, including a disastrously failed attempt to seize Quemoy in late October and the conquest of Hainan in May 1950. An attack upon Taiwan was expected but did not occur, in part because the U.S. Navy interposed part of its Seventh Fleet within the Taiwan Straits after North Korea invaded South Korea in June 1950 (16.5).

Taiwan thereafter undertook frequent small-unit raids against the Chinese mainland and Peking-controlled islands until 1969. She also aided and abetted irregular attacks upon shipping, including by traditionally piratical local islanders. The People's Republic persistently bombarded Taiwan-held islands until 1963.

In summer 1952 the United States helped to train Nationalist military units to mount large amphibious operations against People's Republic island positions. The first major attack occurred against Nanri in October 1952. Other large operations continued until June 1953, just before end of the Korean War. China intensified bombardment of Quemoy and other islands in September 1954. In January 1955 she conquered Ichiang by amphibious assault. Nationalist forces retreated from some outlying islands. Bombardment intensified against Quemoy and Matsu in September 1958. Frequent People's Republic artillery attacks continued until June 1963. Nationalist guerrilla raids continued until July 2, 1969.

The Chinese Islands Conflict involved thousands of fatalities after October 2, 1949. The Taiwan government lost at least 2,000 military personnel during assaults upon Peking-controlled positions. China lost at least 3,000 during attacks upon Taiwan-controlled islands, including 2,000 upon Quemoy in late October 1949.

Brecher, M., J. Wilkenfeld, and S. Moser. 1988. *Crises in the Twentieth Century*, 1: 214–215, 227–228, 242–243, 257.

Butterworth, R. 1976. *Managing Interstate Conflict*, 183–184, 190–191, 249–250.

Chiu, H. 1979. "The Question of Taiwan in Sino-American Relations." In *China and the Taiwan Issue*, ed. H. Chiu, 147–211.

Clough, R. 1978. *Island China*, 96–97.

Day, A., ed. 1987. *Border and Territorial Disputes*, 300–309.

George, A., and R. Smoke. 1974. *Deterrence in American Foreign Policy*, 266–294, 362–389.

Gurtov, M., and B. Hwang. 1980. *China under Threat*, 39–98.

Hinton, H. 1966. *Communist China in World Politics*, 258–272.

Howe, J. 1971. *Multicrises*, 161–282.

Hsieh, C. 1985. *Strategy for Survival*, 78–123.

Kerr, G. 1965. *Formosa Betrayed*, 371–397.

Leckie, R. 1962. *Conflict: The History of the Korean War*, 15.

Kalicki, J. 1975. *The Pattern of Sino-American Crises*, 120–208.

Mendel, D. 1970. *The Politics of Formosan Nationalism*, 135–145.

Segal, G. 1985. *Defending China*, 114–139.
Small, M., and J. Singer. 1982. *Resort to Arms*, 229.
Snyder, E., A. Gregor, and M. Chang. 1980. *The Taiwan Relations Act and the Defense of the Republic of China*, 46–49.
Stolper, T. 1985. *China, Taiwan, and the Offshore Islands*.
Swanson, B. 1982. *Eighth Voyage of the Dragon*, 183–192.
Tong, H. 1953. *Chiang Kai-Shek*, 472–531.
Tsou, T. 1959. *The Embroilment Over Quemoy*.
U.S. Office of Naval Intelligence. 1953. "The Southeast China Coast Today." *The ONI Review* 8 (February): 51–60.

16.7 Tibetan Occupation, 1950–1965

Tibet, independent under the Dalai Lama from the seventh century, was incorporated within China by the Manchu. She regained de facto autonomy following the Chinese revolution of 1912. Tibetans expelled Chinese authorities that year and fought a 1918 Chinese military expedition to a standstill. Most major powers refrained from formally recognizing the the Dalai Lama's government. The United Kingdom, however, maintained a small Indian Army garrison. A representative of the Republic of China government returned to Lhasa in 1935 but exerted little influence and was expelled in 1949.

The People's Republic of China reasserted its claim to Tibet in February 1950, a few months after Mao Tse-tung seized power in Peking at the end of the civil war against the Kuomintang (Nationalist) government. India's prime minister Jawaharlal Nehru mediated inconclusive negotiations between representatives of the Dalai Lama and China's ambassador to India. In September 1950 People's Liberation Army forces began small raids within Tibetan border areas against Kuomintang remnants which had fled China. On October 7, China mounted a full-scale invasion. India protested but withheld her few hundred troops stationed within Tibet. Chinese forces occupied Lhasa in March 1951. In May China imposed a protectorate agreement granting Peking control of defense and foreign affairs. In practice China ruled Tibet under military occupation until she annexed the territory in September 1965.Tibetan tribesmen resisted Chinese efforts to extend central control to outlying areas during the early 1950s. A major uprising began within eastern Tibet in 1956 and eventually reached Lhasa in 1959. The Dalai Lama fled to India in spring 1959. Sporadic resistance continued during the early 1960s.

Persistent Tibetan resistance contributed indirectly to armed conflict between China and India in 1959 (17.10). It also provoked incidents on the unmarked Tibetan-Nepali border. Chinese forces repeatedly intruded within disputed territory claimed by Nepal while pursuing rebellious Tibetan tribesmen. In addition, Chinese troops raided the Nepali village of Gyabria in April 1959 and clashed with Nepali soldiers during the Mustang incident of June 1960.

China's initial occupation of Tibet in 1950–1951 entailed only moderate casualties. Uprising during the late 1950s proved deadly, however, killing tens of thousands of Tibetans and as many as 40,000 Chinese soldiers.

General

Butterworth, R. 1976. *Managing Interstate Conflict*, 149–150, 212–213, 261–264.
Small, M., and J. Singer. 1982. *Resort to Arms*, 99.

China

Ginsburg, G. and M. Mathos. 1964. *Communist China and Tibet*.
Hinton, H. 1966. *Communist China in World Politics*, 281–288.
Lu, C. 1986. *The Sino-Indian Border Dispute*, 43–63.
Patterson, G. 1964. *Peking Versus Delhi*, 100–104, 148–166.
Segal, G. 1985. *Defending China*, 80–91.
Watson, F. 1966. *The Frontiers of China*, 59–61, 131–138.
Whiting, A. 1975. *The Chinese Calculus of Deterrence*, 8–19.

Nepal

Ray, H. 1983. *China's Strategy in Nepal*.
New York Times 4/22/59, 3:3; 6/30/60, 8:4; 7/2/60, 3:1; 7/3/60, 6:3; 7/4/60, 3:5; 7/18/60, 8:5.

Tibet

International Commission of Jurists. 1960. *Tibet and the Chinese People's Republic*.
Moraes, F. 1960. *The Revolt in Tibet*.
Patterson, G. 1960. *Tibet in Revolt*.
Richardson, H. 1962. *A Short History of Tibet*, 169–243.
Richardson, H. 1984. *Tibet and Its History*, 183–258.
Shakabpa, T. 1967. *Tibet: a Political History*, 299–323.
Thomas, L. 1959. *The Silent War in Tibet*.
Walt van Praag, M. 1987. *The Status of Tibet*, 142–188.

16.8 Macao Border Conflict, 1952

Portugal took possession of Macao in 1557. Macao's relationship to China remained ambiguous even after the 1887 Treaty of Peking which acknowledged the enclave but specified neither rights nor boundaries. Macao represented a transit point for Chinese international trade, including after the United Nations called for embargo upon trade with China in 1951 during the Korean War (16.5). Portuguese authorities attempted to restrict smuggling in 1952. Minor incidents occurred from late May, including small arms fire between Portuguese and Chinese border guards July 25–26. Portugal moved troops to the border as did also China. A battle involving Chinese and Portuguese mortars and a Portuguese gunboat took place July 29–30, 1952. Portugal accepted responsibility, paid China compensation and trade resumed. Five Portuguese soldiers were killed July 29–30. Forty Chinese troops also reportedly died.

Dicks, A. 1984. "Macao." In *Leadership on the China Coast*, ed. G. Aijmer, 90–128.
New York Times 7/27/52, 2:7; 7/29/52, 7:5; 7/30/52, 3:5; 7/31/52, 3:2.

16.9 Kowloon Riots, 1956

The United Kingdom acquired the island of Hong Kong from China in 1841 and facing Kowloon Peninsula in 1860. Japan captured the colony in 1941 but surrendered to British civil authorities shortly after armistice in September 1945. Confrontation between the Republic of China on Taiwan and the People's Republic of China in Peking polarized local Chinese communities during the 1950s. On October 10, 1956, local supporters flew flags of the Republic of China on her national holiday. Supporters of the People's Republic immediately provoked riots within Kowloon in protest. Garrisoned British troops intervened for three days, suffering no reported fatalities.

Grantham, A. 1956. *Report on the Riots in Kowloon and Tsuen Wan.*
Miners, N. 1977. *The Government and Politics of Hong Kong*, 32.

16.10 Korean Raids I, 1962–1963

The Korean War ended by truce in 1953 (16.5). A U.N. military force remained thereafter within the Republic of Korea (South Korea), including U.S. troops stationed at some points along the South Korean-North Korean border. Negotiations toward permanent settlement failed to produce agreement. Minor incidents, including small arms fire across the border, occurred frequently. In September 1962 the Democratic People's Republic of Korea (North Korea) began to infiltrate commando units into South Korea, primarily across the

Demilitarized Zone. She continued raids until November 1963. Most actions took place in areas defended primarily by South Korean soldiers but U.S. Army patrols also engaged North Korean infiltrators from July to November 1963. Approximately twenty North Korean military personnel are known to have died and three American soldiers are reported killed.

Butterworth, R. 1976. *Managing Interstate Conflict*, 173–176.
Facts on File 22 (1962): 308, 445; 23 (1963): 267, 298–299, 426.
New York Times 8/3/63, 1:6.

16.11 Korean Raids II, 1965–1971

Truce following the Korean War (16.5) was interrupted by frequent minor border incidents involving the Republic of Korea (South Korea) and the Democratic People's Republic of Korea (North Korea). U.S. troops remained in the name of the United Nations to help police the cease-fire. In 1962–1963 North Korea provoked serious conflict by infiltrating commando units across the Demilitarized Zone (16.10). North Korean cross-border raids resumed in October 1965 and continued until 1971. U.S. Army patrols became directly involved as early as November. South Korean artillery and other small ground forces retaliated against North Korean border positions from April 1967 to December 1970.

North Korea also attempted small seaborne landings on the South Korean coast, contributing to frequent naval incidents and occasional air encounters. In January 1968 North Korea captured the *USS Pueblo* off her coast. She refused to return the ship but eventually released the crew in December 1968. Conflict gradually abated until North Korea ceased serious infiltration in September 1971. An estimated 500 North Korean military personnel died within South Korea between 1965 and 1971. Approximately forty American soldiers were killed within South Korea as were at least ten South Korean troops while attacking North Korean territory.

Brecher, M., J. Wilkenfeld, and S. Moser. 1988. *Crises in the Twentieth Century*, 1: 281, 288.
Butterworth, R. 1976. *Managing Interstate Conflict*, 173–176, 424–425.
Clough, R. 1987. *Embattled Korea*, 104–107.
Koh, B. 1969. "The Pueblo Incident in Perspective." *Asian Survey* 9 (April): 264–280.
Wroth, J. 1968. "Korea." *Military Review* 48 (November): 34–40.
Zagoria, D., and J. Zagoria. 1981. "Crises on the Korean Peninsula." In *Diplomacy of Power*, by S. Kaplan, 357–411.

16.12 Star Ferry Riots, 1966

The United Kingdom's crown colony of Hong Kong suffered violence between Chinese residents supporting the Republic of China and the People's Republic of China in 1956 (16.9). Economic tensions grew within Hong Kong in 1965–1966 due in part to failure of several local financial institutions and widespread fears of inflation. On the night of April 5, 1966, youthful demonstrators gathered in Kowloon to protest a fare increase proposed by the Star Ferry Company which provided transport between Kowloon and Hong Kong Island. Some demonstrators were arrested. Renewed demonstrations the next evening became violent. British troops were called out April 7, 1966, to help contain further riots. Serious disturbances ceased by April 8 and British troops returned to barracks on April 11 without reported fatality.

Lethbridge, H. 1985. *Hard Graft in Hong Kong*, 57–68.
Miners, N. 1977. *The Government and Politics of Hong Kong*, 32.

16.13 Taipa Riots, 1966

Portuguese-ruled Macao experienced border strife with China in 1952 (16.8). On November 15, 1966, a dispute regarding a building project on the island of Taipa administered by Macao led to violence between police and construction workers. The Taipa Kaifong Association demanded government compensation. Supporters of the Taipa workers staged demonstrations within central Macao on December 2. Rioting followed and continued through the next day. Elements drawn from the local Portuguese army garrison supported police efforts to suppress rioting December 2–3, 1966. Eight persons were killed and hundreds were injured, but Portuguese soldiers suffered no fatalities.

Dicks, A. 1984. "Macao." In *Leadership on the China Coast*, ed. G. Aijmer, 90–128.
New York Times 12/4/66, 1:5; 12/5/66, 1:7.

16.14 Hong Kong Riots, 1967

The British Army helped to suppress riots within the Crown Colony of Hong Kong in 1956 (16.9) and 1966 (16.12). Further disturbances erupted within Victoria on Hong Kong Island and within mainland Kowloon in May 1967, precipitated by a local labor dispute. Numerous demonstrations and terrorist attacks followed. The legally constituted

Communist Party of Hong Kong orchestrated many of these events with apparent encouragement from the People's Republic of China. China also provoked minor incidents along the border of Hong Kong's New Territories on the mainland. Britain reinforced its military garrison on June 30, 1967, and actively supported police until the beginning of October 1967. Violent incidents subsided by December. Approximately fifty persons were killed during 1967, including one British soldier.

Blaxland, G. 1971. *The Regiments Depart*, 465–466.
Clutterbuck, R. 1985. *Conflict and Violence in Singapore and Malaya*, 138–141.
Cooper, J. 1970. *Colony in Conflict*.
Lethbridge, H. 1985. *Hard Graft in Hong Kong*, 69–70.
Miners, N. 1977. *The Government and Politics of Hong Kong*, 32.

16.15 Ussuri River Battle, 1969

The Soviet Union formally recognized the People's Republic of China immediately upon proclamation in Peking in October 1949. The two governments signed a 30-year treaty of friendship, alliance and mutual assistance, one of the most explicit of the Soviet Union's foreign commitments, in February 1950. The Soviet Union provided significant military and economic assistance to China during the 1950s. Serious policy disagreements developed by 1959, however, and Soviet military and civilian personnel withdrew. The two states competed for support among third world nationalist and socialist movements during the 1960s. China demanded revision of border treaties signed by the previous Republican regime but negotiations proved unfruitful and were suspended. Frequent minor border incidents occurred from 1960, particularly near Sinkiang. Incidents increased in 1966–1968, many apparently provoked deliberately by Chinese forces.

On March 2, 1969, Chinese troops ambushed a Soviet patrol on disputed Chen Pao (Damansky) Island within the Ussuri River bordering eastern Manchuria. A firefight ensued. On March 15 both states returned to the island in force and waged a fierce short battle. The Soviet Union provoked additional incidents in following months. As late as August 13, 1969, Soviet units of company size or larger harassed Chinese positions at widely scattered points along the frontier. On September 11 Soviet Prime Minister Alexei Kosygin and Chinese Prime Minister Chou En-lai resumed negotiations and border incidents abated. 300 or more Chinese soldiers are believed to have died at Chen Pao; a few more were killed in ensuing incidents. As many as 100 Soviet soldiers were also killed, most during March as well.

An, T. S. 1973. *The Sino-Soviet Territorial Dispute.*
Borisov, O., and B. Koloskov. 1975. *Soviet-Chinese Relations.*
Brecher, M., J. Wilkenfeld, and S. Moser. 1988. *Crises in the Twentieth Century,* 1: 287.
Butterworth, R. 1976. *Managing Interstate Conflict,* 287–288.
Day, A., ed. 1987. *Border and Territorial Disputes,* 288–300.
Gurtov, M., and B. Hwang. 1980. *China under Threat,* 187–241.
Keesing's Contemporary Archives. 1969. *The Sino-Soviet Dispute,* 115–118.
Maxwell, N. 1973. "The Chinese Account of the 1969 Fighting at Chenpao." *China Quarterly* 56 (October/December): 730–739.
Maxwell, N. 1978. "Why the Russians Lifted the Blockade at Bear Island." *Foreign Affairs* 57 (Fall): 138–45.
Robinson, T. 1981. "The Sino-Soviet Border Conflict." In *Diplomacy of Power,* by S. Kaplan, 265–313.
Schmid, A., and E. Berends. 1985. *Soviet Military Interventions Since 1945,* 35–38.
Segal, G. 1985. *Defending China,* 176–196.
Studies in Comparative Communism. 1969. "The Border Issue: China and the Soviet Union, March–October 1969." 2 (July–October): 121–382.

16.16 Poplar Tree Incident, 1976

Persistent minor border incidents followed the truce between the Democratic People's Republic of Korea (North Korea) and the Republic of Korea (South Korea) ending the Korean War in 1953 (16.5). In 1962–1963 and again from 1965 to 1971 North Korean commandos also raided South Korean territory (16.10, 16.11). Further serious incidents occurred in August 1976. On August 5 North and South Korean artillery dueled across their border. On August 18, North Korean soldiers wielding axes and shovels attacked a U.N. work party trimming a poplar tree within the Demilitarized Zone, killing two unarmed Americans. No fatalities are reported among Korean troops.

Day, A., ed. 1987. *Border and Territorial Disputes,* 356–365.
Head, R., F. Short, and R. McFarlane. 1978. *Crisis Resolution,* 149–215.
Zagoria, D., and J. Zagoria. 1981. "Crises on the Korean Peninsula." In *Diplomacy of Power,* by S. Kaplan, 357–411.

16.17 Ussuri River Incident, 1978

Dispute between the Soviet Union and China regarding their far eastern and central Asian boundaries and other policy disagreements contributed to serious border conflict centered in the Ussuri River region during 1969 (16.15). Formal border negotiations then commenced and progressed fitfully through the 1970s amidst continuing minor border incidents. Following the deaths of Chairman Mao Tse-tung and Premier Chou En-lai in 1976, a new Chinese government gradually reduced Communist party controls upon the economy and expanded contacts with western states, aggravating tensions with the Soviet Union. On May 9, 1978, a platoon of Soviet troops, supported by helicopters, landed by night on the Chinese side of the Ussuri River and proceeded inland several miles. A Soviet apology excused the incident as a mistake but it is commonly assumed to represent a deliberate provocation. No fatalities are reported on either side.

Day, A., ed. 1987. *Border and Territorial Disputes*, 288–300.
Maxwell, N. 1978. "Why the Russians Lifted the Blockade at Bear Island." *Foreign Affairs* 57 (Fall): 138–45.

17

South Asia

The United Kingdom attempted to retain control of India in the face of active resistance after World War II (17.1). She withdrew in 1947, partitioning the subcontinent into independent India and Pakistan. Indian efforts to assert control over territories that did not immediately assent to union contributed to conflict involving Hyderabad (17.3), French India (17.4), Portuguese India (17.11) and especially Pakistan. Indo-Pakistani dispute over the princely state of Jammu and Kashmir involved war in 1947–1949 (17.2) and 1964–1965 (17.14). The Bengali War of 1971 (17.17) also pitted India against Pakistan. Disputes concerning Kashmir, the Rann of Kutch and other Indo-Pakistani border areas involved numerous additional engagements between 1951 and the late 1980s (17.7, 17.8, 17.9, 17.13, 17.15, 17.19). Border dispute between China and India contributed to major war in 1962 (17.12) and to less intense conflict in 1959 (17.10), during the Indo-Pakistan War of 1965 (17.14), in 1967 (17.16), and in 1975(17.18). Sino-Indian conflict also related indirectly to Chinese occupation of Tibet (16.7). In addition, Indian forces intervened within Sikkim in 1949 (17.5), within Nepal in 1951 (17.6), and within Sri Lanka beginning in 1987 (17.20) in support of established governments.

17.1 Indian Resistance, 1945–1947

The United Kingdom assembled an empire within India through the cession and conquest of individual states from the seventeenth century. She took direct responsibility for government following the Sepoy Mutiny of 1857–1858. Civil disobedience aimed at inducing British withdrawal, orchestrated in part by the Congress movement, and intermittent violence combined to erode imperial control after World War I. The threat posed by Japanese military operations within Burma and Assam delayed the decision on independence during World War II. After the war, communal riots, guerrilla warfare and occasional mutinies among Indian Army units besieged British authorities. The burden of maintaining order fell mostly upon police although British troops and Indian Army units under British command were frequently called out to assist between October 1945 and March 1947. On August 15, 1947, the United Kingdom relinquished power to newly formed states of India and Pakistan which partitioned the subcontinent. No British soldiers are reported killed during military operations.

Ali, C. 1967. *The Emergence of Pakistan*, 33–236.
Blaxland, G. 1971. *The Regiments Depart*, 15–26.
Brines, R. 1968. *The Indo-Pakistani Conflict*, 18–48.
Butterworth, R. 1976. *Managing Interstate Conflict*, 30–32.
Keegan, J., ed. 1983. *World Armies*, 441–456.
Hodson, H. 1985. *The Great Divide*, 266–288.

17.2 Kashmiri War, 1947–1949

India and Pakistan were founded as separate states at independence in August 1947 (17.1). Individual princely states recognized under the Raj were expected to select whether to accede to the avowedly secular but Hindu-dominated Union of India or to the Moslem-dominated Dominion of Pakistan to the east and west of India. The important state of Jammu and Kashmir on the India-West Pakistan frontier represented an anomaly: a majority of residents were Moslem; the ruling family was Hindu. Maharajah Harasingh delayed a decision concerning accession until October 1947 amidst disturbances and mounting pressures from both directions. A tribal force invaded from Pakistan October 21. Local Moslems organized the Azad Kashmir movement to oppose union with India. On October 26 the Maharajah agreed to cede to India. Indian troops intervened immediately to support Kashmiri accession. Bloody but conspicuously limited war ensued. Pakistan supported the Azad Kashmir movement with arms, money and personnel. Beginning in March 1948 regular units of the Pakistani Army occupied some areas of Kashmir liberated by Azad forces but avoided direct engagement with Indian units. The Indian Air Force occasionally attacked Pakistani territory in 1948, but refrained from major reprisals. A cease-fire took effect January 1, 1949, with Kashmir effectively divided between India and Pakistan. India lost nearly 2,000 soldiers. Pakistan admits no losses among regular military personnel although Pakistani are known to have contributed to Azad Kashmir forces.

Ali, C. 1967. *The Emergence of Pakistan*, 276–315.
Birdwood, C. 1956. *Two Nations and Kashmir*, 38–78.
Blinkenberg, L. 1972. *India-Pakistan*, 74–111.

Brecher, M. 1953. *The Struggle for Kashmir.*
Brecher, M., J. Wilkenfeld, and S. Moser. 1988. *Crises in the Twentieth Century,* 1: 209–210.
Brines, R. 1968. *The Indo-Pakistani Conflict,* 63–84.
Butterworth, R. 1976. *Managing Interstate Conflict,* 91–93.
Chaturvedi, M. 1978. *History of the Indian Air Force,* 64–93.
Day, A., ed. 1987. *Border and Territorial Disputes,* 317–329.
Ganguly, S. 1986. *The Origins of War in South Asia,* 17–55.
Gupta, Sisir. 1966. *Kashmir, a Study in India-Pakistan Relations,* 90–202.
Hodson, H. 1985. *The Great Divide,* 441–474.
Keegan, J., ed. 1983. *World Armies,* 441–456.
Korbel, J. 1966. *Danger in Kashmir,* 44–164.
Lamb, A. 1967. *The Kashmir Problem,* 35–51.
Menon, V. 1961. *The Story of the Integration of the Indian States,* 372–396.
Razvi, M. 1971. *The Frontiers of Pakistan,* 92–104.
Sen, L. 1969. *Slender Was the Thread.*
Small, M., and J. Singer. 1982. *Resort to Arms,* 99.

17.3 Hyderabad War, 1948

The Nizam of the princely state of Hyderabad declined to accede to either India or Pakistan upon independence and partition of the Indian subcontinent in 1947 (17.1). India pressed for union. Hyderabad was wracked by communal disorders that led to thousands of casualties in 1948. Border incidents occurred with neighboring Indian Madras. Indian troops intervened September 11, 1948, and established Indian military administration September 24. Hyderabad was formally incorporated within India in 1949. Approximately 800 Indian soldiers died during two weeks of heavy fighting as did at least a thousand other persons.

Blinkenberg, L. 1972. *India-Pakistan,* 98–102.
Brecher, M., J. Wilkenfeld, and S. Moser. 1988. *Crises in the Twentieth Century,* 1: 213–214.
Brines, R. 1968. *The Indo-Pakistani Conflict,* 59–62.
Butterworth, R. 1976. *Managing Interstate Conflict,* 111–112.
Hodson, H. 1985. *The Great Divide,* 475–493.
Menon, V. 1961. *The Story of the Integration of the Indian States,* 299–371.
Sen, L. 1969. *Slender Was the Thread,* 10–14.
Small, M., and J. Singer. 1982. *Resort to Arms,* 99.

17.4 Mahe Incident, 1948

France established numerous small enclaves within India, including Pondicherry, Karikal and Mahe, beginning in the seventeenth century. These territories were conquered and reconquered by the Dutch, the

British and the French until 1815 when international agreements among the great powers confirmed their status as French possessions. India challenged the standing of French domains shortly after gaining independence in 1947 (17.1). Control of the enclaves passed peacefully to India by the mid-1950s except for an incident involving Mahe in October 1948 prior to scheduled municipal elections. On October 22 a large mob entered from neighboring Madras, seized public buildings, and captured the French Resident. France postponed elections and sent troops by ship from her garrison at Pondicherry. Two dozen French soldiers deployed October 27, dispatched the mob and freed the Resident within a matter of hours without inflicting or sustaining serious bodily harm.

Butterworth, R. 1976. *Managing Interstate Conflict,* 112–113.
Parker, R. 1955. "The French and Portuguese Settlements in India." *Political Quarterly* 26 (October/December): 389–398.
Rajkumar, N. 1951. *The Problem of French India,* 52–57.
New York Times 10/23/48, 4:3; 10/26/48, 12:6; 10/27/48, 5:6; 10/27/48, 25:1.

17.5 Gangtok Occupation, 1949

The East India Company exercised influence over Sikkim from the early nineteenth century. Sikkim formally acknowledged a protectorate under the United Kingdom in 1861 through a treaty signed with the British government of India. Sikkim's status was left undefined upon Indian independence in 1947 (17.1) pending agreement between India and the Maharajah of Sikkim. Negotiations between the two failed to produce an immediate conclusion, in part due to political divisions within Sikkim. A group calling itself the Sikkim State Congress proposed formation of a popularly-chosen government and accession to India. The Sikkim National party opposed union with India. In June 1949 several thousand Congress supporters demonstrated in Gangtok demanding popular governance. An Indian Army unit garrisoned within Sikkim was called out to help protect the Maharajah, whose palace was besieged, and to police the city. Indian forces stood down less than a week later. Leading Congress members were subsequently named to a new ministerial government. In December 1950 Sikkim signed a protectorate agreement with India. No fatalities are reported.

Grover, B. 1974. *Sikkim and India,* 86–91.
Kavic, L. 1967. *India's Quest for Security,* 52.
Maxwell, N. 1972. *India's China War,* 67–68.
Patterson, G. 1960. *Tibet in Revolt,* 214, 232–238.

17.6 Singh Resistance, 1951

The Rana family dominated politics within Nepal from 1847 when the king delegated full governing powers to an office of prime minister for which the Ranas controlled succession. Opposition to Rana power arose within the Nepali Congress movement after World War II. The Nepali Congress enjoyed favor with King Tribhubana Bir Bikram. It also maintained ties with the Indian Congress which formed India's first independent government under Prime Minister Jawarharlal Nehru in 1947. Nehru's government permitted the Nepali Congress to operate within Indian but apparently did not directly aid it.

In October 1950 the Rana government incarcerated Congress members who attempted to organize a terrorist campaign within Katmandu. King Tribhubana took refuge within the Indian embassy on November 6. The Ranas formally deposed the King the next day and installed his grandson on the throne. King Tribhubana flew to India November 10. On November 11 Nepali Congress forces attacked and briefly occupied the Nepali towns of Birganj and Biratnagar near the Indian border. Revolt spread to western Nepal in early January 1951. Nehru mediated a compromise agreement in early February 1951 under which King Tribhubana returned and Rana and Congress leaders formed a coalition cabinet.

A faction of the Nepali Congress associated with K. I. Singh refused to accept the "Delhi compromise" and continued armed struggle against the Ranas. Indian troops deployed in mid-February 1951 at the request of the Nepali government but stood down less than a week later after Singh was taken into custody. Indian soldiers again intervened during early July 1951 when Singh followers mounted renewed resistance. India dispatched police units upon subsequent occasions as late as 1953. No Indian military fatalities are reported.

Jha, S. 1975. *Uneasy Partners*, 57–64.
Patterson, G. 1960. *Tibet in Revolt*.
Patterson, G. 1960. *Tibet in Revolt*, 136–142.
Rose, L. 1971. *Nepal: Strategy for Survival*, 187–201.

17.7 Kashmir Incident, 1951

The Kashmiri War ended by cease-fire on January 1, 1949 (17.2). India occupied part of disputed Kashmir and formally incorporated it as a state of India. Azad Kashmir forces supported by Pakistan and Pakistani troops controlled the remainder of the territory. Pakistan assumed direct responsibility for defense throughout Azad Kashmir beginning in 1949. Minor incidents became commonplace across the Pakistani-Indian line despite efforts of the United Nations Military Observer Group in India and Pakistan. A serious incident occurred in the last week of June 1951 when Pakistani troops ambushed an Indian patrol on the Indian side of the cease-fire line. Pakistan and India each deployed additional forces to the border in July but no further major incidents occurred and reinforcements began to withdraw in August. No Pakistani or Indian fatalities are reported.

Brecher, M., J. Wilkenfeld, and S. Moser. 1988. *Crises in the Twentieth Century,* 1: 220–221.
Burke, S. 1974. *Mainsprings of Indian and Pakistani Foreign Policies,* 120.
Butterworth, R. 1976. *Managing Interstate Conflict,* 117–120.
Gupta, Sisir. 1966. *Kashmir, a Study in India-Pakistan Relations,* 235–244.
New York Times 7/2/51, 2:2; 7/4/51, 4:3.

17.8 Rann of Kutch Crisis, 1956

India and Pakistan disputed control of the Rann of Kutch as well as the state of Kashmir and Jammu (17.2, 17.7) after partition and independence in 1947. The Kutch state including the Rann joined India upon partition. Pakistan claimed that the northern part of the Rann belonged to the Sind state, which joined Pakistan, based upon earlier boundary markings. Protracted negotiations ensued from 1948. Pakistani police established a presence within the Rann's Chad Bet region in early 1956. India brought in regular military forces which proceeded to clear the area beginning in mid-February. Indian patrols were occasionally fired upon during the next month and also mounted small attacks upon Pakistani border positions. Serious fighting occurred at the end of the imbroglio on March 18–19, 1956, by which time regular Pakistani troops had been brought to the border. Pakistani artillery moved into the disputed zone and shelled Indian positions before being silenced by Indian counterattacks. Four Indian soldiers and ten Pakistani troops were reportedly killed.

Asian Recorder 2 (1956): 771.
Butterworth, R. 1976. *Managing Interstate Conflict,* 214.
Razvi, M. 1971. *The Frontiers of Pakistan,* 82.

17.9 Surma River Skirmishes, 1958

Repeated conflict followed partition of British India among independent states of India and Pakistan in 1947. Serious violence arose first on the border of West Pakistan, including involving Kashmir (17.2, 17.7) and the Rann of Kutch (17.8). Smuggling across the Surma River helped to provoke minor incidents on the East Pakistan border also from early 1958, including small arms cross-border fire between Indian and Pakistani guards. India began small military raids upon Pakistani territory at the beginning of June 1958. Pakistan commenced comparable assaults in early August. For two and a half weeks until cease-fire on August 26, 1958, raiding teams repeatedly attacked one another's positions along many miles of the border. At least six Indian soldiers and at least five Pakistani troops died during the skirmishes.

Razvi, M. 1971. *The Frontiers of Pakistan*, 53–54.
Keesing's Contemporary Archives. 1973. *Pakistan from 1947 to the Creation of Bangladesh*, 43–44.
Sen Gupta, J. 1974. *History of Freedom Movement in Bangladesh*, 132–147.

17.10 Longju-Ladakh Events, 1959

Britain and China did not fully demarcate the Sino-Indian border prior to Indian independence in 1947. India and the People's Republic of China advanced conflicting boundary claims in the early 1950s. India established border posts within disputed areas, including advanced positions in the northwest and along the northeast frontier. China built roads in contested regions, including across Aksai Chin in northeastern India. The Chinese occupation of Tibet provoked additional disputes, especially during and after the uprising within Lhasa in 1959 (16.7).

Tibetan refugees fled to India in spring 1959, including Tibet's spiritual leader, the Dalai Lama. China protested alleged Indian support for rebellion and deployed regular troops near India's borders. Indian police aggressively patrolled frontier areas. Minor incidents occurred as early as June 1959. Chinese soldiers intercepted an Indian police patrol within Khinzemane, part of India's Northeast Frontier Agency (Arunachal Pradesh), on August 7. On August 25 several hundred Chinese soldiers captured India's northeast border post at Longju where they remained until October 1962. Minor incidents also occurred elsewhere on the India-China frontier as well as on the borders of Sikkim and Bhutan, Himalayan states under Indian protection. On October 21, 1959, Chinese troops attacked and captured an Indian patrol near Kongka Pass in the Aksai Chin region of Ladakh. Violent subsided temporarily but border dispute remained unresolved. At least five Chinese soldiers died within India during 1959 events as did as many or more Indians.

Brecher, M., J. Wilkenfeld, and S. Moser. 1988. *Crises in the Twentieth Century*, 1: 244–245.

Burke, S. 1974. *Mainsprings of Indian and Pakistani Foreign Policies*, 159–165.

Butterworth, R. 1976. *Managing Interstate Conflict*, 178–181.

Day, A., ed. 1987. *Border and Territorial Disputes*, 279–286.

Eekelen, W. van. 1964. *Indian Foreign Policy and the Border Dispute with China*, 79–92.

Hinton, H. 1966. *Communist China in World Politics*, 288–290.

Hoffmann, S. 1990. *India and the China Crisis*, 3–91.

Kavic, L. 1967. *India's Quest for Security*, 46–51, 62–68.

Lu, C. 1986. *The Sino-Indian Border Dispute*, 64–77.

Maxwell, N. 1972. *India's China War*, 102–134.

Patterson, G. 1964. *Peking Versus Delhi*, 166–199, 250–255.

Richardson, H. 1984. *Tibet and Its History*, 224–234.

Rowland, J. 1967. *A History of Sino-Indian Relations*, 124–132.

Vertzberger, Y. 1984. *Misperceptions in Foreign Policymaking*.

Watson, F. 1966. *The Frontiers of China*, 83–125.

Whiting, A. 1975. *The Chinese Calculus of Deterrence*, 8–10.

17.11 Goan Accession, 1961

Portugal established enclaves on the coast of India beginning in 1505 and retained control of Goa (the capital) and other small territories after India attained independence in 1947. India proposed to absorb Portuguese domains but Portugal refused. In July 1954 an irregular group out of India claiming to represent "Free Goan volunteers" seized control of several enclaves. India denied access to Portuguese authorities who sought to restore control. In August 1955 several thousand demonstrators invaded Goa from India. Police fired upon the crowd, killing fifteen, while Portuguese soldiers stood at standby but took no direct action. The demonstrators withdrew. Tension recurred in 1961 after the Indian Parliament passed legislation to annex former Portuguese enclaves which India had occupied since 1954. Portugal increased her military presence in the area as did India. On December 11 India's prime minister Jawarharlal Nehru demanded that Portugal withdraw from Goa. U.N. Secretary General U Thant attempted to mediate: Portugal agreed; India refused. Minor incidents occurred at the Goan-Indian border beginning December 15. On December 17, 1961, Indian troops invaded Goa and established control the next day when Portugal surrendered. Twenty Indian troops died invading Goa as did forty-five defenders, including at least two Portuguese soldiers.

Brecher, M. 1968. *India and World Politics*, 121–136.
Brecher, M., J. Wilkenfeld, and S. Moser. 1988. *Crises in the Twentieth Century*, 1: 256.

Burke, S. 1974. *Mainsprings of Indian and Pakistani Foreign Policies*, 170–171.
Butterworth, R. 1976. *Managing Interstate Conflict*, 197–198.
Kaul, B. 1967. *The Untold Story*, 295–307.
Kay, H. 1970. *Salazar and Modern Portugal*, 294–328.
Maxwell, N. 1972. *India's China War*, 226–232.
Rao, R. 1963. *Portuguese Rule in Goa*.
Rubinoff, A. 1971. *India's Use of Force in Goa*.

17.12 Sino-Indian War, 1962

Small-scale armed conflict occurred between India and China in 1959 (17.10) within disputed border territory associated with Aksai Chin in northwest India and also India's Northeast Frontier Agency (Arunachal Pradesh). India launched Operation Onkar in 1961 in order to assert military presence within the disputed areas. Indian troops established positions in close proximity to Chinese forces by early 1962. Minor incidents occurred as early as that spring. The first direct confrontation occurred at Galwan in Aksai Chin in July 1962 when Chinese troops deployed around an Indian post recently constructed near a Chinese installation. Small units of Indian soldiers challenged Chinese positions July 20–21 while attempting to resupply Galwan. A similar confrontation near India's northeast post at Dhola led to shooting incidents in late September and to attack by a small unit of Chinese troops in early October.

On October 20, 1962, China launched full-scale offensives against Indian advance positions in both eastern and western regions. India deployed additional troops with American logistical assistance but was forced to withdraw from most disputed areas by the time China declared a cease-fire that took effect November 22, 1962. China sustained more than 1,000 fatalities during month-long major fighting. Although India initially claimed fewer losses, 2,000 or more Indian soldiers apparently died.

Barnds, W. 1972. *India, Pakistan, and the Great Powers*, 165–182.
Brecher, M., J. Wilkenfeld, and S. Moser. 1988. *Crises in the Twentieth Century*, 1: 258–259.
Brines, R. 1968. *The Indo–Pakistani Conflict*, 190–213.
Burke, S. 1974. *Mainsprings of Indian and Pakistani Foreign Policies*, 159–176.
Butterworth, R. 1976. *Managing Interstate Conflict*, 333–334.
Chaturvedi, M. 1978. *History of the Indian Air Force*, 118–128.
Day, A., ed. 1987. *Border and Territorial Disputes*, 279–286.
Eekelen, W. van. 1964. *Indian Foreign Policy and the Border Dispute with China*.
Gurtov, M., and B. Hwang. 1980. *China under Threat*, 99–152.
Hinton, H. 1966. *Communist China in World Politics*, 296–304.

Hoffmann, S. 1990. *India and the China Crisis*, 64–77.
Kaul, B. 1967. *The Untold Story*, 353–445.
Kavic, L. 1967. *India's Quest for Security*, 169–189.
Keegan, J., ed. 1983. *World Armies*, 258–268.
Lu, C. 1986. *The Sino-Indian Border Dispute*, 64–77.
Maxwell, N. 1972. *India's China War*.
Rowland, J. 1967. *A History of Sino-Indian Relations*, 133–173.
Segal, G. 1985. *Defending China*, 140–157.
Small, M., and J. Singer. 1982. *Resort to Arms*, 93.
Vertzberger, Y. 1984. *Misperceptions in Foreign Policymaking*.
Watson, F. 1966. *The Frontiers of China*, 145–161.
Whiting, A. 1975. *The Chinese Calculus of Deterrence*, ix–169.

17.13 Tripura Skirmishes, 1962

Armed conflict erupted frequently between India and Pakistan after partition in 1947, including along the Surma River bordering India and East Pakistan in 1956 (17.9). Accession of Tripura to India in 1949 created problems due to old border disputes predating independence involving states that acceded to East Pakistan. In the early 1960s India and Pakistan each established border posts within disputed areas. During the last week of September 1962 small units of Pakistani soldiers began attacks upon contested Indian border installations. India promptly responded in kind. On October 16 India and Pakistan agreed to a cease-fire in the Tripura region and agreed to withdraw contested border posts. Military engagements ceased by the following day. No military fatalities are reported.

Asian Recorder 8 (1962): 4898–4899.
New York Times 9/27/62, 6:5; 9/28/62, 2:8; 10/14/62, 5:1; 10/17/62, 3:6.

17.14 Indo-Pakistani War, 1964–1965

India and Pakistan disputed various parts of their border, particularly involving West Pakistan, after partition and independence in 1947. Fighting occurred within the Rann of Kutch in 1956 (17.8). The Kashmiri War (17.2) ended in 1949 with India and Pakistan each controlling part of the disputed state of Jammu and Kashmir. Minor incidents and occasionally serious encounters (17.7) occurred along the Kashmiri cease-fire line during the 1950s and early 1960s and eventually sparked major warfare. Pakistan began frequent small raids into Indian Kashmir in February 1964. India followed suit against Azad (Pakistani) Kashmir starting at the end of December 1964. On April 9, 1965, India mounted a ground assault upon Pakistani police posts in the Rann of Kutch. Pakistani troops counterattacked Indian positions in the area the same day. A temporary cease-fire was achieved May 11. In early August 1965 large numbers of irregulars out of Pakistan began infiltrating Indian Kashmir. On August 25 India invaded and captured part of Azad Kashmir. Pakistan counterattacked across the 1949 cease-fire line. The war grew September 5 when India attacked West Pakistan across a broad front.

On September 7 the People's Republic of China condemned Indian attacks upon Pakistan. She also complained of provocations by Indian forces operating out of India's protectorate Sikkim within Tibet, formally annexed to China earlier that year. On September 16 China issued an ultimatum demanding that India withdraw military forces from positions near the Chinese border, including within disputed territory which had been the scene of fighting in 1959 and 1962 (17.10, 17.12). On September 21 Chinese mortars began to shell Indian positions on the border of Sikkim. Indian troops stationed at the Sino-Sikkimese border immediately began shelling Chinese territory in kind.

A cease-fire between India and Pakistan proposed by the United Nations took belated effect September 23, 1965, halting major movements of ground forces. The United Nations Military Observer Group in India and Pakistan (UNMOGIP), present since 1948, was enlarged and the United Nations India-Pakistan Observation Mission (UNIPOM) was established to supervise troop withdrawals. Small skirmishes between Indian and Pakistani forces continued until November 19. Fighting on the Tibetan-Sikkimese border ended December 11, 1965, following two days of small Chinese raids against Indian positions within Sikkim.

2,000–3,000 Indian soldiers died during the Indo-Pakistan War. A similar number of Pakistani troops were killed. Chinese losses included a dozen or fewer fatalities.

General

Brecher, M., J. Wilkenfeld, and S. Moser. 1988. *Crises in the Twentieth Century*, 1: 274–276.
Butterworth, R. 1976. *Managing Interstate Conflict*, 390–395.
Day, A., ed. 1987. *Border and Territorial Disputes*, 317–329.
Keegan, J., ed. 1983. *World Armies*, 441–456.
Small, M., and J. Singer. 1982. *Resort to Arms*, 93.

India

Barnds, W. 1972. *India, Pakistan, and the Great Powers*, 183–208.
Blinkenberg, L. 1972. *India-Pakistan*, 238–263.

Brines, R. 1968. *The Indo-Pakistani Conflict*, 251–400.
Chaturvedi, M. 1978. *History of the Indian Air Force*, 176–147.
Ganguly, S. 1986. *The Origins of War in South Asia*, 57–96.
Gupta, H. 1969. *The Kutch Affair*, 177–213.
Kaul, B. 1972. *Confrontation with Pakistan*, 19–76.

Pakistan

Burke, S. 1973. *Pakistan's Foreign Policy*, 318–357.
Burke, S. 1974. *Mainsprings of Indian and Pakistani Foreign Policies*, 177–190.
Choudhury, G. 1968. *Pakistan's Relations with India*, 258–268, 279–304.
Fricker, J. 1979. *Battle for Pakistan*.
Keesing's Contemporary Archives. 1973. *Pakistan from 1947 to the Creation of Bangladesh*, 88–93.
Korbel, J. 1966. *Danger in Kashmir*, 337–350.
Lamb, A. 1967. *The Kashmir Problem*, 112–134.
Razvi, M. 1971. *The Frontiers of Pakistan*, 83, 123–133.

Sikkim

Grover, B. 1974. *Sikkim and India*, 164–167.
Raghunadha Rao, P. 1978. *Sikkim*, 31–32.

17.15 Kashmir Skirmish, 1967

Dispute over the status of Kashmir provoked armed conflict involving India and Pakistan several times after 1947, including during the Kashmiri War (17.2), in 1951 (17.7) and during the Indo-Pakistan War (17.14). Another skirmish occurred on May 15, 1967. An Indian patrol that included both regular troops and civilian border guards crossed into Pakistani territory north of Sialkot and opened fire on Pakistani border guards. Fighting continued for eight hours and forces on both sides of the border exchanged small arms and mortar fire. Two Indian soldiers are reported killed on Pakistani territory. No Pakistani fatalities are reported.

New York Times 5/20/67, 5:4; 5/21/67, 38:1.
Times (London) 5/20/67, 3c; 5/23/67, 4f.

17.16 Natu La-Cho La Duels, 1967

China and India fought small encounters along the border of India's protectorate Sikkim in 1965 during the Indo-Pakistani War (17.14). Minor incidents continued the following year. The Sino-Sikkimese border, similar to the Sino-Indian border which provoked fighting in

1959 and 1962 (17.10, 17.12), suffered competing claims and incomplete demarcation. China complained about Indian air and ground intrusions during January 1967. Further incidents involving cross-border small arms fire occurred early in September. During the second week of September 1967, Indian and Chinese artillery exchanged fire at Natu La (Natu Pass) on the Sikkimese frontier and an Indian patrol attacked Chinese border positions. China and India exchanged small arms and light artillery fire several times during the following three weeks. Serious engagements ceased after India raided Chinese positions at Cho La (Cho Pass) at the beginning of October. Eighty-six Indian soldiers are reported killed. Chinese losses are estimated variously but presumably included two score or more fatalities.

Grover, B. 1974. *Sikkim and India*, 167–169.
New York Times 9/12/67, 1:1; 9/13/67, 1:2; 9/14/67, 9:1; 9/15/67, 3:2; 9/17/67, 9:1;
    9/17/67, IV, 7:1; 9/24/67, 9:3; 10/2/67, 7:1; 10/3/67, 8:1; 10/5/67, 43:1.
Raghunadha Rao, P. 1978. *Sikkim*, 32–34.

17.17 Bengali War, 1971–1972

Partition of British India upon independence in 1947 resulted in a divided Pakistan to east and west of India. Subsequent Indo-Pakistani territorial disputes provoked repeated armed conflict involving Kashmir and the Rann of Kutch in the west in 1947–1949 (17.2), 1951 (17.7), 1956 (17.8) and 1964–1965 (17.14) and on the Surma River and Tripura boundaries in the east in 1958 (17.9) and 1962 (17.13).

Bengali-populated East Pakistan was culturally as well as geographically distinct from West Pakistan. During the 1960s, the Aswami League led by Sheikh Mujibur Rahman protested West Pakistani control of the central government. The Aswami League swept 1970 elections to select East Pakistani representatives to a proposed National Assembly. On March 1, 1971, the military regime in Karachi postponed scheduled first meeting of the National Assembly. Demonstrations erupted within East Pakistan. Sheikh Rahman was arrested and the Pakistani Army brutally suppressed local dissent beginning March 25, 1971. More than one million refugees fled East Pakistan to India during the next few months. Some returned to fight after obtaining arms and training within India.

The Pakistani Army began sporadic small raids against Bengali sanctuaries within India in late April 1971. Indian artillery occasionally retaliated against East Pakistani territory beginning a few days later. Large Indian Army forces entered border areas of East

Pakistan in early November 1971. Pakistan, in turn, mobilized forces
near West Pakistan's border with India's Punjab. India invaded West
Pakistan November 21. Pakistan counterattacked within the Punjab
December 3 and India launched a major invasion of East Pakistan later
the same day. On December 17, 1971, Pakistani forces surrendered
within the east and a cease-fire was announced in the west. Bengali
nationalists proclaimed independence of East Pakistan as Bangladesh.
Episodic clashes continued on the border of Indian Kashmir and West
Pakistan, including major battle within the Lipa Valley in May 1972.
An effective cease-fire was finally obtained in mid-November 1972.

More than one million civilians are believed killed during the
Bengali war of independence. Total Pakistani military fatalities are
thought to approach 8,000, including nearly 3,000 in contact with
Indian troops. 2,000 to 3,000 Indian soldiers also died.

General

Brecher, M., J. Wilkenfeld, and S. Moser. 1988. *Crises in the Twentieth Century*,
    1: 205–296.
Butterworth, R. 1976. *Managing Interstate Conflict*, 455–458.
Day, A., ed. 1987. *Border and Territorial Disputes*, 317–329.
Keegan, J., ed. 1983. *World Armies*, 258–268, 441–456.
Small, M., and J. Singer. 1982. *Resort to Arms*, 94.

Bangladesh

Payne, R. 1973. *Massacre*.
Sen Gupta, J. 1974. *History of Freedom Movement in Bangladesh*, 258–471.

India

Ayoob, M., and K. Subrahmanyhan. 1972. *The Liberation War*.
Blinkenberg, L. 1972. *India-Pakistan*, 303–324.
Chaturvedi, M. 1978. *History of the Indian Air Force*, 157–174.
Ganguly, S. 1986. *The Origins of War in South Asia*, 97–142.
Jackson, R. 1975. *South Asian Crisis*.
Jagdev Singh. 1988. *Dismemberment of Pakistan*.
Palit, D. 1972. *The Lightning Campaign*.

Pakistan

Attiqur Rahman, M. 1976. *Our Defence Cause*.
Burke, S. 1974. *Mainsprings of Indian and Pakistani Foreign Policies*, 203–215.
Keesing's Contemporary Archives. 1973. *Pakistan from 1947 to the Creation of
    Bangladesh*, 111–127.

Khan, F. 1973. *Pakistan's Crisis in Leadership.*
Rizvi, H. 1981. *Internal Strife and External Intervention.*
Salik, S. 1977. *Witness to Surrender.*

17.18 Tulung Incident, 1975

Troublesome border disputes between China and India provoked fighting in 1959 (17.10) and major war in 1962 (17.12) on both eastern and western frontiers. Indian and Chinese forces also engaged one another on the border of India's protectorate Sikkim in 1965 (17.14) and 1967 (17.16). In December 1962, following the Sino-Indian War, China agreed to withdraw from advanced positions and to administer vacated territory jointly with India through civil authorities. Full demarcation was also promised but repeatedly postponed. Differing interpretations of the 1962 agreement contributed to occasional incidents on the border between China's Tibet and of India's eastern province of Arunachal Pradesh during ensuing years. On October 20, 1975, an Indian military patrol intruded upon Tibet through the demilitarized zone near Tulung and engaged in a firefight with Chinese guards. Four Indian soldiers died but no Chinese fatalities are reported.

New York Times 11/2/75, 15:1; 11/3/75, 4:43; 11/4/75, 5:1.

17.19 Siachen Conflict, 1984–continuing

India and Pakistan divided disputed Kashmir *de facto* during the Kashmiri War (17.2). Frequent minor border incidents followed and also serious engagements in 1951 (17.7), 1964–1965 (17.14) and 1971–1972 (17.17). Conflict penetrated the Karakorum Mountains of far northern Kashmir in spring 1984 as India and Pakistan each attempted to gain control of the remote Siachen Glacier. India and Pakistan began small-unit raids and light artillery attacks upon one another's positions in early June 1984. Frequent skirmishes continued into the 1990s and eventually spread to other border areas. A battalion-sized Pakistani assault in September 1987 attempted unsuccessfully to drive Indian forces from the glacier. Fighting killed a few hundred Pakistani soldiers and a similar number of Indian troops by the end of 1988.

Asian Recorder 30 (1984): 17964, 18040; 31 (1985): 18238, 18444–18445, 18653–18654; 33 (1987): 19401–19404; 34 (1988): 19938–19939; (1989) 20547.
Desmond, E. 1989. "War at the Top of the World." *Time* 133 (July 31, 1989): 26–29.
Gupta, Shekhar. 1985. "Gunfire on the Glacier." *India Today* 10 (July 31, 1985): 78–81.

Laffin, J. 1986. *War Annual 1*, 69–71.
Laffin, J. 1987. *War Annual 2*, 99–100.
Laffin, J. 1989. *The World in Conflict 1989: War Annual 3*, 121–124.

17.20 Tamil War, 1987–continuing

Multicultural Sri Lanka (Ceylon) gained independence from the United Kingdom in 1948, shortly after India and Pakistan. From the beginning, majority Sinhalese controlled most national institutions. Tamil constituted a minority within the society as a whole but a majority within the north. Some Tamil immigrated from India and maintained ties with the Indian state of Tamil Nadu. Most represented indigenous peoples. Militant Tamil separatist sentiment became visible during the 1970s. The Tamil United Liberation Front (TULF), a coalition of Tamil political parties, declared commitment to a separate Tamil state during 1977 national elections. Guerrilla groups formed by the early 1980s, including the Liberation Tigers of Tamil Eelam, the People's Revolutionary Liberation Front and the Eelam Revolutionary Organization and Supporters. Tamil militants fomented violence upon Sinhalese communities and upon national government personnel and installations, including major assaults beginning in July 1983. Sinhalese riots persecuted Tamil in reprisal. TULF members were expelled from parliament and tens of thousands of Tamil fled to India. Efforts of the Sri Lanka army and police to suppress rebellion did not avail. An Indian Peace-Keeping Force commenced operations at the end of June 1987 at the request of the Sri Lanka government. India deployed 70,000 troops by 1988, outnumbering the entire Sri Lanka army. Violence continued into the 1990s. The death toll among civilians and military personnel approached 10,000 by 1989, including nearly 1,000 Indian soldiers killed.

Laffin, J. 1987. *War Annual 2*, 195–205.
Laffin, J. 1989. *The World in Conflict 1989: War Annual 3*, 205–213.
O'Ballance, E. 1989. *The Cyanide War:*.
Vanniasingham, S. 1988. *Sri Lanka, the Conflict Within*.
Wilson, A. 1988. *The Break-Up of Sri Lanka*.

18

Southeast Asia

Several strands of conflict afflicted Southeast Asia after World War II. France fought unsuccessfully beginning in 1945 to regain control of Indochina (18.1). Indochina was divided upon French withdrawal in 1954. Incidents followed on the South Vietnam-Cambodian border during the late 1950s (18.11, 18.14). The Second Indochina War (18.15) began in effect in 1958 and came to involve the United States as well as most states of the immediate region. The Third Indochina War (18.29) followed in 1976 and continued into the late 1980s. Border disputes involving Thailand, Laos and Cambodia surfaced during the First Indochina War (18.1), exacerbated the Third Indochina War (18.29) and also led to conflict upon other occasions (18.21, 18.23, 18.28). Sino-Vietnamese territorial disputes contributed to incidents in 1959 (18.16), to larger engagements in 1974 (18.26) and to major battles during the Third Indochina War (18.29).

The United Kingdom reoccupied Malaya immediately following World War II (18.2) and helped to suppress internal rebellion during the late 1940s and 1950s (18.6). Later Malay efforts to assert control of northern provinces included cooperative military ventures with Thailand between 1969 and 1980 (18.25, 18.30). The United Kingdom reestablished control of Singapore following World War II (18.3) and intervened again occasionally as late as 1956 (18.8, 18.13) during internal disorders.

Persistent instability within Burma provoked international conflict upon numerous occasions. British military forces intervened within Burma from 1946 until independence in 1948 (18.5) Burma was wracked by continuous internal strife and repeated minor international armed conflict after independence. Border dispute with China and Kuomintang exiles contributed to several Sino-Burmese incidents from 1950 to 1969 (18.7, 1812, 18.17, 18.24). Burmese efforts to expel Kuomintang elements led to conflict with Thailand in the early 1950s (18.9, 18.10). Karen insurgency within Burma contributed to further

239

incidents on the Thai border in 1959 (18.18) and 1984 (18.31). Rebellion within western Burma also led to conflict with Pakistan in 1959 (18.19).

Indonesian nationalists won independence from the Netherlands during the late 1940s (18.4). Indonesia subsequently sought to annex other territories initially retained by European colonial powers, including during the conflict over West Irian (18.20), confrontation with Malaysia (18.22) and the Timorese War (18.27).

18.1 First Indochina War, 1945–1954

France acquired protectorates within traditionally independent states of Cambodia, Laos and Tonkin (northern Vietnam) and colonies within Annam and Cochin-China in southern Vietnam between 1863 and 1893. Although these territories each retained a vestige of separate identity, France administered them as one unit after 1900. Sustained opposition to French rule developed starting in the 1920s, especially within Annam and Tonkin. The Vietnamese Independence League, led by Ho Chi Minh, became the most effective resistance group. Its followers were identified colloquially as the Vietminh.

Japan assumed direction of Indochina in 1941, one year after Paris fell to Germany. Japan occupied part of the territory and permitted nominal administration by Vichy France within other areas. The Vietminh opposed both Japanese and Vichy dominion. They grew in strength during World War II due in part to assistance from the United States and the United Kingdom. In March and April 1945, after the Free French were restored in Paris, Japan interned French forces within Indochina and encouraged traditional royal families of Laos, Cambodia and Annam to proclaim independence. Events moved quickly once Japan announced on August 14, 1945 that it intended to surrender. The Vietminh took control of Hanoi on August 19. A Provisional Government associated with but not fully controlled by the Vietminh asserted control within southern Vietnam on August 25, including both Annam and Cochin-China. Ho Chi Minh proclaimed the Democratic Republic of Vietnam in Hanoi on September 2.

China and the United Kingdom divided Indochina for purpose of accepting the surrender of Japanese troops. Chinese units entered the north in late August 1945 and took control of Japanese positions after the formal armistice on September 2. British and British-Indian troops arrived in the south on September 11. French soldiers released from Japanese internment moved promptly against the Provisional Government starting September 20, and fighting ensued within Saigon. British forces intervened and actively helped to suppress anti-French elements until May 1946. In addition, some interned Japanese troops were released and armed for police duty in the south. China, on the other hand, did not directly challenge the Vietminh government in the north and withdrew without major incident at the end of July 1946.

France expanded her forces in late 1945 and by early 1946 regained control of southern Vietnam, Cambodia and most of Laos. French troops entered northern Vietnam in March 1946. Unsuccessful negotiations followed between France and the Vietminh amidst occasional violence. Sustained fighting erupted in the north after French naval forces bombarded Haiphong in November 1946, killing hundreds and possibly thousands of civilians, in retaliation for attacks upon French soldiers.

French-Vietminh conflict became entangled with a Thai-French border dispute in 1946. Thailand seized control of border territories of Laos and Cambodia in 1941 and Japan acquiesced to her claims. France reopened the border question and simultaneously accused Thailand of providing sanctuary to Indochinese rebels. From May to October 1946 France repeatedly raided Thai border villages. Thailand formally agreed to withdraw from disputed areas in December.

Guerrilla warfare and occasional main force battles persisted until 1954. Most fighting took place in northern Vietnam until 1953 when the Vietminh entered Laos in force. The United States subsidized French costs beginning in September 1950. The Vietminh gained increased aid from China after the People's Republic took power within Peking in October 1949. The war became an increasingly controversial political issue within France as casualties mounted.

The battle at Dien Bien Phu was the climactic event of the war. France concentrated elite forces on the Plain of Jars surrounding Dien Bien Phu in 1953. The Vietminh attacked outlying positions in mid-March 1954. The United States considered but did not authorize direct intervention after the Vietminh besieged the central garrison late in March. French forces surrendered at Dien Bien Phu in May. In July 1954, following a change of government in Paris, France accepted a settlement negotiated at Geneva that provided for French withdrawal, recognized the independence of Laos and Cambodia, and partitioned northern and southern Vietnam at the 17th Parallel pending future arrangements.

The First Indochina War cost at least 500,000 fatalities, most of them civilians. As many as 90,000 French military personnel died. Almost forty soldiers under British command were killed in 1945–1946. China suffered no battle fatalities so far as is generally known.

General

Brecher, M., J. Wilkenfeld, and S. Moser. 1988. *Crises in the Twentieth Century*, 1: 223, 226–227.

Butterworth, R. 1976. *Managing Interstate Conflict*, 50–58.
Keegan, J., ed. 1983. *World Armies*, 652–658.
Small, M., and J. Singer. 1982. *Resort to Arms*, 98.

China

Chen, K. 1969. *Vietnam and China*, 99–154.
Hinton, H. 1958. *China's Relations with Burma and Vietnam*, 12–14.

France

Devillers, P. 1952. *Histoire du Viet-Nam de 1940 a 1952*.
Devillers, P. 1969. *End of a War*.
Hammer, E. 1966. *The Struggle for Indochina, 1940–1955*.
Kelly, G. 1965. *Lost Soldiers*, 31–104.
O'Ballance, E. 1964. *The Indo-China War, 1945–1954*.

Laos

Oudone Sananikone. 1981. *The Royal Lao Army and U.S. Advice and Support*, 1–30.
Toye, H. 1968. *Laos: Buffer State or Battleground*, 54–103.

Thailand

Fifield, R. 1958. *The Diplomacy of South East Asia*, 243–245.
New York Times 5/26/46, 14:1; 5/27/46, 1:2; 5/27/46, 4:2; 5/28/46, 8:5; 5/29/46, 8:2,3; 5/30/46, 11:1; 5/30/46, 20:3; 5/31/46, 6:1; 6/30/46, 19:2; 8/10/46, 6:3; 10/13/46, 43:5; 10/14/46, 8:5.
Nuechterlein, D. 1965. *Thailand and the Struggle for Southeast Asia*, 89–91.

United Kingdom

Blaxland, G. 1971. *The Regiments Depart*, 3–4.
Donnison, F. 1956. *British Military Administration in the Far East*, 401–411.
Dunn, P. 1985. *The First Vietnam War*.
Rosie, G. 1970. *The British in Vietnam*.

United States

Billings-Yun, M. 1988. *Decision Against War*.
Gurtov, M. 1967. *The First Vietnam Crisis*.
Spector, R. 1983. *The United States Army in Vietnam—Advice and Support: The Early Years*, 51–214.

Vietminh

Bang, N. 1962. "The Times I Met Him." In *Days with Ho Chi Minh*, 64–103.
Fall, B. 1964. *Street Without Joy*.
Lancaster, D. 1961. *The Emancipation of French Indochina*.

18.2 Malayan Occupation, 1945–1946

The East India Company established scattered settlements on the Malay Peninsula beginning in 1786. These passed to British colonial administration in 1826. The United Kingdom extended control among southern and central Malay territories during the late nineteenth century through protectorate agreements signed with individual local rulers. British domains thus represented a patchwork of colonial settlements, federated and unfederated Malay states. Japan captured the Malay Peninsula at the beginning of 1942. The United Nations allies did not challenge Japanese occupation during World War II except through air raids and clandestine paramilitary operations. British forces returned September 4, 1945, in order to accept the surrender of Japanese troops. Military occupation continued until April 1, 1946. when a civilian government was appointed to administer the Union of Malaya (Malaysia), incorporating all Malay states except Singapore. Four British soldiers died in action during the military occupation.

Clutterbuck, R. 1985. *Conflict and Violence in Singapore and Malaya*, 40.
Donnison, F. 1956. *British Military Administration in the Far East*, 153–170, 375–399.
Paget, J. 1967. *Counter-Insurgency Operations*, 43–47.

18.3 Singaporan Occupation, 1945

The Sultan of Johore ceded Singapore to the British East India Company in 1824. The United Kingdom associated it with her Indian domains in 1830 and established direct colonial control in 1867. Japan conquered Singapore in February 1942 shortly after she captured other Malay territories. British troops deployed to Singapore on September 5, 1945, in order to accept surrender of Japanese forces following armistice ending World War II. Military authorities passed control to civilian colonial administrators a few days later. No serious bloodshed occurred.

Clutterbuck, R. 1985. *Conflict and Violence in Singapore and Malaya*, 40.
Donnison, F. 1956. *British Military Administration in the Far East*, 160–163.

18.4 Indonesian War, 1945–1949

The Netherlands acquired control of the Dutch East Indies gradually between the seventeenth and early nineteenth centuries. Serious rebellions against colonial rule flared and were repressed in the late nineteenth and early twentieth centuries, including an insurrection on Java in 1926. Japan seized the East Indies in early 1942. U.S. forces, supported in part by British and Australian naval and air units, counterattacked coastal areas of remote islands, including former Dutch New Guinea, as early as April 1944. The United Nations allies did not attack heavily populated Java, however, nor Sumatra.

Indonesian nationalists on Java led by Ahmad Sukarno proclaimed an independent Republic of the United States of Indonesia on August 17, 1945, immediately after Japan announced intention to surrender. Australian troops assumed responsibility for disarming Japanese troops on islands east of Borneo beginning September 11, 1945, including West New Guinea and West Timor, and remained until February 1946. British and British-Indian troops arrived on Java for the same purpose at the end of September 1945. The Netherlands claimed the right to restore colonial control within the East Indies but Dutch troops did not appear until the end of October and arrived in large number only in 1946. Nationalists resisted British military occupation and subsequent Dutch efforts to reestablish colonial government. Intense opposition occurred on Java, especially at Surabaya, and to a lesser extent also on Sumatra in late 1945 and early 1946, put down primarily by British-Indian troops. A complex patchwork remained when the United Kingdom withdrew in November 1946. The Dutch government administered some areas and not others. Various nationalist groupings, not all controlled by Sukarno's proclaimed Republican government, held sway in other parts of the Indies.

Guerrilla warfare and negotiations between the Dutch and Republican governments coexisted during the next three years. The Netherlands generally refrained major offensives against Republican positions except during two inclusive "police actions" in 1947 and 1948. On December 27, 1949, the Netherlands formally transferred control of most of the Dutch Indies except West New Guinea (West Irian) to the Republican government.

Tens of thousands of civilians are believed to have died during the Indonesian War. In addition, approximately 400 Dutch soldiers were killed as were almost 600 British and British-Indian military personnel. Australia sustained no reported fatalities.

General

Brecher, M., J. Wilkenfeld, and S. Moser. 1988. *Crises in the Twentieth Century*, 1: 203–204, 207–208, 216.
Butterworth, R. 1976. *Managing Interstate Conflict*, 46–50.
Hartman, T. 1984. *A World Atlas of Military History*, 73.
Small, M., and J. Singer. 1982. *Resort to Arms*, 98.

Australia

Varma, R. 1974. *Australia and Southeast Asia*, 59–100.

Indonesia

Anderson, B. 1972. *Java in a Time of Revolution*.
Jones, H. 1971. *Indonesia: The Possible Dream*, 101–112.
Kahin, G. 1952. *Nationalism and Revolution in Indonesia*.
Kosut, H., ed. 1967. *Indonesia: The Sukarno Years*, 8–32.
Legge, J. 1972. *Sukarno: A Political Biography*, 181–239.
Nasution, A. 1965. *Fundamentals of Guerrilla Warfare*.
Reid, A. 1974. *The Indonesian National Revolution*.
Wehl, D. 1948. *The Birth of Indonesia*.
Woodman, D. 1955. *The Republic of Indonesia*, 200–261.

Netherlands

Dahm, B. 1971. *History of Indonesia in the Twentieth Century*, 110–142.
Gerbrandy, P. 1950. *Indonesia*, 72–191.
McMahon, R. 1981. *Colonialism and Cold War*.
Palmier, L. 1962. *Indonesia and the Dutch*, 46–110.
Taylor, A. 1960. *Indonesian Independence and the United Nations*.
Yong, M. 1982. *H. J. van Mook and Indonesian Independence*.

United Kingdom

Blaxland, G. 1971. *The Regiments Depart*, 4.
Donnison, F. 1956. *British Military Administration in the Far East*, 413–434.

18.5 Burmese Insurgency, 1946–1948

The United Kingdom conquered states previously representing the Burmese Empire during a series of wars from 1826 and annexed them to India in 1885. She also conquered the Shan states extending to Siam (Thailand) by 1891. Burma gained separate colonial status in 1937. Japan nearly captured the territory in 1942. A combined offensive involving Chinese, British and British Indian troops in 1944–1945 reclaimed most of Burma by the end of World War II. British civilian administration was reestablished in October 1945. Aung San, a Burmese nationalist who led the Anti-Fascist Organization resisting Japan during World War II, formed the Anti-Fascist People's Freedom League (AFPFL) in August 1945 in order to oppose continued British rule. The AFPFL recruited paramilitary forces and established a presence within most parts of Burma but its effectiveness was limited by dissension among regional components. The United Kingdom deployed troops in June 1946 to help police control demonstrations and other disorders. British soldiers were called upon for sporadic limited actions until grant of independence on January 2, 1948. No British soldiers are reported killed.

Cady, J. 1958. *A History of Modern Burma*, 427–642.
Donnison, F. 1956. *British Military Administration in the Far East*, 347–373.
Tinker, H. 1956. "Burma's Northeast Borderland Problems." *Pacific Affairs* 29 (December): 324–346.
Tinker, H. 1967. *The Union of Burma*.
Trager, F. 1966. *Burma: from Kingdom to Republic*.

18.6 Malayan Insurgency, 1948–1960

The United Kingdom was driven from the Malay Peninsula by Japanese forces in 1942 and returned following the armistice with Japan in 1945 (18.2). She formed the Union of Malaya (Malaysia) in 1946 among all Malay states except Singapore during military occupation, simplifying pre-World II colonial arrangements. The Union granted uniform powers regarding defense and foreign relations to the British Crown and denied some local rulers the same autonomy they enjoyed before World War II. Several sectors of the population favored greater self-rule or complete independence. On February 1, 1948, the United Kingdom reorganized administration under the Federation of Malaya and returned some powers to local rulers. Federation was opposed by overseas Chinese who feared Malay power as well as by communist factions which resisted any form of continuing British rule.

Britain helped secretly to form the Malayan People's Anti-Japanese Army (MPAJA) during World War II, numbering as many as 7,000 irregular soldiers before being disbanded in December 1945. Opponents of British rule formed the Malayan People's Anti-British Army (MPABA) in 1948, recruited initially from among Chinese and Communist party veterans of the MPAJA. Protracted guerrilla warfare against the Federation government ensued. Emergency regulations passed by the Federal legislature condoned British military intervention which began in June 1948.

British/Federation strategy during the emergency relied upon a combination of locally recruited paramilitary police and Gurkha and other regular army units under British command. Australia:n aircraft joined the effort in August 1950, after Royal Air Force squadrons were transferred to Korea (16.5), as did Australian and New Zealand: ground forces in October 1955. Warfare involved primarily small engagements within and near Malaya's extensive jungles. Violence peaked between 1949 and 1951. Insurgent strength gradually declined thereafter until the emergency was officially declared ended on July 30, 1960.

It is estimated that 10,000 persons died during the Malayan Insurgency, including numerous civilians. Regular British military units suffered approximately 500 fatalities. New Zealand and Australian forces sustained approximately twenty and thirty killed respectively.

Blaxland, G. 1971. *The Regiments Depart*, 73–131.
Butterworth, R. 1976. *Managing Interstate Conflict*, 109–110.
Chin, K. 1983. *The Defence of Malaysia and Singapore*, 8–57.
Clutterbuck, R. 1985. *Conflict and Violence in Singapore and Malaya*, 167–263.
Dewar, M. 1984. *Brush Fire Wars*, 27–44.
King, M. 1981. *New Zealanders at War*, 277–279.
Millar, T. 1978. *Australia in Peace and War*, 237–243.
Millar, T. 1980. "Anglo-Australian Partnership in Defense of the Malaysian Area." In *Australia and Britain*, ed. A. Madden and W. Morris-Jones, 71–89.
O'Ballance, E. 1966. *Malaya: The Communist Insurgent War*.
Paget, J. 1967. *Counter-Insurgency Operations*, 48–79.
Short, A. 1975. *The Communist Insurrection in Malaya*.

18.7 Kengtung Raid, 1950

Mao Tse-tung proclaimed the People's Republic in Peking in October 1949, culminating China's twenty-year civil war. Remnants of Republican (Kuomintang) armies began evacuating mainland China as early as 1948. Some isolated units fled to northern Burma as early as 1949; others retreated to Yunnan within southwest China and eventually also entered Burma.

Burma-Chinese relations were complicated by a disputed, ill-defined boundary which neither fully controlled after World War II. Sporadic cross-border incursions by Republican Chinese forces are reported as early as 1946. The Republic of China claimed large tracts of northern Burma upon Burmese independence in 1948 (18.5). The People's Republic established diplomatic relations immediately with Burma in 1949 and did not at first reassert the Chinese border claim.

China attempted to eradicate Kuomintang resistance within Yunnan from late 1949 as well as among offshore islands (16.6). The People's Republic refrained from major operations against Kuomintang sanctuaries within Burma but occasionally conducted small cross-border forays. On one reported occasion in January 1950 a small People's Liberation Army detachment confronted Burmese troops deep within Kengtung in northern Burma. No fatalities are reported.

Burma (Union) Government. 1953. *Kuomintang Aggression Against Burma.*
Butterworth, R. 1976. *Managing Interstate Conflict*, 99–100, 125–127.
Fifield, R. 1958. *The Diplomacy of South East Asia*, 196–210.
Hinton, H. 1966. *Communist China in World Politics*, 258–272.
Taylor, R. 1973. *Foreign and Domestic Consequences of the KMT Intervention in Burma*, 29.
Teiwes, F. 1969. "Force and Diplomacy on the Sino-Burmese Border." In *The Next Asia*, ed. D. Smith, 197–229.
Tinker, H. 1956. "Burma's Northeast Borderland Problems." *Pacific Affairs* 29 (December): 324–346.

18.8 Hertogh Riots, 1950

The United Kingdom resumed control of Singapore at the end of World War II (18.3) and managed it as a separate colony from Malaya after 1946. Singapore was spared, af first, direct effects of insurgency that broke out elsewhere on the Malay Peninsula in 1948 (18.6). In 1950, a legal dispute involving custody of Maria Hertogh, daughter of Dutch-Indonesian parents raised by a Malay foster family, became a cause célèbre within the Malay community. Demonstrations outside the Singapore Supreme Court on December 12, 1950 led to Malay violence against Europeans and Eurasians after police failed to exert effective control. The Governor called upon locally-garrisoned British Army units to help quell riots. Order was restored the following day. Eighteen persons were killed during the rioting but no British soldiers died.

Clutterbuck, R. 1985. *Conflict and Violence in Singapore and Malaya*, 72–73.
New York Times 12/12/50, 1:7; 12/26/50, 2:3.

18.9 Monghsat Bombing, 1953

Remnants of Republican (Kuomintang) forces resisted the People's Republic of China government proclaimed in Peking in 1949 following protracted civil war. Some Kuomintang elements retreated to Yunnan in southwest China and from there to border territories of Tibet and

Burma, provoking conflict in both areas in 1950 (16.7, 18.7). Several thousand former Kuomintang soldiers loyal to General Li Mi entered Burma during the early 1950s, established fortified positions near Monghsat and Monghai near the Thailand border, and periodically raided Yunnan. The Republic of China on Taiwan, with American assistance and the complicity of Thailand, helped to provide direction and support to Kuomintang remnants within Burma after they arrived.

Burma complained belatedly to the United States and the United Nations in February 1953 about Kuomintang presence after anticommunist Chinese joined attacks upon Burmese government installations. In April the U.N. General Assembly condemned interference by Taiwan and called for the removal of Kuomintang forces, without immediate result. Burma's air force began to bomb Monghsat and Monghai systematically in September 1953. On several occasions in September and October Burmese aircraft also attacked supply lines and refuges within nearby areas of Thailand. No Burmese fatalities are reported within Thailand.

Brecher, M., J. Wilkenfeld, and S. Moser. 1988. *Crises in the Twentieth Century,* 1: 222–223.
Butterworth, R. 1976. *Managing Interstate Conflict,* 125–127.
Taylor, R. 1973. *Foreign and Domestic Consequences of the KMT Intervention in Burma,* 56.
Teiwes, F. 1969. "Force and Diplomacy on the Sino-Burmese Border." In *The Next Asia,* ed. D. Smith, 197–229.
Tinker, H. 1956. "Burma's Northeast Borderland Problems." *Pacific Affairs* 29 (December): 324–346.

18.10 Kuomintang Suppression, 1955

Efforts by the Burmese government to expel Chinese Kuomintang exiles from northern Burma contributed to armed conflict with Thailand in 1953 (18.9). General Li Mi and some followers withdrew to Taiwan in 1954 under pressure from the United Nations. Thousands of former Kuomintang soldiers remained near the Chinese and Thai borders, supported in part by covert assistance from Taiwan and the United States. Further Burmese pacification efforts in 1955 included air attacks upon Kuomintang positions within Burma and the bombing of a Thai border village in March. No military casualties are reported within Thailand.

Butterworth, R. 1976. *Managing Interstate Conflict,* 125–127.
Taylor, R. 1973. *Foreign and Domestic Consequences of the KMT Intervention in Burma.*

Teiwes, F. 1969. "Force and Diplomacy on the Sino-Burmese Border." In *The Next Asia*, ed. D. Smith, 197–229.

Tinker, H. 1956. "Burma's Northeast Borderland Problems." *Pacific Affairs* 29 (December): 324–346.

18.11 Hoa-Hao Resistance, 1955–1956

French Indochina was divided among separate independent states representing Cambodia, Laos, and northern and southern regions of Vietnam in 1954 at the end of the First Indochina War (18.1). Ngo Dinh Diem became President of the Republic of Vietnam (South Vietnam) in October 1955 after Emperor Bao Dai was deposed. The Diem government attempted to suppress domestic elements resistant to central government control, including the Hoa-Hao religious sect. Some leaders of the Hoa-Hao were killed and others fled to neighboring Cambodia. From November 1955 to March 1956 small units of the Army of the Republic of Vietnam occasionally attacked Cambodian territory in pursuit of Hoa-Hao and other dissidents. No Vietnamese military casualties are reported during cross-border actions.

Duncanson, D. 1968. *Government and Revolution in Vietnam*, 220–222.

Fifield, R. 1958. *The Diplomacy of South East Asia*, 304–305, 378–379.

Hinh, N., and T. Tho. 1980. *The South Vietnamese Society*, 32–34.

Leifer, M. 1967. *Cambodia: The Search for Security*, 75, 95–97.

New York Times 3/31/56, 3:6.

18.12 Wa-Yunnan Dispute, 1955–1956

An unmarked and disputed border between China and Burma as well as presence of Kuomintang exiles upon Burmese territory contributed to armed conflict in 1950 (18.7) and to numerous ensuing minor border incidents. China began aggressively to build roads and border posts within its southwestern province of Yunnan near the Burmese frontier in 1955, including within territory that Burma claimed as parts of its states of Wa and Kachin. Chinese troops accompanied construction workers and engaged in occasional skirmishes with Burmese Army patrols beginning in November 1955. Burma protested Chinese actions and bilateral negotiations ensued. Serious incidents ceased in December 1956 when China and Burma announced their withdrawal from disputed border regions pending the outcome of further negotiations. At least four Chinese soldiers died within Burma during 1955–1956.

Butterworth, R. 1976. *Managing Interstate Conflict*, 99–100.

Fifield, R. 1958. *The Diplomacy of South East Asia*, 196–210.

Hinton, H. 1958. *China's Relations with Burma and Vietnam.*

Hinton, H. 1966. *Communist China in World Politics,* 312–315.

Johnstone, W. 1963. *Burma's Foreign Policy,* 187–200.

Kozicki, R. 1957. "The Sino-Burmese Frontier Problem." *Far Eastern Survey* 26 (March): 33–38.

Maxwell, N. 1972. *India's China War,* 210–213.

Nu, U. 1975. *U Nu, Saturday's Child,* 253.

Taylor, R. 1973. *Foreign and Domestic Consequences of the KMT Intervention in Burma,* 54.

Teiwes, F. 1969. "Force and Diplomacy on the Sino-Burmese Border." In *The Next Asia,* ed. D. Smith, 197–229.

Tinker, H. 1956. "Burma's Northeast Borderland Problems." *Pacific Affairs* 29 (December): 324–346.

Watson, F. 1966. *The Frontiers of China,* 79–82, 88–100, 126–130.

Woodman, D. 1962. *The Making of Burma,* 518–539.

18.13 Singaporan Riots, 1956

The United Kingdom administered colonial Singapore separately from Malaya after 1946 and granted limited self-government in 1955. In 1950 the British Army helped to suppress riots that represented in part tension between Malay and Chinese communities (18.8). Singapore was indirectly involved in warfare afflicting neighboring Malaya during the late 1940s and early 1950s (18.6). Some Singaporan Chinese aided the insurgency, including a radical faction within Lee Kuan Yew's People's Action Party (PAP), founded in 1954. Radicals gained influence within Singapore's Chinese-language schools, especially through the Singapore Chinese Middle School Students Union (SCMSSU) which openly recruited jungle fighters. The Singaporan government banned the SCMSSU as well as a few other radical organizations on October 1, 1956, and arrested some leaders. Students seized control of two Chinese schools. On October 26 police expelled occupying students and closed the schools. Roving student gangs resorted to violence the next day and demonstrators gathered on their behalf. Locally stationed British Army units joined police on October 27 and eventually suppressed the rioting by November 1. No British soldiers were killed.

Allen, R. 1968. *Malaysia; Prospect and Retrospect,* 189.

Clutterbuck, R. 1985. *Conflict and Violence in Singapore and Malaya,* 121–138.

18.14 Strung Treng Incident, 1958

The Geneva settlement of 1954 at the end of the First Indochina War (18.1) failed to resolve long-standing border disagreements between

Cambodia and Cochin-China, the latter incorporated within the Republic of Vietnam (South Vietnam). Cambodian representatives voiced border concerns at the Geneva Conference but did not press the matter. Contested control of islands and waterways within the southern Mekong River Delta provoked minor incidents during the mid-1950s. Parts of the northern Cambodian border were also disputed. President Ngo Dinh Diem's efforts to consolidate control within South Vietnam exacerbated tensions when Vietnamese forces raided Cambodian territory in 1955–1956 in pursuit of dissidents (18.11). In late June 1958 South Vietnamese military forces occupied the village of Strung Treng within northern Cambodia. Cambodia protested to the International Control Commission established in 1954 to supervise the Geneva settlement. Vietnam withdrew from Strung Treng by July 1. No fatalities are reported during the incident.

Burchett, W. 1970. *The Second Indochina War*, 43.
Butterworth, R. 1976. *Managing Interstate Conflict*, 207–210.
Leifer, M. 1967. *Cambodia: The Search for Security*, 97–98.
Norodom Sihanouk, P. 1973. *My War with the CIA*, 102–103.
Smith, Roger. 1965. *Cambodia's Foreign Policy*, 159–161.

18.15 Second Indochina War, 1958–1976

Four newly independent states emerged after the First Indochina War ended in 1954 (18.1). Traditional kingdoms were immediately reestablished within Laos and Cambodia. Within little more than a year the Vietminh founded the Socialist Republic of Vietnam within North Vietnam and the Republic of Vietnam was proclaimed within South Vietnam below the 17th Parallel. North and South Vietnam were not soon reunited as originally foreseen.

The Republic of Vietnam never fully pacified the South. Groups sympathetic to the Vietminh engaged in sustained terrorism from 1957. Radical dissidents (called "Vietcong" by the South Vietnamese government) eventually formed the National Liberation Front with North Vietnamese backing. Radical Pathet Lao posed a similar challenge to the Royal Laotian government after 1957.

In December 1958 a battalion of North Vietnamese troops occupied Tchepone near the 17th Parallel within Laos. North Vietnam fortified the area primarily in order to assure supplies to southern insurgents through what the United States later called the "Ho Chi Minh" trail. She maintained forces within the area until 1975 and also periodically assisted Pathet Lao operations. The Laotian government protested but did not directly attempt to dislodge North Vietnamese troops. The

United States provided military and economic assistance to the Laotian government and from the early 1960s also covertly directed irregular anticommunist forces and conducted clandestine air operations. In May 1961, following Pathet Lao conquest of Nam Tha near the Thai border, the United States temporarily deployed large marine and air contingents to Thailand in a dramatic show of force.

Growing insurrection within South Vietnam relied in part upon sanctuaries within neighboring states. Small South Vietnamese army units began small raids upon Cambodia in 1960, where she had previously intervened in 1956 and 1958 (18.11, 18.14), and upon North Vietnam and Laos in 1961. Such cross-border operations continued until 1975. The United States provided military and economic assistance to the South Vietnamese government from the 1950s. American aircraft and military advisors began to accompany South Vietnamese army into battle in 1961. The United States maintained 27,000 "advisors" within South Vietnam by March 1965.

The United States began overt air attacks within Laos in early 1964 and upon North Vietnam in August following a naval incident within the Tonkin Gulf. She began smaller and less frequent attacks upon Cambodia in 1966. These American air raids dropped more bomb tonnage than was delivered by all combatants during World War II before ending in 1973, slightly more upon Laos than upon North Vietnam. China directly assisted North Vietnamese air defense beginning in 1965 and eventually committed more than 30,000 Chinese military personnel.

The United States deployed conventional ground combat units to South Vietnam in March 1965 following a Vietcong attack upon U.S. Marine barracks at Pleiku. American military commitment gradually increased to nearly a half million soldiers by 1968. Australia, New Zealand and South Korea contributed ground combat units during the summer and fall of 1965. Thailand followed suit in 1967. The Philippines provided paramilitary civic action teams. North Vietnam openly committed regular army battalions with South Vietnam by November 1965.

Vietcong and regular North Vietnamese forces seized coastal South Vietnamese cities during the Tet holidays in February 1968. They were soon driven out, but American policy changed direction shortly afterward. At the end of March President Lyndon Johnson invited North Vietnam to negotiate an end to the war. Formal negotiations began in Paris in January 1969. The United States began to reduce her military presence later that year and ceased major ground operations by the end of 1971. An American commando team once raided North Vietnam in November 1970 in an unsuccessful attempt to rescue downed flyers. Australian, New Zealander and Thai soldiers withdrew from South Vietnam by early 1972.

In March 1970 General Lon Nol precipitated expanded warfare within Cambodia by deposing Prince Sihanouk's government and attempting to restrict North Vietnamese transit across Cambodian territory. South Vietnamese armies intervened in support of the Lon Nol's regime and North Vietnamese troops intervened against it. American ground forces entered in April. The United States withdrew soldiers two months later but South Vietnamese and North Vietnamese forces remained entrenched until 1975.

Conflict also expanded within Laos. Small Thai units appeared briefly against the Pathet Lao during June 1969. Several Thai battalions, composed of supposed "volunteers," deployed in March 1970 and remained until January 1973. In February–March 1971 South Vietnamese army units, with American logistical assistance, mounted a large and unsuccessful campaign to destroy North Vietnamese supply lines through Laos, including near Tchepone.

Accords signed at Paris in January 1973 reduced foreign participation but did not immediately end the war. American and South Korean troops withdrew from Vietnam; so did Thai soldiers from Laos. The United States ceased air attacks within North and South Vietnam although she continued raids within Laos and Cambodia until August 1973. North Vietnamese forces remained throughout the region.

The recognized governments of South Vietnam, Laos and Cambodia gradually retreated to a few urban areas during continued fighting. Local insurgents supported by North Vietnamese troops finally toppled all three regimes in March and April 1975. The National Liberation Front established a radical socialist regime within South Vietnam. The Pathet Lao assumed power within Laos as did the Khmer Rouge within Cambodia. The United States intervened briefly to assist the final evacuation of Saigon in April 1975.

International conflict continued on a smaller scale within some areas into 1976. North Vietnamese forces remained active against anti-Pathet Lao elements within Laos until August 1975. American commandos raided a Cambodian port in mid-May 1975 when the Khmer Rouge seized the merchant vessel *Mayaguez*. New Cambodian and South Vietnamese governments jockeyed for position within border areas until January 1976, including a major Cambodian assault upon Hon Troc in early May 1975. In addition, persistent domestic resistance within Laos and Cambodia helped to kindle the Third Indochina War a few years later (18.29).

The Second Indochina War may have killed as many as two million persons, including primarily South Vietnamese civilians. Fighting was less intense within Cambodia and even more constrained within Laos. At least 150,000 North Vietnamese regular soldiers died. The United States sustained almost 60,000 military fatalities. Korea lost approximately 4,000 troops. Thailand and Australia each suffered about 500 killed, and New Zealand 40 fatal casualties.

General

Brecher, M., J. Wilkenfeld, and S. Moser. 1988. *Crises in the Twentieth Century*, 1: 253, 257–258, 271, 273–274, 281–282, 286–287, 291–292, 294–295, 297–300, 306–307.
Butterworth, R. 1976. *Managing Interstate Conflict*, 207–211, 240–246, 275–278, 319–327, 345–348, 360–361, 397–398, 448–450, 464–466.
Dupuy, R., and T. Dupuy. 1986. *The Encyclopedia of Military History*, 1221.
Keegan, J., ed. 1983. *World Armies*, 652–658.
Small, M., and J. Singer. 1982. *Resort to Arms*, 93.

Cambodia

Burchett, W. 1970. *The Second Indochina War.*
Caldwell, M., and L. Tan. 1973. *Cambodia in the Southeast Asian War.*
Chanda, N. 1986. *Brother Enemy*, 11–37.
Chang, P. 1985. *Kampuchea Between China and Vietnam*, 19–43.
Evans, G., and K. Rowley. 1984. *Red Brotherhood at War*, 85–90.
Kiernan, B., and C. Boua, eds. 1982. *Peasants and Politics in Kampuchea*, 166–317.
Kosut, H., ed. 1971. *Cambodia and the Vietnam War.*
Kroef, J. van der. 1979. "The Cambodian-Vietnamese War." *Asia Quarterly* (#2): 83–94.
Norodom Sihanouk, P. 1973. *My War with the CIA.*
Ponchaud, F. 1978. *Cambodia: Year Zero.*
Sak Sutsakhan. 1980. *The Khmer Republic at War and the Final Collapse.*
Tho, T. 1979. *The Cambodian Incursion.*
Vickery, M. 1984. *Cambodia, 1975–1982*, 189–196.

Laos

Brown, MacAlister., and J. Zasloff. 1986. *Apprentice Revolutionaries*, 70–134.
Dommen, A. 1971. *Conflict in Laos.*
Fall, B. 1969. *Anatomy of a Crisis.*
Hinh, N. 1979. *Lam Son 719.*
Main, J. 1972. "The Civil War in Laos." In *The International Regulation of Civil Wars*, ed. E. Luard, 91–107.
Oudone Sananikone. 1981. *The Royal Lao Army and U.S. Advice and Support.*
Stuart-Fox, M. 1986. *Laos: Politics, Economics, and Society*, 23–35.
Thee, M. 1973. *Notes of a Witness.*

Toye, H. 1968. *Laos: Buffer State or Battleground.*
Vongsavanh, S. 1981. *RLG Military Operations and Activities in the Laotian Panhandle.*
Zasloff, J. 1973. *The Pathet Lao: Leadership and Organization.*

United States

Clarke, J. 1988. *United States Army in Vietnam—Advice and Support: The Final Years.*
Clodfelter, M. 1989. *The Limits of Air Power.*
Gelb, L., with R. Betts. 1979. *The Irony of Vietnam.*
Gibson, J. 1986. *The Perfect War: Technowar in Vietnam.*
Head, R., F. Short, and R. McFarlane. 1978. *Crisis Resolution,* 101–148.
Isaacs, A. 1983. *Without Honor: Defeat in Vietnam and Cambodia.*
Kahin, G. 1986. *Intervention: How America Became Involved in Vietnam.*
Lamb, C. 1989. *Belief Systems and Decision Making in the Mayaguez Crisis.*
Lewy, G. 1978. *America in Vietnam.*
Momyer, W. 1978. *Airpower in Three Wars.*
Paust, J. 1976. "The Seizure and Recovery of the Mayaguez." *Yale Law Journal* 85 (May): 774–806.
Rowan, R. 1975. *The Four Days of Mayaguez.*
Schemmer, B. 1976. *The Raid.*
Schlight, J. 1988. *The United States Air Force in Southeast Asia—The War in South Vietnam: The Years of the Offensive.*
Simpson, C. 1983. *Inside the Green Berets.*
Snepp, F. 1977. *Decent Interval.*
Spector, R. 1983. *The United States Army in Vietnam—Advice and Support: The Early Years,* 329–373.
Stanton, S. 1985. *Green Berets at War.*
Tillema, H. 1973. *Appeal to Force.*
U.S. Congress. House. Committee on Armed Services. 1971. *United States-Vietnam Relations.*
U.S. Marine Corps. 1977–1988. *U.S. Marines in Vietnam.*

Vietnam

Burchett, W. 1981. *The China-Cambodia-Vietnam Triangle,* 62–64, 137–164.
Cao, V., and D. Khuyen. 1980. *Reflections on the Vietnam War.*
Gurtov, M., and B. Hwang. 1980. *China under Threat,* 153–186.
Heder, S. 1981. "The Kampuchean-Vietnamese Conflict." In *The Third Indochina Conflict,* ed. D. Elliott, 21–67.
Langer, P., and J. Zasloff. 1970. *North Vietnam and the Pathet Lao.*
O'Ballance, E. 1981. *The Wars in Vietnam, 1954–1980.*
Porter, G. 1975. *A Peace Denied.*
Porter, G. 1981. "Vietnamese Policy and the Indochina Crisis." In *The Third Indochina Conflict,* ed. D. Elliott, 69–137.

Segal, G. 1985. *Defending China*, 158–175.
Sobel, L., eds. 1966–1973. *South Vietnam: U.S.-Communist Confrontation in Southeast Asia.*
Summers, H. 1985. *Vietnam War Almanac.*
Turley, W. 1986. *The Second Indochina War.*
Whiting, A. 1975. *The Chinese Calculus of Deterrence.*

Other States

King, M. 1981. *New Zealanders at War*, 293.
Larsen, S., and J. Collins. 1975. *Allied Participation in Vietnam.*
McNeill, I. 1984. *The Team: Australian Army Advisors in Vietnam.*
Nuechterlein, D. 1965. *Thailand and the Struggle for Southeast Asia*, 138–269.

18.16 Paracels Incident, 1959

China and France settled competing claims to islands within the Tonkin Gulf and South China Sea under a convention signed in 1887. Following French withdrawal from Indochina in 1954, China put forward interpretations of the agreement that conflicted with policies of both the Democratic Republic of Vietnam (North Vietnam) and the Republic of Vietnam (South Vietnam). North Vietnam and China ceased active disputation in 1958 by mutual agreement without formally settling the issue. Disagreement between China and South Vietnam involved primarily the Paracels and Spratly island groups, some of which were also claimed by the Philippines and Taiwan. China established presence among some disputed islands during the mid- and late-1950s. In early 1959 South Vietnam deployed a naval force which landed an armed shore party upon Duncan Island, destroyed a Chinese flag and briefly interned more than fifty Chinese fishermen. During March South Vietnamese ships also harassed Chinese fishermen operating at sea within the area. No fatalities are reported on Duncan Island.

Chang, P. 1986. *The Sino-Vietnamese Territorial Dispute*, 22.
New York Times 3/1/59, 20:4.

18.17 Sino-Burmese Conflict, 1959

Border dispute between China and Burma contributed to armed conflict in 1950 (18.7) and 1955–1956 (18.12). The two governments suspended most activities within disputed areas at the end of 1956 pending a negotiated settlement of the border. Minor incidents continued, however, due in part to remnants of Kuomintang exiles and other dissident tribesmen operating out of Burma who sporadically harassed Chinese territory. Chinese troops raided Burmese territory on several occasions between May and September 1959, allegedly in pursuit of parties pillaging China's Yunnan Province. Chinese raids coincided with onset of armed conflict on the Sino-Indian border (17.10). No Chinese fatalities are reported within Burma.

Butterworth, R. 1976. *Managing Interstate Conflict*, 99–100.
Hinton, H. 1966. *Communist China in World Politics*, 315.
Watson, F. 1966. *The Frontiers of China*, 88–100, 126–130.

18.18 Karen Insurgency, 1959

Burma gained independence from the United Kingdom in 1948 (18.5). The state immediately fractured among tribal and other armed groups. Karen tribesmen persistently resisted government efforts to exert central control, including within areas near Thailand. Remnants of Kuomintang armies driven out of China following civil war also took refuge within northern Burma near the Thai border. Thailand permitted use of her territory by the United States and the Republic of China to help support Kuomintang exiles who harassed the People's Republic of China during the early 1950s. Burmese air forces attacked Thai border areas in 1953 (18.9) and 1955 (18.10) during efforts to expel Kuomintang exiles. Some Kuomintang took up residence within Thailand. Burma and Thailand ratified a treaty of friendship in September 1958. The next month General Ne Win established a caretaker military government replacing Prime Minister U Nu. Ne Win's regime attempted aggressively to subdue Karen de facto autonomy in 1959, including air raids upon Thai border villages during June. No Burmese military personnel are reported killed within Thailand.

Jha, G. 1979. *Foreign Policy of Thailand*, 128–130.
Silverstein, J. 1977. *Burma: Military Rule and the Politics of Stagnation*, 184–185.
Taylor, R. 1973. *Foreign and Domestic Consequences of the KMT Intervention in Burma*, 57.

18.19 Taungbro Incident, 1959

The United Kingdom assumed control of Bengal through the East India Company beginning in 1757. She acquired additional territory to the east at the expense of the Burmese Empire from 1826 and absorbed Burma as a whole by 1890. Burma was reconstituted as a separate colony distinct from India in 1937. Partition of India at independence in 1947 allocated eastern Bengal to Pakistan. Burma gained independence the following year. The understood boundary between Burma and East Pakistan generally followed the wandering course of the Naaf River but was not formally demarcated during the period of British rule. The two states engaged in protracted border negotiations after independence. They signed a friendship treaty in 1953 but reached a definitive border agreement only in 1965. Sporadic border incidents arose as early as 1948 due to alleged Pakistani patronage of the Mujahid movement within Arakan which sought union with Pakistani Moslems. Recurring strife within western Burma provoked repeated flights of refugees to Pakistan during the 1950s, contributing to further incidents. On August 2, 1959, a raiding party out of Pakistan that apparently included Pakistani troops attacked the Burmese border village of Taungbro. No Pakistani military fatalities are reported.

Asian Recorder 5 (1959): 2867.
Razvi, M. 1971. *The Frontiers of Pakistan*, 201.

18.20 West Irian Conflict, 1960–1962

The Netherlands acknowledged the independence of Indonesia and withdrew from most of the Indies in 1949 (18.4). She retained control of West Irian (West New Guinea) pending future negotiations. Indonesia attempted to coerce concession of West Irian in December 1957 by exerting pressure upon Dutch economic interests within Indonesia, including strikes, expulsions and nationalization of Dutch lanholdings. When this did not avail, Indonesia organized a guerrilla campaign within West Irian employing Indonesian soldiers. Attacks began in November 1960. In September 1961 the Netherlands proposed to transfer administration of West Irian to the United Nations pending grant of separate independence or integration with Australian-administered eastern New Guinea. Indonesia announced general military mobilization in December 1961 and increased infiltration into West Irian. In March 1962 Dutch soldiers deployed to assist police in controlling violence. In June, Indonesia conspicuously invested a small number of paratroops. The Netherlands agreed August 15, 1962, to transfer control of West Irian to Indonesia under U.N. supervision. Indonesia lost approximately one hundred military personnel within West Irian, mostly at the hands of police. No fatalities are reported among regular Dutch soldiers.

Agung, I. 1973. *Twenty Years of Indonesian Foreign Policy*, 288–312.

Brecher, M., J. Wilkenfeld, and S. Moser. 1988. *Crises in the Twentieth Century*, 1: 254–255.
Butterworth, R. 1976. *Managing Interstate Conflict*, 292–293.
Henderson, W. 1973. *West New Guinea*.
Jones, H. 1971. *Indonesia: The Possible Dream*, 174–216.
Kosut, H., ed. 1967. *Indonesia: The Sukarno Years*, 49–63.
Lijphart, A. 1966. *The Trauma of Decolonization*.
Mackie, J. 1974. *Konfrontasi: The Indonesia-Malaysia Dispute*, 98–103.

18.21 Preah Vihear Conflict, 1962

Cambodia and Thailand long disputed their border, including land surrounding the Temple of Preah Vihear. French colonial authorities administered the area as part of Indochina during the early twentieth century. Thailand acquired the temple along with two disputed Cambodian provinces in 1941 with approval of Japanese occupation authorities. France coerced Thailand to return seized territories in 1946 during the First Indochina War (18.1). Thai police returned to patrol the temple area in 1949 and strengthened their position in 1956 after Cambodia gained independence from France. Cambodia, with Thai acquiescence, submitted the question to the International Court of Justice following a 1958–1959 diplomatic crisis during which both Cambodia and Thailand deployed military forces to the border. The Court ruled in June 1962 that the temple belonged to Cambodia. Thailand protested the decision and at first refused to withdraw. For several days in mid-August 1962 Cambodia and Thailand each mounted small raids upon one another's positions in the temple area. Thailand belatedly withdrew. No fatalities are reported.

Butterworth, R. 1976. *Managing Interstate Conflict*, 171–172, 294–295.
Nuechterlein, D. 1965. *Thailand and the Struggle for Southeast Asia*, 249–257.
Smith, Roger. 1965. *Cambodia's Foreign Policy*, 140–153.

18.22 Malay Confrontation, 1962–1966

The United Kingdom obtained protectorates on the island of Borneo over Sabah (North Borneo) in 1881 and over Brunei and Sarawak in 1888. The remaining three-quarters of the island represented part of the Netherlands East Indies and was ceded to independent Indonesia in 1949. Britain lost its positions on Borneo to Japan in 1941–1942. She returned in 1945, restored British protection to the Sultan of Brunei, annexed Sabah to the Crown in 1946 and established de facto colonial administration within Sarawak. In 1961 the United Kingdom proposed to federate British territories on Borneo with Malaya. Indonesia and the Philippines both objected based upon their own territorial claims to Borneo. Indonesia encouraged the Sarawak United People's Party (SUPP) and the Sarawak Advanced Youth's Association (SAYA) which expressed opposition among overseas Chinese within Borneo who feared assimilation with ethnic Malay of the peninsula. Indonesia also clandestinely supported the National Army of North Borneo (TNKU) which including forces loyal to A. M. Azahari who claimed to represent all Borneo.

On December 8, 1962 Azahari's forces captured several Brunei towns. The United Kingdom dispatched troops from bases in Singapore to help support the Sultan. First units of British Gurkhas arrived in the area late on December 8 and initiated direct operations by December 10. These, combined with later reinforcements, cleared urban centers of Brunei by December 16. Azahari's forces retreated to remote areas of Brunei and to neighboring Sarawak. Britain extended operations into Sarawak by December 12 and also deployed forces within Sabah as a precaution. She finally pacified Brunei in mid-May 1963. In April 1963 Indonesia began infiltrating regular army commando teams into Sarawak to support opposition forces. Indigenous opposition forces also became active within Sabah and the United Kingdom committed army units there to assist police in mid-August 1963.

On September 16, 1963, the United Kingdom granted independence to Sabah and Sarawak. Both immediately joined the Malaysian Federation. Brunei chose to remain a British protectorate. Indonesia refused to recognize the federation and severed diplomatic relations with Malaya. President Sukarno of Indonesia promised "terrible confrontation". Fighting intensified within Sabah. Beginning in January 1964 Indonesia began large unit operations on Borneo's Malaysian-Indonesian frontiers. British artillery began to shell Indonesian territory by midyear and British commando raids commenced across the border in November in an effort to reduce Indonesian infiltration.

Indonesia began seaborne and later airborne commando raids against the peninsular Malaysia in August 1964. New Zealand and Australian troops garrisoned on the peninsula deployed shortly thereafter to assist the Malaysian Army in capturing infiltrators. In January 1965 Indonesia withdrew from the United Nations to protest the seating of Malaysia's representative. Some Australian forces were dispatched to Malaysian Borneo in February 1965.

"Confrontation" waned in October 1965 when President Ahmad Sukarno's powers were curtailed following violent upheaval within Indonesia. Indonesian raids abated. The United Kingdom ceased cross-border operations in late November. Sukarno was forced to resign office in March 1966. Indonesia and Malaysia signed a peace agreement in August 1966 and overt hostilities ceased.

An estimated 600 Indonesian military personnel died during three years of fighting. Seventy-five British and British Gurkha soldiers were killed. Australia suffered one fatality within Borneo. No New Zealanders are reported killed.

Agung, I. 1973. *Twenty Years of Indonesian Foreign Policy*, 444–506.

Allen, R. 1968. *Malaysia; Prospect and Retrospect*, 157–249.

Blaxland, G. 1971. *The Regiments Depart*, 375–410.

Brecher, M., J. Wilkenfeld, and S. Moser. 1988. *Crises in the Twentieth Century*, 1: 261–262.

Butterworth, R. 1976. *Managing Interstate Conflict*, 344–345, 348–351.

Chin, K. 1983. *The Defence of Malaysia and Singapore*, 58–124.

Dewar, M. 1984. *Brush Fire Wars*, 99–112.

Hyde, D. 1965. *Conflict in the East.*

James, H., and D. Sheil-Small. 1971. *The Undeclared War.*

Jones, H. 1971. *Indonesia: The Possible Dream*, 262–313.

King, M. 1981. *New Zealanders at War*, 279.

Kosut, H., ed. 1967. *Indonesia: The Sukarno Years*, 84–107.

Kroef, J. van der. 1964. "Communism and the Guerilla War in Sarawak." *World Today* 20 (January): 50–60.

Mackie, J. 1974. *Konfrontasi: The Indonesia-Malaysia Dispute.*

Malaysia. Department of Information. 1964. *Indonesian Involvement in Eastern Malaysia*, 47–74.

Millar, T. 1978. *Australia in Peace and War*, 223–249.

Millar, T. 1980. "Anglo-Australian Partnership in Defense of the Malaysian Area." In *Australia and Britain*, ed. A. Madden and W. Morris-Jones, 71–89.

Ranjit Singh, D. 1984. *Brunei, 1839–1983*, 172–180.

18.23 Preah Vihear Clashes, 1965–1966

Long-standing border disputes between Cambodia, and Thailand, contributed to international armed conflict in 1946 during the Indochina War (18.1), and again in 1962 at the Temple of Preah Vihear (18.21). Thailand and Cambodia commissioned a special representative to help resolve their differences in December 1962. Incidents continued and the representative's services were terminated in 1964. In June 1965 a small Cambodian force provoked a minor battle on the Thai side of the border. Cambodia conducted further attacks in January and February 1966. Thai units periodically raided Cambodia from January to April 1966. In early April 1966 Thailand also forcibly reoccupied the Temple of Preah Vihear, awarded to Cambodia by the International Court of Justice in 1962, and held the territory for two weeks before withdrawing. As many as 300 persons are said to have been killed or wounded at or near the border in 1965–1966. Most casualties were due to buried mines and involved police or other civilians. No fatalities are reliably reported among regular military personnel.

Butterworth, R. 1976. *Managing Interstate Conflict*, 171–172, 294–295.
Jha, G. 1979. *Foreign Policy of Thailand*, 117.
New York Times 1/2/66, 72:2; 2/13/66, 9:5; 3/9/66, 5:3; 6/4/66, 5:7.
Times (London) 3/21/66, 9b; 4/9/66, 7c; 5/17/66, 8d; 6/8/66, 8c.

18.24 North Burma Campaign, 1969

China and Burma signed a treaty of friendship and nonaggression in 1960 that resolved some border disputes which had contributed to conflict in 1951 (18.7), 1955–1956 (18.12) and again in 1959 (18.17). The Burmese government failed to establish central control over the northern provinces despite repeated efforts during the 1950s and 1960s. At the same time, the People's Republic of China attempted to exert central control beyond the Han cultural frontier by establishing designated autonomous regions within Yunnan and other southern provinces. Some tribal groups resided on both sides of the Sino-Burmese border. Peking vied with Rangoon for loyalty among some tribal entities not intrinsically identified with either nation. Chinese road-building in far southern Yunnan during the 1960s exacerbated issues of Sino-Burmese border security, including construction within the Ledo area.

In 1969 Burma attempted again to impose central control along its northern border against local tribal resistance. Some dissidents received Chinese military equipment and advice. Between May and November 1969 small detachments of Chinese soldiers drawn from major encampments on China's side of the border participated in occasional skirmishes with Burmese government troops within Burma. More than 100 Burmese soldiers apparently died during the northern campaign of 1969. No Chinese fatalities are reported within Burma.

New York Times 5/9/69, 93:3; 11/23/69, 12:1.
Silverstein, J. 1977. *Burma: Military Rule and the Politics of Stagnation*, 179–180.

18.25 Thai-Malay Border I, 1969–1970

Neither Thailand nor Malaysia fully controlled their border after World War II. Bangkok faced recurrent resistance within southern provinces, including Moslem secessions. Malaya suffered protracted radical insurgency, mostly among overseas Chinese. Malayan

Insurgency (18.6) was declared ended in 1960 but terrorism and banditry continued near the Thai-Malay border, especially after British Borneo joined Malaya to form Malaysia in 1963. In 1965, during confrontation with Indonesia over Malaysian union (18.22), Thailand and Malaysia formally began to share intelligence relating to frontier security. In July 1968 the two agreed to permit "hot pursuit" within one another's territory. From November 1969 to March 1970 Malaysian aircraft repeatedly bombed and strafed border areas of Thailand in pursuit of terrorists. From the beginning to the end of March 1970 Malaysia committed army battalions within Thailand under expanded security agreements and attempted to destroy terrorist bases. At least seven Malaysian soldiers were killed within Thailand.

Jha, G. 1979. *Foreign Policy of Thailand*, 122–128.
New York Times 3/8/70, 3:5.
Tanham, G. 1974. *Trial in Thailand*, 65–68, 100–101.

18.26 Paracels Seizures, 1974

Dispute between China and the Republic of Vietnam (South Vietnam) regarding the Paracels and Spratly islands within the South China Sea provoked incidents on and around Duncan Island in 1959 (18.16). South Vietnam formally incorporated the Paracels within Quang Nam Province in 1961. China protested but otherwise took no direct action at that time. South Vietnam and China each maintained de facto control of some disputed islands during the next dozen years. In September 1973 South Vietnam formally incorporated the main islands of the Spratly group within Phuoc Tuy Province. China protested again. South Vietnam increased naval patrols within the South China Sea in winter 1973–1974. In mid-January 1974, a South Vietnamese patrol boat fired upon Chinese raising a flag on Robert Island, one of the Paracels. A South Vietnamese commando team landed on Duncan Island January 19 and skirmished with a company of Chinese soldiers. China forcibly occupied the Paracels, including Duncan, Robert and Drumond islands, January 20–21. In the aftermath, South Vietnam established presence among some traditionally unoccupied islands of the Spratly group. Three South Vietnamese soldiers died upon Robert January 19. Fifty Chinese troops were reportedly killed during operations January 20–21.

Chanda, N. 1986. *Brother Enemy*, 20–22.
Chang, P. 1986. *The Sino-Vietnamese Territorial Dispute*, 18–19, 25.
Chen, K. 1987. *China's War with Vietnam, 1979*, 42–48.

Day, A., ed. 1987. *Border and Territorial Disputes*, 309–316.
Evans, G., and K. Rowley. 1984. *Red Brotherhood at War*, 44–47.
Segal, G. 1985. *Defending China*, 197–210.

18.27 Timorese War, 1975–1988

Portugal settled coastal areas of the island of Timor during the sixteenth century and claimed the island from 1586. Portugal ceded West Timor to the Netherlands in 1859 but retained East Timor. Japan seized the entire island in 1942. Australia helped to promote guerrilla resistance against the Japanese during World War II. She also helped to restore Dutch colonial authority within West Timor and Portuguese control within East Timor after Japan surrendered in 1945. West Timor passed to Indonesia upon Dutch capitulation in 1949. In 1959 serious riots and demonstrations against Portuguese rule erupted within Viqueque. Portuguese police apparently inflicted hundreds of casualties while suppressing the ill-organized revolt.

On April 25, 1974, a military coup d'etat overthrew the government of Portugal. The new regime in Lisbon sought immediately to end African colonial wars (6.5,10.2,10.4). It also rescinded the long-standing ban against political organization within East Timor. Several political parties quickly appeared. The Frente Revolucionario de Este Timor Independente (FRETILIN) urged unqualified independence for East Timor. The Partido Democratico Unido (PDU), favored by Lisbon, promoted federation with Portugal. The Associacao da Populaca Democratica de Timor (APODETI), supported by Indonesian money and radio propaganda, advocated union with Indonesia. Fighting among FRETILIN and PDU supporters broke out within the capital, Dili, in October 1974, ceased temporarily in January 1975 but resumed in August. Sustained violence spread throughout East Timor as FRETILIN attacked both PDU and APODETI. Some of the later took refuge within West Timor. Portugal refrained from military intervention and abandoned the island a few months later.

In mid-September 1975 small Indonesian military units began sporadic operations within East Timor, primarily on behalf of APODETI, amidst factional fighting on both sides of the border. FRETILIN proclaimed independence from Portugal at the end of November. Indonesia invaded in force a week later. Indonesian armed forces quickly gained control of Dili but encountered protracted resistance within outlying areas. Indonesia formally annexed East Timor in July 1976. War continued until the late 1980s. Indonesia prematurely declared FRETILIN crushed upon several occasions. Finally, in December 1988, Indonesia formally ended its military occupation of East Timor. Total fatalities are not officially reported but are presumed to number tens of thousands, including several thousand Indonesian soldiers.

Amnesty International. 1985. *East Timor.*
Brecher, M., J. Wilkenfeld, and S. Moser. 1988. *Crises in the Twentieth Century,* 1: 312–313.
Budiardjo, C., and L. Liong. 1984. *The War Against East Timor.*
Day, A., ed. 1987. *Border and Territorial Disputes,* 329–336.
Jolliffe, J. 1978. *East Timor: Nationalism and Colonialism.*
Kamm, H. 1981. "The Silent Suffering of East Timor." *New York Times Magazine,* section 6 (February 15, 1981): 35, 56–62.
Laffin, J. 1986. *War Annual 1,* 38–41.
Laffin, J. 1987. *War Annual 2,* 65–69.
Nichterlein, S. 1977. "The Struggle for East Timor." *Journal of Contemporary Asia* 7 (#4): 486–496.
Small, M., and J. Singer. 1982. *Resort to Arms,* 99.
Viviani, N. 1976. "Australians and the Timor Issue." *Australian Outlook* 30 (August): 197–226.

18.28 Mekong River Conflict, 1975

The border between Laos and Thailand has long been troublesome. Siam (Thailand) established indirect control over the Laotian territories at the end of the eighteenth century. She ceded Lao areas east of the Mekong to French Indochina in 1893 and transferred also Sayaboury Province during the first decade of the twentieth century. In 1941, Thailand invaded parts of Laos and Cambodia. Japan, which controlled French Indochina after the German conquest of Paris, acceded to Thai claims. France coerced Thailand to return most territories in 1946, during the First Indochina War (18.1). Thai troops intervened within Laos on behalf of the Vientiene government against Pathet Lao insurgents and North Vietnamese troops during the Second Indochina War from 1969 to 1973 (18.15).

Pathet Lao established control of Laos in March 1975 and established a radical socialist regime. Hmong and other anticommunist guerrilla groups, initially organized by Thailand and the United States during the 1960s, continued to resist the Pathet Lao government after the Second Indochina War. Hmong resistance relied in part upon support among tens of thousands of refugees who fled to Thailand. Old boundary issues regarding the Mekong River were also revived in 1975, contributing to numerous minor border incidents. A serious incident occurred November 17, 1975, when Laotian artillery disabled a Thai patrol boat on the Mekong River. Other Thai vessels returned fire and were aided by Thai aircraft which attacked Laotian shore positions. The fight lasted for several hours. One Thai civilian was killed but no military fatalities are reported on either side.

Day, A., ed. 1987. *Border and Territorial Disputes*, 365–369.
Sanchai, S. 1976. "The Rising of the Rightist Phoenix." *Southeast Asian Affairs* 3: 357–393.
New York Times 7/9/75, 10:4; 11/20/75, 3:1.

18.29 Third Indochina War, 1976–continuing

The Third Indochina War represents a congeries of bilateral conflicts that intersected one another in course. First shots involved Thailand and Laos in May 1976. The Pathet Lao seized power within Laos in spring 1975 near the end of the Second Indochina War (18.15) at the same time as did the Khmer Rouge within Cambodia and the Vietcong within South Vietnam. Resistance to Pathet Lao rule persisted, especially among anticommunist Hmong guerrillas organized and supported by Thailand and the United States from the 1960s. Hmong fled to Thailand in great numbers at the end of the war. Laos charged that Thailand provided aid and sanctuary to those to continuing resistance after 1975. Long-standing boundary disputes between Thailand and Laos also resurfaced in 1975, contributing to a serious incident in November (18.28). Lao military units began systematic attacks upon Thai border positions along the Mekong in May 1976. Thai artillery repeatedly attacked Lao positions from January 1977. Sporadic fighting continued until 1988. Incidents generally involved only air, artillery or commando operations except during the Thai occupation of the disputed Three Villages area in 1984 and during the Ban Rom Klao battles of 1987 and 1988.

North Vietnamese military forces did not fully withdraw from Laos at end of the Second Indochina War although they temporarily ceased overt operations in August 1975. In December 1976 units representing the Socialist Republic of Vietnam (the union of North Vietnam and South Vietnam proclaimed July 2, 1976) resumed direct activity and played an important role in suppressing Hmong and other resistance until the end of 1986. Vietnamese forces also assisted Lao border defense and occasionally exchanged fire with Thai forces.

Meanwhile, conflict erupted between Cambodia and Thailand and between Cambodia and Vietnam. The Khmer Rouge government led by Pol Pot began violent domestic repression in 1975, including forced evacuation of major cities. Khmer Rouge forces pursued refugees across the border into Thailand as early as November 1976. In July 1977 Thai aircraft began retaliatory strikes against Cambodia. Khmer Rouge units also raided villages within Vietnam beginning March 1977. Cross-border operations soon grew to involve entire Cambodian battalions. Vietnam responded by air strikes in June and major counterassaults upon Cambodia beginning in September 1977. She drove Cambodian forces away from the border and mounted a full-scale invasion in late 1978. Vietnamese troops captured Phnom Penh in January 1979, installed a new government under Heng Samrin and occupied most of Cambodia until 1987. Pol Pot's forces fought on after losing the capital. The Khmer Rouge, now a resistance force, received military equipment, financial aid and sanctuary from China, the United States and Thailand during the 1980s.

Violence also erupted between Vietnam and China during the late 1970s. The two states disputed islands within the South China Sea, contributing to armed conflict in 1959 and 1974 (18.16, 18.26), and possessed an ill-defined land border as well as supported rival factions within Cambodia. Vietnamese soldiers attacked a Chinese party at Youyiguan (Friendship Pass) in May 1977. Sustained conflict began the following year. China repeatedly raided and shelled Vietnamese border positions and attacked Vietnamese-held islands in the South China Sea from April 1978 until October 1987. Vietnam responded in kind beginning in August 1978. In February 1979, shortly after Vietnam drove Pol Pot from Pnomn Penh, China invaded northern Vietnam in force. She withdrew one month later after intense fighting. Most important battles took place on Vietnamese territory but a large Vietnamese unit also operated within China for a week during late February. Low-intensity conflict persisted after Chinese ground forces withdrew. In 1981, in 1984 and briefly again in January 1987 China mounted renewed ground offensives against Vietnamese border and island positions. Vietnam counterattacked against Chinese territory during fighting in 1981 and 1984. None of these later episodes matched the ferocity of the 1979 battles, however.

Laos became more deeply involved in regional conflict during China's 1979 offensive. Chinese commandos and artillery besieged the Laotian border in early March 1979. Raids and shelling continued until March 1982 and minor incidents occurred sporadically into the late 1980s. At the same time Laos committed troops within Cambodia in support of Vietnam. She maintained several hundred soldiers there until at least August 1980.

War expanded for Thailand in 1979. Vietnamese troops and Cambodian forces loyal to the Heng Samrin government began small raids upon alleged Khmer Rouge bases within Thailand in March and continued to do so until October 1987. Vietnam also undertook several major operations within Thailand. Most such offensives were brief and many involved both Vietnamese and Cambodian arms, including those in 1980, 1983, 1984–1985, and 1987. Thailand responded primarily defensively until April 1983 when she began sustained air and artillery actions within Cambodia that lasted until October 1987.

The war ended by stages. Vietnam withdrew troops gradually from Laos and Cambodia beginning in 1982. She ceased active operations within Laos by the end of December 1986. She continued against the Khmer Rouge within Cambodia into 1989 but eventually abandoned the effort and acquiesced to a new government. Vietnamese and Thai troops disengaged at the Cambodian border in October 1987 at the same time as did Vietnamese and Chinese forces at the Sino-Vietnamese border. Fighting intensified between Laos and Thailand late in 1987, including serious battles within the disputed Bam Rom Klao area, but ended by cease-fire in February 1988.

80,000 or more soldiers died on foreign soil during the Third Indochina War. More than a million civilians apparently also perished as a result of war during the late 1970s. The Khmer Rouge government was responsible for most deaths among noncombatants; most of its victims were Cambodians. Vietnam sustained approximately 50,000 fatalities during foreign military operations, nearly all within Cambodia. China lost about 20,000 soldiers, mostly during 1979. A few thousand Cambodian troops died abroad, primarily within Vietnam during 1977 and 1978. Laos and Thailand each lost a few hundred soldiers during winter 1987–1988 battles in addition to small numbers of fatalities sustained on other fronts.

General

Brecher, M., J. Wilkenfeld, and S. Moser. 1988. *Crises in the Twentieth Century,* 1: 324–325, 329–330.

Day, A., ed. 1987. *Border and Territorial Disputes,* 309–316, 365–369.

Laffin, J. 1986. *War Annual 1,* 135–141.

Laffin, J. 1987. *War Annual 2,* 119–127.

Laffin, J. 1989. *The World in Conflict 1989: War Annual 3,* 143–153.

Small, M., and J. Singer. 1982. *Resort to Arms,* 95.

Cambodia

Chanda, N. 1986. *Brother Enemy.*

Chang, P. 1985. *Kampuchea Between China and Vietnam.*

Carney, T. 1987. "The Heng Samrin Armed Forces and the Military Balance in Cambodia." In *The Cambodian Agony,* ed. D. Ablin and M. Hood, 180–209.

Jackson, K., ed. 1989. *Cambodia, 1975–1978.*

Kiernan, B., and C. Boua, eds. 1982. *Peasants and Politics in Kampuchea*, 227–317.

Kroef, J. van der. 1979. "The Cambodian-Vietnamese War." *Asia Quarterly* (#2): 83–94.

Schier, P. 1986. "Kampuchea in 1985." *Southeast Asian Affairs* 13:139–161.

Simon, S. 1978. "Cambodia." *Current History* 75 (December): 197–201, 227–228.

Vickery, M. 1984. *Cambodia, 1975–1982*.

China

Chang, P. 1986. *The Sino-Vietnamese Territorial Dispute*, 35–94.

Chen, K. 1987. *China's War with Vietnam, 1979*.

Duiker, W. 1986. *China and Vietnam: The Roots of Conflict*, 63–125.

Jacobsen, C. 1981. *Sino-Soviet Relations Since Mao*, 92–107.

Jencks, H. 1979. "China's Punitive War on Vietnam." *Asian Survey* 19 (August): 801–815.

Ross, R. 1988. *The Indochina Tangle*.

Segal, G. 1985. *Defending China*, 211–230.

Laos

Brown, MacAlister, and J. Zasloff. 1986. *Apprentice Revolutionaries*. 243–260.

Dommen, A. 1985. "Laos in 1984." *Asian Survey* 25 (January): 114–121.

Dommen, A. 1985. *Laos: Keystone of Indochina*, 114–133.

Evans, G. 1983. *The Yellow Rainmakers*.

Stuart-Fox, M. 1982. "National Defense and Internal Security in Laos." In *Contemporary Laos*, ed. M. Stuart-Fox, 220–244.

Stuart-Fox, M. 1984. "Laos in 1983." *Southeast Asian Affairs* 11:179–194.

Stuart-Fox, M. 1986. "Laos in 1985." *Southeast Asian Affairs* 13:165–181.

Stuart-Fox, M. 1986. *Laos: Politics, Economics, and Society*, 94–96, 136–143, 171–193.

Thayer, C. 1982. "Laos and Vietnam." In *Contemporary Laos*, ed. M. Stuart-Fox, 245–273.

Zasloff, J. 1981. "Politics in the New Laos Part II." *American Universities Field Staff Reports* (34).

Thailand

Alagappa, M. 1987. *The National Security of Developing States*, 78–147.

Vietnam

Burchett, W. 1981. *The China-Cambodia-Vietnam Triangle*, 137–209.

Evans, G., and K. Rowley. 1984. *Red Brotherhood at War*.

Heder, S. 1981. "The Kampuchean-Vietnamese Conflict." In *The Third Indochina Conflict*, ed. D. Elliott, 21–67.

Leighton, M. 1978. "Perspectives on the Vietnam-Cambodia Border Conflict." *Asian Survey* 18 (May): 448–457.

Meng, N. 1984. "Vietnam in 1983." *Southeast Asian Affairs* 11:343–368.

O'Ballance, E. 1981. *The Wars in Vietnam, 1954–1980*, 213–227.

Porter, G. 1981. "Vietnamese Policy and the Indochina Crisis." In *The Third Indochina Conflict*, ed. D. Elliott, 69–137.

18.30 Thai-Malay Border II, 1977–1980

Thailand and Malaysia cooperated openly from 1965 in an effort to suppress terrorism and banditry near their border. Agreements reached between 1965 and 1970 provided for joint intelligence operations and for rights to employ police and military forces within one another's territory. Malaysian police frequently entered Thailand during the late 1960s and 1970s. In addition, Malaysian military forces intervened within Thailand during 1969–1970 (18.25). Overt Malaysian military operations resumed within Thailand by the beginning of 1977. From then until June 1980 large units of Malaysian troops repeatedly joined Thai forces in combined operations. Malaysian aircraft also bombed and strafed Thai territory upon a number of occasions. Military activity abated in late 1980 but Malaysian police continued to operate on the Thai side of the border during following years. At least two Malaysian soldiers are known to have died within Thailand during 1977–1980 operations.

Heaton, W., and R. Macleod. 1980. "People's War in Thailand." In *Insurgency in the Modern World*, ed. B. O'Neill, W. Heaton, and D. Alberts, 86–107.

New York Times 5/5/77, 5:4; 7/5/77, 6:6.

Times (London) 1/17/77, 5b; 1/21/77, 71; 4/29/78, 6c; 7/5/80, 5d.

18.31 Maw Pokey Incident, 1984

Karen tribesmen persistently opposed central government efforts to pacify them after Burma gained independence in 1948. Karen insurgency, although internally divided, was especially long-lived within the Irawaddy Delta and areas bordering Thailand. Government attempts to suppress guerrilla activity carried across the Thai border in 1959 (18.18). In 1975 the outlawed Karen National Union (KNU) drew several other minority resistance groups into a National Democratic Front. General Ne Win's government offered general amnesty in 1980. Some rebels accepted the offer but important KNU leaders declined and continued their struggle for autonomy. The Burmese government initiated a major military campaign against KNU strongholds in mountainous areas near the Thai border in January 1984. On March 12, 1984, 200 Burmese troops entered Thai territory in order to attack the Karen base at Maw Pokey. The intruders encountered Thai border police and approximately fifteen Burmese soldiers were killed.

Macdougal, H., and J. Wiant. 1985. "Burma in 1984." *Asian Survey* 25 (February): 241–248.
Washington Post 5/14/84, 2:4.

19

Oceania

Pacific Oceania experienced occasional international armed conflict beginning in the late 1970s, including effects of insurgency among Indonesian Papuans (13.1) upon Papua New Guinea, the Vemarana secession (13.2) within the New Hebrides and the Kanak rebellion (13.3) within New Caledonia. Other conflicts within Melanesia involved disputes concerning territories incorporated within Indonesia and Malaysia, including the Indonesian War (18.4), conflict over West Irian (18.20), confrontation with Malaysia (18.22) and the Timorese War (18.27).

20.1 Papuan Insurgency, 1977

The Netherlands acknowledged Indonesian independence in 1949 (19.4) and ceded West New Guinea (West Irian) to Indonesia in 1962 (19.12). Eastern New Guinea represented the British crown colony of Papua, administered by Australia, and the Australian trust territory of New Guinea until together gaining independence as Papua New Guinea in 1975. The border between Indonesia and Papua New Guinea remained poorly marked and subject to dispute after independence. Indonesian efforts to pacify West Irian encountered serious resistance from the 1960s, especially among ethnic Papuans. Revolt broke out near the Panai (Wissel) lakes in 1969 as it had before as recently as 1956. The separatist Organisasi Papua Mendeka (OPM) also fomented violence in the vicinity of Arso and elsewhere along the Indonesian-Papuan frontier. OPM guerrilla activities increased in early 1977. Indonesia committed a regular army battalion to the border area. Troops raided Indonesian villages believed to support OPM and also repeatedly transgressed the Papuan border. Papua New Guinea tolerated although she did not openly approve minor Indonesian incursions. She protested a raid in mid-May 1977 against a village clearly within Papua New Guinea territory. Border tensions associated with the OPM insurgency continued throughout the 1980s but, so far as is known, Indonesia refrained from further blatant military intervention. No Indonesian military fatalities are reported within Papua New Guinea.

Keegan, J., ed. 1983. *World Armies*, 461–464.
Lagerberg, K. 1979. *West Iran and Jakarta Imperialism*, 10, 110–118.
Premdas, R. 1978. "Papua New Guinea in 1977." *Asian Survey* 18 (January): 58–67.

20.2 Vemarana Secession, 1980

The United Kingdom and France formed a Joint Naval Commission in 1887 to oversee the New Hebrides (Vanuatu, including eighty Melanesian islands host to both British and French settlements. They established joint administration under condominium with headquarters at Port Villa in 1907. The New Hebrides experienced political turbulence during the late 1970s as it approached independence, including nascent secessionist activity by Jimmy Stevens's Nagriamel movement. Repeated attempts from 1975 to form a popular national government proved unsuccessful until November 1979 elections when the Vanaaku Pati (Party of Our Land) won a large majority of the vote.

Vanaaku Pati leader Walter Lini was installed as head of a new local government on November 29, 1979. Britain and France scheduled independence for July 30, 1980. Secessionist movements erupted on outlying islands, supported in part by French-speaking residents. French police thwarted an attempted takeover of the island of Tanna in May. On May 28, Jimmy Stevens proclaimed himself prime minister of the Provisional Government of Vemarana after seizing control of Santo Town on the island of Espirito Santo. Police halted a similar attempt to take control of the island of Aoba on June 27. On July 24, 1980, a combined force of 100 British Royal Marines and 100 French paratroopers deployed to Espiritu Santo where it met no active resistance although Stevens remained at large. The New Hebrides became independent as the Republic of Vanuatu July 30. The Vanuatu flag was raised in Santo Town under guard of Anglo-French troops. Stevens supporters challenged police August 11 and 12 but avoided contact with British and French soldiers.

The Anglo-French force withdrew from Espiritu Santo August 18. It was replaced the same day by military units of Papua New Guinea, assisted by Australians in noncombat roles. Papua New Guinea troops helped to capture secessionists on Santo Espirito and other islands. Operations concluded September 27, 1980, when remaining Stevens's supporters surrendered upon the island of Malekula. Two civilians were killed during Papuan operations but neither the United Kingdom, France nor Papua suffered military fatalities.

Keesing's Contemporary Archives 27 (1981): 30641–30644.
New York Times 7/25/80, 5:2; 7/30/80, 7:1; 8/4//80, 5:1; 8/18/80, 5:6; 8/20, II, 8:2; 8/23/80, 5:2; 8/29/80, 3:1; 9/1/80, 5:3.

20.3 Kanak Rebellion, 1988

France penetrated the southern Pacific islands associated with New Caledonia in the 1850s and established formal colonial control in the 1880s. During the twentieth century, European settlers added to the population composed primarily of native Melanesians (Kanak). In 1984 Melanesians associated with the Kanak Socialist National Liberation Front (FLNKS) began a terrorist campaign to support demands for independence from France. European settlers resorted to counterviolence against Melanesians. France expanded police forces during 1985 amidst growing bloodshed on New Caledonia and associated islands. Despite a September 1987 referendum that reaffirmed majority preference to remain a French territory, Kanak separatists attacked police on the small island of Ouvea April 22, 1988, and seized twenty-seven hostages. France deployed two companies of her Rapid Intervention Force to the area although she did not immediately commit them to action. On April 30 a French patrol boat shelled Kanak forces besieging the town of Pouebe. On May 5 small units of French soldiers accompanied police during a helicopter assault that freed hostages held on Ouvea. Two French soldiers and two policemen died May 5 as did fifteen Kanak dissidents.

Keesing's Record of World Events 34 (1988): 35976–35977.
Laffin, J. 1989. *The World in Conflict 1989: War Annual 3*, 174–178.
New York Times 5/1/88, I, 11:1; 5/5/88, I,17:1; 5/6/88, I,7:1.

International Armed Conflicts, 1945–1988

2. Caribbean

3. Central America

276

6. West Africa

7. Central Africa

8. Horn of Africa

9. East Africa

10. Southern Africa

11. North Africa

12. Persian Gulf

13. Levant

14. Southern Arabia

15. Southwest Asia

16. East Asia

17. South Asia

19. Oceania

General Reference

Bibliographies

Brecher, M., J. Wilkenfeld, and S. Moser. 1988. *Crises in the Twentieth Century*, 2: 207–240.
Brogan, P. 1990. *The Fighting Never Stopped.*
Butterworth, R. 1976. *Managing Interstate Disputes.*
Small, M., and J. Singer. 1982. *Resort to Arms*, 297–372.
Tipson, F. 1974. "Selected Bibliography on Intervention and Civil War." In *Law and Civil War in the Modern World*, ed. J. Moore, 591–620.
Zacher, M. 1979. *International Conflicts and Collective Security*, 222–281.

Atlases

Barraclough, G., ed. 1984. *The Times Atlas of World History.*
Hartman, T. 1984. *A World Atlas of Military History.*
Kidron, M., and D. Smith. 1983. *The War Atlas.*

Political and Military Handbooks

Brecher, M., J. Wilkenfeld, and S. Moser. 1988. *Crises in the Twentieth Century*, 1: 143–346.
Butterworth, R. 1976. *Managing Interstate Disputes.*
Day, A., ed. 1987. *Border and Territorial Disputes.*
Donelan, M., and M. Grieve. 1973. *International Disputes.*
Dupuy, R., and T. Dupuy. 1986. *The Encyclopedia of Military History.*
Jessup, J. 1989. *A Chronology of Conflict and Resolution, 1945–1985.*
Keegan, J., ed. 1983. *World Armies.*
Laffin, J. 1986. *War Annual 1.*
Laffin, J. 1987. *War Annual 2.*
Laffin, J. 1989. *The World in Conflict 1989: War Annual 3.*
Political Handbook of the World. annual 1975–.
Statesman's Year-Book. annual 1864–.
Thompson, R., ed. 1985. *War in Peace.*

Conflict Lists

Bouthoul, G., and R. Carrere. 1976. *Le Defi de la Guerre*, 193–218.
Cable, J. 1981. *Gunboat Diplomacy*, 222–258.

Eckhardt, W., and E. Azar. 1979. "Major World Conflicts and Interventions." *International Interactions* 5 (#1): 75–100.

James, P. 1988. *Crisis and War*, 18–25.

Kende, I., K. Gantzel and K. Fabig. 1982. "Die Kriege seit dem Zweiten Weltkrieg." *DGFK–Hefte* 16 (November): 21–37.

Singer, J. 1991. "Peace in the Global System." In The Long Postwar Peace, ed. C. Kegley, 56–94.

Sivard, R. 1989. "War and War-Related Deaths, 1945–1989." *World Military and Social Expenditures* 13: 22.

Siverson, R., and M. Tennefoss. 1982. "Interstate Conflicts: 1815–1965." *International Interactions* 9 (#2): 147–178.

Small, M., and J. Singer. 1982. *Resort to Arms*, 82–99, 223–232, 297–340.

Stockholm International Peace Research Institute. 1970. "Post-World War II Armed Conflicts and Disputes." *SIPRI Yearbook* 1968/69: 359–380.

Tillema, H. 1989a. "Foreign Overt Military Intervention in the Nuclear Age." *Journal of Peace Research* 26 (May): 179–196.

Zacher, M. 1979. *International Conflicts and Collective Security*, 222–281.

Current World Events

Facts on File. weekly 1940–.

Keesing's Contemporary Archives. weekly and monthly 1931–1987.

Keesing's Record of World Events. monthly 1987–.

New York Times. daily 1857–.

Strategic Survey. annual 1966–.

Times (London). daily 1788–.

Washington Post. daily 1877–.

Latin America and the Caribbean

Child, J. 1985. *Geopolitics and Conflict in South America.*

Dunkerley, J. 1988. *Power in the Isthmus.*

Hispanic American Report. monthly 1948–1964.

Latin America. weekly 1967–1977.

Latin Ameria and Caribbean Contemporary Record. annual 1981/1982–.

Latin America Political Report. weekly 1977–1979.

Latin America Weekly Report. weekly 1979–.

Africa

Africa Contemporary Record. annual 1968/69–.

Africa Diary. weekly 1961–.

African Recorder. weekly 1962–.

Africa Research Bulletin. Political Series. monthly 1985–.

Africa Research Bulletin. Political, Social and Cultural Series. monthly 1964–1985.

Davidson, B. 1978. *Africa in Modern History*, 199–279.

Welch, C., ed. 1970. "Violence and Military Involvement in African States from Independence through 1968." In *Soldier and State in Africa*, ed. C. Welch, 270–301.
Venter, A. 1974a. *Africa at War.*
Zartman, I. 1989. *Ripe for Resolution.*

Middle East

ARR: Arab Report and Record. semimonthly 1966–1978.
Middle East Contemporary Survey. annual 1976/77–.
Blechman, B. 1972. "The Impact of Israel's Reprisals." *Journal of Conflict Resolution* 16 (June): 155–181.
Lenczowski, G. 1980. *The Middle East in World Affairs.*
Pearson, F., and R. Baumann. 1983. "Toward a Regional Model of International Military Intervention." *Arms Control* 4 (December): 187–222.

Asia

Asian Recorder. weekly 1955–.
Asian Survey. monthly 1961–.
Southeast Asian Affairs. annual 1974–.

Bibliography

Periodicals

ARR: Arab Report and Record. semimonthly 1966–1978. ISSN 0003–7451.
Africa Contemporary Record. annual 1968/69–. ISSN 0065-3845.
Africa Diary. weekly 1961–. ISSN 0001-978X.
African Recorder. weekly 1962–. ISSN 0002-0125.
Asian Recorder. weekly 1955–. ISSN 0004-4644.
Africa Research Bulletin. Political Series. monthly 1985–. ISSN 0001-9844. continues *Africa Research Bulletin. Political, Social and Cultural Series*.
Africa Research Bulletin. Political, Social and Cultural Series. monthly 1964–1985. ISSN 0001-9844.
Asian Survey. monthly 1961–. ISSN 0004-4687.

Facts on File. weekly 1940–. ISSN 0014-6641.

Hispanic American Report. monthly 1948–1964. LC 52-220.

Keesing's Contemporary Archives. weekly and monthly 1931–1987. ISSN 0022-9679.
Keesing's Record of World Events. monthly 1987–. ISSN 0950-6128. continues *Keesing's Contemporary Archives*.

Latin America. weekly 1967–1977. ISBN 0023-8724.
Latin America and Caribbean Contemporary Record. annual 1981/1982–. ISSN 0736-9700; 0736-4148.
Latin America Political Report. weekly 1977–1979. ISSN 0309-2992. continues *Latin America*.
Latin America Weekly Report. weekly 1979–. ISSN 0143-5280. continues *Latin America Political Report*.

Middle East Contemporary Survey. annual 1976/77–. ISSN 0163-5476.
Middle East Record. annual, irregular, 1960–1977. ISSN 0076-8529.

New York Times. daily 1857–.

Political Handbook of the World. annual 1975–. ISSN 0193-175X.

Southeast Asian Affairs. annual 1974–. ISSN 0377-5437.
Statesman's Year-Book. annual 1864–. ISSN 0081-4601.
Strategic Survey. annual 1966–. ISSN 0459-7230.

Times (London). daily 1788– .

UN Chronicle. monthly and quarterly 1975– . ISSN 0379-0959. continues *UN Monthly Chronicle.*
UN Monthly Chronicle. monthly 1964–1975. continues *United Nations Review.*

Washington Post. daily 1877–.

Yearbook of the United Nations. annual 1947–. ISSN 0082-8521.

Articles

Arbuckle, Thomas. 1979. "Rhodesian Bush War Strategies and Tactics." *R.U.S.I.: Journal of the Royal United Services Institute for Defense Studies* 124 (December): 27–33. LC 85-014271.

Bell, John Bowyer. 1970. "South Yemen: Two Years of Independence." *World Today* 26 (February): 76–82. ISSN 0043-9134.
Blechman, Barry M. 1972. "The Impact of Israel's Reprisals on Behavior of the Bordering Arab Nations Directed at Israel." *Journal of Conflict Resolution* 16 (June): 155–181. ISSN 0022-0027.
Brown, David J. Latham. 1961. "Recent Developments in the Ethiopia-Somaliland Frontier Dispute." *International and Comparative Law Quarterly* 10 (January): 167–178. ISSN 0004-4687.
Brown, Neville. 1971. "Jordanian Civil War." *Military Review* 51 (September): 38–58. ISSN 0026-4148.
Burrowes, Robert D. 1985. "The Yemen Arab Republic and the Ali Abdallah Salih Regime." *Middle East Journal* 39 (Summer): 287–316. ISSN 0026-3141.
Bustin, Edward. 1983. "Chad: Escalation Leads to Impasse." *The Middle East Annual* 3: 159–184. ISSN 0733-5350.

Cable, Vincent. 1969. "The Football War and the Central American Common Market." *International Affairs* (London) 45 (October): 658–671. ISSN 0020-5850.

Dale, Richard. 1987. "Not Always So Placid a Place: Botswana Under Attack." *African Affairs* 86 (January): 73–91. ISSN 0001-9909.

Davies, Nathaniel. 1978. "The Angola Decision of 1975." *Foreign Affairs* 57 (Fall): 109–124. ISSN 0015-7120.

Dawisha, Adeed I. 1975. "Intervention in Yemen: An Analysis of Egyptian Perceptions and Policies." *Middle East Journal* 29 (Winter): 47–64. ISSN 0026-3141.

Decalo, Samuel. 1980a. "Chad: The Roots of Centre-Periphery Strife." *African Affairs* 79 (October): 491–509. ISSN 0001-9909.

Decalo, Samuel. 1980b. "Regionalism, Political Decay, and Civil Strife in Chad." *Journal of Modern African Studies* 18 (March): 23–56. ISSN 0022-278X.

Depoorter, J. G. 1979. "Kolwezi." *Military Review* 54 (September): 29–35. ISSN 0026-4148.

Desmond, Edward W. 1989. "War at the Top of the World." *Time* 133 (July 31, 1989): 26–29. ISSN 0040-781X.

Diehl, Paul, and Gary Goertz. 1988. "Territorial Changes and Militarized Conflict". *Journal of Conflict Resolution* 32 (March): 103–122. ISSN 0022-0027.

Dommen, Arthur J. 1985. "Laos in 1984: The Year of the Thai Border." *Asian Survey* 25 (January): 114–121. ISSN 0004-4687.

Eckhardt, William, and Edward Azar. 1979. "Major World Conflicts and Interventions." *International Interactions* 5 (1): 75–100. ISSN0305-0629.

Farsoun, Karen, and James A. Paul. 1976. "War in the Sahara: 1963." In *The Struggle for Sahara*, 13–16. MERIP Report no. 45. Washington, D.C.: Middle East Research and Information Project. 26pp. bibliographical references. OCLC 2706294.

Franck, Dorotheo S. 1952. "Pathanistan—Disputed Disposition of a Tribal Land." *Middle East Journal* 6 (Winter): 49–68. ISSN 0026-3141.

Franck, Thomas M. 1976. "The Stealing of the Sahara." *American Journal of International Law* 70 (October): 694–721. ISSN 0002-9300.

Gause, F. Gregory III. 1988. "Yemeni Unity: Past and Future." *Middle East Journal* 42 (Winter): 33–47. ISSN 0026-3141.

Guillemin, Jacques. 1982. "Les Campagnes Militaires Francaises de la Decolonisation en Afrique Sud-Saharienne." *Mois en Afrique* (June): 124–141. ISSN 0035-3027.

Gunter, Michael M. 1988. "The Kurdish Problem in Turkey." *Middle East Journal* 42 (Summer): 289–406. ISSN 0026-3141.

Gupta, Shekhar. 1985. "Gunfire on the Glacier." *India Today* 10 (July 31, 1985): 78–81. LC 75-908882.

Hallett, Robin. 1978. "The South African Intervention in Angola." *African Affairs* 77 (July): 347–386. ISSN 0001-9909.

Henderson, Robert O. 1977. "Relations of Neighbourliness—Malawi and Portugal 1964-74." *Journal of Modern African Studies* 15 (September): 425–455. ISSN 0022-278X.

Holly, Daniel A. 1979. "Le Conflit du Honduras et du Salvador de 1969." *Etudes Internationales* 10 (March): 19–51. ISSN 0014-2123.

Hul, Galen. 1977. "Internationalizing the Shaba Conflict." *Africa Report* 22 (July–August): 4–9. ISSN 0001-9836.

Jencks, Harlan N. 1979 "China's Punitive War on Vietnam: A Military Assesment." *Asian Survey* 19 (August): 801–815. ISSN 0004-4687.

Kamm, Henry. 1981. "The Silent Suffering of East Timor." *New York Times Magazine*, section 6 (February 15, 1981): 35, 56–62. ISSN 0028-7822.

Kende, Istvan, Klaus J. Gantzel and Kai Fabig. 1982. "Die Kriege seit dem Zweiten Weltkrieg." *DGFK-Hefte* 16 (November): 21–37.

Koh, B. C. 1969. "The Pueblo Incident in Perspective." *Asian Survey* 9 (April): 264–280. ISSN 0004-4687.

Kozicki, Richard J. 1957. "The Sino-Burmese Frontier Problem." *Far Eastern Survey* 26 (March): 33–38. ISSN 0362-8949.

Kroef, Justus M. van der. 1964. "Communism and the Guerilla War in Sarawak." *World Today* 20 (January): 50–60. ISSN 0043-9134.

Kroef, Justus M. van der. 1979. "The Cambodian-Vietnamese War: Some Origins and Implications." *Asia Quarterly* (2): 83–94. ISSN 0035-2683.

Leighton, Marian K. 1978. "Perspectives on the Vietnam-Cambodia Border Conflict." *Asian Survey* 18 (May): 448–457. ISSN 0004-4687.

Lellouche, Pierre, and Dominique Moisi. 1979. "French Policy in Africa: A Lonely Battle Against Destabilisation." *International Security* 3 (4): 108–133. ISSN 0162-2889.

Lemarchand, Rene. 1975. "Ethnic Genocide." *Society* 12 (January–February): 50–60. ISSN 0147-2011.

M. K. G. 1954. "The Trieste Dispute." *World Today* 10 (January): 6–18. ISSN 0043-9134.

Macdougal, Hugh, and Jon A. Wiant. 1985. "Burma in 1984: Political Stasis or Political Renewal." *Asian Survey* 25 (February): 241–248. ISSN 0004-4687.

Maghreb Labor Digest. 1963. "Algerian-Moroccan Border Conflict Flares into Open Conflict." 1 (December): 3–9.

Maxwell, Neville. 1973. "The Chinese Account of the 1969 Fighting at Chenpao." *China Quarterly* 56 (October/December): 730–739. ISSN 0305-7410.

Maxwell, Neville. 1978. "Why the Russians Lifted the Blockade at Bear Island." *Foreign Affairs* 57 (Fall): 138–45. ISSN 0015-7120.

Mazrui, Ali A., and Donald Rothchild. 1967. "The Soldier and the State in East Africa: Some Theoretical Conclusions on the Army Mutinies of 1964." *Western Political Quarterly* 20 (March): 82–96. ISSN 0043-4078.

Meng, Ng Shui. 1984. "Vietnam in 1983: Keeping a Delicate Balance." *Southeast Asian Affairs* 11:343–368. ISSN 0377-5437.

Mercer, John. 1988. "The Cycle of Invasion and Unification in the Western Sahara." *African Affairs* 75 (October): 598–510. ISSN 0001-9909.

Metz, Steven. 1986. "The Mozambique National Resistance and South African Foreign Policy." *African Affairs* 85 (October): 491–507. ISSN 0001-9909.

Most, Benjamin, and Harvey Starr. 1983. "Conceptualizing 'War'". *Journal of Conflict Resolution* 27 (March): 137–159. ISSN 0022-0027.

Mylroie, Laurie A. 1989. "After the Guns Fell Silent: Iraq in the Middle East War." *Middle East Journal* 43 (Winter): 51–67. ISSN 0026-3141.

Nichterlein, Sue. 1977. "The Struggle for East Timor: Prelude to Invasion." *Journal of Contemporary Asia* 7 (4): 486–496. ISSN 0047-2336.

Parker, R. H. 1955. "The French and Portuguese Settlements in India." *Political Quarterly* 26 (October/December): 389–398. ISSN 0032-3179.

Paust, Jordan. J. 1976. "The Seizure and Recovery of the Mayaguez." *Yale Law Journal* 85 (May): 774–806. ISSN 0044-3409.

Pearson, Frederic S., and Robert A. Baumann. 1983. "Toward a Regional Model of International Military Intervention: The Middle Eastern Experience." *Arms Control* 4 (December): 187–222. ISSN 0144-0381.

Premdas, Ralph R. 1978. "Papua New Guinea in 1977: Elections and Relations with Indonesia." *Asian Survey* 18 (January): 58–67. ISSN 0004-4687.

Roosevelt, Archie, Jr. 1947. "The Kurdish Republic of Mahabad." *Middle East Journal* 1 (July): 247–269. ISSN 0026-3141.

Rosenau, James N. 1969. "Intervention as a Scientific Concept". *Journal of Conflict Resolution* 13 (June): 149–171. ISSN 0022-0027.

Rossow, Robert, Jr. 1956. "The Battle of Azerbaijan, 1946." *Middle East Journal* 10 (Winter): 17–32. ISSN 0026-3141.

Russett, Bruce J., J. David Singer, and Melvin Small. 1968. "National Political Units in the Twentieth Century." *American Political Science Review* 62 (September), 932–951. ISSN 0003-0554.

Sanchai, Somporn. 1976. "The Rising of the Rightist Phoenix." *Southeast Asian Affairs* 3:357–393. ISSN 0377-5437.

Schatzberg, Michael G. 1989. "Military Intervention and the Myth of Collective Security: The Case of Zaire." *Journal of Modern African Studies* 27 (June): 315–340. ISSN 0022-278X.

Schier, Peter. 1986. "Kampuchea in 1985: Between Crocodiles and Tigers." *Southeast Asian Affairs* 13:139–161. ISSN 0377-5437.

Shehim, Kassim, and James Searing. 1980. "Djibouti and the Question of Afar Nationalism." *African Affairs* 79 (April): 209–226. ISSN 0001-9909.

Simon, Sheldon. 1978. "Cambodia: Barbarism in a Small State Under Seige." *Current History* 75 (December): 197–201, 227–228. ISSN 0011-3530.

Sivard, Ruth L. 1989. "War and War-Related Deaths, 1945–1989." *World Military and Social Expenditures* 13: 22. ISSN 0363-4795.

Siverson, Randolph, and Michael R. Tennefoss. 1982. "Interstate Conflicts: 1815–1965." *International Interactions* 9 (2): 147–178. ISSN 0305-0629.

Stockholm International Peace Research Institute. 1970. "Post-World War II Armed Conflicts and Disputes." *SIPRI Yearbook; World Armaments and Disarmament* 1968/69: 359–380. ISSN 0347-2205.

Stuart-Fox, Martin. 1984. "Laos in 1983: Time for Consolidation." *Southeast Asian Affairs* 11:179–194. ISSN 0377-5437.

Stuart-Fox, Martin. 1986. "Laos in 1985: Time to Take Stock." *Southeast Asian Affairs* 13:165–181. ISSN 0377-5437.

Studies in Comparative Communism. 1969. "The Border Issue: China and the Soviet Union, March–October 1969." 2 (July–October): 121–382. ISSN 0039-3592.

Throup, D. W. 1985. "The Origins of Mau Mau." *African Affairs* 84 (July): 399–433. ISSN 0001-9909.

Tillema, Herbert K. 1989. "Foreign Overt Military Intervention in the Nuclear Age." *Journal of Peace Research* 26 (May): 179–196. ISSN 0022-3433.

Tinker, Hugh. 1956. "Burma's Northeast Borderland Problems." *Pacific Affairs* 29 (December): 324–346. ISSN 0030-851X.

U.S. Office of Naval Intelligence. Department of the Navy. 1953. "The Southeast China Coast Today." *The ONI Review* 8 (February): 51–60. Reprinted in The Declassified Documents Reference System. no. 1975/76A. Washington, D.C.: Carollton Press. microfiche. OCLC 02147532.

Vernier, Bernard. 1965. "La Question Kurde." *Revue de Defense Nationale* 20 (January): 102–122. ISSN 0035-1075.

Viviani, Nancy. 1976. "Australians and the Timor Issue." *Australian Outlook* 30 (August): 197–226. ISSN 0004-9913.

Wheeler, Douglas L. 1969. "The Portuguese Army in Angola." *Journal of Modern African Studies* 7 (October): 425–439. ISSN 0022-278X.

Wild, Patricia. 1966. "The Organization of African Unity and the Algerian-Moroccan Border Conflict." *International Organization* 20 (Winter): 18–36. ISSN 0020-8183.

Wroth, James M. 1968. "Korea: Our Next Vietnam." *Military Review* 48 (November): 34–40. ISSN 0026-4148.

Yong, Mun Cheong. 1978. "Indonesia: A Question of Stability." *Southeast Asian Affairs* 5:107–121. ISSN 0377-5437.

Zasloff, Joseph J. 1981. "Politics in the New Laos Part II: The Party, Political 'Re-education,' and Vietnamese Influence." *American Universities Field Staff Reports* (34). 2 vols. bibliographical references. ISSN 0161-0724.

Edited Books

Ablin, David A., and Marlowe Hood, eds. 1987. *The Cambodian Agony.* Armonk, NY: M. E. Sharpe. 418pp. maps. bibliography. ISBN 0873324218.

Aijmer, Goran, ed. 1984. *Leadership on the China Coast.* London: Curzon Press. 170pp. bibliography. ISBN 0700701621.

Arlinghaus, Bruce E., ed. 1984. *African Security Issues: Sovereignty, Stability, and Solidarity.* Boulder: Westview Press. 229pp. bibliographical references. ISBN 0865316074.

Aruri, Nasseer H., ed. 1975. *Middle East Crucible: Studies on the Arab-Israeli War of October 1973.* Wilmette: Medina University Press International. 479pp. bibliography. ISBN 0914456105.

Beckett, Ian F. W. , and John Pimlott, eds. 1985. *Armed Forces and Modern Counter-Insurgency.* New York: St. Martin's. 232pp. maps. bibliographies. ISBN 0312049242.

Bender, Gerald J., James S. Coleman, and Richard L. Sklar, eds. 1985. *African Crisis Areas and U.S. Foreign Policy.* Berkeley: University of California Press. 373pp. maps. bibliography. ISBN 0520055489.

Black, Joseph E., and Kenneth W. Thompson, eds. 1963. *Foreign Policies in a World of Change.* New York: Harper and Row. 756pp. maps. bibliographies. LC 63-10706.

Blechman, Barry M., and Stephen S. Kaplan. 1978. *Force Without War: U.S. Armed Forces as a Political Instrument.* Washington, D.C.: Brookings Institution. 584pp. bibliography. ISBN 0815709862.

Brown, James, and William P. Snyder, eds. 1985. *The Regionalization of Warfare: The Falklands/Malvinas Islands, Lebanon, and the Iran-Iraq Conflict.* New Brunswick: Transaction Books. 291pp. maps. bibliographies. ISBN 0887380220.

Carter, Gwendolyn M., and Patrick O'Meara, eds 1982. *Southern Africa: The Continuing Crisis.* 2d ed. Bloomington: Indiana University Press. 404pp. maps. bibliographical references. ISBN 0253354005.

Chaliand, Gerald, ed. 1980. *People Without a Country: The Kurds and Kurdistan.* trans. Michael Pallis. London: Zed Press. 246pp. maps. ISBN 090576269X.

Chiu, Hungdah, ed. 1979. *China and the Taiwan Issue.* New York: Praeger. 295pp. bibliography. ISBN 0030489113.

Cohen, Robin, ed. 1983. *African Islands and Enclaves.* Beverly Hills, CA: Sage. 279pp. maps. bibliographies. ISBN 0803919662.

Coll, Alberto R., and Anthony C. Arend, eds. 1985. *The Falklands War: Lessons for Strategy, Diplomacy, and International Law.* Boston: G. Allen and Unwin. 252pp. bibliographical references. ISBN 0043270751.

Cumings, Bruce, ed. 1983. *Child of Conflict: The Korean-American Relationship, 1943–1953.* Seattle: University of Washington Press. 335pp. bibliographical references. ISBN 0295959959.

Davidson, Basil, Joe Slovo, and Anthony R. Wilkinson, 1976. *Southern Africa: The New Politics of Revolution.* Hamondsworth, U.K.: Penguin Books. 374pp. map. bibliographical references. ISBN 0140219633.

Day, Alan J., ed. 1987. *Border and Territorial Disputes.* 2d ed. Burnt Mill, Harlow, Essex, U.K: Longman. 462pp. bibliography. maps. ISBN 0582009871.

Days with Ho Chi Minh. 1962. Hanoi: Foreign Languages Publishing House. 235pp. LC 63-3277/L.

Dunn, Peter M., and Bruce W. Watson, eds. 1985. *American Intervention in Grenada: The Implications of Operation "Urgent Fury".* Boulder: Westview Press. 185pp. bibliographical references. ISBN 0865318689.

Elliott, David W. P., ed. 1981. *The Third Indochina Conflict.* 247pp. bibliographical references. ISBN 089158739X.

Epstein, Howard. M., ed. 1965. *Revolt in Congo, 1960–1964.* New York: Facts on File. 187pp. LC 65-029769.

Farr, Grant M., and John G. Merriam, eds. 1987. *Afghan Resistance: The Politics of Survival.* Boulder: Westview Press. 235pp. bibliography. ISBN 0813372321.

Foltz, William J., and Henry S. Bienen, eds. 1985. *Arms and the African: Military Influences on Africa's International Relations.* New Haven: Yale University Press. 221pp. map. ISBN 0300033478.

Gabriel, Richard A., ed. 1983. *Nonaligned, Third World, and Other Ground Armies: A Combat Assessment.* Westport, CT: Greenwood Press. 276pp. maps. bibliographies. ISBN 0313239053.

Green, Reginald H., Kimmo Kiljunen, and Marja-Liisa Kiljunen, eds. 1981. *Namibia: The Last Colony.* London: Longman. 310pp. maps. index. bibliography. ISBN 0582597358.

Haley, P. Edward, and Lewis W. Snider, eds. 1979. *Lebanon in Crisis: Participants and Issues,* ed. P. Edward Haley and Lewis W. Snider. Syracuse: Syracuse University Press. 323pp. map. bibliographical references. ISBN 0815622104.

Heine, Jorge, and Leslie Manigat, eds. 1988. *The Caribbean and World Politics: Cross Currents and Cleavages.* New York: Holmes and Meier. 385pp. bibliography. ISBN 0841910006.

Higham, Robin, ed. 1972. *Civil Wars in the Twentieth Century.* Lexington: University of Kentucky Press. 260pp. bibliography. ISBN 0813112613.

Hopwood, Derek, ed. 1972. *The Arabian Peninsula: Society and Politics,* ed. Derek Hopwood. London: George Allen and Unwin. 320pp. maps. ISBN 0049530062.

Hoskyns, Catherine, ed. 1969. *The Ethiopia-Somalia-Kenya Dispute, 1960–67.* Dar esSalaam: Oxford University Press for the Institute of Public Administration, University College, Dar es Salaam, Tanzania. 91pp. LC 72-17563.

Jackson, Karl D., ed. 1989. *Cambodia, 1975–1978: Rendezvous with Death.* Princeton: Princeton University Press. 334pp. bibliography. ISBN 0691078076.

Jaster, Robert S., ed. 1985. *Southern Africa: Regional Security Problems and Prospects.* Aldershot, England: Gower. 170pp. ISBN 0566008661.

Kadt, Emanuel de, ed. 1972. *Patterns of Foreign Influence in the Caribbean.* New York: Oxford University Press for the Royal Institute of International Affairs. 188pp. map. bibliographical references. ISBN 0192149881.

Kaplan, Stephen S. 1981. *Diplomacy of Power: Soviet Armed Forces as a Political Instrument.* Washington, D.C.: Brookings Institution. 733pp. bibliography. ISBN 0815748248.

Keegan, John, ed. 1983. *World Armies.* 2d ed. Detroit: Gale Research. 688pp. ISBN 0810315157.

Kegley, Charles W., Jr., ed. 1991. *The Long Postwar Peace: Contending Explanations and Projections.* New York: Harper Collins. 386pp. bibliography. ISBN 0673460932.

Klass, Rosanne, ed. 1987. *Afghanistan, the Great Game Revisited.* New York: Freedom House. 519pp. maps. bibliography. ISBN 0932088163.

Kosut, Hal, ed. 1967. *Indonesia: The Sukarno Years.* New York: Facts on File. 140pp. LC 67-29073.

Kosut, Hal, ed. 1968. *Israel and the Arabs: The June 1967 War.* New York: Facts on File. 216pp. map. LC 68-023430.

Kosut, Hal, ed. 1970. *Cyprus, 1946–68.* New York: Facts on File. 192pp. map. ISBN 0871961830.

Kosut, Hal, ed. 1971. *Cambodia and the Vietnam War.* New York: Facts on File. 222pp. ISBN 087196208X.

Lawless, Richard, and Leila Monahan, eds. 1987. *War and Refugees: The Western Sahara Conflict.* New York: Pinter. 201pp. bibliographies. ISBN 0861879007.

Lemarchand, Rene, ed. 1988. *The Green and the Black: Qadhafi's Policies in Africa.* Bloomington: Indiana University Press. 188pp. map. bibliographies. ISBN 0253326788.

Lenczowski, George, ed. 1978. *Iran under the Pahlavis.* Stanford: Hoover Institution Press. 550pp. bibliography. ISBN 0817966412.

Luard, Evan, ed. 1972. *The International Regulation of Civil Wars.* New York: New York University Press. 240pp. bibliographical references. ISBN 0814749534.

Madden, A. F., and W. H. Morris-Jones. 1980. *Australia and Britain: Studies in a Changing Relationshipp.* London: Frank Cass for the Institute of Commonwealth Studies. 195pp. indexs. bibliographical references. ISBN 0714631493.

Maoz, Moshe, and Avner Yaniv, eds. 1986. *Syria under Assad: Domestic Constraints and Regional Risks.* New York: St. Martin's. 273pp. bibliographies. ISBN 0312782063.

Maull, Hanns W., and Otto Pick, eds. 1989. *The Gulf War: Regional and International Dimensions*. New York: St. Martin's. 203pp. bibliographical references. ISBN 0312037384.

Maurer, John H., and Richard H. Porth, eds. 1984. *Military Intervention in the Third World: Threats, Constraints and Options*. New York: Praeger. 239pp. ISBN 0030711746.

Mesa-Lago, Carmelo, and June S. Belkin, eds. 1982. *Cuba in Africa*. Pittsburgh: Center for Latin American Studies, University Center for International Studies, University of Pittsburgh. 230pp. map. bibliography. ISBN 0916002543.

Moore, John Norton 1974. *Law and Civil War in the Modern World*. Baltimore: Johns Hopkins. 648pp. bibliography. ISBN 0801815096.

Niblock, Tim, ed. 1984. *Iraq, the Contemporary State*. New York: St. Martin's. 283pp. maps. bibliographical references. ISBN 0312435851.

O'Neill, Bard E., William R. Heaton, and Donald J. Alberts, eds. 1980. *Insurgency in the Modern World*. Boulder: Westview Press. 291pp. bibliography. ISBN 0891585982.

Raeburn, Michael. 1978. *Black Fire: Accounts of the Guerrilla War in Rhodesia*. London: Julian Friedmann Publishers. 243pp. bibliographical references. ISBN 0904014215.

Rudolph, James D., ed. 1984. *Mexico, a Country Study*. Washington, D.C.: U.S. Department of the Army. 472pp. maps. bibliography. SUDOC D101.22:550-79/985.

Saikal, Amin, and William Haley, eds. 1989. *The Soviet Withdrawal from Afghanistan*. New York: CambridgeUniversity Press. 177pp. bibliographical references. ISBN 0521375770.

Seiler, John, ed. 1980. *Southern Africa since the Portuguese Coup*. Boulder: Westview Press. 252pp. maps. bibliographical references. ISBN 0891587675.

Smith, David S., ed. 1969. *The Next Asia: Problems for U.S. Policy*, ed. David S. Smith. New York: The International Fellows Program Policy Series, Columbia University. 316pp. maps. bibliographical references. LC 72-81143.

Sobel, Lester, ed. 1966–1973. *South Vietnam: U.S.-Communist Confrontation in Southeast Asia*. New York: Facts on File. 7 vols. OCLC 00412607.

Sobel, Lester A., ed. 1980. *Peace-Making in the Middle East*. New York: Facts on File. 286pp. ISBN 0871962675.

Stuart-Fox, Martin. 1982. *Contemporary Laos*. New York: St. Martin's. 345pp. bibliographical references. ISBN 0312166761.

Suhrke, Astri, and Lela Garner Nobel, eds. 1977. *Ethnic Conflict in International Relations*. New York: Praeger. 248pp. bibliographical references. LC 77-83444.

Tahir-Kheli, Shirin, and Shaheen Ayubi, eds. 1983. *The Iran-Iraq War*. New York: Praeger Special Studies. 210pp. bibliography. ISBN 0030629063.

Thompson, Robert G., ed. 1985. *War in Peace: An Analysis of Warfare from 1945 to the Present Day.* 2d rev. ed. London: Orbis Publishing. 336pp. bibliography. ISBN 085613841X.

United States. Marine Corps. 1954–1972. *U.S. Marine Operations in Korea.* Washington, D.C.: U.S. Marine Corps Headquarters, History and Museum Division. 5 vols. maps. bibliography. LC 55-060727.
United States. Marine Corps. 1958–1971. *History of U.S. Marine Corps Operations in World War II.* Washington, D.C.: U.S. Marine Corps. Headquarters. G-3 Division. Historical Branch. 5 vols. maps. bibliographical references. LC 58-60002.
United States. Marine Corps. 1977–1988. *U.S. Marines in Vietnam.* Washington, D.C.: U.S. Marine Corps Headquarters, History and Museum Division. 7 vols. maps. bibliographical references. LC 77-604776.

Valenta, Jiri, and Herbert J. Ellison. 1986. *Grenada and Soviet/Cuban Policy: Internal Crisis and U.S./OECS Intervention.* Boulder: Westview Press. 512pp. maps. bibliographies. ISBN 0813302358.

Wai, Dunstan M., ed. 1973. *The Southern Sudan: The Problem of National Integration.* London: Frank Cass. 255pp. bibliographical references. LC 72-92980.
Walker, Thomas W., ed. 1982. *Nicaragua in Revolution.* New York: Praeger. 410pp. map. bibliographical references. ISBN 0030579724.
Walker, Thomas W., ed. 1985. *Nicaragua: The First Five Years.* New York: Praeger. 561pp. map. bibliographical references. ISBN 0030695325.
Walker, Thomas W., ed. 1987. *Reagan Versus the Sandinistas: The Undeclared War on Nicaragua.* Boulder: Westview Press. 337pp. bibliographies. ISBN 0813303710.
Welch, Claude E., Jr., ed. 1970. *Soldier and State in Africa: A Comparative Analysis of Military Intervention and Political Change.* Evanston: Northwestern University Press. 320pp. bibliography. ISBN 0810101919.

Monographs

Abd-Allah, Umar F. 1983. *The Islamic Struggle in Syria.* Berkeley, CA: Mizan Press. 300pp. maps. bibliography. ISBN 0933782101.
Abdulghani, Jasim M. 1984. *Iraq and Iran: The Years of Crisis.* Baltimore: Johns Hopkins University Press. 270pp. maps. bibliography. ISBN 0801825199.
Abdullah, Muhammad M. 1978. *The United Arab Emirates: A Modern History.* London: Croom Helm. 365pp. bibliography. ISBN 0064949982.
Abir, Mordechai. 1974. *Oil, Power and Politics: Conflict in Arabia, the Red Sea and the Gulf.* London: Frank Cass. 221pp. map. bibliographical references. ISBN 0714629901.
Adkin, Mark. 1989. *Urgent Fury: The Battle for Grenada.* Lexington, MA: Lexington Books. 391pp. maps. bibliography. ISBN 0669207179.

Agung, Ide Anak Agung Gde. 1973. *Twenty Years of Indonesian Foreign Policy 1945–1965*. The Hague: Mouton. 640pp. bibliography. LC 72-093180.

Alagappa, Muthiah. 1987. *The National Security of Developing States: Lessons from Thailand*. Dover: Auburn House Publishing. 274pp. bibliography. ISBN 0865691525.

Albino, Oliver. 1970. *The Sudan: A Southern Viewpoint*. London: Oxford University for The Institute of Race Relations. 132pp. maps. bibliographical references. ISBN 0192181874.

Al-Fasi, Allal. 1970. *The Independence Movements in Arab North Africa*. trans. Hazem Zaki Nuseibeh. New York: Octagon Books. 414pp. LC 70-096201.

Ali, Choudhri Muhammad. 1967. *The Emergence of Pakistan*. New York: Columbia University Press. 418pp. maps. bibliographical references. LC 67-012535.

Allen, Richard H. S. 1968. *Malaysia; Prospect and Retrospect: The Impact and After-Math of Colonial Rule*. New York: Oxford University Press. 335pp. maps. bibliography. LC 68-031964.

Allfree, P. S. 1967. *Warlords of Oman*. London: Robert Hale. 191pp. map. LC 67-86725.

Alon, Hanan. 1980. *Countering Palestinian Terrorism in Israel: Toward a Policy Analysis of Countermeasures*. Rand report no. 1567. Santa Monica: Rand Corporation. 271pp. bibliography. OCLC 07122068.

Amate, C. O. C. 1986. *Inside the OAU: Pan-Africanism in Practice*. New York: St. Martin's. 603pp. bibliography. ISBN 0312418787.

Ameringer, Charles D. 1978. *Don Pepe: A Political Biography of Jose Figueres of Costa Rica*. Albuquerque: University of New Mexico. 324pp. map. bibliography. ISBN 082630480X.

Amnesty International. 1985. *East Timor: Violations of Human Rights: Extrajudicial Executions, "Disappearances," Torture, and Political Imprisonment, 1975–1984*. London: Amnesty International Publications. 92pp. maps. ISBN 0862100852.

An, Tai Sung. 1973. *The Sino-Soviet Territorial Dispute*. Philadelphia: Westminster Press. 254pp. bibliographical references. ISBN 0664209556.

Anderson, Benedict R. O. 1972. *Java in a Time of Revolution: Occupation and Resistance, 1944–1946*. Ithaca: Cornell University Press. 494pp. map. bibliography. ISBN 0801406870.

Anderson, Thomas P. 1981. *The War of the Dispossessed: Honduras and El Salvador, 1969*. Lincoln: University of Nebraska Press. 203pp. bibliography. ISBN 0803210094.

Anderson, William A. 1975. *Social Movements, Violence, and Change: The May Movement in Curaçao*. Columbus: Ohio State University Press. 175pp. bibliography. ISBN 0814202403.

Anwar, Raja. 1988. *The Tragedy of Afghanistan: A First-Hand Account*. trans. Khalid Hasan. New York: Verso. 286pp. bibliography. ISBN 0860912086.

Appleman, Roy E. 1961. *South to the Naktong, North to the Yalu*. Vol. 1 of The United States Army in the Korean War. Washington, D.C.: U.S. Department of the Army. Office of the Chief of Military History. 813pp. maps. bibliographical references. LC 60-060043.

Apter, David E. 1972. *Ghana in Transition*. 2d rev. ed. Princeton: Princeton University Press. 434pp. bibliographicl references. ISBN 069107545X.

Arfa, Hassan. 1966. *The Kurds: An Historical and Political Study*. London: Oxford University Press. 178pp. bibliography. LC66-073170.

Arnold, Anthony. 1985. *Afghanistan, the Soviet Invasion in Perspective*. Stanford: Hoover Institution Press. 179pp. map. bibliography. ISBN 0817982124.

Ashford, Douglas E. 1961. *Political Change in Morocco*. Princeton: Princeton University Press. 432pp. maps. bibliographical references. LC 61-006285.

Assefa, Hizkias. 1987. *Mediation of Civil Wars: Approaches and Strategies—The Sudan Conflict*. Boulder: Westview Press. 234pp. bibliography. ISBN 081337281X.

Assiri, Abdul-Reda. 1990. *Kuwait's Foreign Policy: City-State in World Politics*. Boulder: Westview. 193pp. maps. bibliography. 081337636X.

Attiqur Rahman, Mohammed. 1976. *Our Defence Cause: An Analysis of Pakistan's Past and Future Military Role*. London: White Lion Publishers. 263pp. bibliography. ISBN 0727401726.

Austin, Dennis. 1966. *Politics in Ghana, 1946–1960*. New York: Oxford University Press. 459pp. maps. bibliography. OCLC 08251411.

Avirgan, Tony, and Martha Honey. 1982. *War in Uganda: The Legacy of Idi Amin*. Westport, CT: Lawrence Hill. 244pp. ISBN 0882081365.

Ayoob, Mohammed, and K. Subrahmanyhan. 1972. *The Liberation War*. New Delhi: S. Chand. 292pp. bibliographical references. LC 72-900309/SA.

Babeeb, Saaed M. 1986. *The Saudi-Egyptian Conflict Over North Yemen, 1962–1970*. Boulder: Westview Press and the American Arab Affairs Council, Washington, D.C. 148pp. map. bibliography. ISBN 0813372968.

Bailey, Clinton. 1984. *Jordan's Palestinian Challenge, 1948–1983: A Political History*. Boulder: Westview Press, 1984. 146pp. map. bibliographical references. ISBN 0813300479.

Bailey, Sydney D. 1990. *Four Arab-Israeli Wars and the Peace Process*. New York: St. Martin's Press. 522pp. maps. bibliographies. ISBN 0312046499.

Baloyra, Enrique A. 1982. *El Salvador in Transition*. Chapel Hill: University of North Carolina Press. 236pp. map. bibliography. ISBN 0807815320.

Barber, Noel. 1974. *Seven Days of Freedom: The Hungarian Uprising 1956*. New York: Stein and Day. 266pp. bibliography. ISBN 0812817303.

Barbour, Nevill. 1962. *A Survey of North West Africa (the Maghrib)*. 2d ed. New York: Oxford University Press. 411pp. maps. bibliography. LC 62-051256.

Bardill, John E., and James H. Cobbe. 1985. *Lesotho: Dilemmas of Dependence in Southern Africa*. Boulder: Westview Press. 224pp. bibliography. ISBN 0865314403.

Baring, Arnulf. 1972. *Uprising in East Germany: June 17, 1953*. trans. Gerald Onn. Ithaca: Cornell University Press. 194pp. bibliography. ISBN 0801407036.

Bar-Joseph, Uri. 1987. *The Best of Enemies: Israel and Transjordan in the War of 1948*. London: Frank Cass. 254pp. bibliographies. ISBN 0714632112.

Barker, Arthur J. 1965. *Suez: The Seven Day War*. New York: Praeger. 223pp. maps. bibliography. LC 65-012314.

Barker, Arthur J. 1980. *Arab-Israeli Wars*. London: Ian Allen. 176pp. maps. bibliography. ISBN 0711009945.

Barker, Dudley. 1965. *Swaziland*. London: Her Majesty's Stationery Office. 145pp. map. bibliography. LC 65-008788.

Barnds, William J. 1972. *India, Pakistan, and the Great Powers*. New York: Praeger. 388pp. bibliography. LC 72-115104.

Barnett, A. Doak. 1963. *China on the Eve of the Communist Takeover*. New York: Praeger. 371pp. LC63-010824.

Barraclough, Geoffrey, ed. 1984. *The Times Atlas of World History*. rev. ed. London: Times Books. 360pp. maps. bibliography. ISBN 0723002614.

Barrett, Leonard E. 1977. *The Rastafarians: Sounds of Cultural Dissonance*. Boston: Beacon Press. 257pp. bibliography. ISBN 0807011142.

Bar-Siman-Tov, Yaacov. 1980. *The Israeli-Egyptian War of Attrition, 1969–1970*. New York: Columbia University Press. 248pp. bibliographical references. ISBN 023104982X.

Bar-Siman-Tov, Yaacov. 1987. *Israel, the Superpowers, and the War in the Middle East*. New York: Praeger. 313pp. bibliography. ISBN 0275923967.

Bar-Yaacov, Nissim. 1967. *The Israel-Syrian Armistice: Problems of Implementation, 1949–1966*. Jerusalem: Magnus Press, the Hebrew University. 377pp. map. bibliography. LC 68-000988.

Beaufre, Andre. 1969. *The Suez Expedition 1956*. trans. Richard Barry. New York: Praeger. 161pp. maps. LC 75-088351.

Becker, Jillian. 1984. *The PLO: The Rise and Fall of the Palestine Liberation Organization*. New York: St. Martin's. 303pp. maps. bibliography. ISBN 0312593791.

Beckwith, Charlie A., and Donald Knox. 1983. *Delta Force*. New York: Harcourt Brace Jovanovich. 310pp. map. ISBN 0151246572.

Bell, John Bowyer. 1969. *The Long War: Israel and the Arabs Since 1946*. Englewood Cliffs, NJ: Prentice-Hall. 467pp. bibliography. ISBN 13540617X.

Bell, John Bowyer. 1977. *Terror out of Zion: Irgun Zvai Leumi, LEHI, and the Palestine Underground, 1929–1949*. New York: St. Martin's. 374pp. bibliography. ISBN 0312792050.

Bell, John Patrick. 1971. *Crisis in Costa Rica: The 1948 Revolution*. Austin: University of Texas Press. 192pp. bibliography. ISBN 0292701470.

Berecz, Janos. 1986. *1956 Counter-Revolution in Hungary: Words and Weapons*. trans. Istvan Butykay. Budapest: Akademiai Kiado. 223pp. bibliographical references. ISBN 9630543702.

Bernard, Stephane. 1963. *Le Conflit Franco-Marocain, 1943–1956*. Bruxelles: Institut de Sociologie, Universite Libre de Bruxelles. 3 vols. maps. bibliography. LC 64-048075.

Bernard, Stephane. 1969. *The Franco-Moroccan Conflict, 1943–1956*. trans. Mariana Oliver. New Haven: Yale University Press. 680pp. maps. bibliography. LC 67-024490.

Beshir, Mohamed Omer. 1968. *The Southern Sudan: Background to Conflict*. New York: F. A. Praeger. 192pp. maps. bibliography. LC 68-017559.

Beshir, Mohamed Omer. 1975. *The Southern Sudan: From Conflict to Peace.* London: C. Hurst. 188pp. maps. ISBN 0903983184.

Bhasin, Vijay Kumar. 1984. *Soviet Intervention in Afghanistan: Its Background and Implications.* New Delhi: S. Chaud. 304pp. bibliography. LC 84-902893.

Bidwell, Robin. 1983. *The Two Yemens.* New York: Longman. 350pp. maps. bibliography. ISBN 0582783216.

Billings-Yun, Melanie. 1988. *Decision Against War: Eisenhower and Dien Bien Phu.* New York: Columbia University Press. 199pp. bibliography. ISBN 0231066228.

Bird, Leonard A. 1984. *Costa Rica, the Unarmed Democracy.* London: Sheppard Press. 224pp. maps. bibliography. ISBN 0900661372.

Birdwood, Chrostopher B. 1956. *Two Nations and Kashmir.* London: Robert Hale. 237pp. OCLC 2054789.

Bitsios, Dmitri S. 1975. *Cyprus: The Vulnerable Republic.* Thessaloniki: Institute for Balkan Studies. 223pp. LC 77-370816.

Black, George. 1981. *Triumph of the People: The Sandinista Revolution in Nicaragua.* London: Zed Press. 368pp. bibliography. ISBN 0862320925.

Blaxland, Gregory. 1971. *The Regiments Depart: A History of the British Army, 1945–1970.* London: William Kimber. 532pp. maps. bibliography. ISBN 0718300122.

Blinkenberg, Lars. 1972. *India-Pakistan: The History of Unsolved Conflicts.* Copenhagen: Munksgaard. 440pp. bibliography. LC 72-197797.

Boley, George E. S. 1984. *Liberia: The Rise and Fall of the First Republic.* New York: St. Martin's. 225pp. bibliography. ISBN 031248352X.

Booth, John A. 1985. *The End and the Beginning: The Nicaraguan Revolution,* 2d ed. Boulder: Westview Press. 363pp. bibliography. ISBN 0813301084.

Borisov, Oleg B., and B. T. Koloskov. 1975. *Soviet-Chinese Relations, 1945–1970.* Bloomington: Indiana University Press. 364pp. bibliographical references. ISBN 0253354102.

Bouthoul, Gaston, and Rene Carrere. 1976. *Le Defi de la Guerre 1740–1974.* Paris: Presses Universitaires de France. 223pp. LC 76-464807.

Bradsher, Henry S. 1985. *Afghanistan and the Soviet Union.* expanded ed. Durham, NC: Duke University Press. 384pp. map. bibliography. ISBN 0822305569.

Braveboy-Wagner, Jacqueline A. 1984. *The Venezuela-Guyana Border Dispute.* Boulder: Westview Press. 349pp. bibliographical references. ISBN 0865319537.

Brecher, Michael. 1953. *The Struggle for Kashmir.* New York: Oxford University Press. 211pp. map. bibliography. LC 54-232.

Brecher, Michael. 1968. *India and World Politics: Krishna Menon's View of the World.* New York: Praeger. 390pp. bibliographical references. LC 68-016083.

Brecher, Michael. 1975. *Decisions in Israel's Foreign Policy.* New Haven: Yale University Press. 639pp. maps. bibliography. ISBN 0300016603.

Brecher, Michael, with Benjamin Geist. 1980. *Decisions in Crisis: Israel 1967 and 1973.* Berkeley: University of California Press. 479pp. bibliography. ISBN 0520037669.

Brecher, Michael, Jonathan Wilkenfeld, and Sheila Moser. 1988. *Crises in the Twentieth Century*. New York: Pergamon Press. 2 vols. bibliography. ISBN 0080349811.

Brines, Russell. 1968. *The Indo-Pakistani Conflict*. London: Pall Mall. 486pp. maps. bibliographical references. ISBN 0269162321.

Brisk, William J. 1969. *The Dilemma of a Ministate: Anguilla*. Columbia, SC: Institute of International Studies, University of South Carolina. 93pp. bibliographical references. LC 72-630038.

Brogan, Patrick. 1990. *The Fighting Never Stopped: A Comprehensive Guide to World Conflicts Since 1945*. New York: Vintage Books. 603pp. maps. bibliographies. ISBN 0679720332.

Brown, MacAlister, and Joseph J. Zasloff. 1986. *Apprentice Revolutionaries: The Communist Movement in Laos, 1930–1985*. Stanford: Hoover Institution Press. 463pp. maps. bibliography. ISBN 0817981225.

Brown, Mervyn. 1979. *Madagascar Rediscovered: A History from Early Times to Independence*. Hamden, CT: Archon Books. 310pp. bibliography. ISBN 02081828X.

Brownlie, Ian. 1963. *International Law and the Use of Force by States*. Oxford: Clarendon Press. 532pp. bibliography. LC 63-003738.

Brownlie, Ian. 1979. *African Boundaries: A Legal and Diplomatic Encyclopaedia*. Berkeley: University of California Press. 1355pp. documents. bibliographies. maps. ISBN 050037952.

Bruce, Neil F. 1975. *Portugal: The Last Empire*. New York: Wiley. 160pp. maps. bibliography. ISBN 0470113669.

Budiardjo, Carmel, and Liem Soei Liong. 1984. *The War Against East Timor*. London: Zed Books. 253pp. bibliography. ISBN 0862322286.

Bueno de Mesquita, Bruce. 1981. *The War Trap*. 223pp. bibliography. ISBN 0300025580.

Bull, Odd. 1976. *War and Peace in the Middle East*. London: Leo Cooper. 205pp. maps. ISBN 0891587063.

Burchett, Wilfred G. 1970. *The Second Indochina War: Cambodia and Laos*. New York: International Publishers. 204pp. map. ISBN 717803074.

Burchett, Wilfred G. 1978. *Southern Africa Stands Up: The Revolutions in Angola, Mozambique, Zimbabwe, Namibia, and South Africa*. New York: Urizen Books. 321pp. maps. bibliographical references. ISBN 0916354253.

Burchett, Wilfred G. 1981. *The China-Cambodia-Vietnam Triangle*. Chicago: Vanguard Books. 235pp. bibliographical references. ISBN 0917702131.

Burke, S. M. 1973. *Pakistan's Foreign Policy: An Historical Analysis*. London: Oxford University Press. 432pp. bibliography. ISBN 0192151797.

Burke, S. M. 1974. *Mainsprings of Indian and Pakistani Foreign Policies*. Minneapolis: University of Minnesota Press. 308pp. bibliography. ISBN 0816607206.

Burma (Union) Government. Ministry of Information. 1953. *Kuomintang Aggression Against Burma*. Rangoon: Ministry of Information, Union of Burma Government. 221pp. maps. LC 60-45289.

Burns, Eedson L. M. 1963. *Between Arab and Israeli*. New York: Ivan Obelinsky. 336pp. LC 63-12370.

Burrowes, Reynold A. 1984. *The Wild Coast: An Account of Politics in Guyana.* Cambridge, MA: Schenkman Publishing Company. 348pp. bibliography. ISBN 0870730371.

Burrowes, Reynold A. 1988. *Revolution and Rescue in Grenada: An Account of the U.S.-Caribbean Invasion.* New York: Greenwood Press. 180pp. bibliography. ISBN 0313260664.

Butterworth, Robert Lyle. 1976. *Managing Interstate Conflict, 1945–74.* Pittsburgh: University Center for International Studies, University of Pittsburgh. 535pp. bibliographies. ISBN 0916002152.

Cable, James. 1981. *Gunboat Diplomacy: Political Applications of Limited Naval Force.* 2d ed. New York: St. Martin's. 288pp. bibliography. ISBN 0312353464.

Cady, John F. 1958. *A History of Modern Burma.* Ithaca: Cornell University Press. 682pp. bibliography. OCLC 00411018.

Caldwell, Malcolm, and Lek Tan. 1973. *Cambodia in the Southeast Asian War.* New York: Monthly Review Press. 446pp. maps. bibliographical references. ISBN 0853451710.

Calvert, Peter. 1982. *The Falklands Crisis: The Rights and the Wrongs.* London Frances Pinter. 183pp. maps. bibliographical references. ISBN 086187272X.

Cao, Van Vien, and Dong Van Khuyen. 1980. *Reflections on the Vietnam War.* Washington, D.C.: U.S. Army Center of Military History. 165pp. LC 79-607979.

Cawthra, Gavin. 1986. *Brutal Force: The Apartheid War Machine.* London: International Defence and Aid Fund for Southern Africa. 319pp. bibliography. ISBN 0904759725.

Chaigneau, Pascal. 1984. *La Politique Militaire de la France en Afrique.* Paris: Publications du Cheam. 143pp. bibliography. ISBN 2903182116.

Chanda, Nayan. 1986. *Brother Enemy: The War after the War.* San Diego, CA: Harcourt Brace Jovanovich. 479pp. maps. bibliography. ISBN 0151144206.

Chang, Pao-min. 1985. *Kampuchea Between China and Vietnam.* Singapore: Singapore University Press, National University of Singapore. 204pp. bibliographical references. ISBN 9971690896.

Chang, Pao-min. 1986. *The Sino-Vietnamese Territorial Dispute.* New York: Praeger Special Studies. 119pp. maps. bibliographical references. ISBN 0030072336.

Charlton, Michael. 1989. *The Little Platoon: Diplomacy and the Falklands Dispute.* New York: Basil Blackwell. 230pp. ISBN 0631165649.

Charters, David. 1989. *The British Army and Jewish Insurgency in Palestine, 1945–47.* New York: St. Martin's. 267pp. map. bibliography. ISBN 0312025025.

Chaturvedi, M. S. 1978. *History of the Indian Air Force.* New Delhi: Vikas Publishing House. 215pp. ISBN 0706906209.

Chen, Jack. 1977. *The Sinkiang Story.* New York: Macmillan. 386pp. maps. bibliography. ISBN 0025246402.

Chen, King C. 1969. *Vietnam and China, 1938–1954.* Princeton: Princeton. 436pp. bibliography. ISBN 0691030782.

Chen, King C. 1987. *China's War with Vietnam, 1979: Issues, Decisions, and Implications.* Stanford: Hoover Institution Press. 234pp. map. bibliography. ISBN 0817985719.

Cheriff Vanly, Ismet. 1965. *The Revolution of Iraki Kurdistan, Part I (From September 1961 to December 1963).* Lausanne: Committee for the Defense of Kurdish Rights. n.p. OCLC 7381904.

Child, Jack. 1988. *Antarctica and South American Geopolitics.* New York: Praeger. 232pp. bibliography. ISBN 02759288861.

Child, Jack. 1985. *Geopolitics and Conflict in South America: Quarrels Among Neighbors.* New York: Praeger. 196pp. bibliography. ISBN 0030014530.

Chin, Kin Wah. 1983. *The Defence of Malaysia and Singapore: The Transformation of a Security System, 1957–1971.* Cambridge: Cambridge University Press. 219pp. bibliography. ISBN 0521243254.

Cho, Soon Sung. 1967. *Korea in World Politics, 1940–1950.* Berkeley: University of California Press. 338pp. map. bibliography. LC 67-014968.

Choudhury, Golam Wahed. 1968. *Pakistan's Relations with India, 1947–1966.* New York: Praeger. 341pp. bibliography. LC 68-025336.

Christian, Shirley. 1985. *Nicaragua, Revolution in the Family.* New York: Random House. 337pp. bibliography. ISBN 0394535758.

Chubin, Shahram, and Sepehr Zabih. 1974. *The Foreign Relations of Iran: A Developing State in a Zone of Great-Power Conflict.* Berkeley: University of California Press. 362pp. map. bibliography. ISBN 0520026837.

Cilliers, J. K. 1985. *Counter-insurgency in Rhodesia.* London: Croom Helm. 266pp. bibliography. ISBN 0709934122.

Clark, Michael K. 1960. *Algeria in Turmoil; The Rebellion: Its Causes, Its Effects, Its Future.* New York: Grosset and Dunlap. 478pp. maps. bibliography. OCLC 01165409.

Clarke, Jeffrey J. 1988. *United States Army in Vietnam—Advice and Support: The Final Years, 1965–1973.* Washington, D.C.: United States Army Center of Military History. 561pp. maps. bibliographical references. LC 87-600379.

Clarke, Stephen J. G. 1968. *The Congo Mercenary: History and Analysis.* Johannesburg: South African Institute of International Affairs. 104pp. bibliography. LC 75-487140.

Clayton, Anthony. 1981. *The Zanzibar Revolution and Its Aftermath.* Hamden, CT: Archon Books. 166pp. bibliographical references. ISBN 0208019251.

Clayton, Anthony. 1984. *Counter-Insurgency in Kenya: A Study of Military Operations Against the Mau-Mau.* Manhattan, KS: Sunflower University Press. 64pp. bibliography. ISBN 0897450612.

Clayton, Anthony. 1988. *France, Soldiers and Africa.* London: Brassey's Defence Publishers. 444pp. bibliography. ISBN 0080347487.

Clodfelter, Mark. 1989. *The Limits of Air Power: The American Bombing of North Vietnam.* New York: Free Press. 297pp. map. bibliography. ISBN 0029059909.

Clough, Ralph N. 1978. *Island China.* Cambridge: Harvard University Press. 264pp. bibliography. ISBN 0674468759.

Clough, Ralph N. 1987. *Embattled Korea: The Rivalry for International Support.* Boulder: Westview Press. 401pp. bibliography. ISBN 0813373247.

Clutterbuck, Richard L. 1985. *Conflict and Violence in Singapore and Malaya, 1945–1983*. Boulder: Westview Press. 412pp. maps. bibliography. ISBN 0813301688.

Cobban, Helena. 1985. *The Making of Modern Lebanon*. Boulder: Westview Press. 248pp. maps. bibliography. ISBN 0813303079.

Cohen, Mark I., and Lorna Hahn. 1966. *Morocco: Old Land, New Nation*. New York: Praeger. 309pp. map. bibliography. LC 65-014062.

Coker, Christopher. 1985. *NATO, the Warsaw Pact and Africa*. New York: St. Martin's. 302pp. maps. bibliography. ISBN 0312560664.

Coker, Christopher. 1987. *South Africa's Security Dilemmas*. New York: Praeger. 112pp. maps. bibliography. 0275927717.

Collins, Joseph J. 1986. *The Soviet Invasion of Afghanistan: A Study in the Use of Force in Soviet Foreign Policy*. Lexington, MA: Lexington Books. 195pp. bibliography. ISBN 0669112593.

Collins, Joseph Lawton. 1969. *War in Peacetime: The History and Lessons of Korea*. Boston: Houghton, Mifflin. 416pp. maps. bibliography. LC 69-015008.

Cooley, John K. 1973. *Green March, Black September: The Story of the Palestinian Arabs*. London: Frank Cass. 263pp. maps. bibliography. ISBN 0714629871.

Cooley, John K. 1982. *Libyan Sandstorm*. New York: Holt, Rinehart and Winston. 320pp. maps. bibliographical references. ISBN 0030604141.

Cooper, John. 1970. *Colony in Conflict: The Hong Kong Disturbances May 1967–January 1968*. 315pp. maps. LC 75-19251.

Cordesman, Anthony H. 1984. *The Gulf and the Search for Strategic Stability*. Boulder: Westview Press. 1041pp. bibliography. ISBN 0865316198.

Cordesman, Anthony H. 1987. *The Arab-Israeli Military Balance and the Art of Operations: An Analysis of Military Lessons and Trends and Implications for Future Conflicts*. Washington, D.C.: American Enterprise Institute for Public Policy Research. 205pp. bibliography. ISBN 0844713783.

Cordesman, Anthony H. 1987. *The Iran-Iraq War and Western Security 1984–1987: Strategic Implications and Policy Options*. London: Jane's. 185pp. maps. bibliography. ISBN 0710604963.

Cordesman, Anthony H. 1988. *The Gulf and the West: Strategic Relations and Military Realities*. Boulder: Westview Press. 526pp. maps. bibliography. ISBN 0813307686.

Cordesman, Anthony H., and Abraham R. Wagner. 1990. The Lessons of Modern War. Boulder: Westview Press. 3 vols. maps. bibliographiy. LC 89-16631.

Cox, Thomas S. 1976. *Civil-Military Relations in Sierra Leone: A Case Study of African Soldiers in Politics*. Cambridge: Harvard University Press. 271pp. bibliography. ISBN 0674132904.

Craton, Michael. 1962. *A History of the Bahamas*. London: Collins. 320pp. maps. bibliography. LC 63-004124.

Crawley, Eduardo. 1984. *Nicaragua in Perspective*. rev. ed. New York: St. Martin's. 200pp. maps. bibliography. ISBN 0312572484.

Crawshaw, Nancy. 1978. *The Cyprus Revolt: An Account of the Struggle for Union with Greece.* Boston: George Allen and Unwin. 447pp. map. bibliography. ISBN 0049400533.

Cruz Sequeira, Arturo J. 1989. *Memoirs of a Counterrevolutionary.* New York: Doubleday. 266pp. ISBN 0385248792.

Cumings, Bruce. 1981. *The Origins of the Korean War: Liberation and the Emergence of Separate Regimes, 1945–1947.* Princeton: Princeton University Press. 606pp. bibliography. ISBN 0691093830.

Curran, Brian D., and Joann Schrock. 1972. *Area Handbook for Mauritania.* Washington, D.C.: U.S. Department of the Army. 185pp. maps. bibliography. LC 72-600188.

Dabat, Alejandro. 1984. *Argentina, the Malvinas, and the End of Military Rule.* trans. Ralph Johnstone. London: Verso. 205pp. bibliography. ISBN 0860910857.

Dahm, Bernhard. 1971. *History of Indonesia in the Twentieth Century.* trans. P. S. Falla. New York: Praeger. 321pp. maps. bibliography. LC 71-095668.

Damis, John. 1983. *Conflict in Northwest Africa: The Western Sahara Dispute.* Stanford: Hoover Institution. 196pp. maps. bibliography. ISBN 0817977813.

Dann, Uriel. 1969. *Iraq Under Qassem: A Political History, 1958–1963.* New York: Praeger. 405pp. maps. bibliography. ISBN 0269670645.

Darlington, Charles F., and Alice B. Darlington. 1968. *African Betrayal.* New York: David McKay. 359pp. map. LC 67-024783.

David, Stephen R. 1985. *Defending Third World Regimes from Coups d'Etat.* Lanham, MD: University Press of America for Center for International Affairs, Harvard University. 92pp. bibliography. ISBN 081914639.

David, Stephen R. 1987. *Third World Coups d'Etat and International Security.* Baltimore: Johns Hopkins Press. 191pp. bibliography. ISBN 0801833078.

Davidson, Basil. 1972. *In the Eye of the Storm: Angola's People.* Garden City, NY: Doubleday. 367pp. maps. bibliography. ISBN 0385031793.

Davidson, Basil. 1974. *Black Star: A View of the Life and Times of Kwame Nkrumah.* New York: Praeger. 225pp. map. bibliographical references. LC 73-016035.

Davidson, Basil. 1978. *Africa in Modern History: The Search for a New Society.* London: Allen Lane. 431pp. maps. bibliographical references. ISBN 0713908742.

Davidson, Basil. 1984. *No Fist is Big Enough to Hide the Sky; The Liberation of Guine and Cape Verde: Aspects of an African Revolution.* London: Zed Press. 187pp. map. bibliographical references. ISBN 0905762932.

Davidson, Scott. 1986. *Grenada: A Study in Politics and the Limits of International Law.* Brookfield, VT: Gower. 196pp. bibliography. ISBN 0566050528.

Dawisha, Adeed I. 1980. *Syria and the Lebanese Crisis.* New York: St. Martin's. 208pp. bibliography. ISBN 0312782039.

Dawisha, Karen. 1984. *The Kremlin and the Prague Spring.* Berkeley: University of California Press. 426pp. map. bibliography. ISBN 0520049713.

Dayan, Moshe. 1966. *Diary of the Sinai Campaign*. Jerusalem: Steimatzky's Agency. 236pp. OCLC 010800634.

Dayan, Moshe. 1976. *Story of My Life*. New York: Morrow and Company. 640pp. ISBN 068030769.

Decalo, Samuel. 1976. *Coups and Army Rule in Africa: Studies in Military Style*. New Haven: Yale University Press. 284pp. maps. bibliography. ISBN 0300019424.

Decalo, Samuel. 1987. *Historical Dictionary of Chad*. 2d ed. Metuchen, NJ: Scarecrow Press. 413pp. maps. bibliography. ISBN 0810810468.

Deeb, Marius. 1980. *The Lebanese Civil War*. New York: Praeger. 158pp. bibliography. ISBN 0030397014.

Denktash, Rauf R. 1982. *The Cyprus Triangle*. Boston: Allen and Unwin. 222pp. maps. bibliographical references. OCLC 08346295.

Deschamps, Hubert. 1961. *Histoire de Madagascar*. Paris: Berger-Levrault. 348pp. maps. bibliography. LC 61-1782.

Despres, Leo A. 1967. *Cultural Pluralism and Nationalist Politics in British Guiana*. Chicago: Rand McNally. 310pp. map. bibliography. LC 67-030674.

Devillers, Philippe. 1952. *Histoire du Viet-Nam de 1940 a 1952*. Paris: Editions du Seuil. 471pp. maps. LC 52-53585.

Devillers, Philippe. 1969. *End of a War: Indochina, 1954*. trans. Alexander Lieven and Adam Roberts. New York: Praeger. 412pp. maps. bibliography. LC 69-012705.

Dewar, Michael. 1984. *Brush Fire Wars: Minor Campaigns of the British Army since 1945*. New York: St. Martin's. 208pp. maps. bibliography. ISBN 0312106742.

Diederich, Bernard. 1981. *Somoza, and the Legacy of U.S. Involvement in Central Ameria*. New York: Dutton. 352pp. bibliographical references. ISBN 0525206701.

Dillon, George M. 1989. *The Falklands, Politics, and War*. New York: St. Martin's. 284pp. bibliography. ISBN 031202035X.

Diskin, Martin, and Kenneth Sharpe. 1986. *The Impact of U.S. Policy in El Salvador, 1979–1985*. Berkeley: Institute of International Studies, University of California. 67pp. bibliography. ISBN 087725527X.

Dominguez, Jorge I. 1989. *To Make a World Safe for Revolution: Cuba's Foreign Policy*. Cambridge: Harvard University Press. 365pp. bibliographical references. ISBN 0674893255.

Dommen, Arthur J. 1971. *Conflict in Laos*. rev. ed. New York: Praeger. 454pp. maps. bibliography. LC 76-145945.

Dommen, Arthur J. 1985. *Laos: Keystone of Indochina*. Boulder: Westview Press. 182pp. maps. inex. bibliography. ISBN 0865317712.

Donelan, Michael D., and M. J. Grieve. 1973. *International Disputes: Case Histories 1945–1970*. London: Europa for the David Davies Memorial Institute of International Studies. 286pp. bibliographies. ISBN 0900362642.

Donnison, Frank S. V. 1956. *British Military Administration in the Far East, 1943–46*. London: Her Majesty's Stationery Office. 483pp. maps. LC 57-001892.

Dowty, Alan. 1984. *Middle East Crisis: U.S. Decision-Making in 1958, 1970 and 1973.* Berkeley: University of California Press. 416pp. bibliography. ISBN 0520048091.

Draper, Theodore. 1968. *The Dominican Revolt: A Case Study in American Policy.* New York: Commentary Report. 208pp. bibliographical references. LC 68-006542.

Drysdale, John G. S. 1964. *The Somali Dispute.* New York: Praeger. 183pp. maps. bibliographical references. LC 64-13122.

Dubois, Jules. 1964. *Danger in Panama.* Indianapolis: Bobbs-Merrill. 409pp. bibliography. LC 64-023196.

Dugard, C J.R. 1973. *The South West Africa/Namibia Dispute: Documents and Scholarly Writings on the Controversy between South Africa and the United Nations.* ed. John Dugard. Berkeley: University of California Press. 585pp. bibliography. ISBN 0520018869.

Dugue, Gil. 1960. *Vers les Etats-Unis d'Afrique.* Dakar: Editions "Lettres Africaines." 314pp. LC 60-45439.

Duiker, William J. 1986. *China and Vietnam: The Roots of Conflict.* Berkeley: Institute of East Asian Studies, University of California. 136pp. bibliography. ISBN 0912966890.

Duncanson, Dennis J. 1968. *Government and Revolution in Vietnam.* London: Oxford University Press. 442pp. map. bibliography. LC 68-019954.

Dunkerley, James. 1982. *The Long War: Dictatorship and Revolution in El Salvador.* London: Junction Books. 264pp. map. bibliography. ISBN 0862450768.

Dunkerley, James. 1988. *Power in the Isthmus: A Political History of Modern Central America.* New York: Verso. 691pp. maps. bibliography. ISBN 0860911969.

Dunn, Peter M. 1985. *The First Vietnam War.* New York: St. Martin's. 392pp. maps. bibliography. ISBN 0312293143.

Dupree, Louis. 1973. *Afghanistan.* Princeton: Princeton University Press. 768pp. bibliography. ISBN 0691030065.

Dupuy, R. Ernest, and Trevor N. Dupuy. 1986. *The Encyclopedia of Military History.* 2d rev. ed. New York: Harper and Row. 1524pp. maps. bibliography. ISBN 0061812358.

Dupuy, Trevor N. 1978. *Elusive Victory: The Arab-Israeli Wars, 1947–1974.* New York: Harper and Row. 669pp. bibliography. ISBN 0060111127.

Dupuy, Trevor N. 1986. *Flawed Victory: The Arab-Israeli Conflict and the 1982 War in Lebanon.* Fairfax, VA: Hero Books. 247pp. maps. bibliography. ISBN 09159790701.

Durham, William H. 1979. *Scarcity and Survival in Central America: Ecological Origins of the Soccer War.* Stanford: Stanford Univeristy Press. 209pp. bibliography. ISBN 08047100007.

Duroselle, Jean Baptiste. 1966. *Le Conflit de Trieste, 1943-1954.* Brussells, Belgium: Editions de L'Institut de Sociologie de L'Universite Libre de Bruxelles. 648pp. bibliography. LC 68-072706.

Eagleton, William. 1963. *The Kurdish Republic of 1946*. London: Oxford University Press. 142pp. LC 63-002313.

Ealy, Lawrence O. 1971. *Yanqui Politics and the Isthmian Canal*. University Park: Pennsylvania State University Press. 192pp. bibliography. ISBN 0271011262.

Earley, Stephen. 1982. *Arms and Politics in Costa Rica and Nicaragua, 1948–1981*. Albuquerque, NM: Latin American Institute, University of New Mexico. 54pp. bibliographical references. OCLC 09005197.

Eddy, Paul, and Magnus Linklater, eds. 1982. *The Falklands War*. London: Andre Deutsch. 274pp. maps. ISBN 0233975152.

Edgerton, Robert B. 1989. *Mau Mau: An African Crucible*. New York: Free Press. 298pp. bibliography. ISBN 0029089204.

Eekelen, William F. van. 1964. *Indian Foreign Policy and the Border Dispute with China*. The Hague: Martinus Nijhoff. 220pp. maps. bibliography. LC 66-50239.

Ehrlich, Thomas. 1974. *Cyprus 1958–1967*. New York: Oxford University Press. 164pp. bibliographical references. ISBN 0198253214.

Eidlin, Fred H. 1980. *The Logic of "Normalization": The Soviet Intervention in Czechoslovakia of 21 August 1968 and the Czechoslovak Response*. Boulder, CO: East European Monographs. 278pp. bibliography. ISBN 0914710680.

El-Badri, Hassan, Taha El-Magdoub, and Mohammed Dia el-Din Zohdy. 1973. *The Ramadan War, 1973*. Dunn Loring, VA: T.N. Dupuy Associates. 239pp. maps. bibliographical references. ISBN 0891581383.

El-Hakim, Ali A. 1979. *The Middle Eastern States and the Law of the Sea*. Syracuse: Syracuse University Press. 293pp. maps. bibliography. ISBN 0815622171.

English, Adrian J. 1984. *Armed Forces of Latin America*. London: Jane's Publishing. 490pp. maps. bibliography. ISBN 0710603215.

Eprile, Cecil. 1974. *War and Peace in the Sudan, 1955–1972*. London: David and Charles. 192pp. bibliography. ISBN 0715362216.

Erisman, H. Michael. 1985. *Cuba's International Relations: The Anatomy of a Nationalistic Foreign Policy*. Boulder: Westview Press. 203pp. bibliographies. ISBN 0813300428.

Erlich, Haggai. 1984. *The Struggle Over Eritrea, 1962–1978: War and Revolution in the Horn of Africa*. Stanford: Hoover Institution Press. 155pp. map. bibliography. ISBN 0817976027.

Evans, Grant. 1983. *The Yellow Rainmakers: Are Chemical Weapons Being Used in Southeast Asia?* London: Verso Editions. 202pp. map. bibliographical references. ISBN 0860910687.

Evans, Grant, and Kelvin Rowley. 1984. *Red Brotherhood at War: Indochina Since the Fall of Saigon*. London: Verso Editions. 312pp. maps. bibliography. ISBN 0860910903.

Evron, Yair. 1987. *War and Intervention in Lebanon: The Israeli-Syrian Deterrence Dialogue*. Baltimore: Johns Hopkins University Press. 246pp. bibliography. ISBN 0801835690.

Fall, Bernard B. 1964. *Street Without Joy*. 4th ed. Harrisburg, PA: Stackpole. 408pp. maps. bibliographical references. LC 64-023038.

Fall, Bernard B. 1969. *Anatomy of a Crisis: The Laotian Crisis of 1960–1961*. ed. Roger M. Smith. Garden City, NY: Doubleday. 283pp. maps. bibliography. LC 68-027115.

Farer, Tom J. 1979. *War Clouds on the Horn of Africa: The Widening Storm*. 2d rev. ed. New York: Carnegie Endowment for International Peace. 183pp. maps. bibliography. ISBN 0870030140.

Farnie, D.A. 1969. *East and West of Suez: The Suez Canal in History, 1854–1956*. Oxford: Clarendon Press. 860pp. maps. bibliography. ISBN 0198223226.

Farnsworth, David N., and James W. McKenney. 1983. *U.S.-Panama Relations, 1903–1978: A Study in Linkage Politics*. Boulder: Westview Press, 1983. 313pp. bibliography. ISBN 0865319693.

Feldman, Herbert. 1967. Revolution in Pakistan: A Study of the Martial Law Administration. London: Oxford University Press. 242pp. bibliographical references. LC 67-077816.

Fifield, Russell H. 1958. *The Diplomacy of South East Asia, 1945–1958*. New York: Harper. 584pp. maps. bibliography. LC 58-8354.

Fitzgibbon, Louis. 1982. *The Betrayal of the Somalis*. London: Rex Collings. 114pp. maps. bibliography. ISBN 0860361942.

Fletcher, Arnold. 1965. *Afghanistan: Highway of Conquest*. Ithaca: Cornell University Press. 325pp. bibliography. LC 65-017709.

Flint, Roy K., Peter W. Kozumplik, and Thomas J. Waraksa. 1987. *The Arab-Israeli Wars, the Chinese Civil War, and the Korean War*. Wayne, NJ: Avery Publishing Group. 130pp. maps. bibliography. ISBN 0895293226.

Foley, Charles, and W. I. Scobie. 1975. *The Struggle for Cyprus*. Stanford: Hoover Institution Press. 193pp. bibliography. ISBN 0817913718.

Forbes, Andrew D.W. 1986. *Warlords and Muslims in Chinese Central Asia: A Political History of Republican Sinkiang 1911–1949*. New York: Cambridge University Press. 376pp. bibliography. ISBN 0521255147.

Fox, Robert. 1985. *Antarctica and the South Atlantic: Discovery, Development and Dispute*. London: British Broadcasting Corporation. 336pp. bibliography. ISBN 0563203323.

Frank, Benis M. 1987. *U.S. Marines in Lebanon 1982–1984*. Washington, D.C.: History and Museums Division, Headquarters, U.S. Marine Corps. 196pp. maps. bibliography. SUDOC D214.13:L49.

Fricker, John. 1979. *Battle for Pakistan: The Air War of 1965*. London: Ian Allan. 192pp. map. ISBN 0711009295.

Friters, Gerard M. 1949. *Outer Mongolia and Its International Position*. ed. Eleanor Lattimore. Baltimore: Johns Hopkins Press. 358pp. maps. bibliography. LC 49-011854.

Fullick, Roy, and Geoffrey Powell. 1979. *Suez: The Double War*. London: Hamish Hamilton. 227pp. maps. bibliography. ISBN 0241101824.

Futrell, Robert F., Lawson S. Moseley, and Albert F. Simpson. 1961. *The United States Air Force in Korea, 1950–1953*. New York: Duell, Sloan and Pearce. 774pp. maps. bibliographical note. LC 61-16831.

Gabriel, Richard A. 1984. *Operation Peace for Galilee: The Israeli-PLO War in Lebanon*. New York: Hill and Wang. 241pp. maps. bibliography. ISBN 0809074540.

Gallicchio, Marc S. 1988. *The Cold War Begins in Asia: American East Asian Policy and the Fall of the Japanese Empire*. New York: Columbia University Press. 188pp. bibliography. ISBN 0231065027.

Gamba, Virginia. 1987. *The Falklands/Malvinas War: A Model for North-South Crisis Prevention*. Boston: Allen and Unwin. 212pp. bibliography. ISBN 004497020X.

Ganguly, Sumit. 1986. *The Origins of War in South Asia: Indo-Pakistani Conflicts Since 1947*. Boulder: Westview Press. 182pp. bibliography. ISBN 0813371090.

Gann, Lewis H., and Thomas H. Henriksen. 1981. *The Struggle for Zimbabwe: Battle in the Bush*. New York: Praeger. 154pp. maps. bibliography. ISBN 0030594448.

Gardinier, David E. 1963. *Cameroon, United Nations Challenge to French Policy*. New York: Oxford University Press. 142pp. map. bibliography. LC 63-023620.

Gause, F. Gregory III. 1990. *Saudi-Yemeni Relations: Domestic Structures and Foreign Policies*. New York: Columbia University Press. 233pp. maps. bibliography. ISBN 0231070446.

Gauze, Rene. 1973. *The Politics of Congo-Brazzaville*. trans., ed. and supplemented by Virginia Thompson and Richard Adloff. Hoover Institution Publications 129. Stanford: Hoover Institution Press. 283pp. ISBN 0817912916.

Gavin, R. J. 1975. *Aden Under British Rule 1839–1967*. New York: Barnes and Noble. 472pp. bibliography. ISBN 0064923371.

Gavshon, Arthur L. 1984. *Crisis in Africa: Battleground of East and West*. Boulder: Westview Press. 320pp. bibliographical references. ISBN 0865316805.

Gelb, Leslie H., with Richard K. Betts. 1979. *The Irony of Vietnam: The System Worked*. Washington, D.C.: Brookings Institution. 387pp. bibliographical references. ISBN 0815730721.

George, Alexander L., and Richard Smoke. 1974. *Deterrence in American Foreign Policy: Theory and Practice*. New York: Columbia University Press. 666pp. bibliographies. ISBN 0231038372.

Georgetown University Center for Strategic Studies. 1965. *Dominican Action, 1965: Intervention or Cooperation?* Washington, D.C.: Georgetown University Center for Strategic Studies. 85pp. map. LC 66-027809.

Gerard-Libois, Jules. 1966. *Katanga Secession*. trans. Rebeca Young. Madison: University of Wisconsin Press. 377pp. bibliographical references. LC 66-022851.

Gerbrandy, Pieter Sjoerds. 1950. *Indonesia*. London: Hutchinson. 224pp. map. LC 51-002997.

Gerteiny, Alfred G. 1967. *Mauritania*. New York: Praeger. 243pp. map. bibliography. LC 67-23574.

Gerteiny, Alfred G. 1981. *Historical Dictionary of Mauritania*. Metuchen, NJ: Scarecrow Press. 98pp. bibliography. ISBN 0810814331.

Ghareeb, Edmund. 1981. *The Kurdish Question in Iraq*. Syracuse: Syracuse University Press. 223pp. map. bibliographical references. ISBN 0815601646.

Ghaus, Abdul Samad. 1988. *The Fall of Afghanistan: An Insider's Account*. Washington, D.C.: Pergamon-Brassey's International Defense Publishers. 219pp. map. bibliographies. ISBN 0080347010.

Gibson, James W. 1986. *The Perfect War: Technowar in Vietnam*. Boston: Atlantic Monthly Press. 523pp. bibliography. ISBN 0871130637.

Gilkes, Patrick. 1975. *The Dying Lion: Feudalism and Modernization in Ethiopia*. New York: St. Martin's. 307pp. bibliography. LC 75-009388.

Gillespie, Joan. 1960. *Algeria, Rebellion and Revolution*. New York: Praeger. 208pp. bibliography. LC 60-14956.

Ginsburg, George, and Michael Mathos. 1964. *Communist China and Tibet: The First Dozen Years*. The Hague: Martinus Nijhoff. 218pp. bibliography. LC 65-84502.

Girardet, Edward. 1985. *Afghanistan: The Soviet War*. New York: St. Martin's. 259pp. maps. ISBN 0312748515.

Glasgow, Roy A. 1970. *Guyana: Race and Politics Among Africans and East Indians*. The Hague: Martinus Nijhoff. 153pp. map. bibliography. ISBN 9024750059.

Gleijeses, Piero. 1978. *The Dominican Crisis: The 1965 Constitutionalist Revolt and American Intervention*. trans. Lawrence Lipson. Baltimore: Johns Hopkins University Press. 460pp. bibliography. ISBN 0801820251.

Glubb, John Bagot. 1957. *A Soldier with the Arabs*. London: Hodder and Stoughton. 460pp. LC 57-059487.

Golan, Galia. 1971. *Czechoslovak Reform Movement: Communism in Crisis, 1962–1968*. Cambridge: Cambridge University Press. 349pp. bibliography. LC 76-163059.

Gordenker, Leon. 1959. *The United Nations and the Peaceful Unification of Korea: The Politics of Field Operations, 1947–1950*. The Hague: Martinus Nijhoff. 306pp. LC 60-004627.

Gordon, David F. 1986. *Decolonization and the State in Kenya*. Boulder: Westview Press, 1986. 266pp. map. bibliographies. ISBN 08133711112.

Gorman, Robert F. 1981. *Political Conflict on the Horn of Africa*. New York: Praeger. 243pp. map. bibliography. ISBN 0030594715.

Grant, Cedric H. 1976. *The Making of Modern Belize: Politics, Society, and British Colonialism in Central America*. New York: Cambridge University Press. 400pp. bibliography. ISBN 0521207312.

Grantham, Alexander W. G. H. 1956. *Report on the Riots in Kowloon and Tsuen Wan, October 10th to 12th, 1956*. Hong Kong: W. F. C. Jenner. 55pp. maps. OCLC 13298512.

Greig, Ian. 1977. *The Communist Challenge to Africa: An Analysis of Contemporary Soviet, Chinese and Cuban Policies*. Richmond, Surrey, England: Foreign Affairs Publishing Company. 306pp. maps. bibliography. ISBN 0900380217.

Griffiths, John C. 1981. *Afghanistan: Key to a Continent*. Boulder: Westview Press. 225pp. bibliographical references. ISBN 0865310807.

Grivas, George. 1965. *The Memoirs of General Grivas*. ed. Charles Foley. New York: Praeger. 226pp. map. LC 65-014586.

Grover, B. S. K. 1974. *Sikkim and India: Storm and Consolidation*. New Delhi: Jain Brothers. 248pp. map. LC 74-903219.

Gupta, Hari Ram. 1969. *The Kutch Affair*. Delhi, U. C. Kapur and Sons. 522pp. map. bibliographical references. LC 70-920002.

Gupta, Sisir. 1966. *Kashmir, a Study in India-Pakistan Relations*. New York: Asia Publishing House. 511pp. bibliography. LC 66-008138.

Gurtov, Melvin. 1967. *The First Vietnam Crisis: Chinese Communist Strategy and United States Involvement, 1953–4*. New York: Columbia University Press. 228pp. bibliography. LC 67-012207.

Gurtov, Melvin, and Byong-Moo Hwang. 1980. *China under Threat: The Politics of Strategy and Diplomacy*. Baltimore: Johns Hopkins Press. 336pp. maps. bibliography. ISBN 0801823978.

Gustafson, Lowell S. 1988. *The Sovereignty Dispute Over the Falkland (Malvinas) Islands*. New York: Oxford University Press. 268pp. bibliography. ISBN 0195041844.

Gutman, Roy. 1988. *Banana Diplomacy: The Making of Amerian Policy in Nicaragua, 1981–1987*. New York: Simon and Schuster. 404pp. bibliography. ISBN 0671606263.

Hadar, Arnon. 1981. *The United Statnes and El Salvador: Political and Military Involvement*. Berkeley, CA: U.S.-El Salvador Research and Information Center. 131pp. bibliographies. LC 83-101377.

Haley, P. Edward. 1984. *Qaddafi and the United States Since 1969*. New York: Praeger. 364pp. map. bibliographical references. ISBN 0030705878.

Hall, William E. 1895. *A Treatise on International Law*. 791pp. bibliographical references. LC 03-000002.

Halliday, Fred. 1974. *Arabia without Sultans: A Political Survey of Instability in the Arab World*. New York: Random House. 539pp. bibliographical references. ISBN 0394715292.

Halliday, Fred. 1979. *Iran: Dictatorship and Development*. Hamondsworth, England: Penguin Books. 348pp. maps. bibliography. ISBN 0140220100.

Halliday, Fred. 1990. *Revolution and Foreign Policy: The Case of South Yemen, 1967–1987*. New York: Cambridge University Press. 315pp. bibliographical references. ISBN 05132856X.

Halliday, Fred, and Maxine Molyneux. 1981. *The Ethiopian Revolution*. London: NLB. 304pp. maps. bibliography. ISBN 0860910431.

Halpern, Jack. 1965. *South Africa's Hostages: Basutoland, Bechuanaland and Swaziland*. Baltimore: Penguin Books. 495pp. maps. bibliography. LC-66-001673.

Hamizrachi, Beate. 1988. *The Emergence of the South Lebanon Security Belt: Major Saad Haddad and the Ties with Israel, 1975–1978*. New York: Praeger. 211pp. bibliography. ISBN 0275928543.

Hammel, Eric M. 1985. *The Root: The Marines in Beirut, August 1982–February 1984.* San Diego, CA: Harcourt Brace Jovanovich. 448pp. bibliography. ISBN 015179006X.

Hammer, Ellen J. 1966. *The Struggle for Indochina, 1940–1955.* Stanford: Stanford University Press. 373pp. map. bibliographical references. LC 66-24065.

Hammond, Thomas T. 1984. *Red Flag Over Afghanistan: The Communist Coup, the Soviet Invasion, and the Consequences.* Boulder: Westview Press. 262pp. bibliography. ISBN 0865314446.

Hanlon, Joseph. 1984. *Mozambique: The Revolution Under Fire.* London: Zed Books. 292pp. bibliography. ISBN 0862322448.

Harbottle, Michael. 1970. *Impartial Soldier.* New York: Oxford University Press. 210pp. maps. bibliography. ISBN 192149830.

Harbottle, Michael. 1971. *The Blue Berets.* Harrisburg, PA: Stackpole Books. 157pp. bibliography. LC 70-179598.

Harrison, Alexander. 1989. *Challenging De Gaulle: The O.A.S. and the Counterrevolution in Algeria, 1954–1962.* New York: Praeger. 192pp. bibliography. ISBN 0275927911.

Hart, Alan. 1989. *Arafat, a Political Biography.* Bloomington: Indiana University Press. 560pp. bibliography. ISBN 0253327113.

Hart, Parker T. 1990. *Two NATO Allies at the Threshold of War; Cyprus: A Firsthand Account of Crisis Management, 1965–1968.* Durham, NC: Duke University Press. 222pp. bibliography. ISBN 0822309777.

Hartman, Tom. 1984. *A World Atlas of Military History 1945–1984.* New York: Hippocrene Books. 108pp. maps. ISBN 0870520008.

Hasou, Tawfiq Y. 1985. *The Struggle for the Arab World: Egypt's Nasser and the Arab League.* London: KPI. 228pp. bibliography. ISBN 0710300808.

Hassouna, Hussein A. 1975. *The League of Arab States and Regional Disputes: A Study of Middle East Conflicts.* Dobbs Ferry, NY: Oceana Publications. 512pp. bibliography. ISBN 0379002904.

Hastings, Max, and Simon Jenkins. 1983. *The Battle for the Falklands.* London: Michael Joseph. 372pp. maps. ISBN 0718122283.

Hastings, Michael. 1970. *Embassies in Crisis: Diplomats and Demagogues Behind the Six Day War.* by "Michael Bar-Zohar." trans. Monroe Stearns. Englewood Cliffs, NJ: Prentice-Hall. 279pp. bibliographical references. ISBN 0132745062.

Hawley, Donald. 1970. *The Trucial States.* London: Allen and Unwin. 279pp. maps. bibliography. ISBN 0049530054.

Haykal, Muhammed Hasanayn. 1975. *The Road to Ramadan.* New York: Quadrangle/New York Times Book Company. 285pp. ISBN 0812905679.

Head, Richard G., Frisco W. Short, and Robert C. McFarlane. 1978. *Crisis Resolution: Presidential Decision Making in the Mayaguez and Korean Confrontations.* Boulder: Westview Press. 323pp. bibliography. ISBN 0891581634.

Headland, Robert. 1984. *The Island of South Georgia.* New York: Cambridge University Press. 293pp. maps. bibliography. ISBN 0521252741.

Heard-Bey, Frauke. 1982. *From Trucial States to United Arab Emirates: A Society in Transition*. New York: Longman. 522pp. maps. bibliography. ISBN 0582780322.

Heggoy, Alf Andrew. 1972. *Insurgency and Counterinsurgency in Algeria*. Bloomington: Indiana University Press. 327pp. bibliography. ISBN 0253330262.

Heitman, Helmoed-Romer. 1985. *South African War Machine*. Novato, CA: Presidio Press. 192pp. ISBN 0891412409.

Helms, Christine M. 1984. *Iraq: Eastern Flank of the Arab World*. Washington, D.C.: Brookings Institution. 215pp. bibliographical references. ISBN 0815735561.

Henderson, Gregory. 1968. *Korea: The Politics of the Vortex*. Cambridge: Harvard University Press. 479pp. maps. bibliographical references. LC 68-025611.

Henderson, William. 1973. *West New Guinea: The Dispute and Its Settlement*. South Orange, NJ: Seton Hall University Press for the American-Asian Educational Exchange. 281pp. bibliography. LC 72-088015.

Henissart, Paul. 1970. *Wolves in the City: The Death of French Algeria*. New York: Simon and Schuster. 508pp. maps. bibliography. ISBN 0671205137.

Henriksen, Thomas H. 1978. *Mozambique: a History*. London: Rex Collings. 276pp. maps. bibliographical references. ISBN 0860360172.

Henriksen, Thomas H. 1983. *Revolution and Counterrevolution: Mozambique's War of Independence, 1964–1974*. Westport, CT: Greenwood. 289pp. map. bibliography. ISBN 0313236054.

Hermes, Walter G. 1966. *Truce Tent and Fighting Front*. Vol. 2 of *The United States Army in the Korean War*. Washington, D.C.: U.S. Department of the Army. Office of the Chief of Military History. 571pp. maps. LC 66-007009.

Herzog, Chaim. 1975. *The War of Atonement, October, 1973*. Boston: Little, Brown. 300pp. ISBN 0316359009.

Herzog, Chaim. 1984. *The Arab-Israeli Wars: War and Peace in the Middle East from the War of Independence to Lebanon*. rev. ed. London: Arms and Armour Press. 403pp. bibliography. ISBN 0853686130.

Heseltine, Nigel. 1971. *Madagascar*. New York: Praeger. 341pp. maps. bibliography. LC 70-079070.

Higgins, Rosalyn. 1969–1981. *United Nations Peacekeeping: Documents and Commentary*. New York: Oxford University Press. 4 vols. maps. bibliographies. LC76-396893.

Hinh, Nguyen Duy. 1979. *Lam Son 719*. Washington, D.C.: U.S. Army Center of Military History. 179pp. bibliographical references. LC 79-607101.

Hinh, Nguyen Duy, and Tron Dinh Tho. 1980. *The South Vietnamese Society*. Washington, D.C.: U.S. Army Center of Military History. 175pp. bibliographical references. SUDOC D114.18:So1.

Hinton, Harold C. 1958. *China's Relations with Burma and Vietnam, A Brief History*. New York: International Secretariat, Institute of Pacific Relations. 64pp. bibliographical references. LC 58-2644.

Hinton, Harold C. 1966. *Communist China in World Politics*. New York: Houghton Mifflin. 527pp. maps. bibliographical references. LC 66-000400.

Hoare, Mike. 1967. *Congo Mercenary*. London: Robert Hale. 318pp. maps. LC 67-96600.

Hodges, Tony. 1982. *Historical Dictionary of Western Sahara*. Metuchen, NJ: Scarecrow Press. 431pp. bibliography. ISBN 0810814978.

Hodges, Tony. 1983. *Western Sahara: Roots of a Desert War*. Westport, CT: Lawrence Hill. 388pp. bibliography. ISBN 088081519.

Hodson, Henry V. 1985. *The Great Divide: Britain, India, Pakistan*. New York: Oxford University Press. 590pp. bibliographical references. ISBN 0195773403.

Hof, Frederic C. 1985. *Galilee Divided: The Israel-Lebanon Frontier, 1916–1984*. Boulder: Westview Press. 134pp. bibliography. ISBN 0813301890.

Hoffmann, Fritz L., and Olga M. Hoffmann. 1984. *Sovereignty in Dispute: The Falklands/Malvinas, 1493–1982*. Boulder: Westview Press. 194pp. maps. bibliography. ISBN 0865316058.

Hoffmann, Steven A. 1990. *India and the China Crisis*. Berkeley: University of California Press. 324pp. maps. bibliographical references. ISBN 0520065379.

Hofstadter, Dan. 1973. *Egypt and Nasser*. New York: Facts on File. 3 vols. map. ISBN 0871962039.

Holden, David, and Richard Johns. 1982. *The House of Saud: The Rise and Rule of the Most Powerful Dynasty in the Arab World*. New York: Holt, Rinehart, and Winston. 569pp. maps. bibliography. ISBN 0030437318.

Horn, Carl von. 1967. *Soldiering for Peace*. New York: David McKay. 402pp. maps. LC 67-017116.

Horne, Alistair. 1987. *A Savage War of Peace: Algeria, 1954–1962*. rev. ed. New York: Penguin Books. 606pp. bibliography. ISBN 0140101918.

Hoskyns, Catherine. 1965. *The Congo Since Independence, January 1960– December 1961*. London: Oxford University Press. 518pp. maps. bibliography. LC 65-002272.

Howe, Jonathan T. 1971. *Multicrises: Seapower and Global Politics in the Missile Age*. Cambridge: M.I.T. Press. 412pp. map. bibliography. ISBN 0262080435.

Hsieh, Chiao. 1985. *Strategy for Survival: The Foreign Policy and External Relations of the Republic of China on Taiwan, 1949–1979*. London: Sherwood. 371pp. map. bibliography. ISBN 0907671136.

Hughes, Colin A. 1981. *Race and Politics in the Bahamas*. New York: St. Martin's. 250pp. bibliographical references. ISBN 0312661363.

Humbaraci, Arslan. 1966. *Algeria: A Revolution That Failed: A Political History Since 1954*. New York: Praeger. 308pp. maps. bibliography. LC 66-021783.

Humbaraci, Arslan, and Nicole Muchnik. 1974. *Portugal's African Wars: Angola, Guinea Bissau, Mozambique*. New York: Third Press. 250pp. maps. bibliographical references. ISBN 0893880728.

Hutchinson, Martha C. 1978. *Revolutionary Terrorism: The FLN in Algeria, 1954–1962*. Stanford: Hoover Institution Press. 178pp. bibliography. ISBN 0817969616.

Hutchison, Elmo H. 1956. *Violent Truce: A Military Observer Looks at the Israeli Conflict, 1951–1955*. New York: Devin-Adair. 199pp. maps. LC 56-009832.

Hutheesing, Gunottam Purushottam. 1961. *Tibet Fights for Freedom; the Story of the March 1959 Uprising as Recorded in Documents, Despatches, Eye-Witness Accounts and World-Wide Reactions.* Bombay: Orient Longmans. 241pp. map. LC 61-066481.

Hyde, Douglas A. 1965. *Conflict in the East: A Background Book.* Chester Springs, PA: Dufour Editions. 127pp. map. LC 65-018352.

Hyman, Anthony. 1984. *Afghanistan Under Soviet Domination, 1964–83.* New York: St. Martin's. 247pp. bibliographical references. ISBN 0312009275.

Ignatev, Oleg K., and Genrikh Borovik. 1980. *The Agony of a Dictatorship.* trans. Arthur Shkarovsky. Moscow: Progress Publishers. 158pp. OCLC 07181465.

Ingrams, William H. 1964. *The Yemen: Imams, Rulers and Revolutions.* New York: Praeger. 164pp. LC 64-106679.

Insight Team of the London Sunday Times. 1974. *The Yom Kippur War.* Garden City, NY: Doubleday. 514pp. ISBN 0385067380.

International Commission of Jurists. Legal Inquiry Committee on Tibet. 1960. *Tibet and the Chinese People's Republic: A Report to the International Commission of Jurists.* Geneva: International Commission of Jurists. 345pp. LC 63-052591.

International Commission of Jurists. 1964. *Report on the Events in Panama, January 9–12, 1964.* Geneva: International Commission of Jurists. 46pp. map. LC 64-54509.

Irving, David J. C. 1981. *Uprising.* London: Hodder and Stoughton. 628pp. bibliographical references. ISBN 0340183136.

Isaacman, Allen F., and Barbara Isaacman. 1983. *Mozambique: From Colonialism to Revolution, 1900–1982.* Boulder: Westview Press. 235pp. bibliography. ISBN 1865313109.

Isaacs, Arnold R. 1983. *Without Honor: Defeat in Vietnam and Cambodia.* Baltimore: Johns Hopkins Press. 559pp. bibliography. ISBN 0801830605.

Ismael, Tareq Y. 1982. *Iraq and Iran: Roots of Conflict.* Syracuse: Syracuse University Press. 226pp. bibliography. ISBN 0815622791.

Ismael, Tareq Y., and Jacqueline S. Ismael. 1986. *The People's Democratic Republic of Yemen: Politics, Economics, and Society, the Politics of Socialist Transformation.* Boulder: Lynne Rienner. 183pp. bibliography. ISBN 0931477964.

Jackson, Robert V. 1975. *South Asian Crisis: India, Pakistan, and Bangla Desh; a Political and Historical Analysis of the 1971 War.* New York: Praeger. 240pp. bibliography. ISBN 0275095606.

Jacobsen, Carl G. 1981. *Sino-Soviet Relations Since Mao: The Chairman's Legacy.* New York: Praeger. 170pp. bibliography. ISBN 0030583462.

Jagan, Cheddi. 1971. *The West on Trial: The Fight for Guyana's Freedom.* New York: International Publishers. 435pp. map. OCLC 00727753.

Jagdev Singh. 1988. *Dismemberment of Pakistan: 1971 Indo-Pak War.* New Delhi: Lancer International. 244pp. maps. ISBN 8170620414.

James, Harold, and Denis Sheil-Small. 1971. *The Undeclared War: The Story of the Indonesian Confrontation, 1962–1966.* Totowa, NJ: Rowman and Littlefield. 201pp. maps. ISBN 0850520800.

James, Patrick. 1988. *Crisis and War.* Kingston, Ontario: McGill-Queen's University Press. 194pp. bibliography. ISBN 0773505741.

Jaquet, Louis G. M., ed. 1971. *Intervention in International Politics.* The Hague: Martinus Nijhoff. 124pp. bibliographical references. LC 78-866515.

Jaster, Robert S. 1985. *South Africa in Namibia.* Lanham, MD: University Press of America. 114pp. map. bibliographies. ISBN 0819146838.

Jaster, Robert S. 1989. *The Defence of White Power: South African Foreign Policy Under Pressure.* New York: St. Martin's. 204pp. bibliographical references. ISBN 0312028296.

Jawad, Saad. 1981. *Iraq and the Kurdish Question, 1958–1970.* London: Ithaca Press. 377pp. map. bibliography. ISBN 0903729776.

Jeffrey, Henry B., and Colin Baber. 1986. *Guyana: Politics, Economics, and Society.* London: Francis Pinter. 203pp. bibliography. ISBN 0931477239.

Jessup, John E. 1989. *A Chronology of Conflict and Resolution, 1945–1985.* New York: Greenwood Press. 942pp. ISBN 0313243045.

Jha, Ganganath. 1979. *Foreign Policy of Thailand.* New Delhi: Radiant Publishers. 195pp. bibliography. LC 79-900898.

Jha, Skhree Krishna. 1975. *Uneasy Partners: India and Nepal in the Post-Colonial Era.* New Delhi: Manas Publications. 344pp. bibliography. LC 75-902423.

Johnstone, William C. 1963. *Burma's Foreign Policy.* Cambridge: Harvard University Press. 339pp. bibliographical references. LC 63-009550.

Jolliffe, Jill. 1978. *East Timor: Nationalism and Colonialism.* St Lucia, Australia: University of Queensland. 362pp. bibliographical references. ISBN 0702214809.

Jones, Griffith B. 1964. *Britain and Nyasaland.* London: Allen and Unwin. 314pp. maps. bibliography. LC 64-006299.

Jones, Howard P. 1971. *Indonesia: The Possible Dream.* New York: Harcourt, Brace Jovanovich. 473pp. map. bibliographical references. ISBN 0151443718.

Jorden, William J. 1984. *Panama Odyssey.* Austin: University of Texas Press. 746pp. bibliography. ISBN 0292764693.

Joseph, Richard A. 1977. *Radical Nationalism in Cameroun: Social Origins of the U.P.C. Rebellion.* New York: Clarendon Press. 383pp. maps. bibliography. ISBN 019822706X.

Julien, Charles-Andre. 1952. *L'Afrique du Nord en Marche: Nationalismes Muselmans et Souverainete Francaise.* Paris: Rene Juliard. 416pp. bibliography. LC 53-3338.

Kahin, George M. 1952. *Nationalism and Revolution in Indonesia.* Ithaca: Cornell University Press. 490pp. maps. bibliography. LC 52-004383.

Kahin, George M. 1986. *Intervention: How America Became Involved in Vietnam.* New York: Alfred A. Knopf. 550pp. maps. bibliography. ISBN 039454367X.

Kalicki, J. H. 1975. *The Pattern of Sino-American Crises: Political-Military Interactions in the 1950s*. London: Cambridge University Press. 279pp. maps. bibliography. ISBN 0521206006.

Katjavivi, Peter H. 1988. *A History of Resistance in Namibia*. Paris: United Nations Educational, Scientific, and Cultural Organization Press. 152pp. maps. bibliographical references. ISBN 085255320X.

Kaul, Brij Mohan. 1967. *The Untold Story*. New York: Allied Publishers. 507pp. LC 67-003064.

Kaul, Brij Mohan. 1972. *Confrontation with Pakistan*. New York: Barnes and Noble. 338pp. maps. OCLC 848117; 15277233.

Kavic, Lorne J. 1967. *India's Quest for Security: Defence Policies, 1947–1965*. Berkeley: University of California Press. 243pp. maps. bibliography. LC 67-016788.

Kay, Hugh. 1970. *Salazar and Modern Portugal*. New York: Hawthorn Books. 478pp. maps. bibliographical references. LC 73-115919.

Kecskemeti, Paul. 1961. *The Unexpected Revolution: Social Forces in the Hungarian Uprising*. Stanford: Stanford University Press. 178pp. bibliography. LC 61-010927.

Keesing's Contemporary Archives. 1969. *The Sino-Soviet Dispute*. New York: Scribner. LC 76-099009.

Keesing's Contemporary Archives. 1973. *Pakistan from 1947 to the Creation of Bangladesh*. New York: Charles Scribner's Sons. 143pp. maps. bibliography. ISBN 0684134071.

Keesing's Publications Limited. 1968. *The Arab-Israeli Conflict: The 1967 Campaign*. New York: Charles Scribner's Sons. 55pp. maps. bibliography. LC 68-009811.

Kelley, Michael P. 1986. *A State in Disarray: Conditions of Chad's Survival*. Boulder: Westview Press. 222pp. maps. bibliography. ISBN 0813303621.

Kelly, George A. 1965. *Lost Soldiers: The French Army and Empire in Crisis, 1947–1962*. Cambridge: M.I.T. Press. 404pp. bibliography. LC 65-024922.

Kelly, John Barrett. 1964. *Eastern Arabian Frontiers*. New York: Praeger. 319pp. maps. bibliographical references. LC 64-13137.

Kelly, John B. 1980. *Arabia, the Gulf and the West*. New York: Basic Books. 530pp. maps. bibliography. ISBN 0465004156.

Kent, Raymond K. 1962. *From Madagascar to the Malagasy Republic*. New York: Praeger. 182pp. bibliography. LC 62-011772.

Kerr, George H. 1965. *Formosa Betrayed*. Boston: Houghton Mifflin. 514pp. maps. bibliographical references. LC 65-020221.

Khadduri, Majid. 1969. *Republican Iraq: A Study in Iraqi Politics since the Revolution of 1958*. New York: Oxford University Press. 318pp. map. bibliographical references. LC 75-447193.

Khadduri, Majid. 1978. *Socialist Iraq: A Study in Iraqi Politics Since 1968*. Washington, D.C.: Middle East Institute. 265pp. bibliographical references. ISBN 0916808165.

Khadduri, Majid. 1988. *The Gulf War: The Origins and Implications of the Iraq-Iran Conflict*. New York: Oxford University Press. 236pp. bibliography. ISBN 0195045297.

Khalidi, Rashid. 1986. *Under Siege: P.L.O. Decisionmaking During the 1982 War*. New York: Columbia University Press. 241pp. bibliography. ISBN 0231061862.

Khalidi, Walid. 1979. *Conflict and Violence in Lebanon: Confrontation in the Middle East*. Cambridge: Center for International Affairs, Harvard University. 217pp. maps. bibliographical references. ISBN 0876740379.

Khan, Fazal Muqueem. 1973. *Pakistan's Crisis in Leadership*. Islamabad: National Book Foundation. 285pp. maps. bibliographical references. LC 73-930368.

Khouri, Fred J. 1985. *The Arab-Israeli Dilemma*. 3d ed. Syracuse: Syracuse University Press. 605pp. map. bibliographical references. ISBN 0815601980.

Kidron, Michael, and Dan Smith. 1983. *The War Atlas: Armed Conflict-Armed Peace*. New York: Simon and Schuster. 124pp. maps. bibliography. ISBN 0671472496.

Kiernan, Ben, and Chanthou Boua, eds. 1982. *Peasants and Politics in Kampuchea, 1942–1981*. Armonk, NY: M. E. Sharpe. 401pp. map. index. bibliography. ISBN 0873322177.

King, Michael. 1981. *New Zealanders at War*. Auckland, New Zealand: Heinemann. 308pp. ISBN 0868633992.

Kirk, George. 1954. *The Middle East 1945–1950, Survey of International Affairs Supplement 1954*. London: Oxford University Press. 338pp. map. bibliographical references. OCLC 4885925.

Kitchel, Denison. 1978. *The Truth About the Panama Canal*. New Rochelle, N.Y.: Arlington House. 240pp. bibliographical references. ISBN 0870004093.

Knapp, Herbert, and Mary Knapp. 1984. *Red, White, and Blue Paradise: The American Canal Zone in Panama*. San Diego, CA: Harcourt, Brace Jovanovich. 306pp. bibliography. ISBN 0151761353.

Kopacsi, Sandor. 1987. *In the Name of the Working Class: The Inside Story of the Hungarian Revolution*. trans. Daniel Stoffman and Judy Stoffman. New York: Grove Press. 304pp. ISBN 0802100104.

Korbel, Josef. 1966. *Danger in Kashmir*. rev. ed. Princeton: Princeton University Press. 401pp. maps. bibliography. LC66-006524.

Korea (Democratic People's Republic) Academy of Sciences. Research Institute of History. 1961. *History of the Just Fatherland Liberation War of the Korean People*. Pyongyang: Foreign Languages Publishing House. 322pp. OCLC 11715714.

Kornbluh, Peter. 1987. *Nicaragua, the Price of Intervention: Reagan's Wars against the Sandinistas*. Washington, D.C.: Institute for Policy Studies. 287pp. bibliography. 0897580400.

Kostiner, Joseph. 1984. *The Struggle for South Yemen*. New York: St. Martin's. 195pp. map. bibliography. ISBN 0312768729.

Kousoulas, Dimitrios G. 1965. *Revolution and Defeat: The Story of the Greek Communist Party*. New York: Oxford University Press. 306pp. maps. bibliography. LC 65-003086.

Krieg, William L. 1987. *Ecuadorean-Peruvian Rivalry in the Upper Amazon*. 2d ed. Bethesda, MD: William L. Krieg. 335pp. maps. bibliography. LC 87-601730.

Kuniholm, Bruce R. 1980. *The Origins of the Cold War in the Near East: Great Power Conflict and Diplomacy in Iran, Turkey, and Greece.* Princeton: Princeton University Press. 485pp. maps. bibliography. ISBN 0691046654.

Kurzman, Dan. 1970. *Genesis 1948: The First Arab-Israeli War.* New York: World Publishing Company. 750pp. maps. bibliography. LC 77-096925.

Kyemba, Henry. 1977. *A State of Blood: The Inside Story of Idi Amin.* New York: Grosset and Dunlap. 288pp. ISBN 044785344.

Lacey, Terry. 1977. *Violence and Politics in Jamaica, 1960–70: Internal Security in a Developing Country.* Totowa, NJ: Frank Cass. 184pp. bibliographical references. ISBN 0714660027.

Lackner, Helen. 1978. *A House Built on Sand: a Political Economy of Saudi Arabia.* London: Ithaca Press. 224pp. maps. bibliography. ISBN 090372927X.

Lackner, Helen. 1985. *P.D.R. Yemen: Outpost of Socialist Development.* London: Ithaca Press. 219pp. bibliography. ISBN 0863720323.

LaFeber, Walter. 1989. *The Panama Canal: The Crisis in Historical Perspective.* updated ed. New York: Oxford University Press. 270pp. bibliographical references. ISBN 0195059301.

Laffin, John. 1986. *War Annual 1.* London: Brassey's Defence Publishers. 187pp. maps. ISBN 008031311X.

Laffin, John. 1987. *War Annual 2.* London: Brassey's Defence Publishers. 246pp. maps. bibliography. ISBN 0080347517.

Laffin, John. 1989. *The World in Conflict 1989: War Annual 3.* London: Brassey's Defence Publishers. 234pp. maps. bibliography. ISBN 0080362656.

Lagerberg, Kees. 1979. *West Iran and Jakarta Imperialism.* New York: St. Martin's. 171pp. maps. bibliography. ISBN 0312863225.

Laitin, David D., and Said S. Samatar. 1987. *Somalia: Nation in Search of a State.* Boulder: Westview Press. bibliography. ISBN 0865315558.

Lake, Anthony. 1989. *Somoza Falling.* Boston: Houghton Mifflin. 317pp. bibliographical references. ISBN 0395419832.

Lall, Arthur S. 1967. *The UN and the Middle East Crisis, 1967.* New York: Columbia University Press. 332pp. bibliographical references. LC 68-008879.

Lamb, Alastair. 1967. *The Kashmir Problem: A Historical Survey.* New York: Praeger. 163pp. maps. bibliography. LC 67-011660.

Lamb, Christopher J. 1989. *Belief Systems and Decision Making in the Mayaguez Crisis.* Gainesville: University Presses of Florida, University of Florida. 304pp. maps. bibliographical references. ISBN 081309006.

Lancaster, Donald. 1961. *The Emancipation of French Indochina.* New York: Oxford University Press. 445 pp. map. bibliography. LC 61-001998.

Landau, Rom. 1956. *Moroccan Drama, 1900–1955.* London: Robert Hale. 430pp. map. bibliography. LC 57-1232.

Landen, Robert Geran. 1967. *Oman Since 1856: Disruptive Modernization in a Traditional Arab Society.* Princeton: Princeton University Press. 488pp. maps. bibliography. LC 66-021835.

Langer, Paul F., and Joseph J. Zasloff. 1970. *North Vietnam and the Pathet Lao: Partners in the Struggle for Laos.* Cambridge: Harvard University Press. 262pp. maps. bibliographies. ISBN 0674626753.

Laqueur, Walter. 1968. *The Road to Jerusalem: The Origins of the Arab-Israeli Conflict, 1967.* New York: Macmillan. 368pp. map. bibliography. LC 68-07517.

Laqueur, Walter. 1974. *Confrontation: The Middle East and World Politics.* New York: Quadrangle/New York Times Book Company. 308pp. maps. bibliographical references. ISBN 0812904540.

Larsen, Stanley R., and James L. Collins. 1975. *Allied Participation in Vietnam.* Washington, D.C.: U.S. Department of the Army. 189pp. LC 74-28217.

Leckie, Robert. 1962. *Conflict: The History of the Korean War.* New York: Putnam. 448pp. LC 62-10975/L.

Lee, David. 1980. *Flight from the Middle East: a History of the Royal Air Force in the Arabian Peninsula and Adjacent Territories, 1945-1972.* London: Her Majesty's Stationery Office. 339pp. bibliographical references. ISBN 0117723568.

Lefever, Ernest W. 1967. *Uncertain Mandate.* Baltimore: Johns Hopkins University Press. 254pp. map. bibliography. LC 67-022890.

Lefever, Ernest W. 1970. *Spear and Scepter: Army, Police, and Politics in Tropical Africa.* Washington, D.C.: Brookings Institution. 251pp. maps. bibliography. ISBN 0815751990.

Legge, John D. 1972. *Sukarno: A Political Biography.* New York: Praeger. 431pp. bibliographical references. LC 77-181868.

Le Gro, William E. 1981. *Vietnam from Cease-Fire to Capitulation.* Washington, D.C.: U.S. Army Center of Military History. 180pp. maps. bibliographical references. LC 80-607143.

Legum, Colin, and Tony Hodges. 1978. *After Angola: The War over Southern Africa.* 2d ed. New York: Africana Publishing Company. 85pp. documents. ISBN 0841902798.

Leifer, Michael. 1967. *Cambodia: The Search for Security.* New York: Praeger. 209pp. bibliographical references. LC 67-018970.

Lemarchand, Rene. 1970. *Rwanda and Burundi.* New York: Praeger. 562pp. maps. bibliography. LC 73-077303.

Lenczowski, George. 1968. *Russia and the West in Iran, 1918-1948.* New York: Greenwood Press. 383pp. maps. bibliographical references. LC 68-23307.

Lenczowski, George. 1980. *The Middle East in World Affairs.* 4th ed. Ithaca: Cornell University Press. 863pp. map. bibliography. ISBN 0801412730.

Leogrande, William M. 1980. *Cuba's Policy in Africa, 1959-1980.* Berkeley: Institute of International Studies, University of California. 82pp. bibliographical references. ISBN 087725513X.

Leonard, Richard. 1983. *South Africa at War: White Power and the Crisis in Southern Africa.* Westport, CT: Lawrence Hill. 280pp. bibliographical references. ISBN 088208108X.

Lethbridge, Henry J. 1985. *Hard Graft in Hong Kong: Scandal, Corruption, the ICAC.* New York: Oxford University Press. 247pp. bibliography. ISBN 0195838963.

Le Vine, Victor T. 1964. *The Cameroons, from Mandate to Independence.* Berkeley: University of California Press. 329pp. maps. bibliography. LC 64-024585.

Le Vine, Victor T. 1971. *The Cameroon Federal Republic*. Ithaca: Cornell University Press. 205pp. maps. bibliography. ISBN 0801406374.

Le Vine, Victor T., and Roger P. Nye. 1974. *Historical Dictionary of Cameroon*. Metuchen, NJ: Scarecrow Press. 198pp. map. bibliography. ISBN 0810807076.

Lewis, Gordon K. 1987. *Grenada: The Jewel Despoiled*. Baltimore: Johns Hopkins Press. 239pp. bibliography. ISBN 0801834228.

Lewis, Ioan M. 1980. *A Modern History of Somalia*. rev. ed. New York: Longman. 279pp. maps. bibliography. ISBN 058264657X.

Lewis, Paul H. 1968. *The Politics of Exile: Paraguay's Febrerista Party*. Chapel Hill: University of South Carolina Press. 269pp. bibliography. LC 68-014358.

Lewis, Paul H. 1980. *Paraguay under Stroessner*. Chapel Hill: University of North Carolina Press. 256pp. map. bibliography. ISBN 0807814377.

Lewis, Paul H. 1982. *Socialism, Liberalism, and Dictatorship in Paraguay*. New York: Praeger. 154pp. map. bibliography. ISBN 0030615631.

Lewy, Guenter. 1978. *America in Vietnam*. New York: Oxford University Press. 540pp. bibliographical references. ISBN 0195023919.

Liebenow, J. Gus. 1987. *Liberia: The Quest for Democracy*. Bloomington: Indiana University Press. 336pp. bibliography. ISBN 0253334365.

Lijphart, Arend. 1966. *The Trauma of Decolonization: The Dutch and West New Guinea*. Yale University Press. 303pp. bibliographical references. LC 66-012506.

Ling, Dwight L. 1967. *Tunisia: From Protectorate to Republic*. Bloomington: Indiana University Press. 273pp. map. bibliography. LC 67-063013.

Liss, Sheldon B. 1967. *The Canal: Aspects of United States-Panamanian Relations*. Notre Dame, IN: University of Notre Dame Press. 310 pp. maps. bibliography. LC 67-022147.

Liss, Sheldon B. 1978. *Diplomacy and Dependency: Venezuela, the United States, and the Americas*. Salisbury, NC: Documentary Publications. 356pp. map. bibliography. ISBN 089712068X.

Listowel, Judith. 1965. *The Making of Tanganyika*. New York: London House and Maxwell. 451pp. maps. bibliography. LC 65-23574.

Little, Tom. 1968. *South Arabia: Arena of Conflict*. New York: Praeger. 196pp. maps. bibliography. LC 68-019644.

Litwak, Robert. 1981. *Sources of Inter-State Conflict*. Vol. 2 of *Security in the Persian Gulf*. Montclair: Allanheld, Osmun for the International Institute for Strategic Studies. 105pp. maps. bibliographical references. ISBN 0865980454.

Lomax, Bill. 1976. *Hungary 1956*. New York: St. Martin's. 222pp. maps. bibliography. LC 76-041633.

Lopes, Carlos. 1987. *Guinea-Bissau: From Liberation Struggle to Independent Statehood*. Boulder: Westview Press. 194pp. bibliography. ISBN 0813305349.

Lorch, Netanel. 1968. *Israel's War of Independence, 1947–1949*. 2d rev. ed. Hartford: Hartmore House. 579pp. maps. LC 71-004189.

Love, Kennett. 1969. *Suez: The Twice-Fought War, a History*. New York: McGraw-Hill. 767pp. maps. bibliographical references. LC 76-081913.

Loveman, Brian, and Thomas M. Davies, Jr. 1985. *Che Guevara, Guerrilla Warfare: With an Introduction and Case Studies.* Lincoln: University of Nebraska Press. 440pp. bibliographical references. ISBN 0803221169.

Lowe, Peter. 1986. *The Origins of the Korean War.* New York: Longman. 237pp. maps. bibliography. ISBN 0582492785.

Lowenthal, Abraham. 1972. *The Dominican Intervention.* Cambridge: Harvard University Press. 246pp. bibliography. ISBN 0674214803.

Lu, Chih H. 1986. *The Sino-Indian Border Dispute: A Legal Study.* New York: Greenwood Press. 143pp. bibliography. ISBN 0313250243.

Luttwak, Edward N., and Daniel Horowitz. 1983. *The Israeli Army, 1948–1973.* Cambridge: Abt Books. 398pp. maps. bibliographical references. ISBN 0890115850.

Mackie, J. A. C. 1974. *Konfrontasi: The Indonesia-Malaysia Dispute, 1963–1966.* New York: Oxford University Press. 368pp. maps. bibliography. ISBN 0196382475.

Mahgoub, Mohamed Ahmed. 1974. *Democracy on Trial: Reflections on Arab and African Politics.* London: Andre Deutsch. 318pp. ISBN 0233964576.

Majdalany, Fred. 1963. *State of Emergency: The Full Story of Mau Mau.* Boston: Houghton Mifflin. 239pp. bibliography. LC 62-052857.

Malaysia. Department of Information. 1964. Indonesian Involvement in Eastern Malaysia. Kuala Lumpur: Malaysia, Department of Information. 83pp. LC 65-66622.

Manley, Robert. 1979. *Guyana Emergent: The Post-Independence Struggle for Nondependent Development.* Boston: G. K. Hall and Company. 158pp. bibliographical references. ISBN 0816190011.

Mannick, A. R. 1979. *Mauritius: The Development of a Plural Society.* Nottingham, U.K.: Spokesman. 174pp. map. bibliography. ISBN 0851242499.

Mansfield, Peter. 1973. The Middle East; a Political and Economic Survey. 4th ed. New York: Oxford University Press. maps. bibliography. ISBN 019215933X.

Maoz, Zeev. 1982. *Paths to Conflict: International Dispute Initiation, 1816–1975.* Boulder: Westview Press. 273pp. bibliography. ISBN 0865319332.

Marcum, John A. 1969–1978. *The Angolan Revolution.* Cambridge: M.I.T. Press. 2 vols. maps. bibliographical references. LC 69-011310. ISBN 062131366 (v. 2).

Markakis, John. 1987. *National and Class Conflict in the Horn of Africa.* African Studies Series 55. New York: Cambridge University Press. 314pp. maps. bibliography. ISBN 0521333628.

Markides, Kyriacos C. 1977. *The Rise and Fall of the Cyprus Republic.* New Haven: Yale University Press. 200pp. maps. bibliographical references. ISBN 0300020899.

Marlowe, John. 1965. *Anglo-Egyptian Relations, 1800–1956.* 2d ed. London: Frank Cass. 468pp. bibliography. LC 66-091017.

Marr, Phebe. 1985. *The Modern History of Iraq.* Boulder: Westview Press. 382pp. bibliography. ISBN 086311196.

Martin, David. 1974. *General Amin.* London: Faber and Faber. 254pp. ISBN 0571105858.

Martin, Lenore. 1984. *The Unstable Gulf: Threats from Within*. Lexington, MA: Lexington Books. 232pp. maps. bibliography. ISBN 0669055581.

Matthews, Kenneth. 1972. *Memories of a Mountain War: Greece, 1944–1949*. London: Longman. 284pp. maps. ISBN 0582103800.

Maxwell, Gavin. 1966. *Lords of the Atlas: The Rise and Fall of the House of Glauoua, 1893–1956*. New York: E. P. Dutton. 318pp. maps. bibliography. LC 66-021307.

Maxwell, Neville. 1972. *India's China War*. Garden City, NY: Doubleday. 537pp. maps. bibliography. LC 79-188296.

McClintock, Michael. 1985. *State Terror and Popular Resistance in El Salvador*. Vol. 1 of *The American Connection*. London: Zed Books. 388pp. bibliographies. ISBN 0862322405.

McDowell, David. 1985. *The Kurds*. 4th ed. London: Minority Rights Group. 32pp. maps. bibliography. ISBN 094669026X.

McFarland, Daniel M. 1978. *Historical Dictionary of Upper Volta (Haute Volta)*. Metuchen, NJ: Scarecrow Press. 217pp. bibliography. ISBN 0810810883.

McMahon, Robert J. 1981. *Colonialism and Cold War: The United States and the Struggle for Indonesian Independence, 1945–49*. Ithaca: Cornell University Press. 338pp. maps. bibliography. ISBN 0801413885.

McNeill, Ian. 1984. *The Team: Australian Army Advisors in Vietnam 1962–1972*. New York: Hippocrene Books. 534pp. maps. bibliography. ISBN 0882549219.

Meade, Edward G. 1951. *American Military Government in Korea*. New York: King's Crown. 281pp. bibliography. LC 51-9103.

Melady, Thomas P. 1974. *Burundi: The Tragic Years*. Maryknoll, NY: Orbis. 110pp. ISBN 0883440458.

Mendel, Douglas Heusted. 1970. *The Politics of Formosan Nationalism*. Berkeley: University of California Press. 315pp. map. bibliographical references. ISBN 0520015576.

Menon, Vapal. P. 1961. *The Story of the Integration of the Indian States*. 3d ed. Bombay: Orient Longmans. 489pp. bibliography. OCLC 260719.

Meo, Leila M. T. 1965. *Lebanon, Improbable Nation: A Study in Political Development*. Bloomington: Indiana University Press. 246pp. maps. bibliography. LC 65-063610.

Mercer, John. 1976. *Spanish Sahara*. London: George Allen and Unwin. 264pp. bibliography. ISBN 0049660136.

Merriam, Alan P. 1961. *Congo: Background to Conflict*. Evanston: Northwestern University Press. 368pp. bibliography. LC 61-011381.

Middlebrook, Martin. 1985. *Operation Corporate: The Falklands War, 1982*. London: Viking. 430pp. bibliography. ISBN 0670802239.

Middlemas, Keith. 1975. *Cabora Bassa: Engineering and Politics in Southern Africa*. London: Weidenfeld and Nicolson. 367pp. bibliography. ISBN 0297769944.

Mikes, George. 1957. *The Hungarian Revolution*. London: Andre Deutsch. 192pp. LC 57-001851.

Milburn, Josephine F. 1977. *British Business and Ghanaian Independence.* Hanover, NH: University Press of New England for University of Rhode Island. 156pp. map. bibliographical references. ISBN 0874511380.

Millar, Thomas B. 1978. *Australia in Peace and War: External Relations 1788–1977.* New York: St. Martin's. 578pp. bibliography. ISBN 0312061188.

Miller, Linda B. 1967. *World Order and Local Disorder: The United Nations and Internal Conflicts.* Princeton: Princeton University Press. 235pp. bibliography. LC 67-016953.

Millett, Richard. 1977. *Guardians of the Dynasty.* Maryknoll, NY: Orbis Books. 284pp. bibliography. ISBN 0883441691.

Miners, Norman J. 1977. *The Government and Politics of Hong Kong.* 2d ed. New York: Oxford University Press. 333pp. maps. bibliography. ISBN 019580371X.

Mitchell, Harold P. 1963. *Europe in the Caribbean: The Policies of Great Britain, France and the Netherlands Towards Their West Indian Territories in the Twentieth Century.* Stanford: Hispanic American Society, Stanford University. 211pp. maps. bibliography. LC nuc65-33165.

Mittelman, James H. 1975. *Ideology and Politics in Uganda.* Ithaca: Cornell University Press. 302pp. bibliography. ISBN 0801409462.

Molnar, Miklos. 1971. *Budapest 1956: A History of the Hungarian Revolution.* trans. Jennetta Ford. London: Allen and Unwin. 303pp. maps. bibliography. ISBN 0049470205.

Momyer, William W. 1978. *Airpower in Three Wars.* Washington, D.C.: Department of the Air Force. 358pp. bibliographical references. LC 78-601817.

Mondlane, Eduardo. 1983. *The Struggle for Mozambique.* London: Zed Press. 225pp. ISBN 086232016X.

Montgomery, Tommie Sue. 1982. *Revolution in El Salvador: Origins and Evolution.* Boulder: Westview Press. 252pp. bibliography. ISBN 0865310491.

Moraes, Frank. 1960. *The Revolt in Tibet.* New York: Macmillan. 223pp. LC 60-6644/L.

Moreno, Jose A. 1970. *Barrios in Arms: Revolution in Santo Domingo.* Pittsburgh: University of Pittsburgh Press. 226pp. map. bibliography. ISBN 822931869.

Morgenthau, Ruth Schachter. 1964. *Political Parties in French-Speaking Africa.* Oxford: Clarendon Press. 445pp. maps. bibliography. LC 65-357.

Moro, Ruben Oscar. 1989. *The History of the South Atlantic Conflict: The War for the Malvinas.* New York: Praeger. 360pp. maps. bibliography. ISBN 0275930815.

Mortimer, Edward. 1969. *France and the Africans: A Political History.* New York: Walker and Company. 390pp. maps. bibliographical references. LC 68-013985.

Moussa, Farag. 1955. *Les Negotiations Anglo-Egyptiennes de 1950–1951 sur Suez et la Sudan: Essay de Critique Historique.* Geneva: E. Droz. 261pp. bibliography. OCLC 4149549.

Munslow, Barry. 1983. *Mozambique: The Revolution and its Origins.* London: Longman. 195pp. map. bibliography. ISBN 0582643910.

Mutawi, Samir A. 1987. *Jordan in the 1967 War*. New York: Cambridge University Press. 228pp. maps. bibliography. ISBN 0521343526.

Nakdimon, Shelomoh. 1987. *First Strike: The Exclusive Story of How Israel Foiled Iraq's Attempt to Get the Bomb*. trans. Peretz Kidron. New York: Summit Books. 353pp. bibliography. ISBN 0671638718.

Nasution, Abdul Haris. 1965. *Fundamentals of Guerrilla Warfare*. ed. Otto Heilbrunn. New York: Praeger. 324pp. maps. LC 65-020502.

Nelson, Harold D. 1972. *Area Handbook for the Chad*. Washington, D.C.: U.S. Department of the Army. 261pp. bibliography. SUDOC D101.22:550-159.

Nelson, Harold D. 1974. *Area Handbook for the United Republic of Cameroon*. Washington, D.C.: U.S. Department of the Army. 335pp. maps. bibliography. SUDOC D101.22 550-166.

Neuberger, Benyamin. 1982. *Involvement, Invasion and Withdrawal: Qadhdhafi's Libya and Chad, 1969–1981*. Tel Aviv: Shiloah Center for Middle Eastern and African Studies. 78pp. bibliography. ISBN 9652240028.

Newell, Nancy P., and Richard S. Newell. 1981. *The Struggle for Afghanistan*. Ithaca: Cornell University Press. 236pp. bibliographical references. ISBN 0801413893.

Newman, P. R. 1964. *British Guiana: Problems of Cohesion in an Immigrant Society*. New York: Oxford University Press. 104pp. map. bibliographical references. LC 64-056438.

Nnoli, Okwudiba. 1978. *Self-Reliance and Foreign Policy in Tanzania: The Dynamics of the Diplomacy of a New State, 1961 to 1971*. New York: NOK Publishers. 340pp. bibliographical references. LC 73-091415.

Norodom Sihanouk, Prince. 1973. *My War with the CIA: The Memoirs of Prince Norodom Sihanouk. as Related to Wilfred Burchett*. New York: Pantheon Books. 271pp. bibliographical references. ISBN 0394485432.

Norris, Katrin. 1962. *Jamaica: The Search for an Identity*. New York: Oxford University Press. 103pp.. LC 62-052774.

Novak, Bogdan C. 1970. *Trieste, 1941–1954: The Ethnic, Political, and Ideological Struggle*. Chicago: University of Chicago Press. 526pp. maps. bibliography. ISBN 0226596214.

Nu, U. 1975. *U Nu, Saturday's Child*. trans. U Law Yone. ed. U Kyaw Win. New Haven: Yale University Press. 358pp. ISBN 0300017766.

Nuechterlein, Donald E. 1965. *Thailand and the Struggle for Southeast Asia*. Ithaca: Cornell University Press. 279pp. bibliography. LC 65-021996.

Nutting, Anthony. 1958. *I Saw for Myself: The Aftermath of Suez*. London: Hollis and Carter. 103pp. LC 58-1308/L.

Nutting, Anthony. 1967. *No End of a Lesson: The Story of Suez*. New York: C. N. Potter. 205pp. map. LC 67-027355.

Nyrop, Richard F., 1969. *Area Handbook for Rwanda*. Washington, D.C.: U.S. Department of the Army. 212pp. maps. bibliography. SUDOC D101.22 550-84.

O'Ballance, Edgar. 1957. *The Arab-Israeli War, 1948*. New York: Praeger. 220pp. LC 57-6649.

O'Ballance, Edgar. 1959. *The Sinai Campaign, 1956.* New York: Praeger. 223pp. LC 60-008717.

O'Ballance, Edgar. 1964. *The Indo-China War, 1945–1954: A Study in Guerrilla Warfare.* London: Faber and Faber. 285pp. maps. bibliography. LC 65-003280.

O'Ballance, Edgar. 1966. *The Greek Civil War, 1944–1949.* New York: Praeger. 237pp. maps. bibliography. LC 66-012479.

O'Ballance, Edgar. 1966. *Malaya: The Communist Insurgent War, 1948–60.* Hamden, CT: Archon. 188pp. map. bibliography. LC 66-031617.

O'Ballance, Edgar. 1967. *The Algerian Insurrection, 1954–62.* Hamden, CT: Archon. 231pp. maps. bibliographical refernces. LC 67-002184.

O'Ballance, Edgar. 1969. *Korea: 1950–1953.* Hamden, CT: Archon. 171pp. map. bibliography. LC 79-004050.

O'Ballance, Edgar. 1971. *The War in the Yemen.* Hamden, CT: Archon. 218pp. maps. ISBN 0208010386.

O'Ballance, Edgar. 1972. *The Third Arab-Israeli War.* Hamden, CT: Archon. 288pp. maps. bibliography. ISBN 0208012923.

O'Ballance, Edgar. 1973. *The Kurdish Revolt: 1961–1970.* Hamden, CT: Archon. 196pp. maps. ISBN 0208013954.

O'Ballance, Edgar. 1977. *The Secret War in the Sudan: 1955–1972.* Hamden, CT: Archon. 174pp. maps. bibliographical references. ISBN 0208016929.

O'Ballance, Edgar. 1978. *No Victor, No Vanquished: The Yom Kippur War.* San Rafael, CA: Presidio Press. 370pp. bibliography. ISBN 0891410171.

O'Ballance, Edgar. 1981. *The Wars in Vietnam, 1954–1980.* new enlarged ed. New York: Hippocrene. 246pp. bibliographical references. ISBN 0882546015.

O'Ballance, Edgar. 1988. *The Gulf War.* London: Brassey's Defence Publishers. 232pp. ISBN 0080347479.

O'Ballance, Edgar. 1989. *The Cyanide War: Tamil Insurrection in Sri Lanka, 1973–88.* Washington, D.C.: Brassey's (UK). 139pp. maps. ISBN 080366953.

Oberling, Pierre. 1982. *The Road to Bellapais: The Turkish Cypriot Exodus to Northern Cyprus.* Boulder: Social Science Monographs. 256pp. maps. bibliographical references. ISBN 0880330007.

Odom, Thomas P. 1988. *Dragon Operations: Hostage Rescues in the Congo, 1964–1965.* Leavenworth, KS: Combat Studies Institute, U.S. Army Comand and General Staff College. 224pp. LC 87-36503.

Ofer, Yehuda. 1976. *Operation Thunder: The Entebbe Raid.* trans. Julian Meltzer. New York: Penguin. 141pp. maps. ISBN 0140523219.

Oliver, Robert T. 1978. *Syngman Rhee and American Involvement in Korea 1942–1960: A Personal Narrative.* Seoul: Panmun Book Company. 508pp. bibliography. LC 79-107504.

O'Neill, Bard E. 1978. *Armed Struggle in Palestine: A Political-Military Analysis.* Boulder: Westview Press. 320pp. bibliographical references. ISBN 0891583335.

Oppenheim, Lassa F. L. 1905–1906. *International Law.* 2 vols. bibliographical references. LC 05019577.

O'Shaughnessy, Hugh. 1984. *Grenada: An Eyewitness Account of the U.S. Invasion and the Caribbean History that Provoked It.* New York: Dodd, Mead. 261pp. maps. ISBN 0396085245.

Ottaway, Marina, and David Ottaway. 1978. *Ethiopia: Empire in Revolution.* New York: Africana Publishing Company. 250pp. bibliographical references. ISBN 084190362X.

Oudone Sananikone. 1981. *The Royal Lao Army and U.S. Advice and Support.* Washington, D.C.: U.S. Army Center of Military History. 182pp. maps. SUDOC D114.18:R81.

Page, Stephen. 1985. *The Soviet Union and the Yemens.* New York: Praeger. 225pp. bibliography. ISBN 0030707382.

Paget, Julian. 1967. *Counter-Insurgency Operations: Techniques of Guerrilla Warfare.* New York: Walker and Company. 189pp. maps. bibliography. LC 67-014266.

Paget, Julian. 1969. *Last Post; Aden 1964–67.* London: Faber and Faber. 276pp. maps. ISBN 0571087205.

Paige, Glenn D. 1968. *The Korean Decision, June 24–30, 1950.* New York: Free Press. 394pp. bibliography. LC 68-010794.

Palit, D. K. 1972. *The Lightning Campaign: The Indo-Pakistan War, 1971.* New Delhi: Thomson Press. 172pp. maps. LC 72-900706.

Palmier, Leslie H. 1962. *Indonesia and the Dutch.* London: Oxford University Press. 194pp. LC 62-001482.

Pastor, Robert A. 1987. *Condemned to Repetition: The United States and Nicaragua.* Princeton: Princeton University Press. 392pp. bibliography. ISBN 0691077525.

Patterson, George N. 1960. *Tibet in Revolt.* London: Faber and Faber. 197pp. LC 60-004625.

Patterson, George N. 1964. *Peking Versus Delhi.* New York: Praeger. 310pp. maps. bibliography. LC 64-12387.

Payne, Anthony, Paul Sutton, and Tony Thorndike. 1984. *Grenada: Revolution and Invasion.* New York: St. Martin's. 233pp. maps. bibliography. ISBN 0312350422.

Payne, Robert. 1973. *Massacre.* New York: Macmillan. 168pp. bibliography. LC 72-092866.

Pedler, Frederick J. 1979. *Main Currents in West African History.* New York: Barnes and Noble Books. 301pp. maps. bibiography. ISBN 0064954994.

Pelcovits, Nathan A. 1984. *Peacekeeping on Arab-Israeli Fronts: Lessons from the Sinai and Lebanon.* Boulder: Westview Press. 181pp. ill. bibliography. ISBN 0865318999.

Pellitiere, Stephen C. 1984. *The Kurds: An Unstable Element in the Gulf.* Boulder: Westview Press. 220pp. bibliographical references. ISBN 089158689X.

Peterson, John E. 1978. *Oman in the Twentieth Century: Political Foundations of an Emerging State.* London: Croom Helm. 286pp. maps. bibliography. ISBN 0064955222.

Peterson, John E. 1981. *Conflict in the Yemens and Superpower Involvement.* Washington, D.C.: Center for Contemporary Arab Studies, Georgetown University. 39pp. LC 82-244844.

Peterson, John E. 1986. *Defending Arabia.* New York: St. Martin's. 275pp. bibliography. ISBN 0313191146.

Petran, Tabitha. 1972. *Syria.* New York: Praeger. 284pp. bibliography. LC 72-088257.

Pettman, Jan. 1974. *Zambia: Security and Conflict.* New York: St. Martin's. 284pp. map. bibliography. LC 74-079129.

Phillips, Wendell. 1967. *Oman: A History.* New York: Reynal and Company. 246pp. maps. bibliographies. LC 68-031978.

Plascov, Avi. 1981. *The Palestinian Refugees in Jordan 1948–1957.* London: Frank Cass. 268pp. maps. bibliography. ISBN 0714631205.

Pogany, Istvan S. 1987. *The Arab League and Peacekeeping in the Lebanon.* New York: St. Martin's. 214pp. maps. bibliographies. ISBN 0312007825.

Polyviou, Polyvios G. 1975. *Cyprus: The Tragedy and the Challenge.* Washington, D.C.: American Hellenic Institute. 222pp. bibliographical references. 222pp. bibliographical references. LC 75-010864.

Polyviou, Polyvios G. 1980. *Cyprus, Conflict and Negotiation, 1960–1980.* New York: Homes and Meier. 246pp. maps. bibliographical references. ISBN 0841906831.

Ponchaud, Francois. 1978. *Cambodia: Year Zero.* trans. Nancy Amphoux. New York: Holt, Rinehart and Winston. 212pp. maps. ISBN 0030403065.

Porter, Bruce D. 1984. *The USSR in Third World Conflict.* Cambridge: Cambridge University Press. 248pp. bibliographical references. ISBN 0521263085.

Porter, Gareth. 1975. *A Peace Denied.* Bloomington: Indiana University Press. 357pp. bibliographical references. ISBN 0253161606.

Posner, Steve. 1987. *Israel Undercover: Secret Warfare and Hidden Diplomacy in the Middle East.* Syracuse: Syracuse University Press. 350pp. bibliography. ISBN 0815602200.

Potholm, Christian P. 1972. *Swaziland: The Dynamics of Political Modernization.* Berkeley: University of California Press. 183pp. map. bibliography. ISBN 0520022009.

Price, David L. 1975. *Oman: Insurgency and Development.* London: Institute for the Study of Conflict. 19pp. bibliography. LC 75-321888.

Prouzet, Michel. 1974. *Le Cameroun.* Paris: Librairie Generale de Droit et de Jurisprudence. 377pp. maps. bibliography. ISBN 2275013474.

Quandt, William B., Fuad Jabber, and Ann Mosely Lesch. 1973. *The Politics of Palestinian Nationalism.* Berkeley: University of California Press. 234pp. maps. bibliography. ISBN 0520023366.

Qubain, Fahim I. 1961. *Crisis in Lebanon.* Washington, D.C.: Middle East Institute. 243pp. LC 61-019686.

Rabinovich, Itamar. 1985. *The War for Lebanon, 1970–1985.* rev. ed. Ithaca: Cornell University Press. 262pp. maps. bibliography. ISBN 0801418704.

Rajkumar, Nagoji Vasudev. 1951. *The Problem of French India*. New Delhi: All-India Congress Comittee. 108pp. map. LC 52-42543.

Ramazani, P. 1978. *Sikkim: The Story of Its Integration with India*. New Delhi: Cosmo. 139pp. bibliography. LC 79-902252.

Ramazani, Rouhollah K. 1972. *The Persian Gulf: Iran's Role*. Charlottesville: University Press of Virginia. 157pp. maps. bibliography. ISBN 0813904064.

Ramazani, Rouhoullan K. 1975. *Iran's Foreign Policy, 1941–1973: A Study of Foreign Policy in Modernizing Nations*. Charlottesville: University Press of Virginia. 507pp. maps. bibliography. ISBN 081390594X.

Ramazani, Rouhollah K. 1979. *The Persian Gulf and the Straits of Hormuz*. Alphen aan den Rijn: Sijthoff and Noordhoff. 180pp. documents. bibliographical references. ISBN 9028600698.

Ramazani, Rouhollan K. 1986. *Revolutionary Iran: Challenge and Response in the Middle East*. Baltimore: Johns Hopkins University Press. 311pp. maps. bibliography. ISBN 0801833779.

Ranjit Singh, D. S. 1984. *Brunei, 1839–1983: The Problems of Political Survival*. Singapore and New York: Oxford University Press. 260pp. maps. bibliography. ISBN 0195825713.

Rao, R. P. 1963. *Portuguese Rule in Goa, 1510–1961*. New York: Asia Publishing House. 242pp. maps. bibliographical references. LC 64-000298.

Ray, Hemen. 1983. *China's Strategy in Nepal*. New Delhi: Radiant Publishers. 122pp. bibliographical references. LC 83-905882.

Razvi, Mujtaba. 1971. *The Frontiers of Pakistan*. Karachi: National Publishing House. 339pp. maps. LC 71-932481.

Rees, David. 1964. *Korea: The Limited War*. New York: St. Martin's. 511pp. maps. bibliography. LC 64-014946.

Reid, Anthony. 1974. *The Indonesian National Revolution 1945–1950*. Hawthorne, Australia: Longman. 193pp. maps. bibliography. ISBN 0582710464.

Reilly, Bernard Rawdon. 1960. *Aden and the Yemen*. London: Her Majesty's Stationery Office. 82pp. LC 60-031565.

Remington, Robin A. 1969. *Winter in Prague: Documents on Czechoslovak Communism in Crisis*. Cambridge: M.I.T. Press. 473pp. documents. bibliography. ISBN 262180359.

Remington, Robin A. 1971. *The Warsaw Pact: Case Studies in Communist Conflict Resolution*. Cambridge: M.I.T. Press. 268pp. documents. bibliography. ISBN 0262180502.

Rennell, Francis J. R. 1948. *British Military Administration of Occupied Territories in Africa during the Years 1941–1947*. London: His Majesty's Stationery Office. 637pp. maps. bibliography. ISBN 837143195.

Reno, Philip. 1964. *The Ordeal of British Guiana*. New York: Monthly Review Press. 132pp. map. LC 64-023143.

Richardson, Hugh Edward. 1962. *A Short History of Tibet*. New York: E. P. Dutton. 308pp. bibliography. LC 61-006023.

Richardson, Hugh E. 1984. *Tibet and Its History*. 2d ed. Boulder, Colorado: Shambhala Publications. 327pp. map. bibliography. ISBN 0877732922.

Rikhye, Indar Jit. 1980. *The Sinai Blunder: Withdrawal of the United Nations Emergency Force Leading to the Six-Day War of 1967*. London: Frank Cass. 240pp. ISBN 0714631361.

Rikhye, Indar Jit. 1984. *The Theory and Practice of Peacekeeping*. New York: St. Martin's. 255pp. maps. bibliographical references. ISBN 0312797184.

Rizvi, Hasan-Askari. 1981. *Internal Strife and External Intervention: India's Role in the Civil War in East Pakistan [Bangladesh]*. Lahore: Progressive Publishers. 313pp. bibliography. LC 82-930539.

Robertson, Terence. 1965. *Crisis: The Inside Story of the Suez Conspiracy*. New York: Atheneum. 349pp. bibliography. LC 65-010914.

Robinson, William I., and Kent Norsworthy. 1987. *David and Goliath: The U.S. War against Nicaragua*. New York: Monthly Review Press. 400pp. bibliography. ISBN 0853457212.

Rock, David. 1987. *Argentina, 1516–1987: From Spanish Coloniazation to Alfonsin*. rev. ed. Berkeley: University of California Press. 511pp. bibliography. ISBN 0520061780.

Rosberg, Carl G., Jr., and John Nottingham. 1966. *The Myth of the 'Mau Mau': Nationalism in Kenya*. New York: Praeger. 427pp. maps. bibliography. LC 66-021793.

Rose, Leo. 1971. *Nepal: Strategy for Survival*. Berkeley: University of California Press. 310pp. bibliography. ISBN 0520016432.

Rosie, George. 1970. *The British in Vietnam: How the Twenty-Five Year War Began*. London: Panther. 144pp. map. bibliographical references. ISBN 0586033939.

Ross, Robert S. 1988. *The Indochina Tangle: China's Vietnam Policy, 1975–1979*. New York: Columbia University Press. 361pp. maps. bibliography. ISBN 0231065647.

Rotberg, Robert I. 1965. *The Rise of Nationalism in Central Africa: The Making of Malawi and Zambia, 1873–1964*. Cambridge: Harvard University Press. 362pp. maps. bibliography. LC 65-019829.

Rothenberg, Gunther E. 1979. *The Anatomy of the Israeli Army: The Israel Defence Force, 1948–78*. New York: Hippocrene Books. 256pp. bibliography. ISBN 0882544918.

Rowan, Roy. 1975. *The Four Days of Mayaguez*. New York: W. W. Norton. 224pp. ISBN 0393055647.

Rowland, John. 1967. *A History of Sino-Indian Relations*. Princeton: D. Van Nostrand. 248pp. map. bibliographical references. LC 66-029857.

Royal Institute of International Affairs. Information Department. 1952. *Great Britian and Egypt, 1914–1951*. new and rev. ed. London: Royal Institute of International Affairs. 216pp. maps. bibliography. LC 52-11636.

Rubin, Neville N. 1971. *Cameroun: An African Federation*. New York: Praeger. 259pp. maps. bibliography. LC 78-150705.

Rubinoff, Arthur G. 1971. *India's Use of Force in Goa*. Bombay: Popular Prakashan. 134pp. bibliography. LC 74-922844.

Rupen, Robert A. 1964. *Mongols of the Twentieth Century*. Bloomington: Indiana University Press. 2 vols. maps. bibliography. LC 63-064522.

Sachar, Howard M. 1976. *A History of Israel: From the Rise of Zionism to Our Time*. New York: Alfred A. Knopf. 883pp. maps. bibliography. ISBN 0394485645.

Sachar, Howard M. 1987. *A History of Israel, Volume II: From the Aftermath of the Yom Kippur War*. New York: Oxford University Press. 319pp. bibliography. ISBN 0195043863.

Safran, Nadav. 1969. *From War to War: The Arab-Israeli Confrontation, 1948–1967*. New York: Pegasus. 464pp. maps. bibliographical references. LC 68-027991.

Safran, Nadav. 1985. *Saudi Arabia: The Ceaseless Quest for Security*. Cambridge: Belknap Press. 524pp. bibliography. ISBN 0674789857.

Saint Veran, Robert. 1981. *Djibouti, Pawn of the Horn of Africa*, by Robert Tholomier. translated and abridged by Virginia Thompson and Richard Adloff. Methuen: Scarecrow Press. 163pp. map. bibliography. ISBN 0810814153.

Sak Sutsakhan. 1980. *The Khmer Republic at War and the Final Collapse*. Washington, D.C.: U.S. Army Center of Military History. 187pp. bibliographical references. LC 79-607776.

Salibi, Kamal Suleiman. 1976. *Crossroads to Civil War, 1958–1976*. Delmar: Caravan Books. 178pp. ISBN 0882060104.

Salih, Halil Ibrahim. 1968. *Cyprus: An Analysis of Cypriot Political Discord*. Brooklyn: Theodore Gaus's Sons. 184pp. maps. bibliography. LC 68-054043.

Salik, Siddiq. 1977. *Witness to Surrender*. Karachi: Oxford University Press. 245pp. maps. ISBN 0195772571.

Sandford, Gregory W. 1985. *The New Jewel Movement: Grenada's Revolution, 1979-1983*. Washington, D.C.: Center for the Study of Foreign Affairs, Foreign Service Institute, U. S. Department of State. 205pp. bibliographical references. SUDOC S1.114/3:J54f/979-83.

Sawyer, Robert K. 1962. *Military Advisors in Korea: KMAG in Peace and War*. ed. Walter G. Hermes. U.S. Department of the Army. Office of the Chief of Military History. Washington, D.C.: Goverment Printing Office. 216 pp. maps. bibliographical note. LC 62-060015.

Schemmer, Benjamin F. 1976. *The Raid*. New York: Harper and Row. 326pp. bibliography. ISBN 0060138025.

Schiff, Zeev, and Ehud Yaari. 1984. *Israel's Lebanon War*. ed. and trans. Ina Friedman. New York: Simon and Schuster. 320pp. maps. indes. ISBN 0671479911.

Schlight, John. 1988. *The United States Air Force in Southeast Asia—The War in South Vietnam: The Years of the Offensive 1965-1968*. Washington, D.C.: United States Air Force Office of Air Force History. 410pp. bibliography. LC 88-14030.

Schmid, Alex P., and Ellen Berends. 1985. *Soviet Military Interventions Since 1945*. C.O.M.T. New Brunswick: Transaction Books. 223pp. bibliography. ISBN 907104212X.

Schmidt, Dana Adams. 1964. *Journey Among Brave Men*. Boston: Little, Brown. 298pp. maps. LC 64-015051.

Schmidt, Dana Adams. 1968. *Yemen: The Unknown War.* London: Bodley Head. 316pp. maps. ISBN 0370004116.

Schnabel, James F. 1971. *Policy and Direction: The First Year.* Vol. 3 of *The United States Army in the Korean War.* Washington, D.C.: U.S. Department of the Army. Office of the Chief of Military History. 443pp. LC 70-609930.

Schoenhals, Kai P., and Richard A. Melanson. 1985. *Revolution and Intervention in Grenada: The New Jewel Movement, the United States, and the Caribbean.* Boulder: Westview Press. 211pp. bibliography. ISBN 0813302250.

Schonfield, Hugh J. 1969. *The Suez Canal in Peace and War, 1869–1969.* Coral Gables: University of Miami Press. 214pp. maps. bibliographical references. ISBN 0870241265.

Schwartz, Harry. 1969. *Prague's 200 Days: The Struggle for Democracy in Czechoslovakia.* New York: Praeger. 274pp. map. LC 69-019700.

Seale, Patrick. 1965. *The Struggle for Syria: A Study of Post-War Arab Politics, 1945–1958.* New York: Oxford University Press. 344pp. maps. bibliography. LC 65-004920.

Segal, Aaron. 1964. *Massacre in Rwanda.* Fabian Research Series 240. London: Fabian Society. 28pp. bibliography. LC 64-004752.

Segal, Gerald. 1985. *Defending China.* New York: Oxford University Press. 264pp. map. bibliographical references. ISBN 019827470X.

Selassie, Bereket Habte. 1980. *Conflict and Intervention in the Horn of Africa.* New York: Monthly Review Press. 211pp. bibliographical references. ISBN 0853455341.

Sen, Lionel Protip. 1969. *Slender Was the Thread: Kashmir Confrontation, 1947–48.* New Delhi: Orient Longmans. 308pp. maps. LC 71-910201.

Sena, Canakya. 1986. *Afghanistan: Politics, Economics, and Society: Revolution, Resistance, Intervention.* Boulder: Lynne Rienner. 206pp. maps. bibliography. ISBN 0931477190.

Sen Gupta, Jyoti. 1974. *History of Freedom Movement in Bangladesh, 1943–1973.* Calcutta: Naya Prokash. 506pp. bibliographical references. LC 74-901242.

Shakabpa, Tsepon W. D. 1967. *Tibet: a Political History.* New Haven: Yale University Press. 369pp. map. bibliography. LC 67-013448.

Shazly, Saad el. 1980. *The Crossing of the Suez.* San Francisco: American Mideast Research. 333pp. maps. ISBN 0960456201.

Sherman, Richard. 1980. *Eritrea, the Unfinished Revolution.* New York: Praeger. 197pp. maps. bibliography. ISBN 0030559219.

Shimshoni, Jonathan. 1988. *Israel and Conventional Deterrence: Border Warfare from 1953 to 1970.* Ithaca: Cornell University Press. 247pp. maps. bibliography. ISBN 0801421209.

Shlaim, Avi. 1988. *Collusion Across the Jordan: King Abdullah, the Zionist Movement, and the Partition of Palestine.* New York: Columbia University Press. 676pp. maps. bibliography. ISBN 0231068387.

Short, Anthony. 1975. *The Communist Insurrection in Malaya, 1948–1960.* New York: Crane, Russak. 547pp. map. bibliography. ISBN 0844803065.

Short, Philip. 1974. *Banda*. Boston: Routledge and Kegan Paul. 357pp. bibliography. ISBN 0710076312.

Shulimson, Jack. 1966. *Marines in Lebanon 1958*. Washington, D.C.: U.S. Marine Corps Headquarters. G-3 Division. Historical Branch. 50pp. maps. bibliographical references. LC 66-61403.

Shwardran, Benjamin. 1960. *The Power Struggle in Iraq*. New York: Council for Middle Eastern Affairs Press. 90pp. LC 60-012973.

Sicker, Martin. 1989. *Between Hashemites and Zionists: The Struggle for Palestine, 1908–1988*. New York: Holmes and Meier. 176pp. bibliographical references. ISBN 0841911762.

Silverstein, Joseph. 1977. *Burma: Military Rule and the Politics of Stagnation*. Ithaca: Cornell University Press. 224pp. bibliography. ISBN 080140911X.

Simmons, Adele. 1982. *Modern Mauritius: The Politics of Decolonization*. Bloomington: Indiana University Press. 242pp. maps. bibliography. ISBN 0253386586.

Simmons, Robert R. 1975. *The Strained Alliance: Peking, Pyongyang, Moscow, and the Politics of the Korean Civil War*. New York: Free Press. 287pp. map. bibliography. ISBN 0029288800.

Simpson, Charles M. 1983. *Inside the Green Berets: The First Thirty Years, A History of the U.S. Army Special Forces*. Novato, CA: Presidio Press. 236pp. ISBN 0891411631.

Skilling, Harold Gordon. 1976. *Czechoslovakia's Interrupted Revolution*. Princeton: Princeton University Press. 924pp. bibliography. ISBN 0691052344.

Skogmo, Bjorn. 1989. UNIFIL: *International Peacekeeping in Lebanon, 1978–1988*. Boulder: Lynne Rienner. 279pp. bibliographical references. ISBN 1555871356.

Slater, Jerome. 1967. *The OAS and United States Foreign Policy*. Columbus: Ohio State University Press. 315pp. bibliography. LC 67-010162.

Slater, Jerome. 1970. *Intervention and Negotiation: The United States and the Dominican Revolution*. New York: Harper and Row. 254pp. map. bibliography. LC 70-095985.

Small, Melvin, and J. David Singer. 1982. *Resort to Arms: International and Civil Wars, 1816–1980*. Beverly Hills, CA: Sage. 373pp. bibliography. ISBN 0803917767.

Smith, George Ivan. 1980. *Ghosts of Kampala*. New York: St. Martin's. 198pp. map. ISBN 0312326629.

Smith, Raymond T. 1962. *British Guiana*. New York: Oxford University Press. 218pp. bibliography. LC 62-004677.

Smith, Roger M. 1965. *Cambodia's Foreign Policy*. Ithaca: Cornell University Press. 273pp. map. bibliography. LC 65-015375.

Snepp, Frank. 1977. *Decent Interval: An Insider's Account of Saigon's Indecent End*. New York: Random House. 590pp. ISBN 0394407431.

Snow, Peter John. 1972. *Hussein: A Biography*. Washington, D.C.: Robert B. Luce. 256pp. bibliography. LC 72-085018.

Snyder, Edwin K., A. James Gregor, and Maria Hsia Chang. 1980. *The Taiwan Relations Act and the Defense of the Republic of China*. Berkeley: Institute of International Studies, University of California. 132pp. bibliography. ISBN 0877255121.

Soggot, David. 1986. *Namibia: The Violent Heritage*. London: Collings. 333pp. map. bibliographical references. ISBN 0860362108.

Somerville, Keith. 1990. *Foreign Military Intervention in Africa*. London: Pinter. 205pp. maps. bibliography. ISBN 0861878906.

Somoza Debayle, Anastasio. 1980. *Nicaragua Betrayed*. Boston: Western Islands. 431pp. ISBN 0882792350.

Spector, Ronald H. 1983. *The United States Army in Vietnam—Advice and Support: The Early Years 1941–1960*. Washington, D.C.: United States Army Center of Military History. 391pp. maps. bibliographical references. SUDOC D114.7/3AD9/941-60.

Spencer, John H. 1977. *Ethiopia, the Horn of Africa and U.S. Policy*. Cambridge: Institute for Foreign Policy Analysis. 69pp. bibliographical references. ISBN 0895490056.

Spencer, John H. 1984. *Ethiopia at Bay: A Personal Account of the Haile Sellassie Years*. Algonac: Reference Publications. 397pp. bibliography. ISBN 0917256255.

Spiller, Roger J. 1981. *"Not War But Like War": The American Intervention in Lebanon*. Leavenworth, KS: Combat Studies Institute, U.S. Army Command and General Staff College. 58pp. maps. bibliographical references. LC 81-602127.

Spinner, Thomas J. 1984. *A Political and Social History of Guyana, 1945–1983*. Boulder: Westview Press. 244pp. maps. bibliographies. ISBN 0865318522.

Stanton, Shelby L. 1985. *Green Berets at War: U.S. Army Special Forces in Southeast Asia, 1956–1975*. Novato, CA: Presidio Press. 360pp. bibliography. ISBN 0891412387.

Stein, Janice Gross, and Raymond Tanter. 1980. *Rational Decision-Making: Israel's Choices, 1967*. Columbus: Ohio State University Press. 399pp. bibliography. ISBN 0814203124.

Stephens, Robert. 1966. *Cyprus, A Place of Arms: Power Politics and Ethnic Conflict in the Eastern Mediterranean*. London: Pall Mall Press. 232pp. bibliography. LC 012987.

Stephens, Robert. 1972. *Nasser: A Political Biography*. New York: Simon and Schuster. 631pp. maps. bibliography. ISBN 0671212249.

Stern, Laurence. 1977. *The Wrong Horse: The Politics of Intervention and the Failure of American Diplomacy*. 170pp. ISBN 0812907345.

Stevens, Richard P. 1967. *Lesotho, Botswana, and Swaziland: The Former High Commission Territories in Southern Africa*. New York: Praeger. 294pp. maps. bibliography. LC 66-018923.

Stevens, Siaka Probyn. 1984. *What Life Has Taught Me*. Bourne End, England: Kensal Press. 448pp. ISBN 0946041121.

Stevenson, William. 1976. *90 Minutes at Entebbe*. New York: Bantam Books. 216pp. ISBN 0553104829.

Stock, Ernest. 1967. *Israel on the Road to Sinai, 1949–1956.* Ithaca: Cornell University Press. 284pp. map. bibliography. LC 67-023764.

Stockwell, John. 1978. *In Search of Enemies: A CIA Story.* New York: W. W. Norton. 285pp. ISBN 0393057054.

Stolper, Thomas E. 1985. *China, Taiwan, and the Offshore Islands.* Armonk, NY: M. E. Sharpe. 170pp. bibliography. ISBN 0873323114.

Stone, Isador F. 1952. *The Hidden History of the Korean War.* New York: Monthly Review Press. 364pp. LC 52-9751/L.

Stookey, Robert W. 1978. *Yemen: The Politics of the Yemen Arab Republic.* Boulder: Westview Press. 322pp. bibliography. ISBN 0891583009.

Stookey, Robert W. 1982. *South Yemen: Marxist Republic in Arabia.* Boulder: Westview Press. 124pp. bibliography. ISBN 0865310246.

Stratton, Arthur. 1964. *The Great Red Island.* New York: Scribner's. 368pp. map. bibliography. LC 64-020055.

Stuart-Fox, Martin. 1986. *Laos: Politics, Economics, and Society.* Boulder: Lynn Rienner. 220pp. maps. bibliography. ISBN 155587004X.

Summers, Harry G. 1985. *Vietnam War Almanac.* New York: Facts on File. 414pp. bibliography. ISBN 081601017X.

Swanson, Bruce. 1982. *Eighth Voyage of the Dragon: A History of China's Quest for Seapower.* Annapolis, MD: Naval Institute Press. 348pp. maps. bibliography. ISBN 0870211773.

SWAPO of Namibia, Department of Information and Publicity. 1981. *To Be Born a Nation: The Liberation Struggle for Namibia.* London: Zed Press. 357pp. maps. bibliography. ISBN 0905762738.

Szulc, Tad. 1965. *Dominican Diary.* New York: Delacorte Press. 306pp. map. LC 65-026188.

Talbott, John E. 1980. *The War Without a Name: France in Algeria, 1954–1962.* New York: Alfred A. Knopf. 305pp. bibliography. ISBN 0394509099.

Talbott, Robert D. 1974. *A History of the Chilean Boundaries.* Ames: Iowa State University Press. 134pp. maps. bibliography. ISBN 0813803055.

Tanham, George K. 1974. *Trial in Thailand.* New York: Crane, Russak. 175pp. maps. bibliographical references. ISBN 0844803189.

Tanter, Raymond. 1990. *Who's at the Helm?: Lessons of Lebanon.* Boulder: Westview. 262pp. map. bibliography. ISBN 081330993X.

Taryam, Abdullah Omran. 1987. *The Establishment of the United Arab Emirates.* New York: Croom Helm. 290pp. maps. bibliographies. ISBN 070994330X.

Taylor, Alastair M. 1960. *Indonesian Independence and the United Nations.* Ithaca: Cornell University Press. 503pp. maps. bibliography. ISBN 0837180058.

Taylor, Robert H. 1973. *Foreign and Domestic Consequences of the KMT Intervention in Burma.* Ithaca: Cornell University Press. 88pp. bibliography. ISBN 0877270937.

Thakur, Ramesh. 1987. *International Peacekeeping in Lebanon.* Boulder: Westview Press. 356pp. bibliography. ISBN 0813373220.

Thee, Marek. 1973. *Notes of a Witness: Laos and the Second Indochina War.* New York: Random House. 435pp. map. bibliographical references. ISBN 0394468368.

Tho, Tran Dinh. 1979. *The Cambodian Incursion.* Washington, D.C.: U.S. Army Center of Military History. 245pp. bibliographical references. LC 79-021722.

Thomas, Gerry S. 1985. *Mercenary Troops in Modern Africa.* Boulder: Westview Press. 157pp. bibliography. ISBN 0865318905.

Thomas, Hugh S. 1967. *The Suez Affair.* London: Weidenfeld and Nicolson. 259pp. maps. bibliography. LC 67-083685.

Thomas, Lowell J. 1959. *The Silent War in Tibet.* Garden City, NY: Doubleday. 284pp. ISBN 0837167760.

Thompson, Virginia M. 1972. *West Africa's Council of the Entente.* Ithaca: Cornell University Press. 313pp. bibliography. ISBN 0801406838.

Thompson, Virginia M., and Richard Adloff. 1957. *French West Africa.* Stanford: Stanford University Press. 626pp. maps. bibliography. LC 58-007722.

Thompson, Virginia M., and Richard Adloff. 1960. *The Emerging States of French Equatorial Africa.* Stanford: Stanford University Press. 595pp. maps. bibliography. LC 60-013871.

Thompson, Virginia M., and Richard Adloff. 1965. *The Malagasy Republic.* Stanford: Stanford University Press. 504pp. map. bibliography. LC 65-021495.

Thompson, Virginia M., and Richard Adloff. 1968. *Djibouti and the Horn of Africa.* Stanford: Stanford University Press. 246pp. map. bibliography. LC 68-21289.

Thompson, Virginia M., and Richard Adloff. 1980. *The Western Saharans: Background to Conflict.* Totowa, NJ: Barnes and Noble Books. 348pp. bibliography. ISBN 0389201480.

Thompson, Virginia M., and Richard Adloff. 1981. *Conflict in Chad.* Berkeley: University of California Institute of International Studies. 180pp. bibliography. ISBN 0877251452.

Thompson, Willard S. 1969. *Ghana's Foreign Policy, 1957–1966: Diplomacy, Ideology, and the New State.* Princeton: Princeton Univeristy Press. 462pp. bibliographical references. LC 68-056322.

Thorndike, Tony. 1985. *Grenada: Politics, Economics, and Society.* Boulder: Lynne Rienner. 206pp. maps. bibliography. ISBN 0931477085.

Tigrid, Pavel. 1971. *Why Dubcek Fell.* London: MacDonald and Company. 229pp. ISBN 0356036030.

Tillema, Herbert K. 1973. *Appeal to Force: American Military Intervention in the Era of Containment.* New York: Thomas Y. Crowell. 260pp. bibliography. ISBN 0690095082.

Tinker, Hugh. 1967. *The Union of Burma: A Study of the First Years of Independence.* 4th ed. London: Oxford University Press for the Royal Institute of International Affairs. 423pp. maps. bibliography. LC 67-095770.

Tong, Hollington Kong. 1953. *Chiang Kai-Shek.* rev. ed. Taipei, Formosa: China Publishing Company. 562pp. LC 56-025496.

Touval, Saadia. 1963. *Somali Nationalism: International Politics and the Drive for Unity in the Horn of Africa.* Cambridge: Harvard University Press. 214pp. map. bibliographical references. LC 63-013817.

Touval, Saadia. 1972. *The Boundary Politics of Independent Africa.* Cambridge: Harvard University Press. 334pp. bibliographical references. ISBN 0674080254.

Townsend, John. 1977. *Oman: The Making of a Modern State.* London: Croom Helm. 212pp. maps. bibliography. ISBN 0312584326.

Toye, Hugh. 1968. *Laos: Buffer State or Battleground.* London: Oxford University Press. 245pp. maps. bibliography. ISBN 0192151584.

Trager, Frank N. 1966. *Burma: from Kingdom to Republic.* New York: Praeger. 455pp. map. bibliographies. LC 65-024936.

Trevaskis, Gerald K. N. 1960. *Eritrea: A Colony in Transition.* London: Oxford University Press. 137pp. maps. LC 60-051042.

Tronchon, Jacques. 1974. *L'Insurrection Malagache de 1947: Essai d'Interpretation Historique.* Paris: Francois Maspero. 399pp. maps. bibliography. LC 75-501394.

Trout, Frank E. 1969. *Morocco's Saharan Frontiers.* Geneva: Droz Publishers. 563pp. maps. bibliography. LC 70-445282.

Tsou, Tang. 1959. *The Embroilment Over Quemoy: Mao, Chiang and Dulles.* Salt Lake City: Institute of International Studies, University of Utah. 47pp. bibliographical references. LC 62-52326.

Turley, William S. 1986. *The Second Indochina War: A Short Political and Military History, 1954–1975.* Boulder: Westview Press. 238pp. bibliography. ISBN 0813303087.

Turner, Robert F. 1987. *Nicaragua v. United States: A Look at the Facts.* Washington, D.C.: Pergamon-Brassey's. 165pp. map. bibliography. ISBN 0080344992.

United Nations Department of Public Information. 1985. *The Blue Helmets: A Review of United Nations Peace-keeping.* New York: United Nations. 350pp. maps. bibliographies. ISBN 9211002753.

U.S. Congress. House. Committee on Armed Services. 1971. *United States-Vietnam Relations, 1945–1967.* A study prepared by the Department of Defense. Washington, D.C.: Government Printing Office. 12 vols. SUDOC Y4.A5/2:V67/3/945-67.

U.S. Department of State. 1951. *The Conflict in Korea: Events Prior to the Attack on June 25, 1950.* Washington, D.C.: Government Printing Office. 35pp. LC 51-6689.

U.S. Department of State and U.S. Department of Defense. 1984. *Grenada Documents: An Overview and Selection.* Washington, D.C.: Government Printing Office. n.p. SUDOC S1.2:G86/2.

Urban, Mark. 1989. *War in Afghanistan.* New York: St. Martin's. 248pp. maps. bibliographical references. ISBN 0312012055.

Valenta, Jiri. 1979. *Soviet Intervention in Czechoslovakia, 1968: Anatomy of a Decision*. Baltimore: Johns Hopkins University Press. 208pp. bibliography. ISBN 0801821681.

Vali, Ferencz. 1961. *Rift and Revolt in Hungary: Nationalism Versus Communism*. Cambridge: Harvard University Press. 590pp. map. bibliography. LC 61-01013745.

Vanderlaan, Mary B. 1986. *Revolution and Foreign Policy in Nicaragua*. Boulder: Westview Press. 404pp. map. bibliography. ISBN 0813370531.

Vanezis, P. N. 1977. *Cyprus: The Unfinished Agony*. London: Abelard-Schuman. 141pp. bibliography. LC 77-471709.

Vanniasingham, Somasundaram. 1988. *Sri Lanka, the Conflict Within*. New Delhi: Lancer. 200pp. bibliography. ISBN 817062052X.

Varma, Ravindra. 1974. *Australia and Southeast Asia: The Crystallisation of a Relationship*. New Delhi: Abhinav Publications. 341pp. bibliography. LC 74-902144.

Venter, Al J., 1974. *Africa at War*. Old Greenwich, CT: Devin-Adair Company. 185pp. bibliography. LC 73-088037.

Venter, Al J. 1974. *The Zambesi Salient: Conflict in Southern Africa*. Old Greenwich, CT: Devin-Adair Company. 395pp. bibliography. LC 74-082701.

Vertzberger, Yaacov. 1984. *Misperceptions in Foreign Policymaking: The Sino-Indian Conflict, 1959–1962*. Boulder: Westview Press. 377pp. bibliography. ISBN 0865319707.

Vickery, Michael. 1984. *Cambodia, 1975–1982*. Boston: South End Press. 361pp. maps. bibliography. ISBN 0896081907.

Vilas, Carlos Maria. 1989. *State, Class, and Ethnicity in Nicaragua: Capitalist Modernization and Revolutionary Change on the Atlantic Coast*. trans. Susan Norwood. Boulder: Lynne Rienner. 221pp. bibliography. ISBN 1555871631.

Vongsavanh, Soutchay. 1981. *RLG Military Operations and Activities in the Laotian Panhandle*. Washington, D.C.: U.S. Army Center of Military History. 120pp. maps. LC 81-10934.

Wagoner, Fred E. 1980. *Dragon Rouge: The Rescue of Hostages in the Congo*. Washington National Defense University Research, Directorate. 219pp. maps. LC 80-600123.

Wai, Dunstan M. 1981. *The African-Arab Conflict in the Sudan*. New York: Africana Publishing Company. 234pp. map. bibliography. ISBN 0841906319.

Wainhouse, David W. 1973. *International Peacekeeping at the Crossroads*. Baltimore: Johns Hopkins. 634pp. maps. bibliographical references. ISBN 0801814782.

Wallace, Elisabeth. 1977. *The British Caribbean from the Decline of Colonialism to the End of Federation*. Toronto: University of Toronto Press. 274pp. bibliography. ISBN 0802053513.

Walt van Praag, Michael C. 1987. *The Status of Tibet: History, Rights, and Prospect in International Law*. Boulder, Colorado: Westview Press. 381pp. maps. bibliogaphy. ISBN 081330394X.

Watson, Bruce W., and Peter M. Dunn, eds. 1984. *Military Lessons of the Falkland Islands War: Views from the United States.* Boulder: Westview Press. 181pp. maps. bibliographical references. ISBN 0865316937.

Watson, Francis. 1966. *The Frontiers of China.* New York: Praeger. 224pp. maps. bibliography. LC 66-012989.

Webre, Stephen. 1979. *Jose Napoleon Duarte and the Christian Democratic Party in San Salvadoran Politics, 1960–1972.* Baton Rouge: Louisiana State University Press. 233pp. bibliography. ISBN 0807104620.

Wehl, David. 1948. *The Birth of Indonesia.* London: George Allen and Unwin. 216pp. maps. LC 49-16619.

Weinberger, Naomi J. 1986. *Syrian Intervention in Lebanon: The 1975–76 Civil War.* New York: Oxford University Press. 367pp. maps. bibliography. ISBN 0195040104.

Weissman, Steve, and Herbert Krosney. 1981. *The Islamic Bomb: The Nuclear Threat to Israel and the Middle East.* New York: Times Books. 339pp. bibliographical references. ISBN 081290978X.

Welles, Benjamin. 1965. *Spain: The Gentle Anarchy.* New York: Praeger. 386pp. map. bibliographical references. LC 65-018081.

Wenner, Manfred W. 1967. *Modern Yemen, 1918–1966.* Baltimore: Johns Hopkins. 257pp. map. bibliography. LC 012420.

Westlake, Donald E. 1972. *Under an English Heaven.* New York: Simon and Schuster. 278pp. bibliography. ISBN 0671213113.

Whetten, Lawrence L. 1974. *The Canal War: Four Power Confrontation in the Middle East.* Cambridge: M.I.T. Press. 520pp. bibliography. ISBN 0262230690.

Whiting, Allen S. 1960. *China Crosses the Yalu: The Decision to Enter the Korean War.* Stanford: Stanford University Press. 219pp. LC 60-015699.

Whiting, Allen S. 1975. *The Chinese Calculus of Deterrence: India and Indochina.* Ann Arbor: University of Michigan Press. 299pp. maps. bibliography. ISBN 0472969005.

Whiting, Allen S., and Sheng Shih-Tsai. 1958. *Sinkiang: Pawn or Pivot?* East Lansing: Michigan State University Press. 314pp. bibliographical references. LC 58-011509.

Wilson, A. Jeyaratnam. 1988. *The Break-Up of Sri Lanka: The Sinhalese-Tamil Conflict.* Honolulu: University of Hawaii Press. 240pp. maps. bibliography. ISBN 0824812115.

Wilson, Mary Christina. 1987. *King Abdullah, Britain, and the Making of Jordan.* New York: Cambridge University Press. 289pp. bibliography. ISBN 0521324211.

Wiseman, Henry, and Alastair M. Taylor. 1981. *From Rhodesia to Zimbabwe: The Politics of Transition.* New York: Pergamon Press. 170pp. bibliographical references. ISBN 0080280692.

Wolfers, Michael, and Jane Bergerol. 1983. *Angola in the Frontline.* London: Zed Press. 238pp. maps. bibliography. ISBN 0862321069.

Wood, J. R. T. 1983. *The Wilensky Papers: A History of the Federation of Rhodesia and Nyasaland and Rhodesia.* Durban: Graham Publishing. 1330pp. bibliography. ISBN 0620064102.

Woodhouse, Christopher Montague. 1976. *The Struggle for Greece, 1941–1949.* London: Hart-Davis, MacGibbon. 324pp. bibliography. ISBN 0246640723.

Woodman, Dorothy. 1955. *The Republic of Indonesia.* New York: Philosophical Library. 444pp. map. bibliography. LC 55-013956.

Woodman, Dorothy. 1962. *The Making of Burma.* London: Cresset. 594pp. LC 62-2969/L.

Wright, John L. 1969. *Libya.* London: Ernest Benn. 304pp. maps. bibliography. ISBN 051039521X.

Wright, John L. 1982. *Libya: A Modern History.* Baltimore: Johns Hopkins Press. 306pp. map. bibliography. ISBN 0801827671.

Xydis, Stephen George. 1973. *Cyprus: Reluctant Republic.* The Hague: Mouton. 553pp. bibliography. LC 72-094514.

Yaniv, Avner. 1987. *Dilemmas of Security: Politics, Strategy, and the Israeli Experience in Lebanon.* New York: Oxford University Press. 355pp. bibliography. ISBN 0195041224.

Yates, Lawrence A. 1988. *Power Pack: U.S. Intervention in the Dominican Republic, 1965–1966.* Leavenworth, KS: Combat Studies Institute, U.S. Army Command and General Staff College.

Yong, Mun Cheong. 1982. *H. J. van Mook and Indonesian Independence: A Study of His Role in Dutch-Indonesian Relations, 1945–48.* The Hague: Martinus Nijhoff. 255pp. map. bibliography. ISBN 9024791413.

Zabih, Sepehr. 1966. *The Communist Movement in Iran.* Berkeley: University of California Press. 279pp. bibliography. LC 66-025348.

Zabih, Sepehr. 1988. *The Iranian Military in Revolution and War.* London: Routledge. 279pp. bibliography. ISBN 0415004764.

Zacher, Mark W. 1979. International Conflicts and Collective Security, 1946–77. New York: Praeger Special Studies. 297pp. bibliographical references. ISBN 0030442613.

Zartman, I. William. 1964. *Morocco: Problems of New Power.* New York: Atherton Press. 276pp. maps. bibliographical references. LC 64-010961.

Zartman, I. William. 1966. *International Relations in the New Africa.* Englewood Cliffs, NJ: Prentice-Hall. 175pp. map. bibliographical references. LC 66-016339.

Zartman, I. William. 1989. *Ripe for Resolution: Conflict and Intervention in Africa.* updated ed. New York: Oxford University Press. 302pp. maps. bibliographies. ISBN 019505931X.

Zasloff, Joseph J. 1973. *The Pathet Lao: Leadership and Organization.* Lexington, MA: Lexington Books. 176pp. bibliography. ISBN 0669867446.

Zolberg, Aristide R. 1964. *One-Party Government in the Ivory Coast.* Princeton: Princeton University Press. 374pp. maps. bibliography. LC 63-012673.

Index

Accra riots, 61
Aden
  Aden riots, 188
  Yemen-Aden War, 192
  See also People's Democratic
    Republic of Yemen-
Aden colony. *See* Aden
Aden independence. *See* Yemen-
    Aden War
Aden Protectorates. *See* South Arabia
Aden riots, 188
Afars and the Issas, Territory of the.
    See Djibouti
Afghanistan
  Afghan revolt, 204
  Moghulgai raid, 203
  Pushtun conflict, 204
  Russo-Afghan War, 205
Afghan revolt, 204
African National Congress
  Anti-ANC raids, 128
  Gabarone raid 1985, 128
  Gabarone raid 1988, 129
  Livingstone raid, 128
  Maputo raids, 126
  Maseru raid, 126
  Matola raid, 124
  Rhodesian War, 123
Agacher battle, 69
Agacher conflict, 66
Albania
  Greek civil war, 46
Al-Dibal incident, 156
Algeria
  Moroccan-Algerian War, 137
  North African War, 134
  Tindouf conflict, 136
  Western Saharan War, 139
  Yom Kippur War, 185

Algerian War. *See* North African
    War
Al-Wadiah battle, 194
Al-Wadiah incident, 198
ANC. *See* African National Congress
Angola
  Rhodesian War, 123
  Southwest African War, 115
Angolan independence. *See*
    Southwest African War
Angolan War. *See* Southwest African
    War
Anguillan secession, 18
Anti-ANC raids, 128
Anti-Youlou riots, 76
Anya-Nya War
  1964, 104
  1966, 106
  1968, 107
  1971, 108
Arab Republic of Yemen
  Ismail's coup, 198
  Najran air raids, 194
  NDF invasion, 199
  South Arabian disorders, 187
  South Arabian revolt, 188
  Yemen-Aden War, 191
  Yemeni conflict, 197
Argentina
  Malvinas War, 42
  Pilcomayo incident, 38
  Snipe Island incidents, 37
Aubame's coup, 77
Australia
  Indonesian War, 244
  Korean War, 211
  Malay confrontation, 261
  Malayan insurgency, 247
  Second Indochina War, 253

346